FAMILY
MATTERS

To my mother, Barbara,
who showed me the meaning of family

FAMILY
MATTERS

A History of Genealogy

MICHAEL SHARPE

Pen & Sword
FAMILY HISTORY

First published in Great Britain in 2011 by
Pen & Sword Family History
an imprint of
Pen & Sword Books Ltd
47 Church Street
Barnsley
South Yorkshire
S70 2AS

ISBN 978 1 84884 559 6

A CIP catalogue record for this book is
available from the British Library

Typeset in Ehrhardt by Chic Media Ltd

Printed and bound in England
by CPI

Pen & Sword Books Ltd incorporates the imprints of
Pen & Sword Aviation, Pen & Sword Maritime,
Pen & Sword Military, Pen & Sword Family History,
Wharncliffe Local History, Wharncliffe True Crime,
Wharncliffe Transport, Pen & Sword Discovery, Pen & Sword Select,
Pen & Sword Military Classics, Leo Cooper, Remember When,
The Praetorian Press, Seaforth Publishing and Frontline Publishing

For a complete list of Pen & Sword titles please contact
PEN & SWORD BOOKS LIMITED
47 Church Street, Barnsley, South Yorkshire, S70 2AS, England
E-mail: enquiries@pen-and-sword.co.uk
Website: www.pen-and-sword.co.uk

Contents

Acknowledgements

I am indebted to many people for their input and feedback as this project has developed. First, I would like to express my gratitude to Rupert Harding and his colleagues at Pen & Sword who have helped to bring this idea to fruition and provided sound advice along the way.

Particular thanks are due to Else Churchill of the Society of Genealogists for her invaluable assistance in locating sources in the Society's library, as well as granting permission to reproduce several illustrations from the Society's collection. I am very grateful to Gordon Honeycombe who entered into correspondence from his home in Western Australia and to Simon Fowler for reviewing the draft manuscript.

Numerous people provided assistance in sourcing images, including Melissa Atkinson of the National Portrait Gallery, Pamela Birch of the Bedfordshire & Luton Archives and Records Service, Patricia Buckingham of the Bodleian Library, and Matthew Jones of the College of Arms.

My friends Roger and Maria Hughes kindly accommodated me on numerous research trips to London and maintained an active interest throughout.

By far my greatest debt is to my wife, Kim. She has lived with the idea of the book since it was first conceived and has supported and encouraged me as I have nurtured it into life. She also gave valuable feedback on the first draft. In this, as in everything else, she has been my inspiration.

Abbreviations

BMD	births, marriages and deaths
BMSGH	Birmingham and Midland Society for Genealogy and Heraldry
BRA	British Records Association
BRS	British Record Society
CFI	Computer File Index
CRO	county record office
EGC	English Genealogical Congress
FFHS	Federation of Family History Societies
FHS	family history society
FRC	Family Records Centre
GOONS	Guild of One Name Studies
GRO	General Register Office
GSU	Genealogical Society of Utah
ICGH	International Congress of Genealogical and Heraldic Sciences
IGD	International Genealogical Directory
IGI	International Genealogical Index
IHGS	Institute of Heraldic and Genealogical Studies
IPS	Identity and Passport Service
LDS	Church of Jesus Christ of Latter-Day Saints
NBI	National Burial Index
NIPR	National Index of Parish Registers
ONS	Office for National Statistics
OPR	Old Parochial Register
OPCS	Office of Population Censuses and Surveys
PCC	Prerogative Court of Canterbury
PRO	Public Record Office
PRONI	Public Record Office of Northern Ireland
RG	Registrar General
RGS	Registrar General for Scotland
SoG	Society of Genealogists
TNA	The National Archives
VCH	Victoria County History

Preface

GENEALOGY, n. An account of one's descent from an
ancestor who did not particularly care to trace his own.
Ambrose Bierce, *The Devil's Dictionary*, 1911

For me it all started with a small spidery diagram sketched on a piece
of brown paper. As a child growing up in Devon I was all too
conscious that our family's roots were elsewhere. We had moved
from Birmingham when I was 5 and some of my earliest memories are of
walking to school through fog-bound Midlands streets alongside the
construction work for the M6 motorway that was cutting a swathe through
the city. The Brummie accents of our family and those who came to visit in
our new Southwest home distinguished us as being different. One such
visitor was my great-uncle Walter ('Wal'), my grandmother's brother. An
inveterate smoker and tea drinker, he would sit in my gran's kitchen
recounting tales of people he had known from his childhood.

Like most Victorian and Edwardian families, his – the Wheelwrights –
was a large household. I sat transfixed as he reeled off uncles and cousins,
grandfathers and stepmothers, and a host of other characters who did not
seem to be related at all. There was his father, George Wheelwright, who
had run a greengrocery business in Aston with Wal's grandfather Josiah,
and an Uncle Albert who had owned a fish and chip shop. Then there was
Auntie Ellen who was big in the Methodist church, a cousin Arthur who
had been killed in the First World War, and a whole series of bachelor
uncles who were 'a penny short of a shilling' and disappeared into grim
Victorian asylums.

In my childish way I would ask Wal to explain more about these people
and he would patiently answer my questions as best he could. Then, one
day I arrived at my grandmother's to find he had drawn out a crude family
tree. On a strip of brown parcel paper – the biggest sheet of paper he could
find – he had drawn long straight lines off which were spurs with people's
names. Here, at last, were George and Josiah, Albert, Ellen, Arthur and a
host of others arranged in family groups, showing the progression of the
Wheelwright family through the ages. To my young eyes it was a revelation.
My family was not just me, my sister, my mum and dad and my gran: we
were just one little sprig on a family tree that went *back* many generations.
This sketch on a piece of parcel paper located me, in 1975, within a lineage

(though I certainly did not know such a word then) that went right back into the nineteenth century. Even my very ordinary family, I now realized, had a history and without that history I would not have come to be.

I rejoiced in the tree for a while but when I looked carefully I noticed gaps. Wal and my grandmother had kept in touch with people as best they could but the vicissitudes of a sprawling urban family were beyond them. Where their collective memory was exhausted, Wal had written on the tree 'Married – no knowledge to whom'. A whole series of cousins – Uncle Albert's offspring – were annotated 'No knowledge of marital development'. This did not seem right to me. If these people had lived, worked and died like our close family, then it ought to be possible to find out more about them.

In 1977 the BBC screened the TV series *Roots*, about the Black American writer Alex Haley's search for his slave ancestry. Then two years later, former newsreader Gordon Honeycombe explained his search for his ancestors in the documentary series *Family History*. My mind was made up: I was going to fill in the gaps on Wal's tree and see what else I could find.

Thus, aged 16, I began researching my family history. I visited record offices and libraries, joined several family history societies, wrote to relatives, and corresponded with specialist archives. I read books, ordered certificates and bought printouts from microfilm indexes. More by luck than intention, I ended up at university in Manchester which was easily within a day's journey of relevant repositories in the Midlands. Many of my Saturdays and university vacations were spent on 'the quest'. Within a few years, I had the Wheelwrights back to 1750 and had started researching other lines as well. From the haze of historical records stepped forward Josiah's scheming second wife who had only married him for his money; a very rich uncle in London who cut the family out of his will; and an unknown branch who had emigrated to America in the 1890s. The overriding picture that emerged was of the sheer grit and determination of a family struggling to make a living in the back-to-back houses of nineteenth-century Brum. I shared my researches with the family who seemed genuinely interested in what had been revealed. Sadly, Wal was not among them, as he died before I had the opportunity to enlighten him on the family's origins.

After leaving university, personal and professional priorities intervened and I put down the family story. Some ten or more years later, soon after the millennium, I decided it was time to brush the dust off the files. In the meantime the family history world had been utterly transformed. Many of the documents that I had toiled over and spent ages finding were now available on the internet and could be searched at the click of a mouse. Commercial businesses were emerging to help people access this data as well as sell them books, computer programs and genealogical indexes. Family historians were talking together on forums and websites to swap information and help each other in their research. Like many others, I have benefited from these developments, using the new technology to extend my research both further back into the past and forwards along collateral lines, in several cases leading to contact with living relatives. Some thirty years after starting out, my quest continues.

Michael Sharpe
Worcestershire, February 2011

Chapter 1

This Ancestry Business

The computer screens are flickering, the cash registers are ringing. People are jostling in the aisles between tightly packed stalls selling everything from books, maps and self-help guides, to computer programs, presentation albums, and genetic tests. Numerous magazine publishers compete for the visitors' attention. Experts are examining military memorabilia and matching it up to regiments and squadrons. Professional researchers are offering eager listeners advice on how to overcome their 'brick walls'.

It is the first day of Who Do You Think You Are? Live 2010 and London's Olympia is buzzing. To one side of the hall a whole series of tables manned by volunteers show off the wares – mainly specialist publications and indexes – of family history societies from across the country. There are companies selling historical tours; record offices, museums and archives publicizing their collections; universities offering vocational courses; and entrepreneurs who think they have spotted an opportunity to make money dating old photographs, binding biographies or preserving documents.

All ages, classes and races are represented. Couples pushing young children in pushchairs and dads holding toddlers above their heads mingle with big-bosomed ladies from the Home Counties, crusty colonels in blazers and silver-haired pensioners with Yorkshire accents. Family history is a democratic pursuit.

Visitors shuttle between the exhibition and a series of seminar rooms where they listen to talks on pet subjects: 'Finding the elusive ancestor', 'Irish genealogy', 'RAF Service records', and 'My ancestor was a gypsy'. Dominating everything in the centre of the hall are the huge stands of the specialist internet companies where punters are crowding to search historical records online.

The internet is why most people are here. The digitization of historical archives over the last ten years has opened up the past as never before. Much of this material comprises the records necessary to trace the history of a family: the census taken every ten years since 1841; the registers of births, marriages and deaths ('hatches, matches and dispatches') that mark out the staging points of an ancestor's life; local and national newspapers that capture everything from personal announcements to notable achievements and even the scandal of court appearances. Records of military service, parish registers, wills, trade and business directories, telephone directories, registers of land – all can be found online and much else besides.

Landmark events such as the 2002 release of the 1901 census online, and the BBC's celebrity genealogy series *Who Do You Think You Are?* – ('WDYTYA') after which the show is named – have helped push the search for ancestry into the public consciousness. According to surveys, around six million people in Britain are researching their family tree and on the internet genealogical information is one of the top categories for online searches. Inspired by our idols and with a wealth of historical data available at the click of a mouse, Britons have discovered a passion for family history.

It has not always been like this. Tracing your ancestry used to be thought of as at best a bit quaint, and at worst outright geeky. It was not something you admitted to in public except, perhaps, at the Christmas dinner table with Aunt Mabel who probably remembered many of the events in question. You had to be a little bit bookish – not to mention endowed with tremendous patience – to probe into your roots in the pre-computer era.

For a start you had to travel, often a long way, to access the records at county record offices, major libraries, specialist local offices, or national repositories in London (or Edinburgh, Cardiff, Belfast). Once you arrived you invariably had to wait to get a seat; this was the furthest reaches of the unreformed public sector, there was no notion of customer satisfaction. Conditions were often poor with bad lighting and equipment that did not work.

Once seated you had to locate the records from poorly maintained and often incomplete catalogues and indexes. If you were lucky you might be able to identify the correct record straightaway, by going to a drawer and getting out the right microfilm or microfiche, but then you would have to wait for a film or fiche reader. If you were unlucky you would have to order up the record from the storeroom, which involved filling in a slip, and waiting some more. Having got the volume or schedule you wanted you were unlikely to be able to locate your family straightaway, since very few records were indexed. It was a matter of searching and browsing, page by page by page, until, if fortune smiled, you found what you were looking for. When the volume was finished with you returned it to the counter and went back to the beginning: another film or fiche; another slip and more waiting; another painstaking search. Records could be copied – using the rather poor technology of the day – but copying was expensive and involved yet another slip and more waiting.

Family history the old way needed a fair amount of money and plenty of time. Only since 1978, for instance, has it been compulsory for churches to deposit their completed registers with a local repository. Before then many were kept at the church – often in very unsatisfactory conditions – requiring family historians to visit individual parishes in order to examine them, a privilege for which clergy could charge. Microfilm has only been widely available since the mid-1950s, a period that also saw the founding of many county record offices.

While recent developments have brought family history to public attention, the growing popularity of ancestor hunting is nothing new. From the formation of the Society of Genealogists in 1911, there has been a steady growth in genealogical enquiry over the last 100 years. Newspapers from the 1960s and 1970s regularly comment on the growing interest in family history research. The opening up of public records, the growth of family history societies, the introduction of microfiche and computers, and later the internet, have helped make family history accessible to all.

How family history went from an obscure, esoteric pastime of gentlemen and scholars to the mainstream pursuit of today is the focus of this book. Our story is about the history of family history itself. Remarkable as it may seem, for a group of people who are concerned with uncovering and recording the past, genealogists have a very limited knowledge of their own origins. Stop the punters in the aisles at Olympia and most would be unaware of the history of the records they consult, the repositories they visit, or the campaigns – sometimes long-fought – that have been waged by previous generations for the right to access the records at all. Few would have heard of nineteenth-century practitioners of their art, such as George Cokayne, William Phillimore or John Horace Round, or twentieth-century pioneers, like George Sherwood and Percival Boyd.

That is the gap the book sets out to fill. We trace the history of genealogy in Britain from the earliest times through to the present day. We show how a field that was once the preserve of an elite few – royalty, peers and society grandees – is now open to anyone and everyone. We look at how campaigners overcame bureaucratic hurdles and gained the right to access public records which we, the people, own; how, long before any form of electronic processing, far-sighted individuals set out to build monumental indexes to the nation's records that remain useful to this day; and how like-minded enthusiasts across the country came together to cooperate in groups and societies for the common good. Family historians blazed a trail in the application of home computers and popular use of the internet. Today, they are in the vanguard of another revolution in gene technology that promises to reshape not just our understanding of the past but also our knowledge of ourselves.

The world of family history is changing more rapidly than ever before. Technology now allows users to undertake a great deal of research from home without ever stepping inside a record office. Email and 'social networking' allow amateur historians to share information and build their family trees together online. New multi-million pound businesses are emerging to service this market and competition to develop the biggest user base is fierce. Historical records that have lain dormant for years are suddenly hot property as companies seek to acquire the best digital content. At the same time, regulatory concerns are emerging regarding privacy and security, which threaten to seriously restrict access to personal data in the future. And over-shadowing all of this is the spectre of 'the new genealogy' based on the application of advanced genetic techniques.

*   *   *   *

The desire to know one's antecedents is a basic human instinct. Since earliest times mankind has sought to connect with his forefathers and an interest in ancestry is found in all nations and periods.

At its most primitive, this desire for connection is expressed through ancestor worship. Veneration of the dead has been practised by societies and cultures around the world, from the prehistoric peoples of Stonehenge through to modern-day Aborigines, and remains an important tenet in various religions. Central to most such societies is the belief that deceased family members continue to exist in an afterlife and can even influence the fortune of the living. Ancestor veneration also has a social function, serving to cultivate kinship values, family loyalty and continuity of the family lineage.

The ancient Egyptians kept records of their pharaohs and dynasties, many of whom were remembered by building pyramids, the most famous historical monuments devoted to the dead. Egyptians believed that the survival of the soul required a physical receptacle for the soul, hence the emphasis on mummification and portraiture.

The ancient Greeks employed genealogy to prove descent from the gods, which was a means of achieving social status. Their methods were hardly scientific, however, consisting primarily of epic poems, such as the *Iliad* and the *Odyssey*, that mixed history and myth. Their neighbours and successors in ancient Rome practised genealogy to distinguish between the patrician class (those with proven noble ancestry) and plebeians (commoners). Aristocratic Romans kept portraits of their male ancestors, a custom shared with other Mediterranean societies. In some cases these portraits would be in the form of death masks which would be worn by surviving family members at festival time. The Romans were also the first to give male children two or three names – personal names and the clan or family name.

The Judaeo-Christian tradition is imbued with genealogies. In Old Testament times ancient lineages were cited to reinforce Hebrew claims to be the Chosen People. The first nine chapters of 1 Chronicles, for example, give genealogies from Adam through Abraham and other patriarchs, concluding 'so all Israel were reckoned by genealogies'. Another notable passage in Genesis 10 (known as the Table of Nations), describes how all the countries of the world came to be populated by Noah's sons after the Great Flood, mentioning some seventy-two people in all. These genealogies serve a number of purposes:

providing origin myths, helping to define early Israel's nationhood, and confirming the authority of its kings and priests. The religious historian Donald Akenson has described the Old Testament genealogical narratives as 'a big imperial engine', exerting a power over succeeding cultures that was virtually impossible to overthrow and in some quarters persists to the present day. He explains their significance thus:[1]

> The Old Testament genealogies are artistic in nature by virtue of their being a massive metaphor. They account for human life, religious practices, and dynastic and geo-political events through a metaphor of biological propagation. Thus, world history necessarily becomes a form of family history. This is a metaphorical framework so strong that the biblical tales could not be told in any other way: if the stories jumped out of the framework of genealogical narrative they would not be biblical.

This theme continues in the New Testament, where the genealogy of Jesus is given twice, with variations between the versions. The Apostle Paul tried to break with the previous tradition and cautioned against 'false doctrines . . . myths and endless genealogies'.[2] In Islam, the genealogy of Muhammad (who had twelve wives) became significant in deciding on the prophet's successor after his death and was a factor in subsequent divisions in the Muslim community.

In more recent times, genealogy has been emphasized by the Church of Jesus Christ of Latter Day Saints (LDS), generally known as the Mormons.[3] According to Mormon teachings, church followers have a responsibility to document their ancestors in order to bring their names to the temple for baptism. In support of this belief, the Mormon church has developed an extensive genealogical organization. From its headquarters in Salt Lake City, it has sponsored work across the world to search out, microfilm and more recently computerize records relating to the ancestry of church members and the population in general. All members of the church contribute to this work either financially or by the personal searches they carry out.[4]

Several Eastern religions promoted ancestor worship and filial piety, so descendants needed to know the identity of their ancestors for religious reasons. Ancestor veneration emerged from a fusion of the teachings of Confucius and Laozi, and ceremonies to honour these ancestors have been held for more than 2,000 years. Genealogies that date back a thousand years are not uncommon among Chinese people today. In 2009, a special committee published the genealogy of Confucius himself. Spanning 2,560 years, it runs to over two million descendants not just in China but around the world.[5] It is accepted by Guinness World Records as the 'longest pedigree in the world', although scholars dispute its authenticity.

Among Native Americans, totem poles were sometimes used as a genealogical record. Found across the Northwest coast, these tall poles, carved from wood, traced the histories of families and clans much like a family crest or family tree. Each figure on the pole represented a special event or characteristic – a totem – associated with the family. Totems often took the form of an animal or spirit. In some tribes, such as the Haida people of the Queen Charlotte Islands, a pole would be erected when a community member died and was decorated with scenes to commemorate their life.

Often the task of recalling and recording a society's or tribe's ancestry has fallen to a class of professional remembrancers – variously described as monks, priests, shamans or griots – who are able to recite lineages going back many generations. In tribal societies, especially, children would either be taught to recite their pedigrees by heart, or else an elder or priest would be called on to preserve the pedigrees for the whole tribe.

One of the most remarkable oral traditions is in the Maori people of New Zealand, who can repeat their pedigree back nearly 800 years to when their ancestors arrived in canoes from other Pacific islands. In one celebrated incident, an aged Maori chief called Tamarau appeared before the New Zealand Land Commission.[6] He supported his people's claim to certain lands by reciting for more than three days pedigrees dating back thirty-four generations and containing more than 1,400 names. The system, known as the *whakapapa*, is distinctive not only for its breadth of genealogical knowledge but also for its inclusiveness: a person only has to show one verifiable Maori ancestor to be admitted to the Maori bloodline. These genealogies continue to be cited in land claims under the Waitangi Tribunal to this day.[7]

The author Alex Haley encountered a similar oral tradition in modern-day Africa. In his book *Roots*, he recounted how the shamans or 'griots' keep the clan genealogies in their heads. In a village in Gambia, he sat entranced as the local griot 'began to recite for me the ancestral history of the Kinte clan, as it had been passed along orally down across the centuries from the forefathers' time'.[8] For the villagers it was a formal occasion, Haley noted, 'as if a scroll were being read'.

A common notion is that we in Britain are all related and that with sufficient research we could trace everyone's family tree back to the Norman Conquest. A little basic mathematics shows this is not as far-fetched as one might think. We are separated from the events of 1066 by some 950 years, equivalent to approximately thirty generations. Theoretically, a person living today would then have had over 100 million ancestors (2 to the power 30), or around fifty million ancestor couples. Compare this to the population of Britain at that time (ignoring the Celtic fringe), estimated to be no more than 1.5 million, made up of three generations: grandparents, parents and children. The middle, parental, generation would have comprised about 600,000 persons, or 300,000 couples, and it is reasonable to assume that the lines of around half of these would have died out at various times since. The surviving lines will lead back to just 150,000 couples, rather than the theoretical fifty million. Thus, we should not be surprised when celebrities on *Who Do You Think You Are?* find links back to William the Conqueror; it is statistically inevitable that any person of English origin today is descended not just from William and his queen but from *everyone* else alive in England at the time. If we could probe deep enough, we would find that we all have royal blood. Adding in Scottish and Welsh ancestors and incomers will affect the figures to some degree, but not sufficient to outweigh the relentless effect of doubling of ancestors from one generation to the next.

One possible objection to this conclusion is that it ignores class divisions and the isolation of families in remote communities. But such criticisms overlook the fact that in England class divisions have never been absolute – this, as we shall see, is one of genealogy's most important contributions to historical study – and that family immobility is largely irrelevant when all female descents are also considered (since a majority of females tended to marry outside their home parish). To the extent these objections are valid, it would show that any given family is descended from even fewer ancestors than if there were full social and geographical movement. Modern genetic techniques are set to cast such extrapolations in a new light, providing further insights on the origins of individual families, the extent to which they moved around, and interrelationships within communities.

* * * *

In general usage, the terms 'genealogy' and 'family history' tend to be used interchangeably, although purists draw a clear distinction between the two. A genealogy, according to the *Concise Oxford English Dictionary*, is 'a line of decent traced continuously from an ancestor'. Genealogists set out to develop a pedigree – a family tree – based on identification of births, marriages and deaths. Family history is wider in scope, aiming to fill out the branches of this tree through investigation of other aspects of our ancestors' lives. It involves genealogical, biographical and historical research, typically resulting in a well-documented narrative history that places one's ancestors in the historical and social context in which they lived. As the British genealogist Don Steel noted: 'Not every genealogist is a family historian, but every family historian must be a genealogist, for a genealogy is the foundation upon which all else rests.'[9] Steel's contemporary Elizabeth Simpson, observed: 'People start off as genealogists, setting out to "collect the set", the 2-4-8-16-32 infinity of ancestors, and all without exception, sooner or later, hit a brick wall. It is then that the real enthusiast becomes a family historian.'[10]
Genealogy – from the Greek *genea*, 'generation' – is certainly the older term, but the distinction is artificial, at least in modern times. Serious genealogists have never been content with placing names on the 'wire frame' of a family

tree. Even in the pre-computer era it was possible to find out a substantial amount about the lives of one's ancestors, as the many written accounts from the late nineteenth and early twentieth centuries bear out. Writing in 1915, the American genealogist Henry Byron Phillips noted that: 'A pedigree is valuable, but immensely more so when associated with the lives of its component members, or as may be said clothed with flesh and blood.'[11] In 1957, Lester Cappon observed that: 'The study of genealogy is something larger than the particular genealogy itself, it is the history of a family in both its immediate relationship and its wider impact on society.'[12]

To the extent early genealogists produced pedigrees rather than written family histories, it was more symptomatic of the difficulties of research rather than any desire to limit their approach. In the days when parish registers were still held in churches, census returns had to be searched by hand and few records were indexed, even a skeleton pedigree could take a considerable time to research with any accuracy. But if a researcher 'got lucky' – for instance by having an ancestor with an unusual surname, coming across a detailed will or newspaper account, or a link into a well-researched line – then (as now) a substantial amount could be found out about them.

The British genealogist George Sherwood, writing in about 1910, was among the first to recognize that the depth of possible research depended on the breadth and quality of available records. 'Our study', he noted, 'is the study of life itself; upon "documents" we have to rely for the knowledge of every episode preceding our own limited experience: all social progress essentially depends upon tradition and writing.'[13]

The novelist Thomas Hardy, who was a keen genealogist, observed how even the most basic information can tell a story:[14]

> Pedigrees . . . arranged in diagrams . . . mostly appear at first sight to be as barren of any touch of nature as a table of logarithms. But given a clue, the faintest tradition of what went on behind the scenes, and this dryness as of dust may be transformed into a palpitating drama. More, the careful comparison of dates alone – that of birth, or death with a kindred marriage, birth or death – will often effect the same transformation, and anybody practised in raising images from such genealogies finds himself unconsciously filling into the framework the motives, passions, and personal qualities which would appear to be the single explanation possible of some extraordinary conjunction in times, events, and personages that occasionally marks these reticent family records.

The term 'pedigree' has snobbish connotations today through its association with pets and livestock. In the eighteenth century, new stockbreeding techniques led to records being kept of the lineages of race horses and prize cattle. These came to be known as pedigreed horses, etc. as against the common sort whose origins were unknown. Thus, 'pedigree' acquired overtones of superiority which 'genealogy' has never had. Prior to the twentieth century such notions were reinforced by the fact that for people it was primarily the genealogies of the nobility and other prominent figures in the written record.

While we are considering the naming of parts, it is useful also to clarify what we mean by 'ancestor', 'family' and 'kinship'. For the genealogist, an ancestor is a person from whom others are descended. A person's ancestry includes all lines of ascent through both male and female lines, as distinct from his/her family which (in Western societies at least) includes only the male line. Until the seventeenth century the term 'family' was used rather loosely and merely signified a household, including any servants and apprentices. Its genealogical usage, referring to people sharing a common male line, contrasts with the more colloquial use which includes close relatives on both the father's and mother's sides, and grandchildren by both sons and daughters. 'Kinship' – a term also used in areas such as anthropology and sociology – refers to the system of social (and other) links between people related either by blood or by marriage. Whatever the ties, kinship was hugely important in the pre-industrial age, with huge implications for how society functioned; this made it necessary for everyone to know who he was and how he related to those around him.

In English the naming of ancestors is rather cumbersome, relying on the prefacing of the word 'grandfather' (or 'grandmother') with one or more 'great'. Latin has a more economical usage based on a series of prefixes (similar to the metric system): grandfather is *avus*; great-grandfather is *proavus*; great-great-grandfather is *abavus*; and great-great-great-grandfather is *attavus*. Certain modern European languages retain a richer system for describing family relationships. Swedish, for example, distinguishes between a *farfar* (paternal grandfather) and a *morfar* (maternal grandfather). Similarly, it is possible to refer to a *faster* (paternal aunt) and a *moster* (maternal aunt). There are also separate terms for grandchildren of each gender, and for nephews and nieces depending on whether they are related through the male or female line.

A sign of our slimmed down family structures is that even this limited terminology is contracting. Forty or so years ago most British families would have been familiar with terms such as 'great-uncle' (a grandparent's brother), 'great-aunt' (a grandparent's sister), or 'second-cousin' (people who share the same great-grandparents other than siblings). They would have encountered these people in their daily lives, even if only at Christmas or family celebrations. In today's nuclear family such extended relationships are rare and even where the relationships exist the terms themselves are seldom used. This contracting vocabulary – what one scholar has called 'the poverty of terminology' – affects how we see and describe our families and kin systems, giving us a much more limited view of family and multi-generational relationships.[15]

The genealogical system used in Britain (and in all Western European societies) where families are associated with both the male and female lines is known as the 'standard double' and is only one of several 'genealogical grammars' identified by anthropologists.[16] Systems found in other cultures and societies include ones where descent is traced through the female line alone (i.e. from mother to mother to mother, so-called matrilineal) and through the male line alone (so-called patrilineal).[17] The former includes many First Nations in North America and several Polynesian island cultures. The latter is found in many regions of the world, especially tribal societies in Africa and Asia. One might think that our own system is patrilineal, in that surnames are handed down through the male line and genealogies have generally been male dominated. But the point with patrilineal systems is that female genealogies do not feature at all and often wives' names are not even recorded. In Britain, women might have had a raw deal from history but at least their names are in the records and if we wish we can usually follow their lines just as well as males.

*   *   *   *

So who are the modern-day genealogists and why do they do it? People set out to trace their ancestry for many and varied reasons. In many cases, the answer is simply curiosity: 'to see what's there'. Surveys show that often the spur is the death of a close relative, such as a parent, grandparent or aunt. The loss itself can leave people with a feeling they did not know the person as well as they should have done. In other cases a discovery in the deceased's possessions – a signet ring with an unknown coat of arms, a book plate in a family Bible, letters and diaries, a piece of silver with an ambiguous dedication, or annotations on photographs – can raise intriguing questions that beg investigation. Sometimes the stimulus is to see whether there is any truth behind a family story or legend that has been handed down over the years.

The idea of the chase appeals to some. Detective stories have long been one of the most popular genres of books, films and TV programmes. Family history is the closest most people will ever get to being a sleuth themselves. Tracing one's family tree always has the potential to throw up something unexpected, such as discovering a lost fortune, or uncovering a famous ancestor (preferably royal), or a link to a momentous national or local event. For others the search is more personal, such as seeking out a sibling given up for adoption or an estranged relative.

Market studies show the average age of a family history researcher in Britain today is 53. Two-thirds are in social categories ABC1, with females slightly better represented than males (57 per cent to 43 per cent). Over nine in ten (93 per cent) use the internet, making online genealogy one of the top ten internet activities (ranked eighth in 2008). The profile appears remarkably stable, despite the apparent widening appeal of family history over the last twenty years. For instance, readership surveys for one of the popular family history magazines during the 1990s showed an average age of 55, with a ratio of 58 females to 42 males. At that time around 60 per cent of the readership was over 50 years of age, figures that tally with membership profiles quoted by today's internet sites. Thus, while online genealogy offers new possibilities for the time-poor, such as those of working age, there is little evidence that it has substantially shifted the overall demographic.

Some commentators have seen the growing popularity of family history as indicative of a need to reaffirm our identity in a rootless world. The trend certainly comes against the background of growing social fragmentation. In the UK, the number of people living alone has risen fourfold in the last forty years to seven million, while one in four families is headed by a single parent. One in ten families are step-families.

With family life fracturing, it is hardly surprising that most Britons have only a tenuous knowledge of their family background. In a 2007 survey, less than half (46 per cent) of people questioned could name their grandparents' birthplace, and one in three (28 per cent) were unable to say whether a relative had fought in a world war.[18] Two in five (41 per cent) were unable to give their grandmothers' maiden names and one in three (36 per cent) had no idea of their grandfathers' professions. These scores were all well below their European counterparts, showing that Britons' knowledge of their personal heritage is among the weakest in Europe.

The notion that someone might *not* be interested in their ancestors has always appalled those who are. Cicero observed that: 'Not to know what happened before we were born is to remain forever a child. For what is the worth of a human life unless it is woven into the life of our ancestors.' Writing in his 1662 opus *The Worthies of England*, the historian Thomas Fuller admonished those who ignored their lineage thus:

> I cannot but condemn the carelessness, not to say ingratitude, of those who can give no better account of the place where their fathers and grandfathers were born, than the unborn child. I could almost wish that a moderate fine were imposed on such heirs, whose fathers were born before them, and yet they know not where they were born.

Similarly, those disposed to dwell on such matters have also wondered how they themselves will be remembered. Thomas Fothergill, Provost of Queens College, Oxford, writing to his brother Richard around 1740, refers to their mutual interest in family history. He then asks whether:[19]

> Some of our posterity may, perhaps, be as inquisitive as we have been, and think it (a hundred years hence) no unpleasing employment to guess at the tempers and characters of us, who have the present period of time allotted to act in.

Lest posterity be in any doubt, Fothergill goes on to recount at length exactly how the family of his time should be remembered.

In days gone by the goal would have been to find the earliest possible ancestor. Nowadays, most researchers take a more lateral view, being as interested in going 'sideways' into co-lateral branches of the family tree as in pursuing the main line. Their aim is not just to go backwards but to come forwards to living relatives with whom they share a common ancestry. These common kin connections can extend to hundreds or thousands of people, although in only a few cases is there personal contact.

Among the most common discoveries made by British family history researchers, one in five (19 per cent) say they have uncovered illegitimate children; one in seven (14 per cent) have family members who had changed their names; and around 7 per cent have family members who were convicted criminals.[20] Other discoveries include secret adoptions (6 per cent), missing family members (6 per cent) and royal blood connections (4 per cent). As the American writer Oliver Wendell Holmes observed, 'We are all omnibuses in which our ancestors ride, and every now and then one of them sticks his head out and embarrasses us.'[21]

*   *   *   *

Most people embark on family history knowing little about what to do or where to begin. The path, however, is well trodden and the beginner has countless 'how-to' books and guides to which to refer.

The best place to start is by talking to relatives. Older family members should be interviewed to confirm their dates and places of birth, and to find out anything they can remember about the family, such as names and dates for their own parents and grandparents and any family legends or stories. Next a researcher should try to locate important family documents, such as birth and marriage certificates, letters and diaries, newspaper cuttings, photograph albums or a family Bible. Armed with this information the searcher can then begin to assemble the basic genealogical facts for their close family and, with luck, further beyond.

Another useful step is to check whether the research has already been done and who else is researching the same or a similar name in a particular locality. Numerous published genealogies, directories and websites exist for this purpose.

A systematic approach is essential. A family historian is likely to consult many thousands of records from all sorts of different sources. The relevance of what is found may not be apparent until many years later, when it will be necessary to review the sources used and what was unearthed. Similarly, others may want to verify your research, or be stimulated to access the same records, or they may want to pick up where you left off. Hence, the serious researcher will adhere to rigorous standards of documentation. They will keep careful records of what searches they have done, even where nothing is found, as well as precise citations for sources where information is obtained (e.g. particular census returns, probate records, etc.). Sometimes 'negative proof' – the ability to rule out certain possibilities as a result of unsuccessful searches – can be used to support the truth of a particular supposition.

Having exhausted the immediate family, the next stage is to start consulting the records. Nowadays, this invariably means the internet. Two of the four most important sources of records – censuses and civil registration indexes – are fully available online through one or more of the commercial family history websites. Many parish registers – another major source – are also available online. For historical reasons, online coverage of the fourth category, wills is more patchy, though improving all the time. Most websites allow access on either a subscription or a pay-per-view basis.

The experienced researcher soon finds that one of the best online resources is other people. Genealogists were among the first and most avid users of electronic communication technology, sharing knowledge and information with each other long before the days of Facebook and MySpace. Today's family historian can tap into a vast online network of researchers who are able to share information, contribute their experiences, provide pointers on where to go and even undertake research for each other.

All of this means that the computer is now essential to the genealogist's art. While it is still possible to pursue research using just pen and paper, all but the most technophobic recognize the huge advantages of personal computers in being able to store, analyse and present their information. As well as the online records and forums, many software programs are available tailored to the needs of genealogists of all levels, from the casual investigator to the professional researcher. These allow the raw genealogical data to be stored and processed, replacing the record sheets that would have been used formerly. Once the data is computerized, a family tree (in a variety of forms) can be produced much easier and quicker than in the past. Specialist online services and marketplaces have also grown up, catering for everything from books and data CDs to genetic tests.

Impressive as they are, the online resources represent just a tiny fraction of the nation's genealogical memory. Britain has one of the richest collections of public records anywhere in the world. From Domesday Book on, kings and clerics through the ages have gathered information on the country and its people, often in meticulous detail. Invariably this was for the purpose of raising taxes to pay for military campaigns or other extravagances. The benefits of their labours have been handed down to us today through a myriad of records that document every aspect of life in Britain over the last millennium. They range from accounts of the annual payments made to feudal lords (known as scutage), vast holdings of manorial records spanning some 800 years, returns from obscure and short-lived tax-raising measures such as the Hearth Tax and Window Tax, to the first population censuses of the early nineteenth century, and modern records of passenger movements to and from the Empire and the New World. Inevitably, some of the resulting panoply of records has been lost along the way through war, fire, flood and outright neglect. But a substantial proportion still remains and is to be found in books, manuscripts, vellum scrolls, card indexes, microfilm and microfiche at specialist repositories up and down the land.

Thus, once the online trail goes cold, the next step for the serious researcher is to beat a path to the various libraries, record offices and archives, both national and local. Organizations with significant holdings include the National Archives (TNA, formerly the Public Record Office) at Kew, county and other record offices in major towns and cities, and Family History Centres across the country run by the Mormon church. These are only the beginning, however. The family historian, as the nineteenth-century genealogist Frederick Snell observed, has 'an unappeasable curiosity for small details',[22] and once sparked into action will seek out evidence wherever it is to be found. Military museums (the military were fastidious record keepers), churches, local history societies, specialist museums and libraries, heritage centres, private and company archives are all grist to the genealogist's mill.

There is no shortage of self-help books and guides for people to consult. Genealogical publishing has experienced a boom over the last thirty years, and at one time it seemed that you could not be taken seriously in the world of family history unless you had written a beginners' guide. Writers such as Jeremy Gibson and Stuart Raymond have developed more extensive series of guides focusing on specific subjects. This publishing bonanza shows signs of having peaked now that information is so freely available online. Periodicals have prospered too and at the time of writing the British market is served by six monthly magazines.

Traditionally, local family history societies have been a valuable source of information and support. Since the early 1960s, genealogists have banded together in locally based societies. Members contribute their knowledge, share their successes and brick walls, identify potential connections with other researchers, and generally extend their learning and understanding. In the 1970s these societies came together in a nationwide federation dedicated to projects of mutual interest, such as indexing and preserving records. Many also produce useful journals and publish directories listing their members' research interests.

In the words of Don Steel, 'Family history is a life sentence. However much you have done, there is always more to do.'[23] While many genealogists will never concede that they are 'finished', at some point most reach a stage where they wish to write up their findings. This might be to share with family members or publish on a website, or even to offer for commercial publication. In any case, it is good practice for researchers to summarize their findings now and again since the process can throw up possible leads and neglected areas. Also, circulating a written account to family members may bring to light new information and reminiscences.

Computer programs can generate narratives based on simple genealogical facts and notes, but any account restricted to key life events – birth, marriage, occupation, migration, etc. – is of little value other than as a work of reference. Producing an engaging and readable account requires considerable historical knowledge, as well as a degree of writing skill. Here, too, technology is opening up new possibilities, with websites and 'social networks' allowing people to collaborate in writing the family narrative.

Once started a genealogical project can go in any number of directions. What began as a personal interest, 'just for fun', can blossom into a lifelong study that draws in people all over the world. Some projects stay small and focused on their original aims, while others develop into more extended trees. Certain researchers opt for depth – a one-name or one-place study, the history of a company or trade, or a full-scale biography of a noteworthy ancestor. It is not uncommon for someone to drop a project for five or ten years and then return to it as time and circumstances allow.

Whichever direction they choose to pursue, genealogists will find that high standards of research, documentation and presentation pay off. With sensitive personal information more freely available and increasing concerns about privacy, family historians also have to confront important ethical questions. Is it acceptable, for instance, to publish the details of living individuals in an online family tree? How far should a researcher go in using information obtained from others? Do they have a right to share such data with third parties?

Not all genealogists are enthusiastic amateurs. Alongside the hobbyist is a relatively small band of professional genealogists who make their living from research. Their clients range from individuals who have hit a 'road block' in their research, or lack the time to do it themselves, to lawyers handling intestacy and inheritance cases. In recent years a new market has grown up among TV production companies making historical and genealogical documentaries. Sometimes professionals will be asked to research a whole family tree, in other cases it is a matter of a specific search, for instance where a client is too distant to visit a particular archive themselves.

Although the number of professionals has increased over recent years, it has not matched the growth in interest in family history overall. For most family historians the prime attraction is in undertaking the quest themselves and only a small minority would contemplate employing a professional researcher. Consequently, the majority of professionals tend to be self-employed or work in small practices of two or three people. Often they are supplementing their income from another source. In such a broad field, many professional genealogists choose to specialize in some way, concentrating on particular periods, areas or occupations, and calling on networks of other researchers where necessary.

The relationship between amateurs and professionals has not always been a happy one. Professionals have derided the sloppy approach of some hobbyists and have complained of being undercut by amateurs who turn to paid research seeking to make a quick buck. The outspoken American genealogist Donald Lines Jacobus, writing in the early 1970s, complained that:[24]

> It is sometimes said of a man who insists on acting as his own lawyer that he has a fool for a client, and too often the same observation is appropriate for a man who insists on being his own genealogist.

He continued:

> Many family histories have been produced by enthusiastic novices, whose enthusiasm is too often the only qualification they bring to the task. The man who would seek the advice and services of a trained expert in any other field of human activity, considers himself quite competent to compile a history of his family. Without previous experience, without knowledge of record sources of information, and often without the kind of mentality capable of handling and arranging infinite detail of facts, names and dates, it is small wonder that his book, more often than not, is a hodge-podge of traditional statements, guesses, and misinterpreted and misplaced records, interspersed with actual proved facts. Occasionally, results are not much better when an incompetent professional is employed.

Enthusiasts, for their part, have complained of professionals who are too ready to run up a bill with little to show for it and offer poor value for money. Such concerns led, in the late 1960s, to the formation of an association to represent the interests of professional genealogists and a movement to improve standards of research among amateurs and professionals alike.

*   *   *   *

Is there a practical value to all this beyond the idle curiosity of knowing one's ancestors? While millions of people engage in genealogy as an enjoyable leisure pursuit, it has benefits in a number of fields.

One of the most visible applications is among lawyers who call on the services of genealogists in intestacy cases. When a person dies without leaving a valid will their estate must be shared out according to certain rules. In the UK, only married or civil partners and some other close relatives can inherit under the rules of intestacy. If there are no identifiable heirs the estate is declared *bona vacantia* (meaning 'vacant goods') and passes to the Crown. The Treasury Solicitor is then responsible for dealing with the estate. The Crown can make grants from the estate but does not have to agree to them. Lawyers and genealogists can use the advertisements on the Treasury Solicitor's website and in national and local newspapers to try to trace beneficiaries, an aspect profiled in the BBC TV series *Heir Hunters*.

In one of the most celebrated cases of intestacy, Ida Wood, widow of a New York newspaper magnate, died in 1933 at the age of 94.[25] Over 1,100 people came forward contesting to be her nearest relatives and claiming a share of her considerable estate. The claimants were a mixture of the genuine, the deluded and the outright fraudulent. The case was eventually settled in 1939 after intense genealogical investigations in America and Europe. Only one of the ten successful claimants knew of Mrs Wood's existence and none had ever met her.

Even where a will is left its terms can be so vague as to require original genealogical enquiry. William Jermy of Bayfield, Norfolk, was storing up a maelstrom of legal activity when in his will, made in 1751, he bequeathed his estate 'to such male person of the name of Jermy as shall be the nearest related to me'.[26] A number of claimants came forward and extensive litigation ensued. The case was still before the courts in 1878 when the Lord Chief Justice commented: 'There probably never was a property in the country the title of which has given rise to such obstinate disputes, or has been the source of much litigation and crime.' The claims rumbled on into the early twentieth century, by which time any fortune associated with the estate had long since vanished.

Another area where genealogy impinges on the law is in peerage and succession claims. Indeed, for a substantial period from the seventeenth through to the mid-nineteenth centuries, the main function of genealogy in Britain was in proving the inheritance of peerages. Genealogists were employed in documenting the lineage of peers and major works began to appear setting these lineages in print. The fact that many such pedigrees were, for various reasons, based on false or erroneous information was the cause of much controversy and brought discredit to the genealogical community of the day. Although the hereditary peerage is much less significant in the life of the nation than it once was, the College of Arms retains a quasi-legal role in relation to peerages.

Charities such as the Salvation Army and the Red Cross employ genealogical techniques in tracing missing or estranged persons. The Salvation Army's Family Tracing Service reunites around 20,000 people every year and claims an 85 per cent success rate.

In the literary world, genealogical perspectives are of great value in biography. This field of writing has expanded significantly over recent years, as we seek more personalized interpretations of both historical and contemporary events. Biographers may wish to ascertain the descent of their subject to get insights into their background and family relationships, and to trace living descendants in the hope of finding useful and hitherto unknown material. They use all the usual genealogical techniques, with a special emphasis on wills which can be a treasure trove of biographical information: lists of legacies to friends and family members, descriptions of possession and property, and even the omissions can say much about the subject's personal relationships.

Scientists and clinicians have turned to genealogy in an attempt to understand the inheritance of various traits and diseases. The Royal College of Physicians estimates that between 2 and 3 per cent of births in Britain result in babies with some form of congenital (i.e. inherited) or genetically determined abnormality. Approximately 13,000 births per year are affected in this way, while some conditions only manifest themselves later in life. Around 5 per cent of the population will have developed a genetic condition by the age of 25. In later life this figure rises to approximately 60 per cent, including conditions in which genetics plays some role.

In the UK, the commonest (although not necessarily the best known) genetic disorders are the heart conditions Familial Combined Hyperlipidaemia (5.0 per thousand births) and Familial Hypercholsterolaemia (2.0 per thousand births). Huntington's disease – a hereditary disorder of the central nervous system – affects about five in ten thousand births. Some genetic disorders vary from one ethnic group to another. The highest frequency of sickle cell anaemia, for example, is to be found in populations with a mid-African background. Cystic fibrosis is most common amongst northern Europeans and their descendants. Many comparatively common forms of blindness, deafness, learning disabilities and malformations are probably caused by a number of different genes.

An interest in how certain traits are passed from parents to their offspring is nothing new. Gregor Mendel founded genetics as the science of inheritance in the mid-nineteenth century, although he studied peas, not humans. From 1890–1920, there was increasing interest in tracing traits in human families, and in a few cases, such as in the study of simple recessive diseases, these studies were placed in the context of Mendelian genetics. Scientists relied initially on studies of fruit flies, mice, and other experimental organisms, and by the 1920s genetic principles were being applied in the selective breeding of livestock. In the early 1930s geneticists such as John Haldane and Ronald Fisher realized that the same techniques could be applied to data on human families and pedigrees.

It was in these early decades of the twentieth century that genealogy faced its darkest hour, through association with the eugenics movement. Eugenicists believed that the selective breeding used in plants and animals could also be applied to humans, with the aim of improving the species. Its advocates sought to counter what they regarded as degenerate or 'dysgenic' dynamics within the human gene pool. The founder of the modern school was Sir Francis Galton, a cousin of Charles Darwin, and at its peak eugenics drew support from many prominent people and a broad spectrum of society. Its proponents included such respected figures as John Maynard Keynes, George Bernard Shaw, Emile Zola, H G Wells, and Marie Stopes. Many leading scientists were also involved with eugenics, including Haldane, Fisher and Karl Pearson, one of the founders of modern statistics.

The movement fed on genealogy; Galton even offered prizes for the biggest compilations of family data. In the United States in particular, where issues of race and immigration were prominent, genealogists provided cover for eugenicists. The president of the National Genealogical Society referred in 1903 to 'the degeneracy and decay of modern society' and the 'negative' influence of immigrants.[27] New solutions to these problems, he argued, lay in the ideas on reproductive choices made possible by the new 'sciences' of genealogy and eugenics. The *Wisconsin Magazine of History* advised its readers in 1923 that the 'only hope of improving the race is through 'selective breeding'', and that questions dealing with racial superiority and traits 'may often profitably be considered with the aid of data compiled and worked out in genealogical study'.[28] Although British genealogists were generally less vocal in their support than their American counterparts, they too became foils for this new pseudo-science.

There was extensive overlap between eugenics and human genetics at this time. Practitioners from both fields published in the same journals and presented at the same conferences. Papers about polydactyly (a congenital condition where patients have an excess of fingers or toes) and cleft lip appeared side by side with papers about pauperism and 'feeble-mindedness'. Each used the pedigree as a tool to demonstrate or prove their hereditarian claims. According to the geneticist Robert Resta:[29]

> Pedigrees permitted eugenicists to objectify the families they studied. Reducing their subjects to geometric shapes reinforced the notion that dysgenic families with their problems of feeble-mindedness, poverty, and squalid living conditions were somehow less than human. Once rendered non-human, dysgenic families were no longer worthy of social and economic support.

This objective display of data helped legitimize eugenics as 'real science'. Starting in the United States in the early 1900s, several countries implemented eugenics policies – sterilizing certain mental patients, for example – as a means of population control. It led ultimately to the atrocities of Nazi Germany where ideas from eugenics legislation were used in support of the mass sterilization of 'defectives' and the extermination of 'undesired' population groups.

Since the discovery of DNA (deoxyribonucleic acid) by James Watson and Francis Crick in the early 1950s, genetics has replaced eugenics as the focus for studies of human inheritance. Modern-day geneticists study the mechanisms by which genes – the blueprint for life – are passed through generations, and how variations in these blueprints are essential for evolution yet can cause disease.

Essentially, genetics is about understanding the consequences of patterns of descent of particular genes. Here family-level studies provide an important link between low-level laboratory experiments and high-level statistical analysis. The geneticist Elizabeth Thompson explained their value:[30]

> One can do genetics in the laboratory, but to relate the DNA sequences of genes to their phenotypic effects we need data on individuals. At the other end of the scale, one can study the genetic characteristics of populations, analysing patterns of differentiation and similarity at the population level. However, the population is a collection of individuals. It is at the individual and family level, in between the population and the test-tube, that the pedigree relationships among individuals affects the patterns of trait occurrences that we can observe.

Hence, the pedigree is a vital tool for geneticists. They have used data on pedigrees to test the distribution of diseases, analyse similarities among relatives, test for genetic linkage among traits, and more generally to understand the genetic basis of various conditions. Major endeavours such as the Human Genome Project, the international effort that mapped all human genes, rely heavily on pedigree relationships.

In contrast to genealogical pedigrees, genetic pedigrees are usually drawn to demonstrate the inheritance of biological traits rather than to identify specific individuals. Scientists have developed their own conventions for this purpose, based on systems of squares and circles, which appear in medical journals and scientific papers.

As the cost of DNA tests has fallen over recent years, a new market has grown up in applying genetics knowledge to traditional genealogy. Genealogical DNA testing can be used to determine the nature of the relationship between individuals in a variety of ways. Direct paternal and maternal lineages, more general geographical and ethnic origins, and patterns of human migration can all be interpreted – to varying levels of detail and accuracy – from an individual's genetic information.

While genetics is the new frontier, genealogy and history have a long-standing association. Genealogy has been called the 'handmaid of history' and although the two might be thought of as natural allies, the relationship between them has often been fraught.

Prior to the mid-nineteenth century, those concerned with studying the past followed a broad amalgam of historical interests. The genealogist, biographer, antiquarian and historian were usually one and the same person. In the late 1800s historical enquiry splintered into roughly three directions. Local historians chronicled the town and the county, leading to the growth of many local history societies. Its practitioners were typically the local clergy or squire who set out to record the natural and local history of their area. History proper became an academic pursuit, with history departments being established in universities and colleges, and professional organizations being set up. Genealogy – the third strand – was left out on a limb, becoming the preserve of a few professionals and a popular pastime for the upper and middle classes.

The interdependence is seen most clearly in the realm of local history. The sources most often used by the genealogist – such as parish registers, wills, manorial records and census returns – are also those of interest to the local historian. In many cases it was the genealogists that got there first and – as we shall see – the fact these records have been preserved and made accessible for all fields of study owes much to the genealogists of previous generations.

Commenting on the value of genealogy to the historian, Cambridge academic Peter Spufford has noted:[31]

> The historian is interested in broad genealogies that give living kinship groups, that enable him to see how and why particular men or particular groups of men were able to bring influence to bear on national policies, on religious opinion, or on village society. Such broad genealogies conversely enable him to see the pressures brought to bear on the individual members of the kinship group by their living relatives. . . .
> Only to a lesser extent is the historian interested in the dead relatives of his subject, and then only if they contributed something to his theme, whether it be something as tangible as land, or as intangible as inherited talent.

Spufford cites numerous examples where, within these confines, the genealogist can throw light on the national narrative. They include the build-up of estates and kinship groups during the feudal period; the problems of the rise of the gentry; tensions between family and personal alignments during the Civil War; the importance of family alliances in eighteenth-century politics; and hereditary ability in civil service and academic dynasties.

The willingness of academic historians, such as Spufford, to entertain the idea that genealogy has anything to bring to the historical party is a relatively recent development. For many years professional historians had little time for a field they saw as amateurish, insufficiently rigorous and lacking context. Historical truth, these academics argued, could be understood only through scientific methods of study, specifically through research, objective analyses and careful documentation. Deriding 'antiquarianism', they sought to professionalize their field by divorcing it from areas outside traditional scholarship.

According to this view, history was, in the oft-quoted words of Thomas Carlyle, 'the biography of great men'. For Carlyle's generation (he died in

1881), it was the nation's leaders who were the 'creators of whatsoever the great mass of men contrived to do or to attain; all things that we see standing accomplished' arose from the 'thoughts that dwelt in the great men sent into the world'. Thus, the historical narrative was around great events and the movers and shakers of past eras: major battles, kings and nobility, treaties, institutions. Scant consideration was given to ordinary people, their environment, social and family relations, work and play.

The snobbery of genealogists did not help their cause. For many the key concern was to establish links to the Conquest, or to nobility or royalty, or to major historical events such as Trafalgar or Waterloo. This snobbery even influenced what records genealogists deemed worthy of preservation. Explaining the policy on copying and publishing parish registers, one editor noted in 1878 that: 'as a genealogical society we are not concerned to find ancestors for families which have risen to the ranks of gentry in recent times: our business is only with the record of those who at the time the entry was made were persons of recognized social position'.[32]

In the absence of clear channels of communication between the two camps, stereotypes took over. Historians tended to see genealogists as fusty antiquarians or busybody maiden aunts. Genealogists were assumed to be over-enthusiastic amateurs too engrossed in chasing down a famous relative to be objective, and prone to sloppy work. Seeing their main output as the unembellished family tree, one 1950s historian surmised that the genealogist 'produces only charts crammed with more notes and dates, bearing obscure numbers, and signifying little to the historian'.[33] For their part, genealogists reproached historians for having only a vague understanding of their methods and for not acknowledging their skills in records research.

Even some genealogists were concerned at their field's poor reputation. Writing in 1913, the American genealogist Charles Bolton asked: 'Are we genealogists writing the lives of people or are we copying records?'[34] A generation later, another American writer, Arthur Adams complained that:[35]

> Many genealogists, falsely so called, do lack a true historical spirit, have no understanding of historical method, and have no vision beyond compiling of names and dates, . . . but a genealogy that doesn't rise above them and reach beyond them has small, if any, excuse for being.

The two sides became estranged, each eyeing the other with suspicion bordering on loathing. The schism persisted until well into the twentieth century.

By the early 1960s, genealogy's contribution in a historical context was beginning to be recognized. In history there was a shift towards social history, with an emphasis on the grassroots and day-to-day human affairs, including the family and history of the family. Genealogists, meanwhile, began to pay greater attention to indexing records (many preserved at local level) and, as more records became available, were able to explore wider family ties rather than linear pedigrees. It was increasingly clear that the two relied on the same records and offered complementary perspectives. Historians could add a wider dimension to family history, providing interpretation and meaning, while genealogists could provide crucial evidence for social history. Having long been maligned and ignored, genealogies came to be accepted as important source material on the family and wider kin relationships.

One of the main drivers of this reconciliation was from a new school of historians who sought insights into population growth and movements, a field of study known as historical demography.[36] How people moved about, trends in births, deaths and marriages, etc. requires inquiry at a very detailed level using large and statistically valid datasets. This area had been closed to historians until the 1950s when scholars realized that genealogical datasets – such as censuses and parish registers – then becoming available offered powerful tools. Rather than focusing on an individual family, they used these data to study whole communities, generating as far as possible huge inter-linked family trees – a technique known as family reconstitution. This was 'statistical genealogy', using large localized datasets converted into machine-readable form as a means of investigating societal behaviour.

Armed with these new tools, social historians were able to offer insights on a whole variety of areas. The balance between population and the supply of cultivable land; the importance of harvest and weather to the community; the raising of children and their relationship to their siblings; sexual mores; relationships between masters and apprentices; attitudes towards the poor; as well as specific demographic issues such as average size of families and life expectancy: all could be informed by a knowledge of the society's demographic character. The process of digging up and experimenting with community and family history cast genealogy in a whole new light.

In the study of migration, for example, these collections provided evidence on the movements of individuals and family groups that could not be obtained by any other means. They were also significant in the opposite context, where families have stayed put: intensive investigation of records of a locality over an extended period of time can yield new understanding of the relationships of families within a community.

Genealogical perspectives have proved especially important in studying social mobility and class. In Britain, in particular, historians have seen class as an important feature of the social and economic structure. Classes were considered to be broadly fixed in their composition with little social mobility up or down. According to the genealogist Sir Anthony Wagner, this represented a conspiracy between thinkers of both conservative and revolutionary traditions that portrayed social classes as 'distinct, self-perpetuating hereditary corporations'.[37]

The conservatives wished to believe that the same families had always been noble, which showed their merit; while the revolutionaries wished to believe that the same families had always been poor, which showed that their poverty was their oppressors' fault and not their own. Even the middle classes, whose social movement up or down was often rapid enough to be visible to the naked eye, did their best to hide this movement in the anonymity of city life.

'All history', Wagner argued, 'is biased by accidents of documentation.'[38] There was, quite understandably, a preference for the ruling classes in the historical record. The lack of documentary evidence on the lives of the lower economic and social strata had led historians to 'uncritical assumptions' about their importance and about the extent of mobility between classes. By ignoring the insights of social historians and genealogists, historians were missing an important part of the picture. Citing his own experience growing up in the early twentieth century, he noted:[39]

I was born into a middle-class, professional family and relations on both sides whom I came to know were of similar occupations and standing. The summary pedigrees, which were shown to me, recorded substantial mercantile antecedents but nothing *lower*. Before I had left school, however, my researches had ferreted out relationships of greater variety and interests – on certain sides rather higher in the social scale than had been expected, others decidedly lower. It surprised me that near kinsman, whose lines in two or three not very great steps had moved some way apart socially, should be not merely estranged but wholly unknown to each other. I wondered if my own family pattern was in this respect unusual. Experience as a genealogist has long since convinced me that it is not.

Genealogy, Wagner concluded, was essential to an understanding of social mobility in Britain, and hence to its social and economic history as a whole. Rather than being the biography of great men, history was better seen as 'a tournament of combining and competing families'.[40] He returned to the theme time and again in his writings, citing as examples the importance of kinship and family links in the economic success of eighteenth-century Quaker industrialists, in the American colonists in the seventeenth and eighteenth centuries, and in prominent thinkers of the nineteenth century. In a radio broadcast of 1960, he asserted his belief that: 'In the microcosm of family history we may hope to discern patterns which illuminate those of classes and nations.'[41]

This view has since come to be widely accepted. Today, family history is seen as a legitimate school in the telling of history and has been joined by other schools eager to invest history with perspectives other than those of the traditional elites.[42] Women's history emerged as a distinct field in the 1960s, offering new insights into the role of women in the family, the community, religion, work and public affairs. It became central to the feminist movement, providing inspiration for political campaigns and a context for understanding women's oppression. Ethnic minority history has explored issues of ethnic and racial identity, such as the role of the individual, the family, and community and kinship relationships within particular ethnic or racial groups. The history of childhood and labour history have also been addressed in this way. In more recent times the term 'community history' has been used to refer to the research and writing of history in a variety of settings outside university history departments.

Issues of family, generational relationships and kinship networks underpin all of these to a greater or lesser extent. Thus, a focus on the family and on intergenerational continuities and discontinuities – aspects that are the lifeblood of family history – brings new insights across the historical spectrum. Some, including in the genealogical community, have even gone so far as to describe current trends as indicative of the 'democratization of history', noting that it is not just the subject matter that is being opened up but also the scholarship. In the internet age anyone can contribute their perspective on historical (and indeed contemporary) events, so wresting the writing of history from professional historians.

Family historians have been in the vanguard of writing 'the people's history'. Over the last fifty years, and over the last decade especially, millions of ordinary Britons have joined the call and started researching their family's origins and background. Perhaps none speaks better for these anonymous masses than a recent contributor to a popular magazine, who described genealogists' motivations with these words:[43]

> When I sit in the quiet churchyards and stroke the stones warmed by the sun or cold and damp after rain, I can feel a connection back to the time when these families were grieving for the person that lies beneath the ground. This brings the meaning of genealogy to life in the need to name and draw a line below what has gone before. Genealogy is, literally, a study of your genes: what has made you what you are. It is history and anthropology and storytelling and a boundless curiosity. It is a determination to remember the past.

*   *   *   *

Chapter 2

The Nation's Memory

Family history is a giant jigsaw puzzle, one where you have no idea of the number of pieces, nor of how the picture will turn out. It involves a process of original historical investigation, gathering information from disparate sources (none of which were compiled with the genealogist in mind), piecing them together to see what picture emerges, and then constantly checking and rechecking against what is already known. In so doing the researcher musters a wide variety of records, ecclesiastical and civil, public and private, central and local, which are probed for their genealogical content.

Many of these records arise from an individual interacting with government in some way. Two important classes of records arise from the functions that have occupied the state since earliest times: collecting taxes and administering the law. In previous centuries the Exchequer dreamt up no end of ingenious ways of raising taxes (Hearth Tax, Window Tax, Land Tax, poll tax, etc.), each of which has associated records. Similarly, the judicial system's attention to detail has resulted in prodigious numbers of documents of value to the genealogist. The military were also meticulous record keepers and kept detailed accounts of an individual's service and career.

A second way in which an individual entered the official record was by being drawn into some act by a public agency. The most obvious examples are the two systems set up by the state specifically to collect information on individuals at key junctures: the civil registration of births, marriages and deaths; and the population census taken every ten years. Other significant acts of record can arise through the buying and selling of property, being party to a will, enrolling at school or university, being admitted to hospital, settling in a new area or country, or any of innumerable everyday activities. In more recent times, it has been recognized that significant sources exist in the private sphere as well, such as records of professional bodies, occupational records and lists of company shareholders.

Many of these institutions are relatively recent inventions, however. For centuries it was the church that dominated life in Britain and where most people left their mark. Parish registers, for recording births, marriages and deaths, were introduced in the sixteenth century and, as we shall see, have undergone significant evolution. While the registers are the most important sources, several other parochial records sat alongside them in the parish chest, such as banns books, marriage licenses, rate books and churchwardens' accounts showing Poor Law relief. The church itself may contain effigies and tombs, while outside in the churchyard are gravestones with monumental inscriptions.

As an island nation, seafaring has always been important for Britain and this has given rise to detailed records of people's movements both entering (immigration) and leaving (emigration) by ship. Often such passenger lists can be matched up with equivalent records elsewhere (e.g. Australia, Canada, USA, Caribbean, New Zealand).

A further class of what we could describe as 'semi-public' records arose in the eighteenth and nineteenth centuries with the growth of newspapers. These are produced privately but document the public sphere. The extent of newspapers in previous eras is difficult to comprehend today. At their peak in the late nineteenth and early twentieth centuries, virtually every small town in Britain had at least one daily newspaper, and large cities like London and Manchester had several. These documented local life in great detail, from general news reports and salacious court cases, to engagements and funerals of local dignitaries.

If exceptionally lucky, the modern-day family historian may also have access to private and family records: letters or diaries written by family members; inscriptions in a family Bible; property deeds (perhaps going back to manorial times); and even pedigrees and family histories compiled by previous generations. Heirlooms, such as medals and plaques, can also yield up useful information.

Weighing the value of all the potential sources available involves the researcher in a trade-off between the richness of the genealogical content and the ease with which any given source may be searched. Parish registers and census returns have very high genealogical content and so should always be searched, even if indexes are not readily available. Certain state papers, such as the printed volumes of Henry VIII's *Letters and Papers*, contain pedigrees from the period, among much else, and although their genealogical content is low they are very well indexed. Between these two extremes lie many classes of records where searching might be worthwhile. A key value of the internet is that it has not only facilitated systematic access to the high value content, but it has significantly expanded the accessibility of the lower value sources as well.

What do we mean by 'value' exactly? In probing these records the genealogist is looking for one of three things: direct links; inferred links; and proof of location. In certain classes of records the genealogical link is stated explicitly: a birth register, for example, will usually specify one or both parents; wills often mention spouses, children, grandchildren and other relations by name; and university, school and apprenticeship records frequently mention the parentage of those admitted. In other cases, proof of kinship is based on inference rather than direct statement. Where two or more individuals cannot be linked to one another directly, it may be possible to link both or all of them by observing patterns in the records. Thus, the tenure of land or property, successive occurrences of a trade, or successive holding of company stock can be used to infer kin relationships. The third class of records are those used to prove an ancestor's location at a given time rather than actual kin relationships. These range from ancient feudal surveys, poll lists and commercial directories, to modern-day telephone directories and electoral rolls. Especially important here are those that give clues to family migrations, such as census returns and (in earlier periods) Poor Law settlement certificates and apprenticeship records.

To these three categories one should add a fourth: records that add 'colour'. Certain sources provide no further facts at all on family relationships (or simply confirm what is readily available elsewhere) but are invaluable for the insight they offer into an ancestor's life. Court and occupational records fall into this category, as well as many military records and newspaper accounts. The extent to which a researcher is interested in such records distinguishes the 'genealogist' (content on compiling a family tree) from the 'family historian' (intent on recording a family's social history). It is here that the internet has had its biggest impact, yielding up a whole variety of sources that allow researchers to fill out their bare-bones biographies into accounts in which family members come alive.

While it is beyond our purpose here to delve into the origins of all these records, it is useful to our story to know how they arose and how they came to be key sources for the genealogists of today. The discussion focuses on the four categories of greatest value to the genealogist and which therefore have become a staple of the genealogical method: parish registers, civil registration, census returns and wills. We go on to briefly review the development of archives and archival legislation.

* * * *

Parish registers are a legacy of Henry VIII's turbulent reign.[1] Henry's split with Rome in order to secure a divorce and the dissolution of the monasteries that followed led him to seek greater control over the new, reformed church. Under an injunction of 5 September 1538, Thomas Cromwell, the Lord Privy Seal, ordered that the church keep records of events within their parishes. Parsons, vicars and curates were required to enter in a book every christening, marriage and burial with the names of the parties concerned. The entries were to be made each Sunday after the service, in the presence of one of the churchwardens. The parish was to provide a parish chest – 'a sure coffer with twoo lockes' – the parson having custody of one key and the wardens the other.

Despite the suspicions they engendered, parish registers were recognized as a useful innovation, a fact that enabled them to survive Mary I's efforts to roll back many of the Protestant reforms. In 1555, and again in 1557, Cardinal Pole – Mary's Catholic Archbishop – directed bishops to check whether registers were being kept, and ordered that the names of godparents should be recorded. Indeed, the Catholic Church all over Europe adopted a similar practice, following a decree to keep records of baptisms first instituted by Cardinal Ximenes, Archbishop of Toledo, in 1497. This was primarily to stem the growing scandal of divorce, where alleged kinship between parties was increasingly being cited as the basis for an annulment.

New orders, or 'cannons', issued by the province of Canterbury were approved by Elizabeth I in 1598 and reissued under James I in 1604, aimed at providing a more adequate framework for how registers were kept and maintained. Register entries were still to be made on Sundays, now in the presence of both churchwardens, and a third lock was to be added to the parish chest, with each warden having the key to his own lock.

Early registers were generally made of paper, sometimes even loose sheets, and so were not easy to preserve. The cannons ordered that parchment should be used instead. Each parish was to purchase new parchment registers and all names from the earlier registers were to be copied into them from the beginning, 'but especially since the beginning of the reign of the late queen'. Some clergy took this to mean that only registers since Elizabeth's accession in 1558 needed to be transcribed. Hence, many parish registers start only from this date. Since the old paper books were destroyed, much valuable information for the period 1538–58 was lost.

In addition, the cannons formalized the system whereby copies of registers were made to be kept in diocesan registries. This had been the custom in some dioceses since early in Elizabeth's reign and was now made general practice. Each year on Lady Day (25 March, the start of the 'legal year') an incumbent was required to submit a copy of their registers to their bishop. Thus, bishops' transcripts (or BTs as family historians call them) provide a valuable check on entries in parish registers for this period and in many cases may be the only surviving copy of a particular register.

During the Commonwealth (1649–60) the law provided for civil marriage, similar in many respects to that of today. Twenty-one days' notice had to be given to a registrar who was elected for each parish. They would arrange for the banns to be 'cried in the market place' or for a notice to be fixed in some public place. The marriage ceremony itself was performed by a Justice of the Peace (JP) or a similar official in the presence of at least two witnesses. On request, the officiating JP could provide the couple with a certificate of marriage which they could take to the registrar to be entered in the parish register.

On the restoration of the monarchy in 1660 all Acts of the Commonwealth became void. The task of keeping parish registers was restored to the clergy and a special Act had to be passed to legalize marriages which had been conducted by JPs.

Over the next 100 years parish registers saw little change. In 1694 a tax on births, marriages and deaths was imposed to help fund the war against France. Ministers were meant to collect the tax and were instructed to expand their registers to cover all such events, not just those within the Church of England. Mass avoidance of the tax led to it being abolished in 1705. A law was passed indemnifying the clergy from the heavy penalties they had incurred by not applying the law effectively.

As support for Nonconformist denominations grew during the seventeenth and eighteenth centuries, the traditional parish registers no longer provided a complete picture for a particular locality. Although the Quakers, the Jews and many of the Free Churches kept their own registers, these were outside the established system and did not have the same validity in law as parish registers.

During the eighteenth century the marriage laws were increasingly seen as unsatisfactory. Not only were the registers themselves inadequate and incomplete, but there was often insufficient preliminary enquiry by the clergy. Marriage was not an essential function of the parish church; it was accepted that marriage was contracted by mutual declaration by the partners, a common-law contract, which did not require a church service. Until 1763, the legal age for marriage was 14 for a boy and 12 for a girl, although parental consent was required up to the age of 21.

Priests failed to follow prescribed procedures, especially in certain enclaves (known as 'liberties and peculiars') operating outside of any ecclesiastical jurisdiction. Legislation in 1694 tackled the worst of the problem but failed to stamp out irregular marriages in the peculiars. Many of these were in the City of London, where a widespread traffic sprang up featuring furtive marriages from all over the country. One such was the Fleet prison, where clergymen imprisoned for debt conducted marriages in the prison chapel. A number of 'marriage centres' grew up in other parts of the country in places where incumbents were willing to flout the rules.

Irregular and clandestine marriage deprived the clergy of their legitimate income, nullified parental authority and threatened the descent of property. Parliament moved to end the scandal and in 1753 passed the Marriage Act which ended the practice of common-law marriage. The Act, generally known as Lord Hardwicke's Marriage Act, specified that a wedding was only legitimate if carried out in an Anglican church; only Quakers and Jews were allowed to conduct their own ceremonies. All marriages had to take place in the home parish of one of the parties and be preceded by the calling of banns or the grant of a licence.

The Act also introduced major changes in how marriage registers were maintained. Records were to be kept of both banns and marriages, and these had to be in proper books of vellum or good and durable paper provided by the churchwardens. Both parties had to sign the register, as did witnesses, and entries had to be recorded in a prescribed form. The registers themselves were to be carefully kept and preserved for public use. These marriage registers were the first to consist of bound volumes of printed forms and contained information on marriages alone. Until then clergy had usually used the same volume for baptisms, marriages and burials.

Another attempt to impose a duty on parish registers was made by the Stamp Act of 1783. This unpopular measure levied a tax of 3d. for every entry of a baptism, marriage or burial. It was extended in 1785 to include Nonconformists before being repealed in 1794.

The next major change – the most significant in the history of parish registers – came with George Rose's Act of 1812. This 'Act for the better regulating and preserving Parish and other Registers of Birth, Baptisms, Marriages, and Burials, in England' was passed on 28 July. Explaining its purpose, the Act stated that:

> Amending the Manner and Form of keeping and of preserving Registers of Baptisms, Marriages, and Burials of His Majesty's Subjects in the several Parishes and Places in England, will greatly facilitate the Proof of Pedigrees of Persons claiming to be entitled to Real or Personal Estates, and otherwise of great public Benefit and Advantage.

Following the success of the printed forms used for marriages under the 1753 Act, Rose's Act extended this requirement to baptisms and burials. From 1 January 1813 separate register books had to be kept for baptisms, marriages and burials, and ministers had to sign each entry. The king's printer provided each parish with new registers printed in the required format together with a copy of the Act. These three books were printed on durable paper and according to the standard layout and numbered entries laid down by the Act.

With the introduction of civil registration in 1837, parish registers became less important as legal documents. They primarily served the needs of the church rather than those of the state. The two systems have since run in parallel, and in the case of marriages a new form of register was introduced to provide the same details as the civil register. Under the Marriage Act 1929 the age of marriage with consent of parents was raised to 16 years for both boys and girls.

After a long campaign by family historians and others, in 1978 the General Synod of the Church of England passed the Parochial Registers and Records Measure as a means of ensuring the long-term care, preservation and access to parish records. Custodians of parish registers and records over 100 years old were required to deposit them in a designated record office (normally the county record office) unless exemption was obtained from the bishop. The measure reflected increased awareness of the value of parish records in historical research of all kinds, as well as recognition that, with the development of archival services, churches were not best placed to store or care for them.

*   *   *   *

The strict conditions on Roman Catholics and Nonconformists imposed under Lord Hardwicke's Act were widely viewed as an over-reaction to the lax situation that existed previously. Many refused to marry within the Anglican church, which was the only way for a marriage to be registered. Similarly, certain Nonconformists used their own baptismal rites, even though their registers could not be accepted as legal evidence. Industrialization and the migration of industrial workers to the cities added to the problem, reducing the number of babies brought for baptism. The result was chronic under-reporting and by the end of the eighteenth century there was growing pressure for national civil registration of births, deaths and marriages.

Various unsuccessful attempts were made but following the constitutional reforms of 1832 the House of Commons appointed a Select Committee to look into the whole system of parochial registration. The Committee recommended the establishment of a system of national civil registration of births, marriages and deaths administered from a central national office. Two bills implementing this were subsequently introduced and passed in 1836 as the Registration Act and the Marriage Act. The General Register Office (GRO) was set up with Thomas Henry Lister as its first Registrar General, appointed under letters patent from William IV. The two Acts came into force in England and Wales on 1 July 1837, just eleven days after the accession of the young Queen Victoria. Similar systems were introduced in Scotland in 1855 and Ireland in 1864.

In the days before local government, one of the major issues to be addressed was how this new system was to be administered at local level. Nothing like it had ever been attempted before. Should the clergy act as civil officers? Should the registrar be an elected officer? Or should the appointment be entirely civil, and how should the appointment be made?

The Poor Law Reform Act of 1834 had introduced Poor Law Commissioners covering several traditional parishes – called 'Unions' – to administer poor relief. Under the 1836 Registration Act these Unions were specified as the basis for registration districts under superintendent registrars, the districts being further subdivided into registrars' districts. The Act further specified that the clerk to the Board of Guardians of each Union should, if suitably qualified, also become the superintendent registrar.

By the end of 1838 the country had been divided into 619 districts, each with a superintendent registrar, about 500 of whom were clerks of Poor Law Unions. Underneath them were 2,193 registrars of births and deaths. Separate registrars were appointed for marriages (although these could also be registrars of births and deaths), who were licensed to conduct civil marriages within the new register offices. All registrars received a fee according to the number of entries made, for issuing certified copies of these entries, and for conducting marriages.

Controversy surrounded the new system and the association between the superintendents' offices and the workhouse did not help in gaining acceptance among the general population. This was particularly so as regards marriage, where a number of clergy circulated posters warning the public that they would have nothing to do with marriages enacted under the Act. It was some time before register office marriages were accepted, especially in areas such as Wales with strong religious ties.

The 1836 Acts made it clear that the system was to be administered centrally. From his office in London, the Registrar General was required to provide 'a sufficient number of register books for making entries of all births, deaths and marriages of His Majesty's subjects in England', according to a specified format. Each register contained space for 500 entries and once completed a volume was returned to the local superintendent registrar. The registers were kept in fire-proof iron boxes, each of which was 'furnished with a lock and two keys, and no more'; one of the keys was kept by the registrar and the other by the superintendent.

Each quarter local registrars were required to send copies of the entries to their superintendents who, after verifying them, were to forward them to the Registrar General, so enabling a national registry to be established. After further processing and checking, a quarterly alphabetical index was prepared for the whole country, with separate indexes for births, marriages and deaths. It is these indexes which have become the key finding aid for family historians.

In the early years of registration about 500,000 births, 125,000 marriages and 360,000 deaths were recorded and indexed each year. In the case of marriage certificates, about a third of the men and nearly half the women were not able to sign their names. The processing of this amount of information, in an age before typewriters, telephones and computers, is a remarkable achievement.

Nevertheless, the system had major shortcomings. Marriage registration, for instance, depended on the regular quarterly cooperation of 15,000 clergy, many of whom had little or no respect for civil registration. They were expected to copy their registers accurately and legibly, and make their returns on time, but many were late or illegible. Being early was just as bad, since the returns would get put on one side by the registrar who would then forget to index them. Other problems affected the registration of births and deaths, where the onus for registration rested with the registrar rather than the family. Consequently, the indexes for the early years are extremely unreliable.

The Births and Deaths Registration Act 1874 made enforcement easier by shifting responsibility for registration from the registrar to the parent, or the occupier of the house, or persons having charge of a child. It also tightened up the registration of illegitimate births by only allowing the father's name to be entered if he attended the register office himself.

The legislation setting up the Scottish registration system permitted registrars to seek more information than was customary south of the border. Expediency led the authorities to simplify the requirements, but nevertheless Scottish sources tend to contain richer seams for family historians. For example, from 1861 birth certificates generally give the date and place of the parents' marriage; death certificates give the name and occupation of the father and the mother's maiden name; and marriage certificates record the names of both parents of the two parties.

Until relatively recently, the civil registration system has seen little change. In 1929 the Local Government Act abolished the fee-based system and replaced it with a salaried service. This applied for all new appointments but gave existing registrars the option to remain fee-paid if they wished; the last registrar appointed under this system was in post until the early 1980s. In 2007 new governance arrangements were introduced making registration solely a local authority function, with the GRO responsible for compiling statistics and general oversight of the system.

In 1970 the General Register Office of England and Wales merged with the government's social survey department to form the Office of Population, Censuses and Surveys (OPCS). In recent years it has had a number of homes until, in 2008, it became part of the Identity and Passport Service (IPS), an Executive Agency of the Home Office.

The GRO and its successors have had an important role in another major class of record of interest to the family historian: the census.

* * * *

Census-taking has a long history.[2] The Babylonians, Egyptians and Chinese all collected statistics about their populations, as did the Greeks and Romans in later times. In Britain medieval surveys, of which Domesday Book was the earliest, were essentially accounts of landholdings, the basis for power under the feudal system. They were never intended to give the authorities a comprehensive picture of the whole population and contain little or no information on named individuals; people were only mentioned as appendages to the land.

Gregory King, a statistician (and also a genealogist) made the first systematic attempt to estimate England's population in 1695. Using figures related to the 1694 Act for improving parish registration, King estimated the number of houses in England and Wales as 1.3 million and the number of people as 5.5 million.

In the mid-eighteenth century the issue of population became the subject of fierce debate. Political radicals and defenders of agricultural interests believed the population had declined since the 'Glorious Revolution' of 1688. The dominance of the Whig aristocracy and the rise of the commercial classes had eroded moral standards, they argued, and led to population decline. Others defended the rise of commerce and claimed that the population had increased over the previous hundred years.

In 1753 Thomas Potter, MP for St Germans in Cornwall, introduced a Census Bill into the House of Commons. It contained provisions to carry out an annual census, to institute registration of births, marriages and deaths, and to count the 'number of poor receiving alms from every Parish and Extraparochial Place in Great Britain'. Critics claimed the bill would be costly and impracticable, and might even lead to new taxation or conscription. Mr Thorton, MP for York, called the measure 'totally subversive of the last remains of English liberty', and added that it would 'acquaint our enemies abroad with our weaknesses'.[3] Although the bill was carried by a large majority in the House of Commons, it was defeated in the Lords.

At this time, censuses were already well established elsewhere. Quebec had completed one as early as 1666 and in the middle of the eighteenth century censuses were also taken in Germany and other European states. Religious opposition meant the United States held out until 1790, with church-goers recalling how the Israelites were afflicted by plague during census-taking in the time of King David. Similar attitudes prevailed in Britain. In the debate on the 1753 bill, Matthew Ridley, MP for Newcastle-upon-Tyne, said his constituents 'looked upon the proposal as ominous, and feared lest some great public misfortune or an epidemical distemper should follow the numbering'.[4]

By the beginning of the nineteenth century it was clear that the population was definitely increasing and the controversy was fuelled by Thomas Malthus's *Essay on the Principle of Population*, published in 1798. Malthus's work shifted the debate from the effect of morality to the relationship between population and society's available agricultural resources. If population grew according to a geometrical progression (2, 4, 8, 16, 32, . . .), Malthus argued, and agricultural production increased according to an arithmetic progression (1, 2, 3, 4, 5, . . .), there would come a point at which social resources would be exhausted and a population would be unable to feed itself.

According to Malthus, this situation would be avoided in practice both by natural means (increased mortality arising from famine and disease) and by preventive checks (fewer births). Late marriage and small families were to be encouraged, although Malthus stopped short of advocating physical contraception which was considered anathema at the time. Only by these means could a Christian society avoid the misery of poverty and disease through over-population. Payments to the destitute, on the other hand, only encouraged early marriage and more births, Malthus believed, leading him to campaign for reform of the English Poor Laws.

Malthus's ideas would have a profound and lasting influence on political, economic and scientific thinking throughout the nineteenth century, including on figures such as Karl Marx, Charles Darwin and Francis Galton. Of most relevance to our story is that it led him and others to press for a census to be undertaken. A succession of bad harvests, increasing emigration and war with the French made it more important than ever for the government to find out how many mouths needed to be fed and how many were working to feed them.

A bill introduced on 20 November 1800 by Charles Abbot, MP for Helston, provided 'for taking an Account of the Population of Great Britain, and of the Increase or Diminution thereof'.[5] It passed through all its stages without opposition and received the Royal Assent on 31 December. The resulting enumeration took place on Monday 10 March 1801 and the first abstracts were released in December of that year. The enumerators, who made house-to-house inquiries, were overseers of the poor or, failing them, leading householders assisted by church officials. As well as enumeration of the population, an attempt was made to obtain data on baptisms, marriages and burials for the whole of the eighteenth century by getting the clergy to count back through their registers.

The exercise was repeated, with very little alteration, in 1811, 1821 and 1831. These early censuses were masterminded by John Rickman, formerly a clerk of the House of Commons, who prepared the abstracts and reports for all four. Like previous surveys, these were merely head counts although some local enumerators collected information on named individuals in order to make their returns. As such they offer little for the genealogist. All this was to change, however, with the census of 1841.

Following the setting up of the General Register Office in 1837, the Population Act of 1840 gave responsibility for the decennial census to the Registrar General. In preparation for the Bill, Thomas Lister ensured that the overseers of the poor – a system dating from Elizabethan times – would no longer be responsible as enumerators; his new registration service would provide the local machinery for administration. The bringing together of these two sets of information, Lister realized, would make it possible for the first time to collect material on a national scale in a uniform and systematic way.

Public pressure for a much more ambitious census was also building in the late 1830s. A committee set up by the London (later Royal) Statistical Society suggested a radical change in organization of the census to take advantage of the new Poor Law and civil registration systems. It recommended the use of an official household schedule listing each individual by name, together with questions relating to their age, gender, marital status, occupation, place of birth, religion and health. The enumerators were to transcribe all this information into books for dispatch to London, rather than making summaries locally, as had been the practice in Rickman's time. Statisticians always want more data and their demands were cut back for fear of making the form too complicated – a real concern in a time when there was no universal system of education and large numbers of people were unable to read and write.

The 1841 Census, as eventually implemented, was a compromise between the recommendations of the London Statistical Society and Rickman's earlier scheme. Local administration was the responsibility of local registrars who would appoint temporary enumerators. They were to gather a much wider range of data on individual members of the population, although not data on religion or health. To avoid double counting, the census was also to be taken on one night of the year rather than, as previously, over a period of time. It thus provides a 'snapshot' of society at a particular moment in time.

For the purposes of the census, the 2,000 or so enumeration districts in England and Wales were subdivided into an appropriate number of subdistricts, each comprising between 25 and 200 dwellings. A total of 35,000 enumerators were appointed for the task. In Scotland, where civil registration had yet to be introduced, supervision of the census remained with parish officials or leading householders such as the schoolmaster. Initially, Lister envisaged that the enumerators would gather all the information themselves through house-to-house enquiries but a pilot enumeration in London showed this would cost far too much. He eventually conceded to the introduction of household schedules, despite reservations as to whether most householders were too illiterate to fill them in, and a supplementary Census Act was passed hastily to authorize their use.

These schedules were delivered to each household a few days before the appointed day. The householder had to fill in the form listing all persons sleeping in the house on Sunday, 6 June 1841; penalties could be imposed for those failing to comply. The enumerator collected the form the following day and checked, as best he could, the schedule was complete and correct. He then transferred the answers to his own schedule following the Registrar General's strict instructions. This took far longer than before since now the enumerators had to record each person's details in the appropriate columns, rather than merely entering numbers in each household.

The machinery and organization of the census established in 1841 remained unchanged until well into the twentieth century (and in important respects through to the present day), although the scope of the enquiry was greatly extended. For the census of 1851, the schedule was expanded, requiring each person's relationship to the head of the household to be stated, as well as their marital status, age, gender, occupation, birthplace and infirmity (whether blind, deaf or dumb). Exact age was to be stated instead of the nearest five-year age group. Better provision was made for enumerating persons on board vessels in harbours and rivers, as well as those serving abroad in the Army, Royal Navy and Merchant Service.

There were also major innovations in the way the census results were presented. For the first time the Registrar General's commentary was accompanied by two substantial volumes of statistical tables containing data grouped according to eleven registration divisions. The reports were illustrated with charts and maps depicting the density of population and the distribution of people by occupation. Correlating the information on occupation and age, William Farr, an Assistant Commissioner for the Census, undertook a ground-breaking analysis on occupational mortality, noting, for instance, the high mortality rates among miners. Another Assistant Commissioner, Horace Mann, concentrated on a supplementary enquiry (which was not a compulsory part of the census) into religion and education. The survey was meant to be concerned with the number and capacity of churches and other places of worship, but Mann could not help passing comment on the nation's spiritual mores; the most important finding, he observed, was 'unquestionably, the alarming number of non-attendants'.[6] Mann's report showed, in black and white, the strong position of Nonconformists in Victorian Britain – they accounted for nearly half of the church accommodation and some 45 per cent of those attending services – and led to calls by the dissenting churches for disestablishment.

Following the introduction of civil registration in Scotland in 1855, a separate Act in 1860 gave the Registrar General for Scotland responsibility for taking the census of 1861. The organization followed similar lines to England and Wales. Over the succeeding years the two Registrars General collaborated closely, ensuring censuses were broadly the same throughout Great Britain.

In England and Wales the content of the census schedules changed little in the decades between 1861 and 1911. Towards the end of the century concern about overcrowding led, in 1891, to a question on the number of rooms per house. This was repeated in 1901 together with a question on the number of people in certain industries working at home and the accompanying report contained for the first time data on the marital status of females with an occupation. In the same year the question on infirmities was modified, with 'idiot' being replaced by 'feeble-minded', and in 1911 it was dropped altogether, it having been finally recognized that the census was not a suitable or reliable means of gathering such information.

The most important change introduced in 1911 was an enquiry into women's fertility. Until then the Registrar General's office had been interested mainly in mortality and morbidity. It was generally believed that mortality was the major factor influencing population growth and that fertility was a constant determined only by the number of marriages. According to the social reformers of the time, intervention by government could prevent death and disease but could have little impact on fertility. When, by the turn of the century, it became clear that the birth rate was falling quite steeply, fertility and infant mortality attracted greater attention. Consequently, for the 1911 census households were asked about the length of marriage and the number of living children born of each marriage, the number still living and the number who had died. These questions were addressed to married women only; widows or single women who had had children did not have to answer.

The 1911 census was the first in which machines were used to process the information. Data were punched onto cards and sorted by machine, which speeded up the whole operation significantly. This new method allowed the results of the census to be presented in more detail than ever before and also the data to be re-sorted to overcome some of the problems associated with the local government boundaries at the end of the nineteenth century.

Despite its inclusion in Great Britain in 1801, Ireland was treated quite differently for census purposes. The first official census was taken in 1821, some twenty years before the rest of the country. As well as names, ages, occupations, and relationships to heads of household, it gave acreages of land and the number of storeys in the house. These wide-ranging enquiries were retained and expanded on in later returns. Unfortunately, these do not provide rich resources for family historians with Irish roots. The returns for 1861–91 were destroyed by government order, and those for 1821–51 were lost in an explosion and fire in Dublin at the time of partition; only a few fragments and some published summaries remain.

The Census Act of 1920 provided for a new legal basis: it was a permanent enactment requiring future censuses in Great Britain to be undertaken at least every ten years. It did not cover Northern Ireland where each census still has to be specially enacted. With increasing numbers of people living in suburban residential areas, there was increasing concern with traffic problems. A question on place of work was introduced for the 1921 census to try to measure daily movements. For the first time there were also questions about the ages and numbers of children under 16, the number of orphans, and about full- or part-time education.

For the fourteenth census, in 1931, enquiries into workplace, orphanhood, dependency and education were dropped. In their place just one new question was added: a requirement to state the place of usual residence. All of these returns were lost during the Second World War, although not, as commonly quoted, through enemy action.[7] Returns for 1941 will not be available either, since plans for that census had to be abandoned due to the war. Hence, family historians of the future face a major gap in the records for the middle of the twentieth century, with no census data available (for England and Wales at least) for a thirty-year period between 1921 and 1951. This is a crucial period when there was much movement from the industrial towns and cities to the suburbs, as well as regional migration as a result of the Depression and the War. Preparations that had already been made for the 1941 survey provided the basis for National Registration, introduced in September 1939. The enumeration then undertaken was used to support a number of wartime measures such as food and clothes rationing and the deployment of labour in the military and essential industries. National Registration was retained until February 1952, by which time it had become the basis for the initial National Health Service registration system.

Later censuses became even wider in scope, reflecting modern government's rapacious desire for information on its citizens. Increasingly sophisticated statistical sampling techniques were applied in developing them and, of course, computers began to be used to process the huge mass of data generated.

Censuses are deemed to be among the most sensitive class of public records, since they contain detailed personal information on individuals. Under archival legislation, they are classified as 'containing information supplied in confidence, the disclosure of which would or might constitute a breach of good faith'. As such, original returns are subject to a one-hundred-year disclosure period, rather than the thirty-year rule now applied to most public records. In recent years, family historians have – with some success – tried to challenge this convention through a series of campaigns for early release. In England and Wales, campaigners succeeded in obtaining the early release of the 1911 census, which predates the 1920 Act, in 2009; similar moves are being proposed in relation to the 1921 survey. Certain information from the 1939 National Registration is also now available (for a fee) from the NHS Information Centre. This is almost certainly the limit, however: individual schedules from the 1951 and later surveys will not be opened to genealogists until the mid to late twenty-first century.

*   *   *   *

Wills are one of the most ancient of the sources used by the family historian.[8] The practice of making a will goes back to Anglo-Saxon times and their development owes much to the early church. Medieval clerics held that it was a matter of conscience to carry out as fully as possible the wishes of the deceased. By the early thirteenth century the church had succeeded in obtaining jurisdiction in testamentary matters. In most cases, probate – the ratification of a will to make it operative – could only be granted by bringing it before one of the ecclesiastical courts.

The Statute of Wills of 1540 allowed greater flexibility in how 'real property' (that is, land and buildings) could be inherited, sweeping away the rather rigid conventions of the feudal period. Owners could 'devise' (the legal term) their property to relatives or friends of their own choosing rather than to the heir stipulated by the law (usually the eldest surviving son). From 1661 this provision applied to land as well. A gift of personal property was termed a bequest, so that a testator devised his real property (in a 'will') and bequeathed his personal property (in a 'testament'). In England a will and a testament could be dealt with in the same document and eventually came to have the same meaning.

If a person died intestate (that is without leaving a will), an application could be made to a court for the appointment of one or more administrators. These were usually the deceased's next of kin, but sometimes business associates, such as partners or creditors, were appointed. The administrators would administer the deceased's estate and divide it among the beneficiaries. If a deceased had few assets and there was no dispute as to who should benefit, the will might not be taken to court – to save the cost of probate. In this case it might only survive in family papers rather than the official records.

Wills can be a rich source for family history. They are prepared with the express intention of acknowledging or confirming relationships, usually specified with legal precision. Where they exist, wills can amplify the tentative family relationships identified through parish registers and census returns. They can throw light on the subject's dealings with family and community members, give very precise details of his household possessions, livelihood and land, and generally bring the character of an ancestor to life.

The nineteenth-century genealogist Stacey Grimaldi was the first to recognize their value. Writing in 1828, he noted that wills[9]

> are the principal and often only records by which families in the middling class of life can trace any dissent prior to the introduction of parochial records; secondly, the quantity of genealogical information in wills is of great value; testaments of men of property almost invariably name two and frequently three or four clear descents of pedigree, whilst the limitation of estates, and bequests of legacies, bring to light kindred who could not otherwise have been traced.

Grimaldi went on to note that elements found in wills, such as the descriptions of estates and the wardship of children, could lead the genealogist onto other important documents. They were, he concluded, 'instruments of great authority'. Having read through around 4,400 wills for the year 1750, the genealogist George Sherwood calculated that they each mentioned an average of ten persons. This made them, he concluded, of great genealogical value, especially in locating people 'just before the introduction into England of the industrial system' which, he said, 'caused great migration. Genealogically, the middle of the eighteenth century is one of the most difficult to bridge.'[10]

Regular series of wills survive in some places from the thirteenth century. The number of persons who left wills varied from time to time and from one family to another; the practice was by no means confined to the wealthy, and in some cases those most expected to leave a will did not. Wills of unmarried women and widows are fairly common and often particularly detailed, but wills for married women are rare before the 1880s. Until the Married Women's Property Act 1882, women were unable to own property in their own name and could only leave a valid will with their husband's consent.

The administration of wills was rather fragmented, being split across 300 or so ecclesiastical courts associated with archdeacons, bishops and archbishops. Some of these had very limited jurisdictions, whereas those for Canterbury and York covered large swathes of the country. The original wills have generally been deposited either in the record office of the ancient diocese concerned or in the relevant county record office (often they are the same place). This is not necessarily the case, however, and in some instances they are to be found in libraries and a host of obscure locations. Guides to holdings have been published to help family historians track them down.

On 12 January 1858 the state took over responsibility for proving wills in England and Wales. Under this new system, the local ecclesiastical courts were abolished and replaced by district registries which undertake filing and probate. Copies of all wills held by district registries are filed with the Principal Registry of the Family Division, part of the High Court of Justice, which for many years had its headquarters at Somerset House in London's Strand, and is now in High Holborn. The Principal Registry itself files original wills proved in London. An annual index is printed and is the first stop for those wishing to locate a will.

The National Archives has a major collection of probate records, including wills proved in the Prerogative Court of Canterbury (PCC), the best known of the earlier courts, which date back to 1383. Other copies of wills survive in family papers and solicitors' collections deposited at local record offices, and in registries of deeds.

Separate systems operated in Scotland and Ireland, the main collections now being deposited in the National Archives of Scotland and the Irish National Archives, respectively.

*   *   *   *

Interest in preserving public records is a relatively recent phenomenon.[11] In medieval times records of the royal court were regarded as part of the King's treasure and were cared for accordingly. Domesday Book – England's oldest public record – was transferred to the royal treasury at Winchester on its completion in 1087, where it was consulted to solve issues of taxation and tenure. Over the next several hundred years it was joined by a multitude of parchment rolls as the apparatus of the medieval state became more sophisticated.

Eventually the main functions of the royal household became split between the Chancery (secretarial), the Exchequer (financial) and the courts of law (legal), each of which developed its own sub-departments and separate records. These nascent departments of state generated huge amounts of documents but gave little thought to how to preserve them. Records were housed at various locations across London and elsewhere. Chancery acquired the King's wardrobes at the Tower of London and New Temple, later moving to the chapel of the Master of the Rolls at Chancery Lane. Exchequer records languished in decrepit rooms at the Palace of Westminster, ravaged by rats, insects, damp and souvenir hunters. These were later transferred to the enlarged Chapter House at Westminster Abbey but a daring burglary there in 1303 convinced the authorities that the Tower was the safest store for public records. Various attempts were made to sort the records – particularly during the reigns of Edward II and Elizabeth I – but often these only served to make the situation worse.

Elizabethan times saw a blossoming of interest in genealogy and antiquities, especially among nobility and gentry keen to establish lineages and title to estates. This brought a new type of record user, the enthusiastic antiquarian, to the record repositories ever more frequently in search of genealogical and historical material. Searchers had to pay fees for searches and copies, the scale of which would be a source of complaint for many centuries to come. In 1589, for instance, George Owen of Pembrokeshire visited the Exchequer hoping to find out about a local lordship. He consulted 'the Book of Domesday' in the Cellars office but found it to be 'very ancient and hard to be read and whoso findeth any things must pay for the copy of every line', while the medieval writing was 'strange and hard for any man to read whether you find [anything] or not'.[12]

At that time the Cellars office was under the control of Arthur Agarde, one of the deputy chamberlains of Exchequer. His *Compendium Recordorum* written in 1610 attempted to list the records in the four Westminster repositories. He wrote of 'a four-fold hurt that by negligence may bring wrack to records, that is to say: fire, water, rats and mice, misplacing'.[13] There was, he added 'yet a last danger worse than some of the former, that is even plain taking of them away'. A later keeper of the records at the Tower, William Prynne, instituted a programme of cleaning and sorting but found his staff were reluctant to touch the filthy bundles 'for fear of endangering their eyesights and healths by the cankerous dust and evil scent'.[14]

In the early eighteenth century Parliament initiated several investigations into the state of record keeping. Lack of space, money, staff and satisfactory buildings were identified as the main problems. For example, a House of Lords

Committee in 1709 found the records of the Court of Wards (an ancient feudal body) to be under a dilapidated roof adjoining the royal fishmonger in Fish Yard, near to Westminster Hall. The fishmonger 'did what he thought fit with the records', which were 'in a perishing condition'.[15] The Queen's Bench records were in a similarly precarious state, being housed in a washhouse-cum-stable, 'which is a very Improper situation for records of such consequence'. In the Chapter House, archives remained 'in a great heap, undigested, without any covering from dust, or security from rats or mice'. Although the solutions to these problems were essentially straightforward, the money to implement them was not easily forthcoming; it would be another hundred years before decisive action was taken.

In 1799 Charles Abbot – the same MP who introduced the Population Act of 1800 – proposed the setting up of yet another Select Committee to inquire into the state of the public records. Abbot was more diligent than most of his predecessors, sending questionnaires to several hundred repositories including the British Museum, Tower of London, offices of county clerks, and chapter houses of cathedrals. His report noted the conditions in which documents were stored, described the repository structure, furnishings and air circulation, and made recommendations for improvements. Most significantly, it was the first inquiry to highlight the importance of written references to the records and recommended the preparation of calendars, indexes, guides and lists. Documents that 'are the most important in their Nature and the most perfect of their kind' should be printed in full or in calendar form, Abbot concluded.[16]

In 1800 the government appointed a royal commission to consider how to implement certain of the Abbot committee's recommendations. As well as being a direct response to the committee's inquiry, this move was spurred by a patriotic concern to protect the nation's heritage during the course of the Napoleonic war, and by the general interest in the past that accompanied the romantic movement.

The Record Commission of 1800 was the first of six successive inquiries into the national records over the period to 1837. At that time there were some fifty repositories in London alone, each with different administrations and traditions, and highly variable standards of preservation. The commissions attempted to improve the physical conditions in which the archives were held by reducing the number of scattered repositories, renovating decaying buildings, and introducing fireproofing and better ventilation. Progress was slow, however, and many of the commissioners' actions were of a temporary nature which only contributed to the confusion and resulted in further losses. Although the commissioners failed in their attempts to introduce a coherent archival policy, they invested considerable sums in transcribing, editing and printing important documents and archival series (mainly from the medieval period) and published some useful compilations of calendars, lists and indexes.

All of this failed to stem the rising tide, however. While the commissioners talked and reported, the volume of records produced by government departments continued to grow and more and more storage space was needed. In 1834 a fire broke out at the Palace of Westminster, resulting in a disastrous loss of records. The subsequent redevelopment work dislodged many others. Describing a visit to Carlton Ride, an old riding school being used for temporary storage, Henry (later Sir Henry) Cole, an Assistant Keeper of Records, recalled documents were 'strewn all over the floor'.[17] He continued:

> It was necessary to mount a ladder to get access to this apartment, the roof was nearly dark, and an area of about 25 feet by 20 was piled up from two or three feet high with documents, all in conflict and confusion. You could not step without sinking among them. The mass was thickly coated with soot, dust and dirt.

The Westminster fire finally served to mobilize public opinion around the need to establish a single national repository in London. The 1838 Public Records Act allowed for the centralization of 'all rolls records, writ books, proceedings, decrees, bills, warrants, accounts, papers and documents whatsoever of a public nature'. A new repository – to be known as the Public Record Office (PRO) – was to be set up under the Master of the Rolls, with responsibility for the records and the terms of public access delegated to a Deputy Keeper.

Despite the good intentions of the Act's sponsors, it failed to solve the problems overnight. There was furious disagreement as to the best site for the new repository, with the Rolls Estate in Chancery Lane, and the Victoria Tower in the new Houses of Parliament both being proposed as potential locations. The Treasury favoured the Victoria Tower option, forecasting unrealistically that it offered sufficient space for the records for several centuries. Sir Francis Palgrave, the first Deputy Keeper, succeeded in dismissing this assertion and his suggestion of the Rolls Estate won out.

Work on the Public Record Office in Chancery Lane began in 1851 according to designs devised by James Pennethorne, a leading architect of the day. Pennethorne's original scheme involved a remodelling of the whole area around Chancery Lane, at the hub of which was to be a large gothic-style record office. But the visionary architect found himself pitched against petty bureaucrats. The Treasury thought the plan too expensive and Pennethorne was forced, reluctantly, to rein in the scheme to fit a more limited budget. Years later he wrote prophetically that 'the necessity for a large library, for large searching rooms etc. etc.; all these things were washed away by economy, and will hereafter have to be provided at greater cost and with less convenience'.[18]

In order to avoid a repeat of the Westminster disaster, the building included the latest fire precautions. It comprised a series of cell-like rooms, each a fireproof unit, with slate shelves for storing the records, all supported on wrought-iron girders. Palgrave thought central heating would be 'positively injurious to the health of those employed', so the safeguards were compromised by the installation of open fires in old-fashioned fireplaces.[19] Later generations of archivists and searchers alike would come to rue this decision as they shivered in the PRO's arctic cold.

Sir Henry Cole wrote approvingly in his memoirs: 'Standing at the corner of Fetter Lane, on the north side of Fleet Street, may now be seen a fireproof stone building full of windows, as strongly built as a fortress: it has an architectural expression full of truth, originality and its purpose, which is highly creditable to the common sense of its architect, James Pennethorne.'[20] The design did not meet with universal approval, however. One commentator complained that 'externally the new building has not much to recommend it on the score of artistic beauty', adding that it did not fit into any recognized style of architecture.

The building was completed in 1858 at a cost of £77,000 and ancient records were moved there from Carlton Ride, the Tower and other London repositories. Almost straightaway it became clear that the space was woefully inadequate. Under the 1838 Act only records of the courts of law were required to be deposited with the new Office but an order of 1852 had extended its jurisdiction to all government departments. This added a voluminous series of extra records for which no space was allotted in the original plan. Palgrave pressed an unwilling Treasury for an extension, a campaign that continued after his death in 1861. Both Parliament and public opinion sympathized with the predicament and additional rooms were added during the periods 1863–8 and 1868–71. A further extension was added in 1892–5, which involved a controversial decision to demolish the medieval Rolls Chapel.

Although having no formal training, Palgrave had long experience in archival practice, having been Keeper of Exchequer Records at the Chapter House before being appointed at the PRO. He recognized from the beginning that modern administrative papers were just as important to the archivist, and ultimately to the historian, as the ancient records in his care. In 1851 he quashed a proposal to destroy the records of the first ten-yearly census, to the relief of latter-day family historians. Documents from across the legal and administrative system began to accumulate at Chancery Lane, which became known as the 'Strongbox of the Empire'.

In these early days readers were seen as little more than an inconvenience, to be tolerated rather than encouraged. *The Globe* newspaper commented that the PRO was 'the least known of public institutions' and thought it 'could be mistaken for a lunatic asylum or prison'.[21] Around twenty to thirty persons a day frequented the poorly heated and unlit search rooms, mostly lawyers' clerks with a few bewhiskered antiquarians and a handful of record agents. Women, especially married women, were rarely seen. Walter Rye, a professional genealogist, recalled how he had had to work 'in a long unpleasant room with low tables and high backless forms which cramped the searcher's legs if he were anything above a dwarf in stature. A searcher then had to pay a shilling for each search.' As the light failed, searchers had to abandon their work and exit via an unlit corridor, leaving the assistant keepers to 'play out time' over a hand of cards. The Victorian PRO was a place to be endured, not enjoyed.

At least amateur inquirers did not have to pay for their displeasure. A petition sent by the Society of Antiquaries in 1851, and signed by luminaries such as Charles Dickens, Thomas Carlyle and Thomas Macaulay, had led to search fees for historical or antiquarian inquiry being dropped. However, these so-called 'literary' (as opposed to legal) readers were reminded that:[22]

> The time of the various officers and other persons employed in the PRO is so wholly engrossed by the performance of their present duties, that it will not be possible for the officers to assist any literary inquirers beyond the production of documents.

Under the house rules of 1875 reasons for which persons might be excluded from the search rooms included: 'insolence to the officials or using violent or offensive language; careless or wilful damage to any public document; and offensive habits of any kind, or want of personal cleanliness'.

Palgrave was succeeded as Deputy Keeper by Sir Thomas Duffus Hardy. The two had been arch rivals and Hardy was determined to take the Office in a new direction. Although much work remained to be done in sorting and cataloguing the records, Hardy chose to concentrate on editing and publishing instead. Time and again he opted to divert his time and energies to editorial projects rather than more urgent issues of preservation and cataloguing. Nevertheless, his tenure saw an expansion of the Office's accommodation and, in 1877, a new Public Record Office Act, which addressed the accumulation of obsolete and obsolescent departmental records. On his death in 1878, Hardy was succeeded briefly by his brother William, and then in 1886 by Henry Maxwell-Lyte.

Maxwell-Lyte's appointment was to mark a new phase in the Office's development. Then just 37 years old, he was the first graduate to become Deputy Keeper, and the first, and for many years the only, historian in the PRO. Over the previous half century the Office had largely achieved its original objective of securing the custody of the ancient records. Maxwell-Lyte sought a new direction, promoting the scholarly use of the records and improving the conditions under which they were accessed. He had electric lighting installed in the search rooms, as well as the first lift. Most importantly, he initiated a comprehensive series of calendars and lists that helped diffuse knowledge of the Office and its work around the world.[23] At his retirement in 1926, after a forty-year tenure, Maxwell-Lyte left the Office in a very much stronger state than he had found it and the PRO continued to operate in his image until at least the Second World War.

By this time major repositories had also been established elsewhere. The Scottish Record Office predated the PRO by a considerable period, having been completed in 1827 at a central site in Edinburgh's new town. The building, known as the General Register House, was built partly using monies appropriated from confiscated Jacobite estates. Established by royal charter in Aberystwyth in 1907, the National Library of Wales serves as the repository for ecclesiastical documents, private deposits and certain series of public records relating to the principality. Archives in Ireland have had a troubled history, frequently falling victim to the conflicts that have beset that island. Following partition, the Public Record Office of Northern Ireland (PRONI) was established in 1924 and serves as the main archive repository for the province. Other important repositories include the British Library, the National Library of Scotland, and diocesan and county record offices.

A series of Royal Commissions held between 1910 and 1919 again investigated archival issues but came up with few solutions. In the meantime, the First World War and modernization of the state increased administrative burdens, while a growing curiosity for social inquiry and historical research continued to bring new demands. It was not until 1954 that a government-appointed committee under Sir James Grigg came up with actionable reforms. The Grigg committee's report formed the basis for the Public Record Act 1958, which provides the main framework for archival legislation through to the current day.

The Act gave the PRO custody of all public records, whether legal or departmental, although responsibility for the selection and transfer of material rests with individual departments. A fifty-year rule was introduced, whereby all records would automatically be disclosed to the public after a statutory period. This was modified almost immediately to allow the release of First World War material, and again in 1967 to become the thirty-year rule we have today.[24]

Archival policies could be updated but attitudes would prove harder to change. One staff member recounted how as late as the 1960s a rigid class system existed inside the Office:[25]

> Curatorial staff were better than clerical staff and clerical staff were better than conservators, photoprinters and messengers. 'Our Old Etonian' was worshipped as a god. In addition, a certain special kudos was attached to those who applied themselves to editing of medieval records. The older the better. Scant regard was had for anything post 1485 (frivolous and modern) and work on modern and near contemporary records was seen as little more than base paper-keeping.
> . . . For us, officers of the archive of Empire, work took a low priority,

indeed no-one seemed to have any concern as to whether or not we produced anything at all.

Genealogists, who by this time made up a substantial proportion of the Office's client base, were particularly derided. These tweedy eccentrics and genteel old ladies in black hats were 'not serious scholars (like we were) and should not be allowed to take up our valuable time'.

The issue of accommodation still loomed large, and in 1969 the government announced the building of a new record office in Kew, southwest London. The five-storey concrete building opened its doors on 17 October 1977, complete with sixty-nine miles of shelving, and has been much extended since. Its stark 1970s façade has become familiar to millions through TV documentaries.

Ironically for an organization devoted to conserving the past, the Public Record Office itself has not been preserved. In recent years, the Office has been amalgamated with other government bodies 'specialising', to quote the website, 'in particular aspects of managing information'. The occupant of Kew's unlovely building now furnishes an equally unlovely name: the National Archives (abbreviated to TNA).

*   *   *   *

Chapter 3

The Crane's Foot

In Britain, as in other societies, the first pedigrees were handed down by word of mouth. During pagan times, the passing on of histories was the role of the bards who travelled the country singing songs, telling stories and reciting poems; genealogy was just another type of story. Since virtually nothing was written down, the lineages the bards recited were a mixture of fact, hearsay and outright myth. With the arrival of Christianity, this priestly class became assimilated into the church and monks took on the role of recording the lines of royalty and prominent nobles. By Anglo-Saxon times these royal houses were linked to the Bible and classical antiquity. According to the traditional pedigrees, mainly enshrined in the Anglo-Saxon Chronicle, English kings were descended from Woden, who in turn was a direct descendant of Noah.

All of this changed after the Norman Conquest. The feudal system established by the Normans divided the country among a new noble class who had tenure over the land. The fate of these manors and estates was decided by descent, under the principle of primogeniture, and hence pedigrees became hugely significant as a legal proof of entitlement. The epitome of this was Domesday Book, compiled in 1086 by William the Conqueror as a survey of land held by his barons. In fact, the Domesday inquest, from which the book was culled, was only one of a series of regional and national surveys during the medieval period. The last and most exhaustive of these was the Hundred Rolls survey of 1279–80, which described in minute detail every landholding in the country from those of the King to the poorest peasant. Much of this survey has been lost or damaged but the parts that survive are an invaluable source for the period.

As the Norman legal and administrative systems developed many other classes of records were introduced, several of which remained on the statute well into the modern era. The Plea Rolls, which date from 1193, record actions brought under the Common Law and heard in the King's Court ('Curia Regis') and the courts that grew out of it, namely the courts of Common Pleas, King's Bench and the Exchequer. The Pipe Rolls record the annual accounts rendered to the Exchequer by the sheriffs in each county and entered up each Michaelmas by the Exchequer clerks; a continuous series survives from 1155 through to the 1830s. The Close Rolls contain copies of letters and deeds, including many conveyances, issued by the monarch through the royal Court of Chancery. And the Patent Rolls comprise registered copies of letters issued by the royal court, dealing with everything from international treaties, to the ward of lands and creation of peerages, and charters of incorporation. Running from 1200, in the reign of John, to the middle of the twentieth century, they are the longest unbroken set of archives anywhere in the world.

From the start of the Plea Rolls onwards, the many lengthy statements of descent in lawsuits demonstrate the importance of genealogy within the Norman state. Most such statements are confined to three or four generations, but occasionally they cover five or six generations or more. These early pedigrees still rested primarily on oral transmission, although some of the earlier ones at least are likely to have been compiled from written evidence. The compilers were clerks and monks who had access to the few documents then existing, such as charters, chronicles and monumental inscriptions, from which they worked out pedigrees retrospectively.

The word 'pedigree' is itself Norman in origin. Early illustrations of familial relationships depicted the subject at the bottom with their offspring (usually only sons were shown) above, connected to the father by radial lines. To the medieval mind, the resulting wiry diagram looked like the foot of a crane ('grue' in Middle French), and so the diagrams became known as *pied de grue* ('the crane's foot'). The word first entered the English language around 1410 as 'pedegru' or 'pedegrewe', which later morphed into 'pedigree'.[1] Surnames came into common usage between the twelfth and fourteenth centuries, partly in response to the increase in the use of written records, but took some time to become fully established.[2]

* * * *

In the Middle Ages, the role of genealogy went well beyond simply determining the tenure of land. Issues of succession and inheritance were seen as essential in maintaining order in feudal society. Genealogies, initially for royalty and later for other nobles and members of the gentry, were a means of enforcing power and privilege. Royal genealogies helped shape national identities and national histories. Kings and the governing classes looked to romances, prophecies and historical writing to shape how their actions were viewed and genealogies permeated all three. Medieval scholars now see them as crucial in shaping chronicles and myths, and in creating propaganda, not just for rulers but for families who relied upon them for security in an uncertain world.

English romances involving legendary historical figures such as Havelok the Dane, King Arthur and Joseph of Arimathea were influenced by genealogical structure derived from chronicles.[3] For instance, in the late thirteenth-century romance *Havelok the Dane*, a fictitious king of England, Athelwold, dies without a male heir. He leaves the throne to his daughter Goldeborw on condition she marry the tallest man in the land. Goldeborw's treacherous guardian marries her off to one such suitor, who turns out to be Havelok, the unknowing son of another king. The story reflects feudal England's interest in the lawful right of royal succession and the general preoccupation with law and order. Similar themes are found in the Arthurian romances written during this period. These stress not only Arthur's own right to the English crown – left vacant by his heirless status – but also the lineage of the Grail keepers, culminating with Lancelot and his son Galahad.

For these medieval writers the boundaries between romances and allegories (fiction) and historical chronicles (fact) were blurred. A prime example of this is the chronicle known as the prose *Brut*, one of the most widely read Anglo-Norman chronicles.[4] It offers a history of England from the fall of Troy, when Britain was supposedly settled by the Trojan prince Brutus, through to the contemporary medieval period. The chronicle describes each reign in turn and, although most versions contain few if any genealogical charts, its message is one of continuity. England has an unbroken lineage, its readers are invited to believe, from the time of Brutus right through to the Plantagenet rulers of the period. One of its key sources was Geoffrey of Monmouth's *Historia Regum Britanniae* ('A History of the Kings of Britain'), completed in 1139 at the time of the civil war between Stephen and Matilda.[5] The *Historia* is imbued with allegorical tales and prophecies, many of a genealogical nature.

Anglo-Norman rolls showing royal genealogies were important to those families' claims to the throne of England and were used to propagate their own version of history.[6] They asserted the Plantagenets' position as the descendants and not just the successors of the Anglo-Saxon kings, at a time when their legitimacy was still questioned by some. Later these rolls aimed to increase the King's prestige by emphasizing the monarchy's increasing Englishness as a result of intermarriage. At a time when Anglo-Saxons and Normans were still races apart, genealogies that stressed common origins and interests helped to build in England a national history and a national identity.

If genealogies could be used to record history, they could also be used to shape it. At various times during the Middle Ages those in power turned to genealogy as a source of propaganda; a body of evidence that could be marshalled to their own ends. The master of this approach was Edward I, who as part of his attempt to claim the Scottish throne twice sent out calls to English monasteries and cathedrals for evidence to back up his claim. The request for 'everything that he finds touching in any way our realm and the rule of Scotland' was vague and yielded a wide variety of responses. The Scots were not going to take this lying down and tabled evidence of their own: king-lists claiming to go back some 2,000 years, showing Scotland had long been an independent nation.[7]

Royal genealogies also played a crucial role in that most turbulent period of English history, the Wars of the Roses.[8] With the houses of Lancaster and York pitted against each other, issues of legitimacy were proffered by both sides. After his father's execution in 1460, Edward of York relied heavily on both prophecy and genealogy in his campaign to oust Henry VI. Edward's coronation in 1461 was commemorated by a magnificent genealogy, now in the Philadelphia Free Library,[9] that emphasizes his superior bloodline. By placing his ancestry within the framework of world history as it was understood at the time, he could claim hereditary and God-given rights to the throne of England; the roll asserts Edward's claim to the crowns of France and Spain as well.

At a time when few people could read or write, the main record keepers were the monks. Monastic communities used genealogical information in part to bolster the reputation of their monasteries, but also to preserve the genealogies – whether real or fictitious – of their benefactors for future generations. Such lineages were found not just in narrative texts but also in collections of charters and important legal documents known as 'cartularies', and in other records. With their focus on the home institutions, rather than national events, modern historians have often dismissed these monastic chronicles as rather insular, although they are now being reappraised as a source of local, manorial and family history. In the words of one contemporary scholar, such narratives 'insert a monastery within the continuous blood-line that anchors it to the symbols of power and authority'.[10]

A celebrated example of monastic records being used as documentary evidence for proof of ancestry was the case of *Scrope versus Grosvenor* in 1387.[11] This was one of the earliest heraldic law cases brought in England and centred on the fact that two knights, Sir Richard Scrope, 1st Baron Scrope of Bolton, Yorkshire, and Sir Robert Grosvenor from Cheshire, were both using the same coat-of-arms. The case was heard before a chivalric court and several hundred witnesses were called, including the King of Castile, the playwright Geoffrey Chaucer, and several members of the English nobility. Two of the witnesses were canons from Bridlington. Asked if they had heard of Richard Scrope's ancestors, the canons testified that their priory had possessions given by the Scrope family and they produced charters carrying great seals depicting knights on horseback, as used by 'those of the Conquest'. The case was eventually decided in Scrope's favour, though neither party was happy with the decision and in the end Richard II himself had to rule on the matter.

The Scrope case is illustrative of how, during the late Middle Ages, genealogy became associated with heraldry. Heralds were originally the King's messengers and had been employed on ceremonial duties and diplomatic missions. They were also responsible for recognizing and recording coats-of-arms during tournaments. By the late thirteenth and early fourteenth centuries they were making records of this armour.

Heraldry – the study of arms – is intrinsically bound up with genealogy since the right to bear arms is hereditary, i.e. it passes to the bearer's descendants. Only the eldest son inherits the original coat-of-arms, other family members having to vary the arms according to complex rules. Similarly, the union of two armorial families entitles the offspring to juxtapose the arms of both the father's and the mother's families, again according to strict heraldic rules. Thus, after just a few generations a coat-of-arms can become a walking family tree. Since a right to arms had often to be proved by pedigree, a concern with the one was bound in time to lead to the other.

In 1415 the office of Garter King of Arms was created to oversee the work of the heralds and in 1484 the College of Arms was established under a charter granted by Richard III. The first Garter, William Bruges, set about honouring the order and the knights appointed to it by setting up a series of enamelled stall plates of their arms in the chapel at Windsor. He also commissioned a painted record of the arms of all the knights from the foundation of the order in the 1340s through to his own time. This would have involved him in research to identify former knights, although according to Wagner several of these pedigrees were erroneous.[12]

Noble families had used genealogical chronicles to give themselves prestige and support their claims to inherited property since at least the twelfth century.[13] These were sometimes in the form of roll chronicles displaying genealogies of prominent families alongside the royal line. Other materials are to be found in letters and in petitions pleading rights to certain lands. Examples exist both in Anglo-Norman – the dialect of Old French used by the ruling class until the fifteenth century – and in Middle English – the tongue of the middle and lower classes.

The gentry's attitudes to genealogy evolved considerably in the period after 1370 in response to widespread social change.[14] As the feudal system loosened its grip in the wake of the Black Death, wealth and power began to disseminate beyond the nobility towards a new administrative and merchant class. Traditional boundaries between the high-born and those of more humble origins became less distinct. A person could aspire to gentility through a variety of means, such as service to the state or in the military, and need not rely on paternal lineage.

By the middle of the fifteenth century an embryonic 'genealogy industry' can be detected, with scribes (probably heralds) producing standardized genealogical trees for clients with enough time and money to spend on them.[15] These would be taken out and pored over among family and friends, like a modern-day photograph album. The introduction of paper as a cheaper alternative to parchment, more efficient working practices among scribes and the increasingly entrepreneurial attitude of stationers all contributed to this printing boom, although it was nowhere near 'mass production' in the modern sense.

The oldest books of pedigrees which can reliably be claimed to be the work of heralds date from around 1480. A notable collection of pedigrees relating to northern families was compiled for the most part around 1490, probably by John Writhe, Garter King of Arms, or his son and successor, Sir Thomas Wriothesley. Another important example is a manuscript volume compiled by William Ballard, who as March King of Arms in the same period recorded genealogical details of the nobility and gentry for several English counties.

The gentry's deep interest in genealogy was not always written down, however. The oral tradition was still strong and monks, as local guardians of aristocratic knowledge, could be called on to provide documentary proof where it were needed. Formal records, whether in paper, stone or glass, were the exception rather than the rule and are often a sign of a lineage in crisis. Either someone faced being the 'last of the line', and so wished to preserve their memory, or they felt their dynasty was being challenged in some way. As the historian Jon Denton has noted:[16]

> For the most part, gentry families did not need to produce physical genealogies. Those that did either had an illustrious descent and feared it might be lost or wished to invent one for reasons of social insecurity.

Some of the most insecure were the newly wealthy families who had no proud lineage to record or transmit. Many aspired to gentility and began assuming its trappings to show they 'had arrived', including fabricating a suitable pedigree. The increasing role of the heralds meant 'rising families could bolster their gentility in return for a fee'. Grants and petitions for arms from 'nouveau' families increased significantly after the 1450s, with written genealogies as central evidence. On the other hand, more long-established families, whose arms and lineage were well known in a locality, had no need to seek confirmation from the heralds and were less likely to commit their genealogies to paper.

By the early sixteenth century the rivalry between the ancient and nouveau gentry was clear for all to see. Rising literacy rates, continued expansion of the merchant class, greater opportunities for advancement generally, plus release of monastic lands, swept away the old order and created much fluidity and social change. Established gentry emphasized longevity of land tenure to set themselves apart and vied with the newly risen who invented their own social fictions. Paternal ancestry and genealogy underpinned this discourse – a situation that would pertain in England for the next 300 years.

Under the Tudors government became more centralized and the royal court began to take vigorous steps to control the way arms were being used. In 1530 Henry VIII instructed the officers of arms to visit particular counties in order to register arms and pedigrees of the nobility and gentry and to remove honours from those who had no right to possess them. Thus began a series of tours of inspection throughout England and Wales, known as heraldic visitations, which continued through to the late seventeenth century.

Over a period of 160 years the officers of arms toured the forty counties of England inquiring into the usage of arms and demanding documentary evidence of the claimant's right to use them. There was no apparent system in these visitations, but the closer you lived to London the more likely you were to get a knock on the door. The appalling state of the roads and the ever-present risk of highway robbery meant the heralds found it much safer and more convenient to stay in the Home Counties. Kent, for example, was visited five times between 1530 and 1663, and on three of these occasions by the Clarenceux King of Arms in person. Similarly, Essex was visited six times between 1550 and 1650. Far-off Westmorland, on the other hand, was only ever visited twice. Likewise, Cornwall and Cumberland received just three visits, and Durham four.

Having arrived in the county, the visiting herald would take up residence with the principal gentleman of the neighbourhood and begin to proclaim his presence and the purpose of his visit. Deputies would be sent around the county to require or request the local gentry to come in for registration. This was a major task in itself but only then could the main business of registration begin.

Visitations were the first formal and systematic investigations of family histories. Claimants were asked for dates of birth, marriage and death of their ancestors and any other information which supported their claim to bear arms. Then, as now, very few people could give these dates without consulting documents or other persons. Consequently, few of the early visitation pedigrees go back beyond three generations, and often they are limited simply to a statement of paternity. In some cases arms are given with only the names of the families who bore them. Where no satisfactory evidence could be produced the arms were 'respited for proof'; the family was given six months to find proof of their right to arms, after which they would be taken away.

Under the Visitation Commissions, the officers of arms had draconian powers to deal with offenders who were found to be using arms without authority. They could deface and mutilate monuments bearing the arms, proclaim publicly that the arms should not be borne, and require the bearers to disclaim their right to use them. In practice, they exercised discretion – and often a fair amount of bias – in how these powers were applied. Social position was everything. Persons who lived in the style expected of an English gentleman were allowed arms, others were not. For example, in the visitation of Rutland 1681–82, the list of disclaimers includes a farmer, a schoolmaster, an attorney, a draper and a wealthy yeoman.

The use of arms without formal authority from the College of Arms was fairly commonplace during this period. This was not out of any desire to evade the law but simply a matter of ignorance and a reflection of the practical difficulties and expense in visiting London to apply for a grant. For these well intentioned – or simply naive – families the visitations were nothing to fear. The heralds were accustomed to accepting arms not granted by the College provided that they had been borne for a sufficient period (generally at least sixty years or two generations) and that the users were members of the gentry. In heraldry this is known as the 'right to arms by prescription'.

In focusing on genealogy as an area for original inquiry, the heralds were staking out new territory and learning their trade as they went. Those of Tudor times were not chosen for their skills in genealogy and the difficulties in acquiring information were considerable. They would accept sworn statements back to the grandfather and for earlier records of descent would quote or copy original sources such as grants, deeds and seals. Monastic records were consulted and the occupation of houses, stained glass and memorials would also be taken as evidence. Nevertheless, the pedigrees of the early heralds were often pretty bare.

In retrospect, we now know that many of the pedigrees entered in the visitation registers were wrong, either because they relied on scant or erroneous information or, in certain cases, they were deliberately fabricated. The use of fictitious documents for genealogical or other purposes was nothing new. People had resorted to forgery throughout the Middle Ages, usually to secure titles to land. Perhaps none went further than the Wellesbourne family of Buckinghamshire, who in their efforts to prove descent from Simon de Montfort, Earl of Leicester, not only forged medieval deeds and seals, but also placed a fabricated thirteenth-century effigy in the local church. It would require a canny herald to refute these claims.

The question arises as to whether the heralds were complicit in such acts. The Elizabethan herald Richard Lee is widely believed to have fabricated the descent of the Spencers – one of England's most aristocratic families – from the medieval Despencers. According to the Victorian critic Horace Round:[17]

> He took from the records Spencers and Despencers wherever he could lay hands on them, fitted them together in one pedigree at his own sweet will, rammed into his composition several distinct families, and then boldly certified the whole as gospel truth.

Such outright deceits were the exception, however. More typical was the case of Sir William Dethick, a contemporary of Lee, who defended himself against accusations of producing false pedigrees by arguing that he was merely acting on the proofs provided by the claimant – though he obviously did not feel it was his job to challenge these. A generous view is that the heralds did not question enough what was presented to them; but this was in an age when, on the whole, standards of critical scholarship in any field had yet to be established. Where erroneous information was taken it was more a matter, as Wagner observed, of 'real evidence [being] interpreted in too optimistic a manner'.[18]

As the heralds became more experienced, the reliability and veracity of visitation pedigrees improved significantly. So too did their presentation. Early visitation records use a narrative form, where a pedigree is set out as a descriptive text. By the late sixteenth century this had given way to the rectilinear form – or 'dropline' family tree – with which most people are now familiar. This innovation is generally attributed to Robert Glover, Somerset Herald, who was using it in visitation entries during the 1570s, although Sir Thomas Wriothesley had occasionally employed this form several years before. It proved much more practical and by 1618 had wholly superseded both the narrative form used since the 1530s and the medieval 'crane's foot' representation with radiating lines.

The foundation myths advanced by Geoffrey of Monmouth and the prose *Brut* gradually gave way to a more scholarly view of history. As the Renaissance told hold, educated Englishmen engaged in systematic inquiry into the country's people and its past, while accepting the Bible's account that the world was some 4,000 years old. These investigators, who were known as 'antiquaries', concerned themselves with more or less anything to do with Britain and its people. Antiquarian studies were much slower to emerge in Britain than in its continental neighbours, however. An independent critical faculty was not looked on favourably in early Tudor England, where clerics and educated laymen inherited a respect for written authority that had persisted since the Middle Ages. It was not until the late sixteenth century that a distinct English antiquarianism began to emerge.[19]

Foremost in this movement was William Camden, who was appointed as Clarenceux King of Arms in 1597. Camden was an antiquary with a broad range of interests and is widely credited as the first true English historical scholar. His seminal work was *Britannia*, a topographical and historical survey of Great Britain and Ireland, first published in 1586. Written in Latin, *Britannia* gives a county-by-county description of Britain in the late Tudor period and relates it to its classical Roman heritage. His intention, he said, was 'to restore antiquity to Britaine, and Britaine to . . . its antiquity'. The book was immediately popular, going into seven editions by 1607, each one incorporating much additional material. The first English translation of 1610 reached an even wider audience and inspired many later county surveys.

Camden was following in the footsteps of John Leland (1506–52), who is often referred to as 'the father of English local history'. Appointed Royal Antiquary by Henry VIII (the only person ever to hold that post), Leland spent six years in the 1540s travelling through England and Wales, making records of the remains of ancient buildings and monuments. He also made attempts to save manuscripts put at risk by the dissolution of the monasteries by having them transferred to the King's library. Leland's collections – most of which are held at the Bodleian Library in Oxford – are an invaluable source on the local history and geography of England, as well as for archaeology, and social and economic history.

The middle to late Elizabethan period saw a new generation of scholars – of which William Camden was one – who sought to build on Leland's foundations. Laurence Nowell, an antiquarian and cartographer, collected and transcribed Anglo-Saxon documents and compiled the first Anglo-Saxon dictionary. In 1570, William Lambarde published *Perambulation of Kent*, the first history of a British county. And between 1605 and 1610 John Speed, a historian and cartographer, published the first series of fifty-four individual county maps of England and Wales.

In about 1585 notable figures formed the College of Antiquaries as a debating society on historical and antiquarian matters. This was banned in 1604 by James I, who was suspicious of any ideas which he thought might play to English patriotism. Meetings were resumed in 1707 at the Bear Tavern in London's Strand and the organization was formally re-established in 1717, as the Society of Antiquaries of London, with the aim of encouraging 'the ingenious and curious' in the field of 'Bryttish antiquitys'. A Royal Charter granted in 1751 enabled members to call themselves Fellows, and in 1781 the Society moved to prestigious new premises in Somerset House, which it shared with the Royal Academy of Arts and the Royal Society before moving to its current home at Burlington House. Outside of London, provincial societies, such as the Spalding Gentleman's Society (founded in 1712), provided meeting places for antiquarians, at least some of whom had genealogical interests.

Antiquarians were keen to explore time and place in a whole variety of ways, including through the study of landscape, geography, archaeology and history (especially local history). Genealogy and heraldry were seen as subjects of increasing interest, partly because they met the demands of local readers of antiquarian works, and partly because many antiquaries were heralds.

Augustine Vincent, a pupil of Camden, helped cement the place of genealogy within antiquarian studies by introducing a knowledge of the public records. Vincent had worked in the Tower Record Office, the main repository for public records at the time, under Sir John Borough and later entered the College of Arms. Having a foot in both camps, he was able to consult the records in proving pedigrees. His manuscript collections, now held by the College, include more than thirty volumes of extracts from records such as the Patent Rolls, Close Rolls, Inquisitions, Pleas and Fines. He put this knowledge to good use in defending his master against a fellow herald, Ralph Brooke, who was an avid critic of Camden's work. Vincent's recognition of public records as original documentary sources for the tracing of pedigrees was thus a landmark in the history of genealogy in Britain.

This period also saw the first written family history, an account of the Berkeley family of Berkeley Castle, Gloucestershire, compiled by John Smyth of Nibley around the 1630s. Smythe's *Lives of the Berkeleys* was based partly on public records and partly on the family's own papers and charters. It remained in manuscript for many years, however. The first family history to be published did not appear until 1685 and included many forged charters and fictitious pedigrees.[20]

In Wales the Tudor antiquaries arrived in time to encounter the last of the bardic tradition that had once existed all across Celtic Britain. An account of the inhabitants of north Wales from this period notes that the people would congregate on Sundays and holidays to listen to bards singing 'songs of the doeings of their Auncestors'.[21] They were able to recite their own pedigrees at length, 'howe eche of them is discended from those theire ould princes'. Such recitals were popular entertainment, but also helped bind the community together by emphasizing ties of kinship and reminders of a shared past. This preoccupation with the genealogy of the common man, rather than the gentry, gave the Welsh a particular identity that set them apart and became a source of ridicule for their English cousins. In a play written around 1700, the dramatist Sir John Vanburgh portrays a herald who claims to 'know every man's father, Sir, and every man's grandfather, and every man's great-grandfather'. When asked how this was, he proclaims that his mother was from Wales, 'a country in the world's back-side, where every man is born a gentleman, and a genealogist'.[22]

By the early 1600s there was a network of antiquarians throughout Britain, with a scholarly approach to documents and versed in legal training. Genealogy was a core interest of these scholars, underpinning as it did the study of local history, family history and claims to property and peerages. Foremost amongst this generation was Sir William Dugdale, a Warwickshire gentleman and herald who lived at Blythe Hall, near Birmingham. Friends found him a place in the College of Arms where he had an illustrious career, ending up as Garter King of Arms in 1677.

From a genealogical point of view, Dugdale's most important works were *The Antiquities of Warwickshire* (published in 1656) and *The Baronage of England* (published in 1675–6). The former was the most detailed study then undertaken of the history of an English county, while the latter was the first attempt to catalogue the pedigrees of barons and peers. Both would provide models of their kind. His other notable publication, *Monasticon Anglicanum* – a collection of documents relating to the English monasteries – is of more limited genealogical value.

During his early career Dugdale undertook extensive searches in the public records. These foundations enabled him to exercise great skill not only in collecting evidence but also in the way in which he marshalled it to prove (or disprove) his case and draw appropriate conclusions. His pedigrees in the *Antiquities of Warwickshire* and the *Baronage* are accompanied by detailed references so that readers can verify the facts stated for themselves. He thus established the principle – now familiar to every serious student of family history – that every statement made should be backed up by evidence from contemporary records. 'How hard a matter it is', he wrote to a friend in July 1651, 'to sifte out ye truth in these matters of Genealogye.'[23] This insistence on documentary evidence did not stop him from being deceived by spurious records on rare occasions, such as the claim that the Earls of Denbigh (the Feilding family) were descended from the Habsburgs. But by all objective measures his standards were far above those of his contemporaries, both in Britain and continental Europe.

Later scholars accused Dugdale of plagiarism and though he relied greatly on the work of other scholars, such a charge is exaggerated. Indeed, he seems to have exercised extreme caution in referencing others' work, including his predecessors and colleagues at the College, and was only prepared to accept sources – such as Glover and Vincent – who he judged came up to his own exacting standards. He particularly admired Smyth's work on the Berkeleys, which he described as being 'written in a historical way which I heartily wish may be a pattern for some others to follow'.[24]

Dugdale is noted in particular for his thoroughness. In his *Warwickshire* volume, as the historian Philip Styles observed, he acknowledged as sources:[25]

> those obscure people, descended from younger sons or belonging to families of mere yeoman origin, whose small estates had been acquired within the last three generations. They number, on a rough estimate, rather more than a quarter of the whole. . . . That such men were beginning to take an interest in history and genealogy was a notable sign of the times.

Dugdale's work as a herald – and a rather strict one at that – came at the very end of the heraldic visitations. The overthrow of James II in the 'Glorious Revolution' of 1688 brought major changes to the monarchy and to Parliament. The visitations were not popular with the gentry and since the sovereigns who came after James owed their thrones to the gentry-dominated Parliament, they did not feel secure in issuing new commissions into arms. William III, George I and George II were also foreigners and had problems fully understanding the customs of their new kingdom. Thus, the tradition of heraldic visitations died out.

The visitations had in effect been a system of compulsory registration. Their cessation opened the way to the system we have today, whereby the registration of genealogical information in relation to armorial bearings is purely voluntary. In the intervening period a practice has built up whereby it is possible to register a pedigree with the College of Arms for genealogical purposes alone – as a recognition of authenticity – irrespective of any heraldic entitlement. Thus, despite the end of the visitations, the genealogical component of the heralds' work grew rather than decreased. Indeed, from the mid-eighteenth to the early twentieth century the heralds were invariably the most accomplished genealogists in the land.

*   *   *   *

In the years after Dugdale's death in 1686 the prominence of genealogy waned as antiquaries' attentions were directed elsewhere. New interests came to the fore, such as archaeology, natural history and topography, and genealogy's star was eclipsed. Keen genealogists continued to carry the torch, but none came close to repeating Dugdale's achievements and overall the level of scholarship fell far short of that reached during the time of the visitations. Robert Thoroton's *Antiquities of Nottingham*, published in 1677, followed the principles Dugdale had set out in his *Warwickshire* volume but was altogether a less substantial work. Other writers, such as James Wright, Sir Robert Atkyns and Ralph Thoresby, printed some useful and interesting material though genealogical content was lacking.

The genealogies published in antiquarian local and county histories served a wider purpose than simply recording family lineages: they helped reinforce the invisible bonds of deference that bound society together. Edward Hasted noted that 'relationship of family extended, by the preservation of pedigrees, promotes a chain of society and good will that often affords assistance and support to every link of it'.[26] On the other hand, some individuals became wary of allowing access to their family records in case such knowledge gave rise to legal challenges to their estates.

The most important contribution of this period came from Peter Le Neve, Norroy King of Arms and first president (1717–24) of the revived Society of Antiquaries. By the end of the seventeenth century a new clientele was emerging who had made their fortunes in trade and commerce. Many of these were offshoots of known families, but others were of humble origins. For instance, one of Le Neve's clients, Sir William Milman, who was knighted in 1705, was the son of a shoemaker from the Strand. In 1699 Sir Comport Fitch, whose father had been a carpenter and had grown rich rebuilding London after the Great Fire, registered a pedigree showing descent from an Essex yeoman.

Until this point, genealogists had been concerned almost exclusively with landed families and so had grounded their research on knowledge of records of land tenure. Le Neve recognized this was no longer sufficient for tracing the pedigrees of the new commercial class and he began to investigate the use of parish registers. First established in 1538, parish registers were now 'old' enough to take more obscure pedigrees some way back.

Le Neve, together with a colleague at the College, Samuel Stebbing, became an expert in their use. They made extracts from parish registers and consulted a range of other sources, copying wills, noting monumental inscriptions, interviewing family members and fitting all this evidence together as best they could. It is an early and elementary instance of what has since become commonplace in the genealogical method. Church monuments had always been used but Le Neve and Stebbing recognized that those in the churchyard could also be important for humbler families.

The mantle was taken up by Ralph Bigland, Somerset Herald, who drew attention to the genealogical value of parish registers, wills and monumental inscriptions in tracing the origins of those not of noble birth. He set out his views in a pamphlet published in 1764: *Observations on Marriage, Baptism and Burials, as preserved in Parochial Registers . . . Interspersed with divers Remarks concerning proper Methods necessary to preserve a Remembrance of the several Branches of Families, &c.* Here he advocated the inclusion of much greater detail in church registers and called for better safekeeping and detailed indexing of such records.

Bigland was himself of relatively humble origins. Born in Stepney, Middlesex, in 1712, he served as apprentice to a cheesemaker and maintained commercial interests throughout his life. As a supplier to the allied armies during the War of the Austrian Succession (1740–8), he travelled to Flanders where he began to take an interest in antiquarian matters. He travelled the whole of England, accumulating historical information and recording the inscriptions on everything from great monuments to modest gravestones. Much of his attention focused on Gloucestershire, where he copied or had copied nearly all the inscriptions in the county's parish churches. These were published posthumously in his *History of Gloucestershire*, which is notable for its extensive (and virtually unique) collection of churchyard epitaphs dating back to the time of Elizabeth I.

Bigland began to think about a change of career and in 1757 entered the College of Arms. A skilled draftsman and methodical genealogist, he climbed steadily through the College hierarchy, ending as Garter King of Arms 1780–4. With his friend and colleague Sir Issac Heard, he helped to re-establish the College as the centre of genealogical study in England. He died at his rooms in the College and was buried in Gloucester Cathedral; he had already drafted his own, genealogically informative, monumental inscription.

While the newly risen families provided additional scope for the genealogist, the nobility and gentry remained an important market. The number of published peerages proliferated during the course of the eighteenth century, with both historic families and the newly ennobled alike wanting to see their pedigrees in print.

The peerage writer Arthur Collins published the first edition of his *Peerage of England* in 1709 and remained its editor through to the third edition in 1756. Collins was industrious and well qualified, but was no match for Dugdale in his standards of scholarship. Reluctant to deflate family pride, he was quite happy to take, without question, old heraldic pedigrees given to him by ennobled houses. Thus, fallacies which had up to now been private within the records of the College or families themselves, made it into print and became a matter of public record. The notion – which we see today with the internet – that 'if it's written down it must be true' took hold. Myths and errors were perpetuated in later works and with each repetition became all the more difficult to dispel.

Other peerage volumes of the period – Thomas Wotton's *Baronetage* (published in 1727 and 1741) and Joseph Edmondson's *Baronagium Genealogicum* (published in 1764 based on earlier work by Simon Segar) – suffered similar flaws.

As interest in antiquarian matters grew, genealogical and other enquirers found a new outlet through the pages of the *Gentleman's Magazine*. It was founded by the publisher Edward Cave in 1731 to preserve 'for universal Benefit and Information' items from the many pamphlets and newssheets then circulating in London and elsewhere. Writing in the preface to the first number, Cave described the purpose as being:[27]

> to treasure up, as in a Magazine, the most remarkable Pieces on the Subjects . . . , or at least impartial Abridgements thereof, as a Method much better calculated to preserve those Things that are curious, than that of transcribing.[28]

It was an immediate success and, despite what to modern eyes is an exceptionally dry style, soon became required reading for the literary classes. For its founder it became an all-consuming passion. Dr Johnson famously said of Cave that 'he never looked out of the window but with a view to the *Gentleman's Magazine*'.

The magazine was sufficiently established to survive Cave's death in 1751 and in 1778 his sister sold a share of the company to John Nichols, a printer and writer. Nichols was proprietor of one of London's largest printing houses, having acquired the publishing interests of William Bowyer, his former master. The firm held important government contracts and was also printers to high-profile institutions such as the Society of Antiquaries and the Royal Society. In 1773, before Nichols took full control, the government commissioned the Bowyer press to print a type facsimile of the Domesday Book. He designed the type and saw the work through the press during the ten years it took to produce.

Nichols became the sole printer of the *Gentleman's Magazine* and took over much of the editorial responsibilities, before acquiring full editorial control in 1792. He expanded the publication considerably, doubling the size of each issue so as to print longer reviews, as well as giving space to literary and antiquarian contributions from readers. He was fascinated with the minutiae of people's lives and under his editorship the columns of the magazine became packed with biographical facts and anecdotes which he would invite readers to check and comment on. Obituaries were given particular prominence, to the extent that he became known as 'John Nichols, the death hunter'.

Nichols's love of antiquarianism, as well as his expertise as a printer and editor, put him at the centre of the late eighteenth century's awakening to all things historical. His circle included Johnson's biographer James Boswell, the historian Edward Gibbon and man of letters Horace Walpole. While printing a volume entitled *History and Antiquities of Dorset*, he met Richard Gough, a pioneer local historian. The two men shared a passion to unmask Britain's antiquities and became firm friends. Over a period of twenty years they travelled the country together visiting sites of historic interest and collecting material for publication. Gough was a frequent contributor to the *Gentleman's Magazine* and the two collaborated on various projects. After Gough's death in 1809, Nichols as his executor oversaw the bequest of his enormous collections of local history to the Bodleian Library.

Nichols's later years were marred by ill-fortune. In 1807 he fell and fractured his thigh – an injury from which he never fully recovered – while the following year his printing office and warehouse off Fleet Street were destroyed by fire, with the loss of much uninsured stock. Yet at the age of 63 and with the help of his son, John Bowyer Nichols, he was able to recover his business and continue his numerous personal printing enterprises. Although not a biographer, in the traditional sense, his works contain more biographical information than all his contemporaries combined. 'Every book', he is noted as saying, 'should contain within itself its necessary explanation.'[29]

After Nichols's death in 1826, John Bowyer Nichols became sole owner of the printing house. He continued the association with the *Gentleman's Magazine* and in 1833 purchased the remaining shares from the descendants of Edward Cave and elsewhere. He published most of the early nineteenth-century county histories, in which he took a personal interest, and was an active and popular antiquary. However, it was not until the tenure of his son, John Gough Nichols, that the company focused more specifically on genealogical material. By the 1840s, the firm of J B Nichols & Son was at the centre of a publishing boom that would drive genealogy forward.

* * * *

Chapter 4

Societies and Peers

By the early nineteenth century, peerage volumes of the sort initiated by Dugdale and Collins were more than just academic interest. The chronicling of the peerage and baronetage (hereditary knighthoods which rank one step below peers) had drawn attention to the fact that a large number of titles were unclaimed. This was because they were either *dormant* – the rightful heir could not be traced – or were *in abeyance* – the title was suspended between co-heirs each of whom had a legitimate claim. The situation was particularly acute for a certain type of medieval barony known as being 'created by writ'.

Wealthy and powerful families had come to see the House of Lords as a select club, entry to which was highly sought after. An ancient barony could provide the key to the door and rich claimants were prepared to spend very large sums to win the prize. Faced with these abuses, the Lords' authorities had to impose exacting standards of proof over those they admitted. Thus, written accounts of the peerage came to be not only scholarly works but also important legal references.

In a society obsessed with gossip and one-upmanship, they also met the needs of those intent on social climbing. Volumes on the peerage and baronetage abounded and were popular reading in drawing rooms up and down the land. Mrs Bennett-type characters would peruse them to find an eligible bachelor for their daughters – preferably one with a sizeable estate – and Mr Bennett could reflect on how even those in high society could be laid low. Sir Walter Elliot, in Jane Austen's *Persuasion* was one 'who, for his own amusement, never took up any book but the Baronetage; there he found occupation for an idle hour, and consolation in a distressed one'.

Two of the most famous peerage works started around this period. John Field Debrett published the first edition of *The Correct Peerage of England, Scotland and Ireland* in 1802 and his *Baronetage of England* in 1808.

Of Huguenot extraction, Debrett had been apprenticed to William Davis, a Piccadilly bookseller and publisher, and later moved to another bookseller, John Almon. Almon was one of many publishers printing peerage volumes and in 1790 passed the editorship of his *New Peerage* to Debrett. He put his name to the two small volumes and personally edited fifteen editions, the last appearing in 1823, after his death.

Despite the success of his publishing ventures, Debrett was plagued by money problems and was twice declared bankrupt. His obituary in the *Gentleman's Magazine* described him as 'a kind, good-natured, friendly, man, who experienced the vicissitudes of life with fortitude. He had full opportunity of acquiring a large fortune, but from too much confidence and easiness of temper, he did not turn it to the best account.'[1] He died penniless in November 1822 after a long illness.

In due course Debrett's *Peerage* was united with the *Baronetage* in a single volume. Initially full lineages were presented but these were later dropped in favour of summaries of succession and more descriptive accounts of current families and title holders. Both works, usually published in one volume, still flourish, and Debrett's name is used in a wide variety of reference books.

Debrett's main rival, Burke's *Peerage*, was genealogically more ambitious, and because of that more controversial. Its originator, John Burke, was born in Ireland to a gentry family; his father was a justice of the peace and his mother the daughter of a doctor from County Westmeath. After a classical education, Burke moved to London where he devoted himself to literary pursuits. He contributed articles to periodicals and produced a volume of poetry before publishing the first of his genealogical volumes in 1826.

Until that time printed peerages had divided peerage titles into those of England, Scotland and Ireland, and then listed them in order of precedence within each country. In 1825 Nicholas Harris Nicolas, a peerage lawyer and antiquary, had produced *A Synopsis of the Peerage of England* with each title listed alphabetically. Burke decided to adopt this arrangement and in his *Peerage*, published the following year, listed the baronets and entire peerage alphabetically, irrespective of rank.

Burke's Peerage – full title *A General and Heraldic Dictionary of the Peerage and Baronetage of the United Kingdom* – was immediately popular. Its size grew rapidly, with the number of pages of pedigrees increasing from 359 in 1826 to 1,300 for the 4th edition in 1833. Nine editions appeared between 1826 and 1847, after which it became an annual. With the exception of 1918–20, *Burke's Peerage* was produced every year from 1847 through to 1940. A further nine editions have been published since then, the most recent (the 107th) in 2003.

In 1837 Burke published a companion work in four volumes, *A Genealogical and Heraldic History of the Commoners of Great Britain and Ireland*, renamed in subsequent editions *Burke's Genealogical and Heraldic History of the Landed Gentry* (generally referred to simply as *Burke's Landed Gentry*). This never became an annual publication, but many editions have appeared. It at first comprised the principal untitled landowning families and gradually became more comprehensive.

In the 1st edition of the *Peerage* John Burke stated that he was 'deducing the genealogical line of each house from the founder of its honors'. In subsequent editions this was changed to 'deducing the genealogical line of each house from the earliest period'. In expanding the scope of the work in this way Burke laid the foundations for much later criticism. Moving from founders of titles, who were generally well known and well documented, to 'the earliest period' of the house concerned, which was much more difficult to substantiate, opened the door to myth and intrigue. Burke accepted uncritically fictional and inaccurate information on the origins of families, either supplied by subjects themselves or printed in earlier works, particularly those by Collins (who in turn had copied the heralds of earlier periods).

After Burke's death in 1848, editorship of the *Peerage* and the *Landed Gentry* was taken over by his son (John) Bernard Burke. Energetic and ambitious, Bernard trained as a lawyer, was admitted to the bar and later entered the College of Arms. In 1853, on his appointment as Ulster King of Arms, he moved to Dublin, where he helped in cataloguing and arranging the Irish State Papers. He built up a substantial genealogical practice and produced a number of popular books on genealogy and heraldry, including *Anecdotes of the Aristocracy, Family Romance, and Vicissitudes of Families*. He was knighted in 1854.

Sir Bernard was no scholar, lacking both knowledge as a medievalist and a critical mind. As the number and size of publications under the Burke imprimatur grew, so did their inaccuracies. This was especially apparent in the *Landed Gentry*, which being a new compilation was riddled with unreliable information that Burke was unable, or unwilling, to filter out.

An anonymous pamphlet published in Edinburgh in 1865 finally took Burke to task. Its author is now widely accepted as being George Burnett, a Scottish genealogist and peerage lawyer, who had recently entered the office of the Lyon King of Arms. Entitled *Popular Genealogists or the Art of Pedigree-making*, the pamphlet set out to expose the inaccuracies in genealogical peerage works and Burke was the main target.

'It was the fashion among the wits and philosophers of last century', Burnett began, 'to throw ridicule on the subject of pedigree . . . Since that time, however, genealogical studies have entered a new phase.'[2] He continued:

> It has become an admitted fact that the history of the leading families of the country is an important part of the history of that country. A race of learned and accurate investigators have sprung up, who, approaching genealogy in a critical spirit, have brought entirely new resources to bear on it. Rejecting all that is not borne out by authentic evidence, they have applied themselves to the patient examination of the national records, the archives and chronicles of the monasteries, and the contents of private charter-chests. Each source has yielded its quota of facts, and

these facts have been woven into genealogical biographies. Heraldry itself, after having been abandoned to coach-painters and undertakers, has again come into favour, having been found to be a valuable, if not indispensable aid to the knowledge both of family and of national history.

Burnett asked how far this 'genealogical revival' was being extended to peerage volumes, and in particular to Sir Bernard Burke 'the most voluminous of our popular writers on genealogical topics'. Burke's position, both as editor of these commercial publications and as a holder of one of the highest heraldic offices in the land, represented a particular problem, in Burnett's opinion, since it imparted 'a stamp of authority which they would not otherwise possess'. Burke, Burnett maintained, was failing to follow proper critical standards:[3]

An account, either of the peerage families, or of the untitled gentry of Britain, must, if properly drawn up, be a work of great historical value. It would presuppose high genealogical qualifications on the part of its author, including patience, carefulness, and a scrupulous regard to truth. It would be based on an attentive examination of title-deeds, contemporary documents, and the public records, and its statements would be checked by reference to every available source of information. While due weight would be allowed to conclusions arrived at by genealogical critics of tried skill and accuracy, no mere dictum of the representative family, however unimpeachable in point of veracity, would be received without investigation.

Turning to Burke's reliance on the peerage works of earlier authors, such as Dugdale and Collins, Burnett noted:[4]

Since their day, the materials for arriving at truths have been so greatly extended, the public records have become so much more accessible, and so much light has been thrown on family history by the labours of genealogical antiquaries, that it is obviously desirable that the standard works should be replaced by others written under advantages which the older writers never possessed, and embodying the results of the genealogical literature which has been accumulating since their date.

After this Burnett really set to work, citing numerous examples of inaccurate pedigrees, misconstrued ancestry and erroneous use of arms, starting from the royal line and working down. His sharpest criticism was reserved for the *Landed Gentry*, where 'the immense majority of the pedigrees' were 'utterly worthless'.[5] The errors contained in the *Peerage* were as nothing to the 'fables' encountered here, where 'families of notoriously obscure origins have their veins filled with the blood of generations of royal personages of the ancient and mythical world'. One example was the Coulthart pedigree, which Burke attributed as being derived from Coulthartus, a Roman lieutenant who 'settled in North Britain in the time of Tacitus'.

Burke failed to take the criticisms to heart and made little attempt to weed out the myths surrounding early pedigrees. Twelve years later, in 1877, an Oxford scholar, Edward Freeman, again tried to take him to task. Freeman was widely acclaimed as the historian of the Norman Conquest and, writing in the *Contemporary Review*, showed the absurdity of Burke's claims regarding the early ancestry of families such as FitzWilliam, Leighton, Wake, and Stourton. Like Burnett, he took particular exception to the fact that Burke's senior position in the College gave his editorship a quasi-official approval. 'From Sir Bernard Burke', he wrote, 'we have a right to expect historical criticism and we do not get it.'[6]

Joseph Foster, a London-based genealogist and antiquary, decided he could do better. In 1879, with his friend Edward Bellasis, who occupied a junior position at the College, Foster produced his own *Peerage, Baronetage and Knightage*. Building partly on an earlier work, he set out to show how accurate an annual peerage could be made. Foster was no medievalist and in many ways was overly ambitious in trying to tackle such a monumental task without any proper grounding in medieval genealogy or heraldry. Even so he rooted out many of the mythical ancestries prevalent in earlier works and introduced a new section dealing with baronetcies of doubtful creation, appropriately entitled 'Chaos'. His pedigrees were accompanied by attractive new artwork, although this drew criticism from purists in the College.

Only four issues of Foster's *Peerage* appeared, the last in 1883. A series of *Pedigrees of the County Families of England* was planned but only four, one for Lancashire and three for Yorkshire, were published. Foster focused instead on the works for which he would become best known: a series of transcripts relating to the universities and the professions. The most important of these was *Alumni Oxonienses*, an eight-volume edition of the Oxford matriculation register starting in the year 1500, published in two four-volume series in 1887 and 1891. This was the first published register of the alumni of a British university. It built on the work of his friend and collaborator Joseph Lemuel Chester, which Foster supplemented with his own researches. The university recognized him with the award of an honorary MA degree in 1892. A further work, *Oxford Men and their Colleges* followed and he also published works on the bar (*Men at the Bar*, 1885), Gray's Inn (*The Register of Admissions to Gray's Inn 1557–1859*, 1889), and the clergy (*Index Ecclesiasticus*, 1890).

An American by birth, Chester first visited England in 1858. A brief period in the militia had given him the title of 'colonel', an appellation by which he was known for the rest of his life. Although the business interests that had prompted his journey did not materialize, he settled in London, working first as a journalist and writer and later as a researcher. American families were increasingly curious about their English ancestry and as a London-based investigator he was ideally placed to make searches for US clients. In 1862 he obtained permission to examine all Prerogative Wills before 1700 (then at Doctors' Commons) and to make copies. He spent the next twenty years exploring these and other records for the origins of American settlers.

Chester's output was prodigious. His transcript of the Oxford matriculation registers, which formed the basis for Foster's later work, was made between 1866 and 1869. He made extensive extracts from parish registers, including editing and annotating the registers of Westminster Abbey published in 1876 and dedicated to Queen Victoria. At his death in 1882 he left eighty-seven volumes of parish register extracts, seventy of which were carefully indexed, and a further twenty-four volumes of pedigree collections. These were bought and presented to the College of Arms by his literary executor, George E. Cokayne.

With Chester's death the New England Historic Genealogical Society (NEHGS) felt the need for 'a competent person in London to make genealogical researches for the English ancestry of American families'. Henry FitzGilbert Waters, a genealogist with experience of the main English repositories, was offered the post for a modest salary. He accepted and from 1883 to 1899 made regular contributions to the *Register*, the Society's journal, detailing searches among English records and paying particular attention to the wills at Somerset House. These were reprinted in 1901, in two volumes running to some 1643 pages, as *Genealogical Gleanings in England*. Waters worked methodically, 'keeping a sharp look out for everything possibly indicative of the slightest connection with known American families'. Probably his most pleasing discovery was unearthing the origins of John Harvard, the founder of his university. The NEHGS continued to sponsor research in Britain until well into the twentieth century.

* * * *

With the blossoming of interest in all things historical, by the mid–nineteenth century genealogy was for the first time being practised as a profession in its own right, outside of the College and the main publishing houses. These independent practitioners had a small market for their wares. Advertising was in its infancy, so there were no general customers as such. Income was from two sources: private commissions from wealthy individuals (relatively rare) and subscriptions to their own self-produced publications.

Prospective clients generally had to be appealed to in person. A common method was to make a tour of the large houses in a county or locality, fortified if possible by recommendations from some kind-hearted nobleman, and try to persuade each owner to subscribe for one or more copies of the forthcoming work. The buyer would, of course, be more inclined to subscribe if he (it was invariably a he) found his own name in the book and here the vendor had to be adroit. At the moment, he would admit, the name did not appear but he had recently discovered an unsuspected marriage which gave the aspirant admission to the pedigree of some far more illustrious family. Thus, the gentry would subscribe and in the next edition would acquire a pedigree connecting them to an earl, a duke, or even royalty.

This sort of approach, with variations, was often very successful. One practitioner was William Berry, who started his career as a clerk at the College of Arms before retiring, at the age of 36, to become a professional genealogist. He is best known for his county genealogies published in small folio volumes, at 5 or 6 guineas each. Eight such volumes covering the Home Counties appeared over the period 1830–42.

In the volume for Sussex Berry had to handle the Newingtons, a well-to-do Puritan family, who took their name from the village of Newenden. They refused to subscribe to the new book unless their existing records were smartened up in some way, a challenge that was grist to Berry's mill. He told them that an ancestor had married 'the heiress of the glorious Culpepers, who owned many of the finest estates in Kent and Sussex'. To prove this assertion he simply inserted the heiress into the Newington pedigree and inserted the supposed husband into the Culpeper pedigree, so that each falsehood proved the other. To give the husband the necessary social position, he is declared (without a shred of evidence) to have been a knight associated with Ticehurst church. The Miss Culpeper whom Berry selected was a real person but probably never married, while her supposed husband must have been 80, if he ever existed.

Berry was not always so unscrupulous and in fact produced some useful work. His *Encyclopedia Heraldica, or Complete Dictionary of Heraldry*, brought out in numbers between 1828 and 1840, was a valuable contribution to the study of heraldry, embracing contents from Joseph Edmondson and other writers, with much original material. Next he began to issue, in 1832, his *Genealogical Peerage of England, Scotland and Ireland*. This was a carefully compiled family history, with beautiful engraved coats of arms, but had to be abandoned after the fourth issue due to lack of subscribers.

Controversy surrounded the launch of his *County Genealogies* series when the Kent volume was very poorly reviewed in the *Gentleman's Magazine*. Berry brought an action for libel against the publishers, J B Nichols & Sons, but when the case reached court, in November 1830, the jury decided almost immediately, without having heard any rebutting evidence, in favour of the defendants.

Not surprisingly, practices such as these meant professional genealogists acquired a poor reputation and were often viewed as charlatans and quacks. The lawyer William Turnbull wrote in 1839 of the genealogist Thomas Banks that he was:[7]

One of the busy, meddling, troublesome and officious individuals, professing themselves 'Genealogists', who tend so much to perpetuate blunders and misrepresentations in matters of general and family history, if indeed they do not wittingly aid and abet in the fabrications of impostures.

Although the Public Record Office had yet to be established, there was increasing interest in what records were available and how they could be used. In 1828, Stacey Grimaldi, a peerage lawyer of forty years standing, drew on his experiences in publishing England's first genealogical textbook, entitled *Origines Genealogicae or, the Sources Whence English Genealogies May Be Traced*. He followed this up in 1835 with a series of lectures, which in turn were published as *Lectures on the Sources from which Pedigrees may be Traced*.

A more substantive work was *A Manual for the Genealogist, Topographer, Antiquary and Legal Professor*, by Richard Sims, a curator at the British Museum, first published in 1856. 'The study of Heraldry and Genealogy', wrote Sims in the preface, 'is beset with difficulties sufficiently great to deter all but the most enthusiastic, from the pursuit of an employment to all appearances so dry and unprofitable.'[8] 'Nevertheless', he continued, 'the number of students in this useful department of history is undoubtedly on the increase; hundreds of persons derive pleasure from this mode of passing their leisure hours.' Tellingly, he also noted that 'there are very many' who toiled to 'establish a claim to wealth or title, long since apparently within their grasp'. Sims went on to explain the purpose of his volume, which by the 3rd edition in 1888 ran to some 500 pages.

Starting with Domesday Book, Sims's *Manual* describes in exquisite detail the various sources available and their value to the genealogist. The list seems alien to a modern eye: parish registers receive just 14 pages and wills even fewer. Census returns – which were less than fifteen years old at the time of the 1st edition – are nowhere mentioned, nor are civil registration records. Instead, some 25 pages are devoted to court and state records, 50 pages to the various classes of medieval rolls, and 140 pages to heraldic collections including the heralds' visitations, and county and family histories.

* * * *

At a time when the educated classes banded together around all sorts of causes, it was perhaps natural that genealogists began to talk about a society of their own. Two such societies, the London Genealogical Society and the Heraldic and Genealogical Society of Great Britain and Ireland for the Elucidation of Family Antiquity, functioned briefly around 1850 but were short-lived. A correspondent to *Notes and Queries* in 1852 noted how he had been appointed a corresponding member of the London Genealogical Society, 'but on going to their rooms one morning, found the concern had "vanished into thin air"'.[9]

A more substantive body, the Genealogical and Historical Society of Great Britain, was formed in 1853 by a group of London gentlemen and scholars.[10] Its Committee of Research met every Monday at 18 Charles Street, off St James's Square, its duties being:

> to make researches relating to Genealogy and Family History from Public and Private Records and manuscripts; to collect evidences of family descent and antiquity; and to form manuscript compilations for the Society.

Genealogical and historical information relating to its fellows was purportedly collected and compiled into 'several elaborate pedigrees, commencing with the ninth and eleventh centuries, and brought down to the present time'. The Society appears to have petered out sometime during the early 1860s. According to Sims, 'No profit is made by the Society in any of its transactions, except by the sale of its publications to non-subscribers';[11] this, no doubt, was the reason for its early demise.

This frenzy of activity in the early 1850s was most likely prompted by developments in the United States, where the NEHGS had been founded in 1845 by a group of Boston merchants and book dealers. It was the first society anywhere in the English-speaking world to focus primarily on genealogy rather than other aspects of historical studies. In January 1847 the Society began publication of the *New England Historical and Genealogical Register*, a quarterly journal that continues to the present day, making it the world's longest running genealogical publication.

Despite the lack of support for an association, genealogy was increasingly an activity that people were prepared to engage in themselves, as opposed to commissioning research from the College or from professional genealogists. As one correspondent to *Notes and Queries* noted in 1858: 'inquirers now no longer are satisfied with pedigrees of exorbitant price compiled from evidence in the College of Arms, and without references to accessible proofs, but wish to satisfy themselves, and to obtain incontestable and ostensible proofs'.[12] This immediately presented problems, however, in terms of the time and cost involved. Not only would researchers have to travel great distances, but they would also have to pay to see original documents, such as wills and parish registers. This was expensive 'when performed even by the most liberal of the clergy or registrars'.

The correspondent, who identified himself only as 'Caedo Illud' (pseudonyms were common in these nineteenth-century publications), proposed that the journal set aside a special section devoted to such queries. Readers would be able to send in their inquiries for proposals for 'gentlemen to search for one another, on mutual terms'. Thus, a person living in one parish would be able to swap information with someone living in another where he had an interest. Or someone living near a cathedral library would be able to request information from a person occupied in researches at the British Museum, Tower Record Office or other repository.

Many people wrote in support of the scheme, but its cooperative spirit failed to strike a chord with the more hardened Victorian gentlemen. Meetings and discussions were one thing, actually volunteering to work for someone else was quite another. It would, replied a correspondent identified as 'Caedo Hoc.', 'be found very difficult to put into practice':[13]

> It would assume that in all localities wherever records are to be found, reside a number of disinterested and unemployed individuals who are willing to render gratuitous services as copyists in a labour of love at the beck and call of any one possessing the *cacoethes scribendi*,[14] and as we must assume, to a certain extent, the *amor nummi*, or else a considerable lack of the same precious commodity. Barters may do very well in an infant state of society, but it has always receded with civilization; and it is anything but complimentary to the present era to resume that this species of literary traffic would be either appreciated or sustained by the public generally.

There was also the problem of equivalency – one party might require a simple search while the other might ask for a transcript that would take days to make. Other correspondents pointed out the need for care in consulting and copying old documents: 'I have had occasion to correspond with clergymen in England and have seldom found one able to decypher [sic] the registers under their custody before the middle of the seventeenth century.'

While this proposal for an organized exchange of information never saw the light of day, there was no shortage of journals for British genealogists to consult. From the early 1830s a plethora of periodicals began to appear devoted wholly to genealogical, heraldic and topographical materials. John Gough Nichols was behind several of these. As well as being editor of the *Gentleman's Magazine*, he was both editor and publisher of *Collectanea Topographica et Genealogica*, produced in eight volumes between 1834 and 1843. This was followed by three volumes of *The Topographer and Genealogist* (1863–74), and eight volumes of *The Herald and Genealogist* (1863–74). The last of these was the most ambitious, being designed to succeed not only the other two but also the antiquarian side of the *Gentleman's Magazine*. Whereas its predecessors had been devoted mainly to printing existing materials such as documents, record extracts and old pedigrees, *The Herald and Genealogist* contained critical discussions, book reviews and essays written for it on heraldic and genealogical topics. With its high editorial standards, *The Herald* did much to put Victorian genealogy on a credible footing, countering the more flamboyant approach of publishers such as Burke.

Nichols was not the only publisher to try his hand with genealogical journals. This period is littered with antiquarian and genealogical periodicals, most of which turned out to be short-lived. Invariably they had Latin names to give intellectual weight.

Collectanea Genealogica et Heraldica was launched in 1881 by Joseph Foster, editor of Foster's *Peerage, Baronetage and Knightage*. It contained printed transcripts of legal and other registers and genealogical researches, and was a vehicle for much trenchant criticism of contemporary genealogy. Only three volumes ever appeared and it ceased publication in 1885.

Rather more long-lived was *Miscellanea, Genealogica et Heraldica*, launched in 1866 by Joseph Jackson Howard. It offered a 'true Miscellany', being devoted 'exclusively to transcripts from original and inedited documents relating principally to Genealogy and Heraldry'. Howard aimed to meet the demand for information among the new middle and upper-middle classes whose families, unlike the nobility and gentry, had only 'sprung into notice in the second half of the sixteenth and early years of the seventeenth centuries'. Each issue was a hotchpotch of information, containing everything from readers' pedigrees, to wills, grants of arms, funeral certificates and parish register extracts – and all totally unindexed. The chances of a subscriber finding anything of relevance to their researches in any given issue must have been very slim. It survived more or less unaltered until 1938, although only through the benevolence of its publisher.

The high critical standards championed by Nichols in *The Herald* were taken up by George William Marshall in *The Genealogist*, launched in 1877. As with *Miscellanea*, *The Genealogist* included original transcripts but also indexes to collections of primary sources such as wills, pedigrees and other periodicals. This made the density of genealogical information much greater, and hence increased the chances that a reader would find something of relevance in a particular issue. Unlike its rival, *The Genealogist* was something to be read rather than browsed. It became the mouthpiece for the critical school of genealogy that had been founded by Nichols some fifty years before, debunking myths and arguing at every opportunity for genealogists to aspire to high standards of scholarship.

A barrister who later entered the College of Arms, Marshall was an active supporter of genealogical projects. He edited the first seven volumes (1877–83) of *The Genealogist* himself before turning his attention to his most important work, *The Genealogist's Guide*. This was basically a huge bibliography providing references to printed pedigrees in existing published sources. These included journals, peerage books, heraldic visitations, county histories, record society publications, as well as privately printed family histories and even private Acts of Parliament. Marshall's qualification for inclusion – one which was taken by authors of many similar works that followed – was that the pedigree had to show descent of three generations in the male line.

First published in 1879, *The Guide* as it soon became known, was immensely useful at a time when few other indexes of genealogical material were available. Further editions followed in 1893 and, shortly before Marshall's death, in 1903. It remained an essential reference work until well into the twentieth century and still has some currency.

* * * *

Victorian genealogists were obsessed with the heraldic visitations, which fed into a wider interest during the period to rediscover Britain's medieval past. In 1869 the Harleian Society was formed for 'the publication of the Heraldic Visitations of Counties, and any manuscripts relating to genealogy, family history, and heraldry'.[15] It was named after Robert Harley, Earl of Oxford, who built up a substantial collection of visitation manuscripts. His original collection had been carried on by his son Edward, who bequeathed it to the nation in 1753.

Prime movers in this new enterprise were Joseph Howard, George Marshall and Joseph Chester. The inaugural meeting was held on 28 May 1869 at 8 Danes' Inn, London, in the Council Room of the Surrey Archaeological Society. The Duke of Manchester agreed to be president and Sir George Armytage, one of a long line of Yorkshire antiquarians, was elected secretary.

As usual for this period, the Society operated on a subscription model. Individuals or organizations would pay an annual fee for which they would receive all of the Society's publications – however many, or few, that might be. Such was the interest, however, that the Society found immediate and substantial support. By the end of the first year there were 169 subscribers, and by 1871 numbers had risen to 264, including the first overseas member, the Minnesota Historical Society.

The Society's first volume was the Visitation of London, carried out by Robert Cooke, Clarenceux King of Arms, in 1568. Five hundred copies were printed at a cost of £87. Thereafter publication proceeded at the rate of roughly one volume per year. Not all of these were county visitation books, other issues being Peter Le Neve's *Pedigrees of the Knights*, and several volumes of marriage licences. In 1877 a separate section was established for the publication of parish registers, following the publication in 1875 of Chester's *Registers of Westminster Abbey*. These visitation and registers sections remained separate for many years and were only amalgamated, as Harleian Society Publications, New Series, in 1979.

The Harleian was the most successful of many publishing societies formed during this period. The Camden Society, named after William Camden, was founded in London in 1838 to publish early historical and literary materials, both unpublished manuscripts and new editions of rare printed books. In the words of its constitution, it aimed 'to perpetuate and render accessible whatever is valuable but at present little known amongst the materials for the Civil, Ecclesiastical or Literary History of the United Kingdom'. Again, it was supported by subscriptions, initially £1 per annum. From an original 500, membership peaked at 1,250 in 1845. By the 1880s the Society was experiencing serious financial problems, brought about in part by a project to create a general index to its first 100 volumes. In 1896, it merged with the Royal Historical Society.

The Surtees Society, covering the northeastern counties, was founded in 1834 in honour of Richard Surtees, a historian and antiquary from County Durham. It has published continually ever since and to date has produced some 200 volumes relating, as its rules say, to 'the Ancient Kingdom of Northumberland'. Many county and local antiquarian societies published journals featuring genealogical articles to a smaller or larger degree, according to the fluctuations of fashion and individual interest. Some of these in turn set up subsidiary series for publishing record material.

Other societies, both national and local, grew up for the publication of particular classes of record. In 1883 the Pipe Roll Society was founded, at the instigation of the Public Record Office, for publishing the medieval Pipe Rolls. Publication of medieval ecclesiastical records was the speciality of the Canterbury and York Society, founded in 1904. Another class of societies was concerned with special sections of the population, such as the Huguenot Society founded in 1885, the Jewish Historical Society of England founded in 1893 and the Catholic Record Society founded in 1904.

Of all the societies set up during this period the Index Library and its successor the British Record Society proved the most influential. The driving force was William Phillimore, a 34-year-old solicitor from Nottingham. Phillimore had immersed himself in local history and genealogy from an early age and spent his undergraduate vacations working on his family history. While at Oxford he published his first book on church bells in his native Nottinghamshire. After graduating he practised as a solicitor in London but as he became more financially secure devoted increasing amounts of time to his genealogical interests. In 1887 he published *How to Write the History of a Family*, a ground-breaking work that for a generation was seen as the standard genealogical textbook.

All the major historical publishing enterprises of the day – such as the Camden Society, the Harleian Society and the Pipe Roll Society – were concerned with producing a limited number of select documents in full. Phillimore felt that a different approach was needed: not more printed records, but *printed indexes* to the records already existing at the Public Record Office and elsewhere. No indexes to the British public records were then being produced and the previous efforts under the Record Commissioners had stopped some fifty years before.[16]

He enlisted the help of Walford Selby, a long-serving official at the Public Record Office and one of the founders of the Pipe Roll Society. Selby had worked at the PRO for over twenty years and was by then superintendent of the search room, with an intimate knowledge of the collections. Together they came up with a new scheme for the publication of a 'series of indexes to the principal English Records'. After enlisting the financial backing of Charles Clark, a legal publisher, they launched their scheme in 1888 under the grand title of The Index Library.

With Phillimore installed as editor, the pair began to publish indexes of everything they could lay their hands on. They chose as wide a range as possible so as to appeal to the maximum number of people. Their first issue, dated January 1888, comprised a calendar of Chancery Proceedings from the reign of Charles I, an index of papers from the Commonwealth period, and an index to late sixteenth- and early seventeenth-century records from the Signet Office. These were all transcriptions of manuscript indexes already in the PRO and easily accessible to Selby. Their efforts were offered to the public at 2 shillings each or a guinea a year for twelve instalments.

Initially the aim was to publish existing indexes only available in manuscript form, rather than compile new indexes of their own. They soon ran into problems, however, since the quality of the indexes was not what they had been expecting. Writing to one of their sources, Phillimore noted:[17]

> These indexes, unfortunately, have been done very badly, and the only thing which can be said in their favour is, that a bad index is, perhaps, better than none at all. They were evidently compiled by persons unable to read the handwriting of the Stuart period, and unacquainted with even the elements of indexing.

Some of the old indexes, for example, were only divided up by the first letter of the names and arranged within each letter chronologically, rather than strictly alphabetically. Soon they found themselves checking and compiling indexes rather than simply copying them, making the whole enterprise much slower and more costly than anticipated. Financial problems set in and were exacerbated by Selby's unexpected death from typhoid in 1889 at the age of 45.

Phillimore endeavoured to carry on alone for a while, but Charles Clark stepped in and suggested the Index Library's subscribers should be invited to form a society to continue the work. This they did and the British Record Society (BRS) came into being on 28 November 1889. With the scheme now on a firmer footing, many new subscribers signed up. Phillimore became the first Secretary and remained the General Editor of its publications for four years.

In 1890 the BRS merged with an older body, the Index Society, which had run into financial trouble. It had been founded in 1877 by Henry Wheatley, a bibliographer and topographer, to produce indexes of scientific, artistic and literary works. Wheatley had been the first secretary of the Early English Text Society and has been described as the 'father of modern indexing'.

The BRS set to work to fulfil its mandate, its first publications being six volumes of indexes to Chancery Proceedings and twelve volumes of indexes to Inquisitions Post Mortem. But Phillimore and the Society were being overtaken by events. At the PRO the new Deputy Keeper, Henry Maxwell-Lyte, was determined to breathe new life into what was by then a moribund institution. He embarked on major building works and at the same time launched various ambitious publishing schemes. These included a series of lists and indexes, produced progressively from 1892. Starting with the major series of medieval records – Patent Rolls, Close Rolls, Fine Rolls, Inquisitions Post Mortem, Curia Regis Rolls – Maxwell-Lyte set in train a whole series of calendars and indexes opening up a readily accessible core of dated information about people and events. Official lists and indexes to other classes of record followed.

This massive public effort made the original intention of the BRS redundant almost as soon as it had started. Nevertheless, Phillimore and Selby deserve much of the credit. Their initiative had helped stimulate official action that, with public resources at its disposal, could be infinitely more effective than anything done in the private sphere. As the scale of the official indexing was extended, so the need for the Society's original activities diminished.

In any case, Phillimore's attentions were already elsewhere. The preservation of provincial records had been a long-standing interest for him. As early as October 1889, when county councils were formed, he had written to *The Times* suggesting that this was an ideal opportunity to act to preserve local records. 'In every county town there should be provided a suitable building under the direction of the county council to be styled "The County Record Office" and under the responsibility of a county archivist', he wrote.[18] He even prepared bills to promote their foundation. This was a radical suggestion at the time, since the only 'local' record office then in existence was that for London at Guildhall. It would be another quarter of a century before Phillimore's idea began to materialize.

He took the opportunity of the BRS's incorporation in 1892 to enlarge the declared aims. No longer would it be concerned merely with indexing but would also be permitted 'to take any measures necessary or desirable for the protection or preservation and custody of any records or documents in the nature of records'.

In the succeeding years Phillimore became involved with a wide range of local or specialist societies, initiating several of them. At his instigation, a Scottish section of the BRS was set up in 1896 to publish indexes to Scottish wills and records and this became totally independent, as the Scottish Record Society, two years later. In 1897 he founded the Thoroton Society (named after Robert Thoroton) to print historical records from his native Nottinghamshire, followed in 1904 by the Canterbury and York Society for printing episcopal registers of the dioceses of England and Wales. He was also active in the foundation of parish register societies in Shropshire and Staffordshire and made failed attempts to start others in Gloucestershire, Bristol and Derbyshire. From 1897 he had his own publishing business, Phillimore & Co., to publish the parish registers of various counties as well as the constant stream of books and pamphlets that emanated from Phillimore's own pen.

Phillimore's involvement with parish registers had begun a few years earlier, as a committee member of the Parish Register Society. His view that marriage registers should be printed first of all, and that indexing could be delayed until a later date, was not shared by colleagues. He decided to continue on his own and from 1894 began to publish a whole series of registers – most of them marriage registers – which later came to bear his name. Over the next twenty years, until his death in 1913, he and his co-compilers (local enthusiasts were recruited to copy their local registers) produced a total of 237 volumes of printed registers, covering 1,200 parishes in thirty counties.

Concern over the preservation of parish registers had been building throughout the nineteenth century.[19] As early as 1764, Ralph Bigland, Somerset Herald, had pondered the most effective way of preserving registers for posterity. In a letter to the *Gentleman's Magazine* in 1819, Dr Thelwall of Newcastle reported that a friend of his had a great number of bishops' transcripts in his possession. When asked where they came from, he said that they had been given to him by his cheesemonger, and that the transcripts 'Had been allowed, through the negligence of their keeper, to obtain the distinguished honour of wrapping up cheese and bacon.'[20]

A Parliamentary Select Committee looked into the issue in 1833. Sir Thomas Phillipps, a wealthy and eccentric antiquary and publisher, told the committee that all parish registers up to the year 1700 should be transferred to the British Museum and that a modern transcript of each should be made at the expense of the parish. Phillipps had been printing copies of parish registers – the first in England to do so – through his Middle Hill Press since the 1820s.

In a paper read before the Statistical Society in 1850, the Revd E Wyatt Edgell suggested that all parish registers should be transcribed. Extensive correspondence on the subject took place in the pages of *Notes and Queries* from the 1850s onwards. One correspondent, Edward Peacock, thought that 'The best course to pursue would be to have them all printed, but the expense would be so very great that I despair of ever seeing the project put into execution.'[21] By 1857 a bill was prepared requiring details of all baptisms, marriages and burials from 1750 to 1837 to be copied on forms supplied by the Registrar-General and lodged with the General Register Office. Transcription would be entrusted to the clergy, who would be paid out of the poor rates for their efforts. In the end the proposed bill was dropped and, to the detriment of modern-day genealogists, the grand scheme never happened.

It was clear something needed to be done and in 1889 the Congress of Archaeological Societies and the Society of Antiquaries appointed a committee to look into the whole issue of transcription and publication of parish registers. The committee's report, published in 1892, began by noting that parish registers 'contain matter of the greatest value not only to the genealogist, but also to the student of local history, and through these to the general historian'. 'It is to be regretted', the committee continued, 'that sufficient care has not been taken in the past of these documents, which have too often been thoughtlessly destroyed.' Transcription was necessary, the committee said, not only to guard against loss but also to make them more accessible, since many were 'not easily deciphered, and require careful examination, even from experts'.[22]

The committee went on to list the relatively few register transcripts known to exist at that time, which it divided into five categories: registers published as separate works; registers printed in other books and periodicals; original registers and bishops' transcripts in the British Museum Library; registers of other churches in all classes; and parish registers transcribed in manuscript.

Where Phillimore led others followed and by the time of the Congress of Archaeological Society's second report, four years later, its updated list was very much longer. Not only had Phillimore begun his marriage registers with a complete set for Gloucestershire, but the Parish Register Society was also producing a series of its own. The committee felt encouraged, if not over-optimistic:[23]

> The supposed impossibility of ever transcribing the whole of the parish registers of the United Kingdom is imaginary. . . By enlisting and encouraging local effort, the very desirable object may be obtained at no great distance of time.

The committee's point about an expert eye being required was well made. Although some of the early transcripts were of unimpeachable accuracy, others were not so. A review of the *Records of Preston Parish Church* published in *The Reliquary* in 1892 described the quality as 'lamentable'.[24] Several entries had been omitted, apparently because they were too difficult to decipher. This rendered the transcript, in the reviewer's opinion, 'worse than worthless'. Not only was this 'a great pity and misfortune' for the transcriber concerned, but it was 'also likely to throw discredit on other printed copies of registers elsewhere'.

The Reliquary was one of many periodicals to regularly print register extracts and copies. John Bowyer Nichols's *Collectanea Topographica et Genealogica* was the first to plough this furrow, in 1835 printing a seven-page extract from the parish registers of St Olave, Hart Street, London. The theme was continued in later publications such as *The Genealogist* and *Miscellanea Genealogica et Heraldica*, as well as county, local history and archaeological journals. Since only the upper classes would subscribe to periodicals such as these, the extracts were often highly selective, featuring only the grand and glorious and their servants.

When the Harleian Society printed its first volume of register transcripts in 1878, its editor W. Granville Leveson-Gower confronted this need for selectivity head on. 'Our object', he wrote in the preface, 'is to obtain as large a mass of genealogical information as possible in the shortest possible time.'[25] Publishing every register in its entirety would be 'a very great mistake', Leveson-Gower argued, since:

> We shall encumber our Volumes with a large mass of useless and uninteresting matter, and spend money, both in printing and copying, which might be much better employed. To say nothing of the entries of 'vagrants', 'rogues', persons in '*ignoti cognominis*', and such like, which will fill our pages. I maintain that as a Genealogical Society we are not concerned to find ancestors for families which have risen to the ranks of gentry in later times; our business is *only with the record of those who at the time the entry was made were persons of recognised social position.* I am aware that to prepare complete and trustworthy abstracts of Parish Registers will require Editors of considerable experience and of local knowledge, and that even then some important entry may occasionally be omitted; but surely this will be a lesser evil than the publication of so many names which have no interest or value whatever. [Emphasis added.]

'No interest or value': in other words, only the pedigrees of society's elite were *worth* documenting and the upper classes should not sully themselves by mixing the names of their ancestors with those who were of lower birth. If even the class that had 'risen to the ranks of the gentry in later times' were not entitled to know who their ancestors were, what hope was there for the rest of the masses?

Such pomposity would prove hard to dislodge, but not everyone shared these views. Writing in the same year as Leveson-Gower, the Worcestershire genealogist and historian John Amphlett observed that all 'good families can tell who their forefathers were, where they lived and whom they married'.[26] 'Good' did not necessarily mean high-born and 'depends much more on the number of its known generations than any other condition'. Amphlett detected a widespread curiosity about ancestry even if people did not have the wherewithal to probe the matter:

> of the mass of the people below the class immortalized in such books as Burke's *'Landed Gentry'*, but few know whence they come, or anything at all about their antecedents. And yet among all ranks of people, from the highest to the lowest, there is some curiosity upon the subject,

which, though usually languid, is always ready, should circumstances so direct, to burst into a flame.

'No one', he concluded, 'is too humble in station to make care about such things necessary.'

Another benefactor of the parish register movement was Frederick Arthur Crisp, a wealthy businessman and passionate genealogist, who supported a vast number of works from his private press in Denmark Hill, south London. Between the 1890s and his death in 1922 he published twelve volumes of Essex parish registers, ten for Suffolk, together with a miscellaneous range of transcripts from parishes across the country. With a businessman's eye, he cleverly publicized these through a frequently updated *List of Parish Registers and Other Works*. Here he listed the principal surnames in each printed register – up to a thousand at a time – so as to whet people's appetite. The register volumes themselves would be produced in print-runs of between ten and one hundred copies and cost between 5 shillings and 4 guineas. With appropriate courtesy and gratitude, each entry was accompanied by a paragraph of thanks to the incumbent concerned for permission to use the original material.

Crisp's output was prodigious and of a very high quality. Each publication was printed on handmade paper and in a limited edition, often with a full or half vellum binding. As well as parish registers, he published twenty-one volumes of heralds' visitations (produced with Joseph Howard), a visitation of Ireland, and important collections of marriage licenses and apprentice indentures. Starting in 1897 he also produced his own journal of genealogical miscellany, *Fragmenta Genealogica*, published irregularly until 1909. Many of the items to attract his attention were from obscure sources that would never make commercial sense, but out of altruism he published them nonetheless. His obituary noted that his 'time, patience, taste, and money . . . enabled him to produce so valuable a collection of works'.[27]

*   *   *   *

In the 1880s, the Literary Search Room of the Public Record Office, over which Walford Selby presided, was a bustling place. Over the previous half century, since the PRO's formation in 1838, the records of the nation had gradually been brought together from repositories all over London into one central complex around Chancery Lane. With them came an eccentric group of older officials, some as fusty as the records under their care. Selby was one of the younger and more approachable members of staff, together with Hubert Hall, who was becoming a recognized authority on medieval Exchequer records.

The searchers in the Literary Search Room were largely genealogists: James Greenstreet (founder with Selby of the Pipe Rolls Society) was a frequent visitor, as were scholars such as John A C Vincent and William Stubbs (regius professor of modern history at Oxford), and antiquaries such as Walter Rye. The growth of the Empire and booming trade generally brought the PRO much work, in everything from disputes over mineral and other rights to peerage claims. The Legal Search Room was frequented by record agents who prepared the ancient evidence for legal cases, in place of the officials who at one time were allowed to undertake this work. As well as those on official business, the prospect of finding legal nuggets buried in the ancient documents attracted a fair share of crackpots and mavericks. One searcher, calling himself 'Plantagenet' Harrison, was a general in the Peruvian army, a giant of a man who wore a cowboy hat and claimed to be the Duke of Lancaster.[28] There were also two strange Welsh gentlemen who periodically retired to worship on the Welsh mountains and returned in foul-smelling sheepskins.

Into this intellectual party in the early 1880s entered John Horace Round, a historical writer and researcher who would pioneer a new school of historical genealogy. Round was fresh out of Oxford, where he had received a first in modern history at Balliol (a new subject on the curriculum at the time) and was intent on carving out a career as a professional historian. To help subsidize his writing career, he took commissions as a searcher, helping out in commercial and peerage cases, and became a frequent visitor to the PRO.

Round began contributing papers on genealogical and historical subjects to the main periodicals of the time such as *The Genealogist* (then edited by Selby), *The Antiquary* and the *Antiquarian Magazine*. In 1883, when Selby formed the Pipe Rolls Society, Round joined him as auditor and he also edited some of its volumes. He helped Phillimore on the Index Library, which developed into the British Record Society, and was involved with him in the Canterbury and York Society. Outside of the genealogical sphere, Round was also involved with the Selden Society for printing documents illustrative of the history of English law. He was a frequent contributor to two new publications of the period: the *English Historical Review* and the *Dictionary of National Biography*.

Round's early life had been plagued by tragedy and ill-health. He was born in Brighton in 1854 into a wealthy political family; his great-grandfather had been recorder of Colchester and his grandfather had been an MP. His mother, Laura, died when he was 10, leaving the young John Horace and his sister, Violet Grace, to be brought up by their father (also called John). John Round senior fell into a deep depression after his wife's death and had little time for the children. John Horace too was a sickly child and had to be educated at home. At the insistence of his uncle, who saw how the boy was becoming isolated, Round was sent to preparatory school in Brighton where he gained new confidence.

William Stubbs, Round's mentor, was a great advocate for genealogy, which was snubbed by most academics at the time. There was, thought Stubbs, 'nothing in this that need be stigmatised as vain and foolish'.[29] On the contrary, tracing family histories was 'a very natural instinct, and it appears to me to be one of the ways in which a general interest in national history may be expected to grow'. The tutor left a lasting impression on his pupil.

After leaving Oxford, Round channelled his energies into his historical passion: the medieval period and in particular a study of the records of English medieval government. He became a recognized authority on Domesday and helped organize the commemoration of its 800th anniversary in 1886. His two most important historical works were: *Geoffrey de Mandeville*, an examination of a major figure during the reign of Stephen (published in 1892); and *Feudal England*, a collection of essays tracing the history of English feudalism from the Norman Conquest (published in 1895). This interest in the feudal period brought him into conflict with Professor Edward Freeman, another of his tutors, with whom he disagreed vehemently.

For Round, in studying the Anglo-Norman period, genealogy and history went hand in hand. As his protégé and friend Sir Frank Stenton wrote:[30]

> He founded the modern study of Domesday book. His insistence on the importance of family history gave a new value to genealogical studies. . . . He was the first modern historian to base a narrative on charters, and all subsequent use of these materials has been influenced directly or indirectly by his work. . . . His work gave a new direction and precision to the studies which he had followed, and its permanent value is becoming clearer as the controversies in which he engaged are fading out of memory.

The 'controversies' to which Stenton refers were many and legendary. The spat with Freeman was long running and was continued by Freeman's supporters even after his death. It was just the first of many celebrated disputes, some justified, others not, that Round engaged in throughout his life. He fell out with Hubert Hall, an Assistant Keeper at the PRO, over an obscure medieval document known as the 'Red Book of the Exchequer', which they worked on as joint editors. Late in life he quarrelled with his long-standing friend Walter Rye over points that most observers took to be minor and petty. Rye fought back, complaining of Round's 'violent and offensive language' and producing a list of fifty-seven persons whom Round had abused in print. Writing to one of his 'victims', whom he had attacked as a poor scholar and a plagiarist, Round offered this grudging truce:[31]

> Do not let us quarrel. For myself, I stand on sure ground, and experience has taught to me that I have no cause to fear a fight. But my wish is to live in peace. At the same time it is no good for anyone to look down on me. I know a great deal more than anyone imagines.

Stention thought 'the violence with which he attached other scholars of whose work he disapproved' to be Round's 'least attractive quality', and attributed it to his poor health.[32]

Round's most vitriolic attacks were directed at that bugbear of critical genealogists – Burke's *Peerage*. After Sir Bernard Burke's death in 1892 the editorship of his illustrious publication passed to his son, Henry Farnham Burke. The *Peerage* itself was largely unreformed and still contained many inaccuracies. Like his father, Henry (later Sir Henry), occupied a key position at the College, so bringing quasi-official authority to Burke's volumes; he eventually became Garter King of Arms in 1919.

Starting in 1893 and over a period of many years, Round unleashed a series of ferocious attacks against Burke's, drawing attention to its 'errors, mis-statements and absurdities'. He returned to the theme time and again in his writings, especially towards the latter part of his life when he focused more on genealogy than history. Burke's was riddled with spurious pedigrees, Round argued, most of which dated from the late medieval or Tudor periods. These genealogical concoctions were of four types:[33]

> Those that rested on garbled versions of perfectly genuine documents, . . . those which rested on alleged transcripts of wholly imaginary documents, those which rested on actual forgeries expressly concocted for the purpose, and lastly those which rested on nothing but sheer fantastic fiction.

Round set out his criticisms of Burke's and others, and his own arguments to place the critical study of genealogy on a sound and historical basis in a seminal paper, 'Historical Genealogy', delivered to the International Congress of Historical Studies held in London in April 1913.[34] Genealogy, Round argued, must be seen as a branch of historical study in its own right and must be based on the same principles of rigorous research as other historical disciplines. No one could call themselves a genealogist, he maintained, 'who cares for nothing but the pedigree of his own family'. In particular, he thought that genealogy was of great value for topographical and local history:

> The topographer should always have a pedigree by his side, and the genealogist a local map. When you have once grasped the method of combining the two studies, you will be surprised at the results. The history of a manor, though a blank for generations or even for centuries, can be traced, by the help of genealogy, with precision, through the history of another manor in what may be a distant county.

Thus, a sound grasp of the feudal system was a prerequisite for studying the medieval period. By studying the system of land tenure it was possible to trace the pedigrees not only of the lords who were tenants-in-chief, but also of their under-tenants much further down the social scale. Modern genealogy, Round asserted, began with the death of Richard III, when family history became disconnected from land tenure. Thereafter, 'genealogy now becomes a study based on other sources than the records of manorial descent'.

Next he turned to the Tudors, 'the great age of the pedigree-makers, of whose concoctions not a few have survived to the present day'. Elizabeth I herself had set the example, Round maintained, with 'a Tudor pedigree deduced from Adam'. He went on to denounce Lord Burghley, who he said was 'pedigree mad', her Lord Chancellor, Sir Christopher Hatton, as well as 'that notorious herald, "William Dethick, Garter"'. In what became his most quoted line, Round exclaimed: 'These frauds I have set myself to expose with infinite labour, nailing them up one by one, as a gamekeeper nails his vermin.'

Turning to the poor scholarship that persisted at Burke's, Round cited the case of[35]

> Mr Smith, a successful business man, of whom it was no secret that his father was of lowly origin. Suddenly, in Burke's *Landed Gentry* (1894) it was revealed to the world that he had a gorgeous pedigree, beginning at the Norman Conquest, and that he was heir-male of the body to Sir Mychell de Carington, Standard-bearer, on crusade, to King Richard the First. . . . The same work was able to announce, four years later (1898), that 'the descent is recorded in the Heralds' College in an unbroken line for over 700 years.' The great history of the family, published more recently, explained that the earlier ancestors of those *before* the standard-bearer had failed to satisfy the strict tests now required by the heralds. . . . But the standard-bearer, at least, was proved. Well, it is my painful duty to assure you that no such person is known.

Round was not prepared to accept tradition as the basis for a pedigree unless fully supported by hard evidence.[36]

> To some, 'tradition' is a sufficient warrant for a vague but lengthy descent, although there is, perhaps, no 'authority' so unworthy of credit. Indeed, the so-called 'tradition' is really, in most cases, the guess of some speculative antiquary or even of a member of the family itself, at no remote period.

In his criticisms of Burke's, Round was egged on – if he needed any encouragement – by another genealogist and publisher, George Edward Cokayne. Some thirty years older than Round, the two had meet through the circle of searchers at the PRO and became firm friends. Cokayne (or 'G.E.C.' as he was widely known) was a herald – appointed Norroy King of Arms in 1882 – and an active member of the Society of Antiquaries. He was a close friend and professional partner of Joseph Chester and on his death acquired much of Chester's extensive collection of manuscripts.[37]

Although known more for his industry than his scholarship, Cokayne recognized the weaknesses in existing peerage volumes and as early as 1870 began collecting material for his own original work. The fruit of his labours, entitled the *Complete Peerage*, was published in eight volumes from 1887 to 1898.[38] Cokayne's aim was to give a full historical and genealogical account of all peerages created in the whole of the British Isles from the Conquest to the time of publication. Earlier peerages had only covered those titles existing or extinct at the time of writing or had dealt only with one country, such as England or Ireland. Rather than attempt full, and often inaccurate, accounts of the whole family, Cokayne confined himself to the public life of the title holders and their direct heirs only, using original sources as far as he could.

The *Complete Peerage* was an immediate success and passed out of circulation almost as soon as it was published. Round thought highly of the new work – to which he had also contributed – and in 1901 paid tribute to it in his *Studies in Peerage and Family History*. 'If Sir Bernard Burke flattered the vanity of his patrons, the opposite tendency is visible in G.E.C.', Round wrote, '. . . for pretentious affections he is pitiless.'[39] Round's friend and collaborator Oswald Barron described Cokayne's work as being: 'A rill of concise statement flowing above a savoury sediment of notes.'[40] Fictitious ancestors, he added, were 'shadows who have no place in his scheme of peerage-making, save perhaps for passing reference in one of those notes whose piquancy goes far to explain the high price with which the *Complete Peerage* is honoured in booksellers' catalogues'. Round, though, disapproved of the vehemence with which his friend condemned those who falsified history, which he thought 'a subject for regret in a work of reference'.[41]

A 2nd edition of the *Complete Peerage* was begun in 1910, this time by Cokayne's nephew, Hon. Vicary Gibbs. A banker and also a keen genealogist, Gibbs had supplied information for the 1st edition. He invested in original and exhaustive research, particularly relating to the minor baronial families, improving the work's scale and accuracy but pushing up costs. By 1916 four volumes had been produced, at his own expense, but in 1919 with rising costs and increasing ill-health he was forced to hand over the enterprise to Herbert Arthur Doubleday, his assistant editor. Doubleday (another of those with whom Round fell out) continued the work, financed by various means, producing six further volumes before his death in 1941. The *Complete Peerage* remains in publication, in more modern formats, to the present day.

Doubleday, with Round, was also instrumental in launching the last great historical project of the nineteenth century: the *Victoria County History (VCH)*.[42] By the 1890s histories had been printed for most of the English counties. Following in the tradition of William Camden and William Lambarde, over the previous century and a half the scope of county histories had grown considerably, taking in not just historical figures and events but also geology, prehistoric and Roman antiquities, architecture and other matters. Genealogy remained an important element and featured prominently in works such as Robert Surtees's *History of Durham* (1816–40), George Baker's uncompleted *History of Northamptonshire* (1822–41) and Joseph Hunter's *Hallamshire* (1819) and *Deanery of Doncaster* (1828–31).

Many of these works showed high standards of scholarship, yet their scope and plan varied significantly and, especially for those that were the work of one hand, were biased in one way or another. Doubleday, the son of a wealthy businessman and himself a noted antiquary, came up with the idea of a general series of county histories produced cooperatively by many writers according to a uniform plan. His scheme was launched in 1899 and later, with royal approval, took the title *Victoria History of the Counties of England*. It was to be produced by his own publishing house, Archibald Constable & Co., which he had founded with his uncle in 1891.

Round was involved in the *VCH* from the outset and in the ten years from 1899 to 1908 it occupied the majority of his time. Although never a staff member, he served as consultant, author and editor, providing input out of all proportion to the modest fees he received. He helped to recruit authors and editors and in many respects the early *VCH* was fashioned in his image, especially in its coverage of Domesday. He had a hand in no fewer than forty-two of the seventy-four volumes produced up to 1914, relating to twenty-seven counties, and helped shape this mammoth historical project more than any other individual of the period.

In his later years Round turned his attentions increasingly to peerage matters. He advised on issues of procedure relating to the coronation of Edward VII, helped in the formulation of the first official list of baronets issued in 1913, and wrote a series of reports on individual claims to peerages. In 1914 he was appointed Honorary Historical Adviser to the Crown in peerage matters, a post he held until 1922, when he resigned because of ill-health. His scrutiny of claims to peerages in abeyance did much to bring them back under control, and thus helped to protect the reputation of the House of Lords during a period of considerable political and social change.

Round's last significant genealogical venture came in 1902, when he and Oswald Barron persuaded Doubleday to launch a new quarterly journal, *The Ancestor*, devoted to genealogy and heraldry. Published by Constables, this aimed to bring into genealogical periodicals the high standards of scholarship that Round had long espoused, and to prepare the way for the 'pedigree' volumes of the *VCH*. It has been called 'the most sumptuous and distinguished periodical ever devoted to its subject in England'.[43].

The Ancestor was virtually a two-man band. Barron, a journalist, was officially the editor but Round was constantly at his side and contributed over forty articles, notes, and reviews for the journal during its four-year run. They made for an odd couple; Round was tall and imposing, Barron short and erratic. The two were lifelong friends, but Barron, who came from a humble background, lacked Round's confidence and appetite for controversy. In 1903 a reader protested that *The Ancestor* was 'not a serious genealogical magazine but

. . . a vehicle for [Round's] personal animosities'.[44] In a later letter, the same correspondent noted that Round did not know when to stop and had 'gone on and on, till judge and jury have grown weary and restive'.

As Round frightened away other contributors, the journal became increasingly reliant on the two men and in issue 6 their articles comprised over 100 pages. By 1905 this, together with Doubleday's departure and the increasing demands of the *VCH* for both men, became too much and *The Ancestor* closed. They intended to resurrect it as an annual publication, but such a phoenix never rose from the ashes. Writing in the final issue, Barron attributed its demise to the fact that[45]

> There has not yet arisen in England a body of antiquaries large enough to sustain amongst them by their pens a quarterly magazine of family history which shall combine with original critical research, matter that has interest for the larger public.

In other words, the world was not ready for them. This was far from the case, however. On the contrary, there were many younger genealogists (as opposed to 'antiquaries') who were only too ready to engage in original critical research in a manner that was of interest to the public at large. Had Barron and Round been more outward-looking – and Round less pugnacious – they could have led the movement they had helped to inspire. As it was, it would fall to others to lead genealogy into the new century.

Horace Round never married and had few women friends. He was plagued by ill-health throughout his life and became increasingly invalid. Headaches, influenza, bronchitis and numerous other ailments all assailed him, and towards the end of his life he had a major intestinal operation. He died on 24 June 1928 at his house in Hove after contracting pneumonia, and was buried at the family estate at West Bergholt, Essex, four days later. Arthur Oswald Barron continued as a record searcher and writer. He was a leading authority on medieval heraldry and in 1937 entered the College of Arms as Maltravers Herald Extraordinary. In his later years he was to be found at the PRO, reading a medieval roll 'as the ordinary man reads his newspaper'[46] – a throwback to a bygone age.

*   *   *   *

Chapter 5

Gentlemen Genealogists

On a cold December night in 1895 a young genealogist called George Frederick Tudor Sherwood sat down at his desk at Lyster's Temperance Hotel, Northampton, and penned a letter to his wife. Then just 28 years old, Sherwood had already been a professional genealogist for six years. As a boy growing up in Berkshire he had been fascinated by genealogy and history and knew it was his calling. At the first opportunity, he set up his own practice as a genealogist and record agent and began to advertise his services. It was an itinerate life, involving frequent travel around the country to visit libraries, repositories (mainly probate courts) and churches, often taking him away for weeks at a time. In one six-month period during 1897, for instance, he visited Winchester, Wells, Andover, St Asaph, and Peterborough. In the letter to his wife, Sophia, he imparted something of the frustration and loneliness in being away from his home and young family:[1]

> After a stiff day's work at the Probate Registry – 10 to 5 – I have just finished tea – chop, mince pie and coffee – and a pipe. A cold sleety, windy night. . . . With another day's work I shall finish, but am afraid in regard to Hadden the search will not give us the information we want. . . . How is my little woman getting on? I hope tomorrow evening to get a train that will land me home not later than 10.

Sherwood was typical of the new breed of researchers that took to the stage during the Edwardian era. Inspired by Round's 'historical genealogy', they shared his rigour and commitment to high evidential standards. But these were businessmen, not academics. While Round's interest in pedigrees was as a scholarly pursuit, this new generation was concerned with building genealogy as a profession.

In contrast to their Victorian forebears, who tended to rely on subscription publishing for much of their income, the new professionals earned their living from private commissions. As previously, the clients were generally upper and upper-middle class families, who would engage a professional genealogist to research their pedigree as best they could using the very limited records of the time. Whereas before the genealogist might have embellished his findings to flatter the client, those of the late nineteenth and early twentieth century were more scrupulous. Snobbish attitudes persisted in some quarters, but the professional was no longer prepared to indulge the client and presented their results as they found them. Indeed, a rallying point for this new generation was the belief that genealogy could and should be applied just as much to the masses of middle and working class people as to the peerage and nobility.

Working with records on a continual basis, professionals developed expertise in specific fields or in the records of particular counties or regions, which they would share with others. A certain camaraderie developed and they would discuss the growth of their craft both in person and through correspondence in relevant journals. They began to converse about the poor working conditions in the PRO and other repositories; the urgent need for better calendars and indexes; and the opportunities to marshal new types of record for genealogical purposes, such as censuses, newspapers, monumental inscriptions, and ships' passenger lists.

American clients seeking to enquire into their British roots were a ready source of income for professionals. With the exchange rate then at five dollars to one pound, this was an expensive undertaking and sometimes they clubbed together in family associations to share the costs. This account by the Maltby Association from 1915 describes their experiences in employing the genealogist Gerald Fothergill in the search for Yorkshire ancestors:[2]

> Mr Fothergill visited York in July 1910, and read all the wills 'round Retford for about fifteen years – no matter what the testator's name, in the hope of getting a mention of Maltby, but obtained only one. This used one ten pound note. The second ten pounds he used in going around Retford. He personally saw the record of William Maltby's baptism – '16 March 1644–45'.

Noting that much more work remained to be done, the Association appealed for further contributions. '£10 ($50.00) is about the smallest sum one can send, and if some of the members who have not already contributed to this good work would care to assist in subscribing to this fund it would be greatly appreciated.'

Fothergill was another of the new generation, being two years younger than Sherwood. He had a particular interest in American emigration and was amongst the first to study early passenger lists. He discovered a wealth of material in Treasury Records at the Public Record Office and also at the British Museum, for which he negotiated publication. Comprising around 6,000 names, these were published between 1906 and 1912 by the NEHGS as *Passenger Lists to America*.

Fothergill was a man of great energy and enthusiasm, although this occasionally got him into trouble. In 1907 he used the columns of *Notes and*

Queries to explain that he was preparing a supplement to George Marshall's *Genealogist's Guide* and invited correspondents to send him the titles of any books containing genealogies that ought to be included.[3] He had no formal association with the *Guide* and was doing the work off his own back. Marshall's son Isaac, who by then owned the copyright, accused Fothergill of 'misleading the genealogical public'. He made clear there was no formal association and advised readers that an official update was already under way. Chastened, Fothergill wrote back that he[4]

> had no intention of infringing copyright. What I think of doing is to index pedigrees in books issued since the last edition of 'the Guide' and perhaps some not included in that book. I am sorry if my paragraph has misled any as to the ownership of yours in Marshall's *Genealogists' Guide*.

Sherwood shared this enthusiasm and recognized the importance of indexes in making the wealth of information available in public records more accessible to the genealogist. But he also felt that a proliferation of disparate indexes – each held in separate places and using different conventions and notations – had its limitations. In a letter to *Notes and Queries* in June 1901, he observed:[5]

> It is quite impossible for an individual, in making a genealogical search, to encompass a tithe of the existing indexes which are likely to assist him, contained as they are in hundreds, if not thousands, of scattered books of various classes, MSS. [manuscripts], and records, whose numbers are increasing every year.

What was needed, he said, was one great 'consolidated index' covering all genealogical material and this could be achieved through collective effort. He set out a proposal for such a scheme:

> Let a club be formed, and let each member devote himself to names beginning with one particular letter of the alphabet, proceeding to the formation of a 'consolidated index' of all names beginning with that letter. Thus one member takes A names, another B names, and another C names, and so on to Z. Each copies upon a system, from every index he can lay hands on – small indexes preferred – the names beginning with his especial letter. The system is perfectly simple, but not easily explained. I will send a specimen sheet, showing the method of arrangement, to any who propose to join. Members would be expected to work upon a uniform plan, and undertake to examine their respective indexes for names in which other members happened from time to time to be interested. If only fifteen join a start could be made, but there is plenty of scope for ten times that number.

Sherwood clearly felt the scheme was in keeping with the scientific thinking of the times, with the increasing emphasis on the classification and organization of knowledge. To emphasize the point he ended his letter by quoting at length from a recent review in the *Daily Chronicle* newspaper on the value of catalogues and indexes. The quote concluded:

We are waking up to the necessity of classification and organization in the world of books. . . . On all sides there are signs that the near future will be signalized by the systemizing of the knowledge we already have, rather than by great strides in the direction of further gains.

'These remarks', he noted, 'apply with peculiar force to genealogical research.'

Charles Allan Bernau, a businessman who worked at the Baltic Exchange in the City, had other ideas on how to make the genealogist's life easier. His scheme was for an *International Genealogical Directory* that would allow amateurs and professionals alike to make contact with each other and share their researches.

Bernau had developed an interest in genealogy as a boy whilst visiting relations in Jersey, where he was fascinated by tales of a pirate ancestor. Seeking to combine his private passion with a business venture, he began work on his Directory around 1906. Its purpose, Bernau explained, was 'to provide an up-to-date list of the names and addresses of those, of whatever nationality, who are interested in genealogy' and (this part was printed in bold type for emphasis) **'to introduce to each other those who are interested in the history of the same families,** so that they may enter into correspondence, without it being necessary for them to seek a further introduction'.[6]

This was not the first such directory, as Bernau himself acknowledged. Whereas existing works were house publications of particular societies, his project was much more ambitious in scope. Nevertheless, he used these earlier works as a source of contacts. H E Woods of the NEHGS sent him a copy of that Society's *A List of Genealogies in Preparation*. This he used to contact American genealogists, acknowledging that 'it is largely to Mr Woods that we are indebted for the fact that America is so well represented in this "Directory"'. He also consulted membership lists of about twenty other societies, such as the Huguenot Society of London.

Altogether, Bernau sent around 7,200 letters to people known to, or likely to, have an interest in genealogy in Europe, America and elsewhere. He received around 1,400 replies from genealogists both amateur and professional.

Learning as he went along, Bernau realized that the initial batch of forms, sent out in November and December 1906, had no directions on how they were to be completed. As a result he was inundated with contributions quite outside the original scope of his scheme and requests for explanation. On the 1907 forms he attempted to correct this by providing explanations on all the points correspondents had misunderstood. That they bewildered many soon became apparent, as correspondents completed the new forms 'according to their own fancy, ignoring all the instructions'.[7] One of the first to be returned had written on it: 'Why all these complicated directions?'

Bernau arranged the directory into six parts. Part I contained the names and addresses of the correspondents, each of whom was given a unique number. 'No name has been included without written permission having first been obtained', he noted. Part II listed surnames of almost 4,500 families being researched by these correspondents. Each entry contained the reference number or numbers of correspondents interested in that name, which could be cross-referenced against part I. A third section 'which was not included in the original scope of the work' was added listing specific queries and memoranda, again cross-referenced to part I. Three further sections contained reference information of a more general nature, such as addresses of relevant societies, offers of publications for sale or exchange, and lists of privately printed family histories and pedigrees. Advertisements from publishers and professional researchers and record agents were also carried.

The concept of cooperation was so new to genealogists that Bernau felt at pains to describe at length not only how to use the directory itself, but also the etiquette involved in contacting fellow researchers. Thus, he advised his contributors to 'always send a stamped, addressed envelope', to state their wants 'both precisely and concisely', and not to expect an immediate reply.

In the days when even a telephone directory was a novelty, the prospect of using such a listing to contact a complete stranger seemed to go against all social norms. One contributor asked: 'You surely do not intend your book to act as a social introduction, but only for purposes of correspondence.' To which Bernau replied: 'Of course. Even if you find that a genealogist living in the same street as yourself is interested in one of your families, this book gives you no permission to do anything but write to them.' Another correspondent was concerned that inclusion in the directory would 'lead to my being pestered with circulars which I do not want'. Yet another feared that having their name published could lead to 'the possibility of being let in for correspondence with people one may not care to know. I had a painful experience of the sort lately, when an individual whom I had helped to some useful knowledge soon began to pester me with requests for loans!' Again, Bernau prescribed the wastepaper basket but requested that correspondents let him know confidentially if the complaint related to a fellow contributor to the book.

Bernau urged professional genealogists to exercise caution in how they used the directory. Although shying away from using a 'distinctive mark' to identify professionals, he made it clear they were expected to 'abide by the etiquette of their profession', which meant being upfront about any fees incurred for advice or research arising from correspondence with contributors.

The publication was originally to be called the *International Genealogical and Heraldic Directory* but Bernau changed the title to the shorter form when an American publisher tried to imitate it. The *International Genealogical*

Directory (or *IGD*) was an immediate success and went through three editions, being curtailed only by the paper shortages brought about by the First World War. By the time the war ended Bernau had other preoccupations and did not return to the project. Nevertheless, the model he adopted, of separately listing correspondents and their research interests and cross-referencing between them, remains the basis for most genealogical directories through to the present day.

Sherwood had also taken up publishing and in 1907 launched *The Pedigree Register* as a platform for 'authenticated genealogies and family history'. He welcomed the efforts of his friend Bernau and gave the *IGD* a glowing review. After again emphasizing his view that 'simple organisation might easily facilitate research into pedigree and family history', he noted: 'no genealogical work of reference of greater value than this to the ordinary amateur has ever been issued'.[8] The directory, said Sherwood, 'gives the ordinary person, with no opportunity for research at first hand, and merely by putting pen to paper, the means of addressing his inquiries in the right direction'.

The success of the directory proved to Bernau the immense interest in genealogical matters and convinced him to explore other ventures. While many of the new amateur genealogists were of the middle or professional class, their families had not always been so. Many had come from modest and even poor backgrounds and through hard work or good fortune had prospered in Victorian Britain. The slide in the other direction could be just as great, with the debtors' prison and the workhouse a constant prospect. Could this poor class – these common men – also be traced through genealogy? If so, how far?

Bernau began to apply himself to such questions and penned an article as part of a series of reference guides called the *Genealogical Pocket Library*. In *The Genealogy of the Submerged* Bernau set out, in the most authoritative form to date, how one might go about tracing the ancestry of the common man.[9] 'As most families, if fully traced, will be found to include those who have sunk as well as those who have risen, genealogists must expect to find in the course of their researches many fresh skeletons for their family cupboards', he wrote in the introduction.

Using his own parish of Walton-on-Thames as an example, he went on to describe 'the splendid records which are in existence in some parishes concerning the condition and actions of those who in the past were guilty of "the crime of poverty"'. These included parish bonds, certificates of settlement issued by churchwardens and overseers of the poor, removal and affiliation orders, apprenticeship and related documents, and Poor Law and workhouse records. This amounted, Bernau concluded, to a wealth of information which hitherto had been overlooked. Indeed, in parishes where such records had survived: 'the task of tracing a family in the lowest stratum of society will be easier than compiling the pedigree of one in the upper middle class'.

This focus on the lower and middle classes was occupying Sherwood too. Writing in *Notes and Queries* in 1906, he expressed the wish 'to correspond with any-one interested in the genealogies of middle-class families, with a view to the systematic exchange of manuscript copies of unpublished pedigrees'.[10] He was only too well aware that genealogy had a poor reputation in some quarters and was sorely in need of an image makeover if it was to attract a new clientele.[11]

> If we can dispel the common idea, that genealogy is a study ministering to vainglory, pretence and social exclusiveness, a great step in advance will be gained. If genealogy teaches anything it teaches the absurdity of claims for consideration based on long descent: the proof that evidence exists today to show the descent and illustrate the career of almost every English-born person for the last four or five hundred years, and only awaits indexing, is one of the purposes we set before us.

Another means for researchers to share their knowledge and resources was suggested by the professional genealogist Edward Dwelly. In a letter to *Notes and Queries* he explained his proposal for a Genealogical Circulating Library.[12] Those with 'large collections of heraldic works' could lend them to others for a small fee, Dwelly suggested. Persons interested in a certain district or county could join together to advertise their services, he went on. 'A library comprising books for the whole of England and Wales would be within the means of very few, but numbers of amateurs could give mutual help by lending each other the works connected with a particular district.'

This scheme was hardly practical, however. Few private individuals would be prepared to risk lending expensive genealogical works from their collections. One correspondent – who identified himself only as Leo C. – proposed that the London Library, which already had a 'fine nucleus of genealogical and kindred works' presented a potential alternative.[13] 'If a hundred or more persons interested in genealogy would combine and make an arrangement to offer themselves as individual subscribers upon certain conditions, the prospect of such a number of new subscribers would cause the London Library to give special attention to genealogical works.' He suggested forming a committee to explore the idea and draw up specific proposals.

While this suggestion never came to fruition, the time was ripe for a more collective approach. For the first time since the 1850s, people began to talk seriously about the need for a society dedicated to genealogical inquiry. Bernau and Sherwood had long been considering such a move and entered into correspondence on the issue as early as 1906. They had perhaps been influenced by developments in the United States, where a National Genealogical Society had been formed in April 1903. In the words of its prospectus, it was 'Prompted by the belief that organisation by those having common aims and needs would be of mutual benefit and might secure access to or copies of official records where individual effort would not.' Its principal aims included publishing records to benefit researchers at a distance; ensuring access to records; creating a 'card index bureau' or 'clearinghouse' to facilitate the exchange of information; and establishing a genealogical library.

Writing to René Droz, Vice-Chancellor of the Convention Internationale d'Héraldique – the international body representing heraldry – in September 1908, Bernau stated he was a 'firm believer in united action in all matters connected with genealogy and heraldry'.[14] Droz wrote back saying he supported Bernau's opinions and proposed setting up an international society covering both subjects. Any British society would be a branch of this wider international organization.

Bernau responded:[15]

> After careful consideration my feeling on the matter is that the time is not yet quite right for the actual formation of such a society. Before I started circularising about the Directory in 1906 I had a long correspondence with my friend Mr. Sherwood, who is one of our leading and most enthusiastic genealogists. His views coincided with mine. That is to say, we both thought that the best policy would be to lead up to the subject by degrees and not to launch the scheme until the genealogical and heraldic public had become accustomed to the idea of international cooperation in their hobby and profession. I then decided to bring out three editions of the Directory. On the publication of the third edition (1911), I propose to broach the scheme of an International Society.

Professing that he had 'made a few notes', Bernau observed that subscriptions should either be 'nominal', a few shillings or so, or 'heavy' so as 'to permit of offices being taken, a library formed, a secretary engaged'. Status could be bought, rather than earned, with those paying a modest amount being admitted as members and those paying a higher subscription allowed to call themselves fellows. A library would be its main function, since 'few can afford all the new genealogical and heraldic works published in the publications of the various societies'.

In a further letter to Droz, dated 17 September 1908, Bernau wrote:[16]

> The County Secretary is an important factor. For instance, if among my County Secretaries, I appointed Mr. H Maxwell Wood (who is an Hon. Secretary for the Durham and Northumberland Parish Register Society) as Secretary for the counties of Durham and Northumberland, you will understand how local friendships and already established connections would lead to the (Society) obtaining many members in his district.

Thus, even while working on his Directory, Bernau was already looking to the longer term and saw it as just one part of a grander scheme. Furthermore,

Sherwood clearly shared these ambitions. The spark that would lead them to implement their plan came from an unexpected quarter.

In April 1910 a correspondent, W V Morten, wrote to *Notes and Queries* advising readers that a new society was being set up aimed at preserving 'old and current records of the Civil Service'.[17] He offered to provide information to anyone wishing to consult this collection and asked readers to inform him of any meritorious service by civil servants so that he could record the details.

In a reply to Morten, the Hertfordshire antiquarian William Blyth Gerish acknowledged that, while this was an excellent scheme, its scope should not be limited to the Civil Service.[18]

> There seems to be room in this kingdom for a society similar in several respects to the New England Historic Genealogical Society. For instance, the increasing quantity of genealogical memoranda, both privately printed and in manuscript, has no habitat; and if a society did no more, in return for a moderate subscription, than secure a permanent repository, it would not have been founded in vain. Many of us have collected material for a history of our family, which, when the last summons comes, will most probably be destroyed; but if there were a society in existence, a clause in the collector's will would ensure the MSS. being handed over to it. Perhaps Mr. C. A. Bernau, as a genealogical expert, would favour us with his opinion.

This was the trigger Bernau had been waiting for. In a two-page memorandum published in *Notes and Queries* on 21 May, Bernau unveiled his scheme to the world.[19]

With the title *A Genealogical Society for the United Kingdom*, the memorandum set out some of the options for such a body and how it might operate. It was essential, Bernau noted, that it be given 'careful consideration' by a committee rather than being the work of one man. The main expenses to be met would be the salary of a 'competent librarian' and one or two assistants; the rent of a room or suite of rooms in London; and the purchase of genealogical works of reference. These would be covered by revenues obtained from membership subscriptions, the sale of publications, bank interest, and fees for searches undertaken by the librarian.

Members would be able to bequeath or donate their manuscript collections to the society for safe preservation. All such manuscripts would be indexed (for surnames and place names) and their references entered onto a central card index. Finally, Bernau noted austerely that the funds of the society 'should not be wasted in dinners or excursions, nor should there be any obligation on the Society to issue an annual volume to its members'.

The next step would be to set up either a society or a company and invite 'the many thousands in the United Kingdom who are interested in genealogy' to join. Around fifty people would be needed to get it going, each paying a guinea towards the initial expenses. This, Bernau thought, would be enough to convince 'the genealogical public' that they were 'not being asked to join what is vulgarly called a "one-man show"'.

Bernau received many letters of support for his proposals, the most fulsome of which came from Sherwood.[20] Keen to stamp his own imprimatur on the new venture, Sherwood stated that in its work the society should give priority to collecting and indexing rather than printing. 'Its primary function should be the compiling of one great Index to genealogical, biographical, and local documents, on the Card Index system.' Recent work in compiling the *New English Dictionary on Historical Principles* provided useful experience here, Sherwood explained. Another priority for the society would be to maintain a register of experts in particular fields, as well as a list of record searchers across the country.

For Sherwood the new society provided an opportunity to break, once and for all, with the pretences of the past. The new class of amateur historians was interested not just in their lineage but in how and where their ancestors worked and lived.

> There are many people who are deeply interested in their surroundings (local history), for whom the word 'genealogy' has no attraction. We must impress upon this class that genealogy implies no more (and no less), than the discovery of what their own personal blood-relationships may be to scenes, places, and events, and the men and women who took part in them – that a pedigree is not, as commonly supposed, an affair of mere vaingloriousness and pretence.

The ideal for such a society, Sherwood concluded, was 'the ready production, to any inquirer, of a body of direct reference to documentary evidence concerning any place or family in the kingdom.'

Events unfolded quickly following the publication of Bernau's memorandum. In early June, Sherwood hosted a meeting of interested parties in his offices at 227 The Strand. This meeting turned out to be one of the most important in the history of British genealogy, yet surprisingly there is no written account. While both Bernau and Sherwood refer in correspondence and reports to five people attending, they are never named. One suggestion is that, in addition to Bernau and Sherwood, those in attendance were Sir William Bull MP, Edgar Briggs (a solicitor), and Gerald Fothergill.[21] Other sources favour Richard Holworthy (a genealogist), William Crow and William Blyth Gerish.[22] Whoever was there, the decision was taken to put Bernau's plan into action.

In August 1910 a prospectus was issued seeking fifty founders and fellows to provide a fund to incorporate the Society and requesting others to offer themselves for election as fellows, members and associates. Founders were asked to pay £2.2.0, members £1.1.0, and 'corresponding associates' 10s.6d (half-a-guinea). The Society was being founded, according to the proposal, 'In the belief that systematic working is better than the casual tunnelling and mining of amateur fossickers.'[23] It would, through collective effort, 'bring to the ordinary inquirer, with the least expenditure of time and energy, a body of evidence, and direct reference to documentary evidence, concerning any place or any family in the kingdom'. A notice was also published in the September issue of Sherwood's *Pedigree Register*. Of this prospectus, Bernau later conceded to Gerish 'there was not much in it – just an outline of the Society'.

Early subscribers included Sir Thomas Troubridge, Bt., Dr Vere L. Oliver and Mr Samuel Bircham, as well as the professional genealogists James Reginald Glencross and Frederick Snell. By early October thirty-six supporters had been signed up and the target of fifty Founder Fellows was reached by the end of November. Lady Elizabeth Cust,[24] Marquis de Liveri et de Valdausa and René Droz were invited to become Vice-Presidents, of whom only the Marquis accepted.

Writing to the Marquis on 26 November, Bernau stated:[25]

> The Fifty Founders were obtained almost immediately (and) . . . the Marquis of Tweeddale has accepted the post of President of the Society. We are now hard at work electing an Executive Committee of Eleven . . . and preparing the Memorandum and Articles of Association.

The following day Bernau wrote to George Latimer Apperson, editor of *The Antiquary*:[26] 'I do not know whether you would like to be the first to announce that this important new Society will be incorporated at the end of December, if not before.' And on 3 January 1911, Gerish wrote to Bernau:[27] 'I observe in *The Antiquary* this month that you have practically succeeded in floating the proposed Society of Genealogists. Please accept my congratulations.'

Bernau replied that 'a very full prospectus' would be issued as soon as possible after the incorporation, 'which still awaits the leisure of the Board of Trade'.[28] He expressed the hope that Gerish would become a member rather than the corresponding associate as 'only Members can become Local Secretaries and you are just the man to act as Local Secretary for Hertfordshire'. In this letter Bernau also reported that Sherwood had been appointed Honorary Secretary, suggesting that the key officers were already in place.

The Society was finally incorporated on 8 May 1911 as the Society of Genealogists of London. In a letter to Lady Cust, Bernau explained that the name 'is based on the Society of Antiquaries of London'; the 'of London' was dropped in 1914.[29] Seven people signed the Memorandum of Association, the legal instrument bringing the Society into existence. Naturally Bernau, Fothergill and Sherwood signed as sponsors of the plan. They were joined by Cyril Beachcroft and Edgar Briggs (both solicitors), Frank Evans (a barrister), and Frank Hitching (an 'author of genealogical works'). Sir Henry White, the King's solicitor, acted for the new entity.

In another letter to Apperson, on 20 May 1911, Bernau observed:[30]

> The Society of Genealogists has now been incorporated and Mr. George Sherwood, the Honorary Secretary, 227 Strand, is ready to receive contributions for the library at that address. The first meeting of its Executive Committee was held on Thursday evening and I waited until that was over and I knew all was in order before writing this to you. There is every sign that the Society is going to be a great success.

Of the initial fifty subscribers there were four peers of the realm, two military officers, two clergymen, fourteen solicitors or in other professions, and ten academics or prominent members of antiquarian or historical societies. Most of the remainder were gentlemen or justices of the peace. Seven of the founder fellows were professional genealogists: Bernau, Fothergill and Sherwood as well as Ronald Audley Dixon, James Reginald Glencross, Richard Holworthy and Frederick Snell.[31] Lady Cust was the only woman amongst the fifty Founder Fellows.

Two of the initial officers only served for very short periods. The first President, the Marquess of Tweeddale, the Most Honourable William Montagu, died in December 1911, and one of the Vice-Presidents, the Rt. Hon. John Allan, Baron Llangattock, died in September 1912. Tweeddale was succeeded in 1913 by the Rt. Hon. George Fitz-Roy Henry (Lord Raglan), while a series of new Vice-Presidents was appointed, including Sir Henry Maxwell-Lyte, doyen of the Public Record Office.

In addition to Bernau, Fothergill and Sherwood, the first executive committee included Glencross, Snell and Briggs, as well as William Bradbrook, a Member of the Royal College of Surgeons and frequent contributor to genealogical publications.

Writing again to Gerish, on 26 April 1912, Bernau noted: 'the Society of Genealogists (which started as a result of your letter to *Notes & Queries*) is making excellent progress and there can now not be the slightest doubt that it has come to stop'. Genealogy in Britain at last had a home.

* * * *

The new Society exuded the confidence of the Edwardian era. The Articles allowed for no fewer than fourteen committees, each comprised of a chairman, members and honorary secretary. Five of these were concerned with the library, of which the most important was the committee dealing with the Consolidated Index. According to the prospectus, this was to 'constitute the chief, key and ready means of access to the Society's collections'. The aim was to prepare one integrated index of surnames and places, covering both the Society's own holdings and those of official repositories across the country. All information was to be recorded on paper slips compiled according to a unified scheme. 'The Committee will receive such index-slips, query any when necessary, sort them alphabetically, and hand them to the Librarian to be sorted in with the great Consolidated Index.'

Other library committees dealt with printed volumes, manuscripts, documents (meaning deeds, letters and papers), and the 'Subject Index on Cards'. This latter was intended to provide a unified index to the mass of published genealogical material, such as Sims's *Manual for the Genealogist*, Walter Rye's *Records and Record Searching* and Bernau's *Genealogist's Pocket Library*, and periodicals such as *The Topographer* and *The Antiquary*. Other committees had remits in relation to 'cataloguing pedigrees' (updating the work in Marshall's *Guide*), recording monumental inscriptions, and acquiring and indexing parish registers.

No aspect was too obscure or too trivial to escape the Society's attentions. Thus, there were committees for school, college and apprenticeship records; for recording fly-leaf inscriptions in family Bibles; for heraldry; for collecting records of migration and change of residence; and for representing family associations. A fifteenth committee – on Irish records – was added within a few months of incorporation. Shortly after a Committee for Amateur Genealogists was also discussed. This was intended to 'advise beginners how to set to work', but never got off the ground.

A Committee on Local Records was envisaged as part of the original scheme. This was to be drawn from members across the country who were invited to submit their names as honorary local secretaries for their county, district or parish. 'It is hoped that this branch of our activities will be looked after, as it will undoubtedly be one of the most useful', the Prospectus explained. The words proved prophetic, for while local representation was essential for comprehensive coverage the system was never fully implemented. This lack of a local dimension was to haunt the Society for decades to come.

Books, documents and manuscripts began to flood into George Sherwood's office at 227 The Strand, to the point where the limited space was soon overwhelmed. Among these early works, Mrs V T C Smith compiled forty-three volumes on West Indies records and Frederick Snell bequeathed fifty-one volumes of Berkshire material.

It was clear new premises were required and in 1914 the Society made its first move, from The Strand to 5 Bloomsbury Square, a fine Georgian house near the British Museum. Its first-floor rooms were more spacious and provided a more comfortable environment for the increasing library and index-slip collections. According to Sherwood, they offered 'some of the advantages of a quiet club'.

Quarterly reports of the Society's activities were published, initially in the *Pedigree Register* and from September 1913 in *The Antiquary* so as to give them greater visibility.

The triumvirate of Bernau, Fothergill and Sherwood proved a powerful combination. Bernau was the strategist: he had thought long and hard about how to bring the Society into being and used all his connections from the *IGD* and other activities to bring this about. Sherwood was the consummate administrator, with a keen eye for detail and not afraid to roll his sleeves up to get things done. Fothergill was the publicist, putting the Society's case on the public stage and always relishing a fight with the archival establishment.

This alliance was not to last for long, however. Having established the Society, Bernau was never deeply involved in its activities. He only served on the executive committee for four years, from 1911 to 1915, took little interest in the work of the subcommittees and never delivered a lecture. Instead he embarked on another great project of his own.

By this time Bernau had given up his job at the Baltic Exchange to become a professional genealogist. While researching at the PRO he realized that the Chancery records were a much-neglected source. These records related to various court cases from the eighteenth and early nineteenth centuries, listing the names of both plaintiffs and defendants. The official calendars – where they existed – tended to list just one plaintiff and defendant in each case, when in fact a document might mention up to a dozen names. As such they provided an important source for genealogists covering the difficult period before civil registration and the census returns.

Bernau began transcribing original documents, working through the Chancery Proceedings for 1714–1800 and then other classes, some for earlier periods: Chancery Depositions, Exchequer Depositions and Town Depositions. His daughter Rosa and her friends were recruited to help out. Since no ink was allowed in the search rooms, documents were copied first into notebooks in pencil and then copied again in ink onto slips. Later the information was compiled directly onto slips in pencil, to save handling.

The slips were sorted into alphabetical order with each spelling separated by a dividing card typed by Bernau's wife, also called Rosa. Over a period of about fifteen years, from 1914 to 1929, around 4.5 million slips were compiled in this way, building into what eventually became known as the Bernau Index. In the later years other sources were added as well, including genealogical publications such as: *The Ancestor*, *The Genealogist*, and *Miscellanea Genealogica et Heraldica*; various tax and military records; poll books; naturalization certificates; and wills from certain registries.

The index was made available to enquirers through the Genealogical Co-operative Club, a scheme whereby researchers, whether professional or amateur, could subscribe to get the references to a surname in which they were interested. Subscribers could also pay for additional suits or bundles of records to be searched and indexed on their behalf.

Bernau gradually drifted away from the Society he had founded, devoting himself to his professional research before retiring to Cornwall. He offered his index to the Society 'for a very modest sum' and the purchase was completed a few weeks before his death in December 1961. Another of the Founders, Richard Holworthy also died in that year, his membership having long lapsed. Apart from serving on a number of subcommittees, he too played very little part in the Society's affairs after incorporation.

George Sherwood, on the other hand, relished the opportunities. With the Society up and running he could at last get to work on his 'Consolidated Index'. His original intention had been for a vast compendium of genealogical information, gathering together in one place all the available facts about everyone who had ever lived from the medieval period through to the nineteenth century. It would record baptisms, marriages, burials, wills, monumental inscriptions, lawsuits and all kinds of other miscellaneous details.

Fittingly enough, Sherwood provided the first entry in the form of a batch of 5,528 slips delivered in September 1911 covering manuscripts relating to his own family name. Thereafter, the index – which soon became known as the Great Card Index – grew rapidly. It was an ambitious and laborious undertaking, which relied heavily on volunteers. After the slips had been received and their source carefully logged, they had to be manually sorted into order, a slow and painstaking business. Many people contributed entries over the years, sometimes recording their names at the bottom of the slips, and to encourage others to help out 'sorting parties' were held.

To capitalize on these efforts, the Society launched a service to members whereby, for a small fee, all the slips relating to a particular surname could be typed. Two copies were made, one being sent to the member and the other retained by the Society and then bound. The typed slips were removed from the index and replaced by a note of the volume and page reference to the typed list.

With limited resources and ambitious plans, the Society relied heavily on volunteers in all its activities and the quarterly and annual reports continually carried requests for more people to get involved. Certain tasks could be done at home, such as enveloping and indexing deeds, slip-indexing printed volumes, manuscripts and heraldic works, and cataloguing pedigrees. Other tasks required attendance at the Society's rooms in London, primarily sorting slips into the Great Card Index. Certain activities could be done locally but away from home, such as transcribing documents at repositories, and recording monumental inscriptions in local churchyards.

At the suggestion of Dr Moor, a series of talks on genealogical topics was introduced. The first was given by Moor himself on 22 October 1915, when he presented a paper on 'Modern Uses of Armorial Bearings'. George Sherwood's review of the talk, published in *The Pedigree Register*, noted that:[32]

> Dr Moor's treatment of the subject was surprisingly interesting; much more so than the title would lead one to expect. The lecture, while learned and instructive, was enlivened by humour and a lightness of touch, all of which evoked high praise from competent authorities present.

This was followed in 1916 by papers by Henry Wood on 'Elementary Welsh Genealogy', the Revd Henry Denny on 'Anglo-Irish Genealogy', and by Sherwood on 'How to Make Pedigrees Interesting'. Anticipating their longevity, the Annual Report noted:[33]

> The reading of these papers has proved extremely interesting and attractive, and will, we have no doubt, result in time in a collection of great value to the genealogist, one indeed which no student of our science can afford to ignore.

Talks and lectures soon became a staple of the Society's work, a tradition that continues through to the present day. Where possible the texts of the lectures were published and offered for sale, providing much-needed extra income.

The Society also began to apply itself in the public arena, lobbying for the release of records and improvements in the conditions under which genealogists could access them. Their first target was the census returns. Within months of incorporation a committee was set up to communicate with the Registrar General and others to gain access to the returns from 1841 and 1851, which were still confidential. Gerald Fothergill was the main protagonist, having raised the issue of their release on a number of occasions. The formation of the SoG strengthened his hand and he wrote again to the Home Office, on the Society's behalf, requesting they be disclosed.

Pressure to allow the census returns to be searched had been building for some time. In the early 1900s a solicitor called William Haworth had sought to use information from the 1861 census to disprove an inheritance claim brought against the Duke of Portland.[34] An Irish widow, called Annie Druce, claimed her late husband was the rightful heir to the 5th Duke of Portland, who died unmarried in 1879. She started to refer to herself as the Duchess of Portland and, with five children to support and very little money, began a series of legal actions to assert her claim. After much correspondence with Somerset House, Haworth was able to show that Druce was an impostor. The case became a *cause célé`bre*, not least because Haworth himself ended up in litigation against the then Duke (which he lost) claiming breach of contract.

The General Register Office had vigorously resisted any moves to access census information, partly because they thought it would create too much work but also because no one was entirely sure where all the original returns were located. The Superintendent of Records, Mr A R Bellingham, said the GRO had only given way in the Druce case because they 'thought it was for a good purpose'. He added: 'generally speaking we do not favour these returns being searched and we refuse over and over again'. They were, he said, of a confidential nature 'for all time'.

Even without the Druce case, the issue of what to do with the early censuses was beginning to occupy the administrative minds at the GRO. Completion of the 1901 census had created major storage problems, leading the Office to offer the 1871 and 1881 returns to the PRO in order to make room. The PRO, however, refused to take them unless the GRO also handed over the 1841–61 returns. This created something of a panic at Somerset House. Enquiries revealed that various census documents had been stored in the lofts over the House of Lords' Committee Rooms. When officials from the Census Office and the Office of Works visited in 1903 they found about 100 iron-bound boxes containing the 1841 returns for England, Wales and Scotland. A further series of boxes held the 1861 census of England and Wales. Some months later the books for 1851 were located in one of the GRO's vaults at Somerset House. Those for 1871, 1881 and 1891 were also housed there, though in highly unsatisfactory conditions: the vaults were furnished with rough wooden shelving and traversed by water mains and with the electrical wiring in wooden casings.

The Registrar General had all the books for 1841–81 brought together and taken to the cellars at Queen Anne's Chambers in Tothill Street, Westminster. Hundreds of heavy cases were forced open and their contents arranged on wooden storage racks. Damp affected some of the cases and all were covered in years' worth of dust. The books were arranged so that they were available for reference, but it was not intended as a place for regular searches.

With the passing of the Old Age Pensions Act of 1908, the pension authorities requested that they be allowed to search the census to verify the ages of claimants. Since there was no room at the GRO, a new home had to be found. After a good deal of correspondence between the Treasury, the Local Government Board and the Public Record Office, the latter agreed to take the returns for 1841 and 1851 and to make them available on the payment of fees. The Under-Secretary of State at the Home Office advised Gerald Fothergill of the decision in a letter dated 6 June 1912:[35]

> I am directed by the Secretary of State to say that he has authorised the production to the public in the search room at the Record Office of the enumeration schedules of the 1841 and 1851 Censuses, on payment of fees fixed by the Master of the Rolls viz. 1s. for one piece, and 2s.6d. for each set of 10 pieces.

Once news got out searches in the returns increased rapidly. Between August and December 1912 over 4,000 searches were made, and the PRO had to apply to the Treasury for additional staff. The following year there were over 12,000 searches, the number rising further in 1914. The situation was repeated at the General Register Office in Edinburgh and the PRO in Dublin, where the respective returns for Scotland and Ireland had also been made available. At the same time, the GRO had to deal with unprecedented numbers of requests for birth certificates, with about 100,000 searches a year being made in connection with the new old age pension.

Although it was a victory of sorts, the Society had been only one voice of many in demanding access to the census information. Most searches were in relation to pension claims rather than genealogy and so it would long remain. Moreover, although the safety of the 1841 and 1851 censuses was assured, there was no certainty whatever that later censuses would be preserved. The GRO continued to claim that its confidential records were outside the scope of the 1838 Public Records Act and it would be many years before family historians could come to rely on access to the ten-year census.

Eager to build on the momentum, the Society also requested that 'Parish Registers of England and Wales, before 1 July 1837, be vested in the Master of the Rolls, deposited at the Public Record Office, and be open to inspection under the same conditions as the other national archives are'.[36] This battle would be much more protracted and would not be fully resolved until the 1970s.

The Royal Commission on Public Records provided the Society with its greatest opportunity on the public stage. Launched in 1910, under the legal historian Sir Frederick Pollock, the Commission's remit was to inquire into the status and management of all public records. The SoG's executive committee appointed Fothergill and Glencross to represent it in dealings with the Commission and sent a letter outlining its position.

New indexes, both printed and manuscript, should be lexicographical, the committee argued, and indexing of seventeenth- and eighteenth-century records in particular should be speeded up. Class lists should be placed on open shelves for the public to consult, while the time taken to produce the records 'should be carefully considered'. The 'weeding and destruction of important records' should be very carefully supervised, and medieval and early modern records needed to be cleaned. Finally, the Society insisted all records should be open for 'literary' (i.e. non-legal) searches at most 100 years after their deposition, and in special cases from an earlier date.

The picture of archival practice in Britain uncovered by the Commission was not a happy one. Witness after witness testified to the poor state of the archives, both in London and across the country. Documents were kept in inappropriate conditions and were often dirty or damp. There was a severe lack of calendars and indexes, and for wills in particular the records could only be consulted on payment of a fee. Repositories had limited and irregular opening hours, and search rooms were equipped with insufficient tables or chairs and little light. Clerks often discouraged professional searchers altogether, hoping to pocket enquirers' search fees themselves.

When Fothergill appeared before the Commission, on 23 January 1913, he focused his evidence on the practices and conditions in the Literary Search Department at Somerset House.[37] There was 'practically no arrangement' of the records, Fothergill noted, and many people were turned away due to lack of space. Searchers were only allowed to see eight registers in a day and paid a fee of one shilling for the privilege. 'In London sometimes you can deal with eight registers in an hour, and it is no hardship on the messengers to produce more if required, because half the day they have nothing to do.'

The fee should be abolished, Fothergill continued, as should the long six-week closing during the summer. He had raised a petition on both these issues. This had met with some success, he went on, as in the summer of 1912 the search room had remained open. There should be no fees for producing original records, Fothergill maintained, only for searches. Better indexes to the records were needed and should be made available in the search rooms, as they were at the Public Record Office.

District probate registries were hardly any better. Registrars could often refuse appointments for weeks at a time and had very limited opening hours – typically 11 am–3 pm. Furthermore, they were only open two days a week, and often not on consecutive days. This was a particular inconvenience to professional researchers like Fothergill: 'You either have to kick your heels about in the town for the greater part of the week or pay your fare back to London.'

Turning to the conditions at Somerset House, he noted that the premises were not fireproof – an issue he had confirmed through a question in the House of Commons – yet smoking was allowed within the building. Overall, Fothergill said, there was a conflict between the Principal Registry's day-to-day work as an arm of the legal system and the Literary Research Department's role as a repository for historical records. The Department was 'out of touch with its object of existence', he concluded, while admitting he had been 'an awful agitator' for reform.

Elizabeth French, the London-based record searcher for the NEHGS, contrasted the situation in Britain with that in the United States.[38] State, county and town authorities did not distinguish between literary and legal searches and all offices were open to the public 'without permit or appointment during the usual office hours, from 9 to 5', she told the Commission. 'There are no fees of any kind to anybody to see any public records', Miss French continued. In Massachusetts, printed indexes of probate were available up to 1900, arranged by county. Wills, administrations and inventories were recorded in folio volumes on open shelves for a searcher to consult and 'he may see a hundred in a day if he chooses'. 'There are seats for about 30 searchers, several more than are ever in use at one time.' Civil records of birth, marriage and death were also similarly available for public access. While the situation was not the same across all of America, it pertained broadly, at least across New England.

Summarizing her experiences, Miss French noted:

> In conclusion, I may say that owing to the longer office hours, and the greater facilities and encouragement given to searchers, as well as the absence of 'red tape', it is possible to accomplish an amount of work in one week in these Massachusetts Archives which it would take at least four weeks to accomplish in any similar archives in England. But the work in the English archives is much more interesting than the American archives, owing to their greater antiquity.

Sherwood used his evidence to the Commission to campaign against the fee structure at the General Register Office. Some years earlier on behalf of a client he had undertaken a search for entries of the name Boddington. The search took five days for which he had to pay the Registrar General's fees of £5, while his own time cost a further £7.10s.0d. Although some 3,774 entries were identified, the search failed in its primary objective of pinpointing people to particular locations, Sherwood told the Commission.[39] This was: 'First by reason of the inadequate indexes. Second, because inspection of the records themselves is not now allowed, though it was formerly. Third, because the fee . . . for certified copies of the records required would have approached £500.' He added: 'The Indexes are entirely inadequate and insufficient to identify the persons named therein.' What was required was 'the material extension of facilities to the Public for the examination of their own Registers and Indexes; the provision of more detailed indexes; [and] the placing of other copies of the printed Indexes elsewhere than at the Registrar General's Office, and providing ready access to them'.

In other evidence to the Royal Commission, Mr Ridsdale, a professional record agent, said he had been told that access to the registers had been stopped in about 1898 because the Registrar General thought the system was open to abuse. Agents for life insurance companies would merely check the cause of death and not buy certificates. There were also concerns that attendants might be bribed to alter a register, for whatever reason. The restricted access was a great hindrance to professional searchers, Mr Ridsdale said, since it prevented them from pursuing pedigree cases in the way they would wish. There was a risk that 'very often great injustice might be caused simply from parties not being able to get information which is in the registers and could be found if the solicitor could see them'. He added: 'My opinion is that people ought to be allowed to see the registers, because they are public registers, and are of enormous importance.'

Sherwood pressed home the point in a review of the Commission's Second Report, published in 1914. Writing in *The Pedigree Register*, he again set out the genealogist's manifesto for the public records and mounted a vociferous attack on those who sought to deny access.[40] The Report showed 'there are great masses of public records still held up from public use', Sherwood maintained. He continued:

> There is still the same doleing out with one hand and keeping back with the other which characterises the small person in office: the same unwillingness to understand, when not passively hostile, what the record-searcher wants. What he wants is simple enough. He wants Class Lists or Inventories of all records. He wants ready and easy production of bundles, volumes and rolls. He wants Indexes and more Indexes, and Calendars of the contents of the said bundles, volumes and rolls, but he will often make indexes for himself if only he is allowed access, and can be kept quiet for quite a long time with such simple humouring.

There were, he said, three principles to be observed for recordkeeping and record-searching to be put on 'an honourable basis'. First, public records had to be distinguished from private collections, which were the concern of the Historical Manuscripts Commission. Secondly, all public records, wherever they were held, should automatically become freely accessible when they reached a certain age. This threshold could be fifty, seventy or a hundred years but needed to be clearly laid down. Thirdly, class lists or inventories of all public records needed to be compiled and made available at an affordable price.

> These Class Lists or Inventories should not be hidden away, but boldly put on open shelves and the public instructed to ask for them as the veritable key, abstract, and brief chronicle, of what may or may not be seen.

While great strides had been made at the PRO through the influence of Hubert Hall, other repositories were not so advanced. They needed to adopt the same system, both in indexing their collections and improving accommodation for searchers, which was often limited or non-existent. If this situation continued, and no ready public access could be given, once they reached a certain age such records should automatically be deposited at the PRO.

'Free public access to public records of any age is a public right', Sherwood argued, 'and if it is withheld that is because nobody with enough public spirit has come forward to contest it in the Courts. After all, what are records but "scraps of paper," binding individuals (or bodies corporate) for the public good? If record-keepers have the power to deny access what becomes of public safety?'

The Commission continued its work until 1919 but against the background of the First World War achieved little. On the central issue of access to original registers, the Commissioners noted in their final Report that:

It is true that the Act of 1836 provides that the indexes may be searched on payment of a fee, and that this provision would seem to imply (as the Registrar General contends) that the actual registers shall not be searched. Nevertheless, the Act permits the local registers to be searched by the public on payment of a fee, and in practice this was permitted at the General Register Office itself prior to the year 1898. . . . We see no good reason in principle for forbidding searchers to take copies at their own risk. The existing restriction rests merely on financial grounds and we think that it should be removed.

Nothing happened and it would prove to be just the first salvo in a long-running campaign by genealogists for access to the records of civil registration.

*   *   *   *

The outbreak of 'the Great War' had relatively little effect on the Society's affairs. The membership was generally of advancing years, and thus of an age that was not called on to perform active service. Although the annual reports from the period list certain casualties, the losses seem light compared to the roll calls found on war memorials across the land. Labour and materials of all kinds were in short supply, which curtailed the printing of certain indexes and the regular reports. Voluntary work also suffered as members concentrated on issues closer to home.

Membership grew steadily throughout the war, at the rate of around fifty new members per year. In 1913 there were 257 members, including 121 fellows and life fellows and 49 corresponding associates. After the initial push for subscriptions following incorporation, the qualification for fellowship was raised so that a member could not 'now be elected a Fellow until he has been a Member for a year, and has shown himself to be a valuable Member'. Certificates of Membership were issued at 1s. each, valid for one year. These were 'small enough to go into the waistcoat pocket, and can be shown to clergy when Members are searching, and wish to show that they are literary and not legal searchers'.

During the emergency many of the Society's subcommittees had, of necessity, ceased to function. The original scheme was far too unwieldy and with the war over the opportunity was taken to restructure. The previous fifteen committees were replaced by just four: Finance, Index (covering all aspects of transcribing and indexing records), Library and Heraldry.

Sherwood, who was well above fighting age, became more absorbed than ever in genealogical projects – both for the Society and on his own behalf – which provided a welcome distraction from the grim wartime situation. Despite the paper shortages, in 1916 he decided to launch a new journal. *Dramatis Personae* was a collection of snippets of information gleaned from wills, newspapers and other documentary sources, at the 'trifling cost' of 1s. per week. Keen as ever for family history to receive the recognition it deserved, Sherwood stressed that the results were 'bound up with Local History, and of equal value to anyone who takes an interest in his own surroundings'. The journal aimed to provide 'the *human colour* so necessary for the historian', he explained, adding: 'There's fun in many of the details, too. We must get our fun where we can.'

Concern over the preservation of provincial records was growing and was one of the main questions enquired into by the Royal Commission. Since William Phillimore had first raised the idea in 1889, there had been calls for county councils to take responsibility for storing and preserving archives relevant to their jurisdiction. Under Phillimore's scheme, such bodies would be overseen by a county archivist and travelling inspectors from the PRO. The county councils were reluctant to take on this work and many saw district probate registries as more suitable candidates. In Bedfordshire, however, the issue began to gain traction due to the vision of Dr George Herbert Fowler.

Fowler was a scientist by training. He was born in Lincoln in 1861 where his father, Revd John Fowler, was headmaster of the grammar school.[41] After graduating in natural sciences from Keble College, Oxford in 1884, George studied at Owen's College, Manchester, and eventually gained a doctorate from Leipzig University. An academic career as a marine zoologist followed, including spells as director of the Marine Biological Association Laboratory at Plymouth, and later as Assistant Professor of Zoology at University College London. With the oceanographer Richard Norris Wolfenden, he founded the Challenger Society for Marine Science in 1903, eventually retiring from UCL in 1909 at the age of 48.

On receiving an inheritance from his parents, who died within two years of each other, in 1906 Fowler moved to the country and bought The Old House, a sixteenth-century manor house at Aspley Guise in Bedfordshire. He started to restore the property and became interested in its history and that of the nearby village. This led him to the Bedfordshire archives where he eventually located the early title deeds, allowing him to trace the history of the house and of the families who had owned and occupied it. In 1912 Fowler published his study of some early Bedfordshire families in *The Genealogist*.

Despite settling in the country, Fowler had no intention of a leisurely retirement. His interest in archives aroused, he stood for and was elected to the Bedfordshire County Council in 1912 and within a few months was appointed to the County Records Committee. Within a year he was elected its chairman and set about reinvigorating what had become a rather moribund body.

Like many counties, Bedfordshire had no coherent policy for the care of its records, then referred to as 'county muniments'. On their formation in 1889 the county councils were charged with the care of the records of their predecessors, the county Quarter Sessions. To these were added other classes of official records, such as the plans of proposed railways, and copies of enclosure awards and maps. A few counties, including Bedfordshire, undertook comprehensive surveys and even started publishing catalogues and indexes. Others became involved in listing parish records or publishing older Quarter Sessions documents. The schemes were of varying utility, but all skirted around the problem of how to care for records at the local level.

Fowler, the scientist, applied himself to the task. In his first report as chairman of the Records Committee, presented in January 1914, he set out in detail what was required:[42]

> The ideal Muniment Room will be arranged by classes so that anyone can learn in a few minutes where to lay hands on any paper required, and so that each new bundle of papers, when added to the archives, finds a place ready to receive it.

He went on to propose that archives from private families, estates and local solicitors should also be acquired, if necessary sacrificing old printed material, such as Acts of Parliament, to make space. The physical conditions in the muniment rooms were also important, Fowler observed. Steel joists would be required to help bear the expected loads; electric wiring should be in fire-protective casing; and ventilation needed to be much improved so as to avoid mould.

Important issues of policy did not escape Fowler's attention either. It was, he thought, essential that documents be made available to researchers free of charge and he wrote this condition into a clause on the deposit forms finalized in 1914. He even considered guidelines for the retention of records, suggesting that certain bills and vouchers more than ten years old be destroyed. Thus, within the space of little over a year, Fowler had laid down most of the principles of modern archival practice.

He set about transforming the existing two muniment rooms into a model records office, a task essentially complete by the outbreak of the First World War. As the war unfolded Fowler returned to London to take up intelligence work at the Admiralty, returning to Bedford only for the occasional meeting. A volunteer and unpaid, he regularly worked ten-hour days preparing charts for use by the submarines then being introduced into the Royal Navy. He found the work 'intensely interesting, but exhausting'. His efforts were recognized with a CBE and he is thought to have declined a knighthood.

On leaving the Admiralty, in March 1919, Fowler at once resumed work in the muniment rooms and a third room was eventually added. By 1922 he had been at the task for ten years, with only an ageing assistant for support. The need for new blood was all too apparent but there was no training for work with records: 'The only method is to train on the spot some young person who has a natural bent towards historical study, who is orderly, methodical and neat-fingered. This training I am prepared to give.'[43] After a short recruitment process, Fred Emmison, a 16 year old from the Bedford Modern School, was appointed. His starting salary was to be £52 per annum, rising to £100 in the second year and £300 on completion of his training.

Emmison was a well-judged appointment. He learnt quickly and injected new energy into the work of cataloguing the collections and making new acquisitions. A particular effort was made to acquire manorial records following changes in the laws relating to manors and title to property. Many of these documents were held by solicitors who had neither the time nor inclination to sort them themselves. Fowler found that if Emmison made an appointment to visit the solicitor in person, they were more likely than not to let him walk away with all he wanted.

Fowler, meanwhile, was working on what was to be one of his greatest legacies. *The Care of County Muniments* is a guide to recordkeeping intended, as he told the Records Committee in November 1923, 'to call the attention of other county councils to the value of their Records'.[44] It set out the principles of archival practice Fowler had pioneered in Bedford, covering acquisition policy, cataloguing, storage, conservation and the provision of records to the public. He presented the copyright to the County Councils Association, which distributed copies to all its members. It was the first handbook for the care of local archives and by 1939 was in its 3rd edition, remaining in use until well after the Second World War.

With growing and more accessible collections and a new building, the number of visits by external readers increased rapidly, from 12 in 1922 to over 550 in 1937. In 1930 the service officially became the Bedfordshire County Record Office, the first such to bear that name, and as the decade progressed Fowler handed over more of the running of the service to Emmison.

Following Fowler's death in 1940, it fell to Emmison to spread his ideas more widely. This happened slowly at first. By 1938 only a dozen county record offices had been established with full-time salaried staffs ranging from one to six members. The movement did not really take hold until the 1950s, becoming an essential foundation for the popularity of family history in the second half of the twentieth century.

*   *   *   *

Back in London, the Society of Genealogists was gradually growing in confidence. By 1923 membership had reached 500. The library had over 5,000 books in addition to many thousands of loose manuscripts, and the Great Card Index contained nearly two and a half million references. Under Sherwood's supervision, work also began on a new catalogue to the Society's collections, arranged in sixty-eight divisions. A series of *Quarterly Queries* was being produced whereby members could submit enquiries relating to their own researches for publication in a quarterly pamphlet. Replies had to be sent to the

Society, unless otherwise requested, which forwarded them to the enquirers periodically. Beginning in 1916, this series was edited for many years by the Revd Thomas Dale.

As the *Quarterly Queries* accumulated over time, they built into a useful snapshot of the members' interests. An analysis made by Sherwood in 1929, covering 861 queries received up to 1925, showed almost half (393) related to the period 1700–1800 and almost a third (237) to the period 1600–1700. This compared to just 68 queries pre-1500; and 66 to 1800 or later. Thus, there was a great preponderance for the eighteenth century, which Sherwood again took as justification for 'more lists and indexes affecting this period'.

From a high water mark in the late Victorian period, the number of genealogical periodicals had been gradually declining. Production problems brought about by the First World War and a declining interest in the subscription model led many publications to close. In 1922, *The Genealogist*, one of the last surviving genealogical and antiquarian periodicals in Britain, ceased publication. The editor, H W Forsyth-Harwood, had kept it afloat throughout the war but fell into debt and when peace came could bear the costs no longer. An appeal for additional subscribers drew little response and he had no choice but to close. Originally started by George Marshall in 1877, *The Genealogist* had been an important part of Britain's genealogical scene for forty-five years. In his final editorial Forsyth-Harwood wrote that 'the magazine will be much missed both here in England and in the United States, and I trust that when happier times come an effort will be made to revive it'.[45]

Its closure left a big void in terms of genealogical publishing. The Society of Genealogists considered acquiring the rights to the journal but eventually decided to start its own publication instead, expanding on the quarterly report. *The Genealogists' Magazine* was first published in April 1925 and has been the house magazine of the Society ever since.

Writing in the Preface to the first issue, the Society President, Lord Farrer, introduced the journal thus:[46]

> Owing to the lamented decease of many useful record prints during the War period, there is room for a carefully edited and indexed periodical publication . . . and, if backed by a responsible Society, such a permanent record publication of pure Genealogy will aid the sister crafts of History and Heraldry.

Under its first editor, the Revd Henry Denny, the *Magazine* soon established its own character and became a valuable journal of record for genealogical studies. Early issues were dogged by production problems, however, which Denny felt necessary to defend.[47]

> It has proved to be no easy matter, even under the most favourable circumstances, successfully to maintain a *Magazine* of this kind in the

past. The pathway of Genealogy for the last three generations is strewn
with the wreckage of publications like our own, most of which had a
short life and a hard one. We venture, therefore, to express the hope that
our readers will try to refrain from any unnecessary criticism, giving us,
rather, all the forbearance and practical help possible.

In case his readers were in any doubt about how hard he was working, Denny
went on to give a lengthy account of the processes involved in compiling each
issue.

As well as the 'Quarterly Queries', regular features included 'Quarterly
Notes' (news-type items), and 'Manuscript Accessions' (listing all new material
received by the library). There was also a list of new members, but addresses
were not added until much later. Among the forty pages were eight pages of
advertisements where professional genealogists, such as Fothergill, Sherwood
and Glencross, offered their services alongside booksellers and heraldic
stationers.

Some of the contents of these early editions seem esoteric to modern eyes.
The medievalist Walter Rye provided a long-running series of articles
recording the Rolls of Battle Abbey, which date from the Norman Conquest,
and there were frequent articles on medieval genealogy and manorial records.
A feature from December 1925 discussed graphology (the study of
handwriting), which was considered to be a legitimate means of studying
hereditary traits. Lists of bookplates and of portraits offered for sale in auction
houses were also regular features.

By the end of the fourth volume, in December 1928, Denny noted that
whereas it had initially been regarded by some as a 'side-show', the *Magazine*
had 'undoubtedly become firmly established as an integral part of the work of
the Society of Genealogists, and we may confidently look forward to the day
when it will become a much larger and more important publication'.[48]

Another innovation, introduced in early 1929, were Discussion Meetings
where members presented brief papers (rather than a full lecture) on topics of
personal interest. Each paper was followed by a short discussion. This 'new
experiment', reported the *Magazine*, 'proved an undoubted success. The brief
lectures reached a high level of excellence and produced very interesting
discussions.'[49]

Expanding the range of genealogical sources was a keen concern and here
the Society achieved an early coup through the assiduous eye of Gerald
Fothergill. In an effort to search out original records, Fothergill would read
Acts of Parliament and then try to identify what records would have resulted
from them. In 1921 he found an Act from the reign of Queen Anne imposing
a tax on apprenticeship indentures. He took the Act to the Inland Revenue
Department at Somerset House and asked if the records still survived. The
officials managed to locate a series of registers of apprenticeships covering the

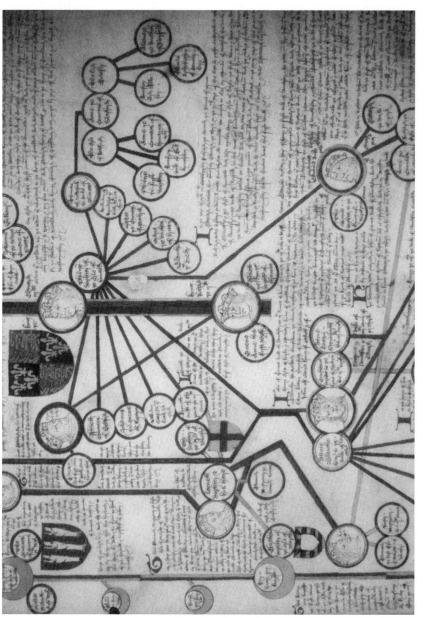

Medieval roll showing the genealogy of the Percy family (with 'cranes foot' representations) (Bodleian Library)

Sir William Dugdale (1605–86), English antiquarian and herald (National Portrait Gallery, London)

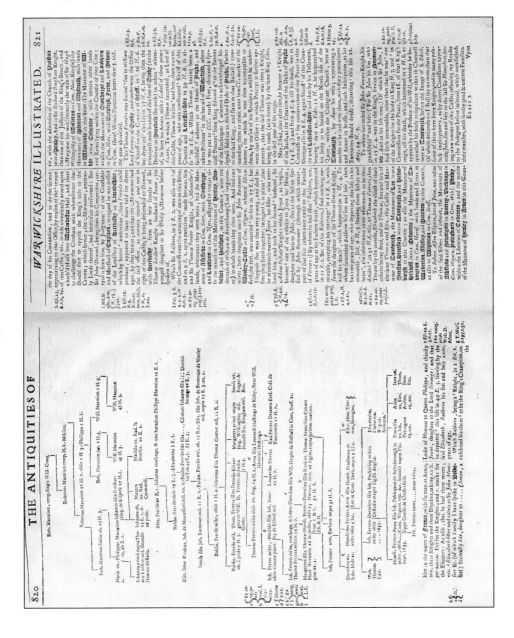

Extract from Dugdale's *Antiquities of Warwickshire*, showing the descent of the Ferrers family of Tamworth Castle (note references and notes in the margins)

Ralph Bigland
(1712–84), as
Somerset Herald,
was one of the first
to use parish
registers for
genealogy (National
Portrait Gallery,
London)

Title-page of Richard
Sims' *Manual*, first
published 1856

A MANUAL

FOR THE

GENEALOGIST, TOPOGRAPHER, ANTIQUARY,

AND

LEGAL PROFESSOR,

CONSISTING OF

DESCRIPTIONS OF PUBLIC RECORDS; PAROCHIAL AND
OTHER REGISTERS; WILLS; COUNTY AND FAMILY
HISTORIES; HERALDIC COLLECTIONS IN
PUBLIC LIBRARIES, ETC. ETC.

BY

RICHARD SIMS,

OF THE BRITISH MUSEUM,

*Compiler of the "Index to the Heralds' Visitations," the "Handbook to
the Library of the British Museum," etc.*

SECOND EDITION.

LONDON:
JOHN RUSSELL SMITH,
36, SOHO SQUARE.
MDCCCLXI.

Sir (John) Bernard Burke (1814–92), controversial editor of *Burke's Peerage* (National Portrait Gallery, London)

George Edward Cokayne (1825–1911), known as 'G.E.C.', compiler of *The Complete Peerage* (College of Arms)

John Horace Round
(1854–1928), fierce
critic of Victorian
genealogy (National
Portrait Gallery,
London)

The Registry of Wills, Somerset House, London, 1875 (Illustrated London News Ltd/Mary
Evans Picture Library)

George Sherwood
(1867–1958), one of the
founders of the Society of
Genealogists (Society of
Genealogists)

Percival Boyd
(1866–1955),
compiler of
Boyd's Marriage
Index (Society of
Genealogists)

Percival Boyd standing in front of the Great Card Index and volumes of his Marriage Index
(Society of Genealogists)

George Herbert Fowler
(1861–1940), pioneer of
county record offices
(Bedford & Luton Archives
Services)

Microfilming of
parish registers,
c.1940 (Society of
Genealogists)

227 The Strand (1911–14). The Society was initially given two rooms in the premises of George Tudor Sherwood (Society of Genealogists)

5 Bloomsbury Square (1914–33) (Society of Genealogists)

3 Chaucer House,
Malet Street (1933–54)
(Society of
Genealogists)

37 Harrington Gardens,
South Kensington
(1954–84) (Society of
Genealogists)

The Search Room at the Public Record Office, Chancery Lane, 1967 (Getty Images)

Sir Anthony Wagner (1908–95), as Garter Principal King of Arms (National Portrait Gallery)

SoG representatives around the Phillimore & Co. stand at the Heritage '74 show, Brighton, August 1974. From left to right: Cecil Humphrey-Smith; Noel Osborne (Editorial Director of Phillimore); Jeremy Gibson; Don Steel; Peter Spufford (Society of Genealogists)

Publicity leaflet for Gordon Honeycombe's *Family History* television series, 1979 (BBC Archives, Caversham)

Fiche from the *International Genealogical Index*, 1992 (Church of Jesus Christ of Latter-Day Saints)

BERRY, CHRISTOPH

COUNTRY ENGLAND   COUNTY: DERBY   AS OF MAR 1992   PAGE   2,299

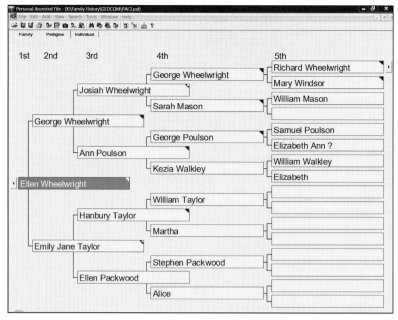

Personal Ancestral File (PAF), one of the earliest family history software programs (Church of Jesus Christ of Latter-Day Saints)

Family history today: Who Do You Think You Are? Show 2009, Olympia Exhibition Centre, London (Michael Sharpe)

period 1710–1811. These registers were a goldmine for the genealogist; they showed the name of the apprentice and of his or her father or guardian, the name and place of residence of the master, the trade to be learnt, the term of years, and the premium paid.

Fothergill immediately recognized their genealogical value and reported back to the Society's executive committee. The priorities were twofold: first, to try to get the authorities to open the records for inspection; and secondly, to index them so as to improve their utility to genealogists. At the Society's behest, the Registrar General agreed to transfer the registers to the Public Record Office where they were made available for public access. The Committee itself voted £100 towards indexing them on slips. To supplement this a fund was opened to which members of the Society were asked to subscribe and the sum of £48 6s. was raised in the first year.

Work then began on transcribing and indexing about one million entries, a laborious task that had to be accommodated alongside the existing work on the Great Card Index. By the end of the year 25,000 slips had been extracted and by 1923 this had risen to around 140,000. The project, which became known as *The Apprentices of Great Britain*, was not completed until the early 1930s. The final index was in two series, 1710–62 and 1762–74, all the index slips being sorted by the artist Duncan Moul. Fothergill did not live to see the result; he died in November 1926 after a long illness.

Members were not expected to miss any opportunity for enlarging the Society's indexes. An editorial from *Genealogists' Magazine* of March 1928 observed:[50]

> At this time of the year many people will be holiday-making in the country or by the sea. May we make a suggestion to our members for a profitable use of this leisure? You will, no doubt, visit old churches, perhaps in remote districts, off the beaten track, and you are sure to find in them or in their churchyards epitaphs and coats of arms which will strike you as being worth recording. A postcard to the Secretary of our Society will elicit information as to whether the inscriptions in that particular place have already been gleaned. If they have not, devote a little time to the task yourself, and forward the results for our Library.

The author went on to suggest that travellers might wish to use their excursion to call on the local clergy to examine their registers, record monumental inscriptions in the graveyard, seek out local antiquaries, or scour through the parish magazines for useful information. An editorial of the same period drew attention to the wealth of private records languishing in country houses and came up with a rather novel proposal for how they might be copied:[51]

> We would venture to suggest that of the many educated women without husbands or careers who belong to our ancient families or have access to

the houses of such, a large number might, at the cost of very little personal trouble, take in hand this work, to the benefit alike of themselves, of the families concerned and of the genealogist and historian.

With members contributing slips in ever larger numbers the Great Card Index grew steadily and its coverage increased, so that it became an indispensable reference point for genealogists of the day. Its place was soon to be eclipsed, however, by another index of even greater scope and ambition, and which was all the more remarkable for being the work of one man.

Percival Boyd joined the Society of Genealogists in September 1922, aged 56. After being educated at Sutton Valance, Uppingham and Clare College Cambridge, he entered the family firm of J C Boyd Ltd, merchants and warehousemen, at Friday Street in the City of London. Boyd was the fifth generation of his family to join the company, which dealt mainly in cotton goods, and eventually became chairman and managing director. As a young man one of his interests was cycling. He joined the Cyclist Touring Club in the days of the high bicycle and when safety bicycles arrived was one of the earliest owners. He was also an avid collector of British and colonial stamps. All of this fell by the wayside once he joined the Society.

Boyd had studied maths at Cambridge and had the mathematician's predisposition to logic and order. He conceived the idea of an index to all the marriages that had taken place in England before 1837, and within a year of joining the SoG had started writing index slips. He soon found he could copy about a thousand names a day. With an estimated thirty million marriages to index, at that rate, he calculated, the work would take him around a hundred years!

A lesser man would have stopped there and then but Boyd pressed on, applying himself coolly and methodically to his self-appointed task. He worked mostly at his home at Upper Warlingham, Surrey, using copies of registers sent to him, so avoiding the need to travel all over the country to work from original documents. Notice of the work was given to members in the *Genealogists' Magazine* of September 1925:[52]

> An attempt is being made to solve one of the greatest difficulties met with in genealogical research – that of finding the record of lost marriages. To this end a marriage index has been commenced by Mr. Percival Boyd, who is carrying out the work under the auspices of the Society of Genealogists. . . The nucleus will be supplied by indexing all printed parish registers (irrespective of whether the books are themselves indexed) and forming a single card index to all the printed registers for each county, thus avoiding an immense amount of search work. To this nucleus will be added the names from manuscript copies of parish registers which have not hitherto been copied. The first step

will be the addition of the Bishops' Transcripts where the Registers are lost or incomplete.

The marriage slips were sorted first by men's names, in groups by county, each county being divided into periods of twenty-five years. These were then typed by paid assistants, sorted again by women's names, and then typed again. Fifteen counties were treated in this way, though none of them was covered completely, the results being bound into green volumes. Additional entries for these and other counties were sorted together and typed in a series of miscellaneous volumes, bound in red.

By 1928 Boyd had finished ninety-eight volumes containing almost one million names and the index was growing at the rate of 10,000 names a week. The time had come to announce his scheme to the world, which he did through a publication entitled *A Marriage Index on a New Plan*.[53] This initial list covered some 863 parishes (not all complete) in Cornwall, Cumberland, Derbyshire, Devon, Durham, Middlesex, Norfolk, Shropshire and Somerset. Spare blank pages were included at the back to which later printed lists could be added. There was also a pocket in the back cover containing index search forms. A copy was sent to every member of the Society – of which Boyd was by then chairman – free of charge and additional copies were offered for sale at 1s.6d.

Explaining the index's value, Boyd noted that although the chance of finding a marriage was only around one in fifty, even when unsuccessful 'the searcher knows that his search has covered some hundreds of parishes, and this book will give him the names of those parishes'.

As the work proceeded others came forward to share the burden, transcribing original registers and sending the results to Boyd for inclusion. Collaborators included Haydon Whitehead (for Suffolk registers), the Revd Evelyn Young (for Cambridgeshire), Henry Wood (for Durham and Northumberland), and Norman Hindsley (for Yorkshire).

Although the Society was the main point of access, Boyd was keen for the index to be available around the country. A copy of the Cornwall and Devonshire sections was sent to Devon and Cornwall Record Society and housed at the City Library in Exeter. Wood arranged for a copy of the Durham section to be available in Newcastle and Boyd gave a copy of the Middlesex section to the Guildhall Library.

By 1935 300 volumes, containing 3.5 million names had been completed, and by the time of Boyd's death in the mid-1950s there were some 534 volumes with more than 7 million entries from around 4,300 parishes. As the work principally of one man it is unsurpassed in the history of genealogy in Britain – and probably anywhere in the world.

In an interview in the *London Evening News* on 29 July 1937, Boyd explained his motives thus:[54]

I'm not interested in pedigrees, although my index will help a lot of people to trace their ancestors. No, I'm doing it because, to me, the lives of ordinary men and women are the real history of England. Not the dates of reigns and battles that we were taught at school. People were born and got married and died whether there were wars or not; only you don't hear about them in the history books.

*   *   *   *

The inter-war years saw a series of reforms in property law that alarmed genealogists and historians. The reforms were designed to tidy up the law of owning or holding real estate, and strip away the accumulated anachronisms of centuries. One of the most significant measures was the Law of Property Act 1922, by which the medieval systems of land tenure through the institution of the manor, in decline for centuries, were finally abolished. Another was the Land Registration Act 1925, which greatly simplified land registration practices in England and Wales. Provided title had been registered, those needing to prove title in a piece of land had only to produce deeds and documents back to the date of registration, rather than to time immemorial.

Thus, from a practical, legal point of view, there was no longer any reason for keeping runs of manorial court rolls or old title deeds, perhaps spanning several centuries. An industry grew up turning these ancient parchment documents into lampshades, to the horror of historians and antiquarians. The Law of Property (Amendment) Act 1924 went some way in alleviating the threat to manorial records by vesting responsibility for manorial documents in the Master of the Rolls. The then incumbent of that office, Ernest Pollock, set up a register of all such manors in England and Wales and enlisted the help of the Law Society, the Society of Genealogists and others to help compile it. Nevertheless, concern remained that there was no general provision or policy for historical records other than those of central government.

The British Record Society (BRS) was the only national organization equipped to take on this role. Since its formation by Phillimore and others in 1888, the BRS had focused on the publication of documents and calendars of documents of national interest held in the country's public records offices, and on encouraging the proper care and preservation of historical sources. By 1928 many in the BRS believed that the first part of this mission had essentially been fulfilled and the preservation of surviving documentary sources was more urgent. At the same time it was clear that the issue went wider than the society's existing remit, requiring the involvement of a growing number of local and specialist record-publishing societies. Nor was it an appropriate body to lobby and campaign on controversial matters.

It was decided to found a new organization which would appeal to these much wider interests. Thus, in 1932 the British Records Association (BRA) was established to deal primarily with the preservation and care of archives not in national collections.[55] The BRA set up a Records Preservation Section, with George Fowler – the pioneer of local archives – as chairman. Drawing partly on Fowler's experiences with the Bedfordshire solicitors, eventually a system was devised to organize the return of documents held by London solicitors to the proper provincial repositories. Much valuable work on document storage, repair, classification and cataloguing was also undertaken.

* * * *

The Society of Genealogists in the inter-war years was a place of serene gentility. At 5 Bloomsbury Square the atmosphere was more that of an intimate club than the headquarters of a learned society. The building had a beautiful staircase and Adam decorations showing dimly through the gloom of the accumulated dust of years. The staff had plenty of time to give to the relatively few members who visited, which was just as well as the library catalogue was small and inaccurate while the staff were conversant with the contents of the library shelves. No research was done for members and very little was being done by the Society as a body to add to the collection of parish register transcripts, although individual members did some work on their own account. The magazine was run by a committee who did all the work of preparing it for press, aided by an assistant who came in specially for the purpose. At 4 pm tea was dispensed to all those who happened to be in the rooms at the time.

One aspect was not so congenial. With the continual expansion of the indexes and acquisition of other collections space was becoming very tight. If the Society was to continue to grow its library new premises would have to be found.

In 1932 the Library Association acquired premises in Upper Malet Street, close to University College, and began converting it into offices, to be called Chaucer House. The Association was keen to share the premises with other societies and offered the SoG a twenty-one-year lease. Chaucer House was ideally situated from the Society's point of view, being 'surrounded by seats of learning'. As well as the Library Association, it shared the building with the Museums Association, while University College, the National Central Library, the Institute of Historical Research and the British Museum were all close by.

The Society took possession in spring 1933. Its offices were on the third floor and had access to a lift for its many aged members. At around 1,750 square feet the space was almost 50 per cent greater than at Bloomsbury Square and allowed all the facilities to be housed on one floor. Partitions were erected to create three rooms: a large library, an Index Room and a small office for the secretary. Committee meetings were held on a lower floor and there was also a large Council Room which the Society could hire for lectures.

A reception was held on 10 October to mark this new departure in the Society's development, attended by around 200 members and their friends. No alcohol was served, just tea in the Library Association's 'beautiful and spacious rooms'.[56] Lord Hanworth, Master of the Rolls, was the guest of honour and delivered an address on the work of his office and of the Public Record Office generally. As was usual for the period, the event was reported in *The Times* and other newspapers. An exhibition was also held at which members 'lent some of their treasures for the delectation of the guests'. Amongst these exhibits were tapestry maps of Old London, a collection of heraldic china, and pedigrees laid out on large sheets of vellum and adorned with emblazoned shields and heraldic beasts. The event was marred only by the absence of the President, Lord Farrer, through illness.

Oiling the wheels of the Society at this time was the new Secretary, Kathleen Blomfield. As Miss Kathleen Bell, she was appointed the Assistant Secretary in November 1930, having worked previously at the College of Arms. She succeeded almost immediately as Secretary on the resignation of the previous incumbent due to ill-health. In 1933 she married the distinguished anaesthetist Dr Joseph Blomfield. She remained with the Society for twenty years, during which she greatly increased the scope of its activities.

Under Blomfield's influence, and with the new premises, the 1930s brought expansion and change. Several long-standing members disappeared from the scene, due to ill-health or old age, and the Society gradually came to rely more on paid staff, bringing a more professional and also more commercial approach.

Following the deaths of the Revd Thomas Dale and Walter Gun, the *Genealogists' Magazine* became the responsibility of the staff – primarily Blomfield – with the editorship more of an honorary position. The Annual Report for 1932 noted that the *Magazine*'s 'value as an advertising medium is beginning to be more and more appreciated by those who desire to get in touch with genealogists', allowing the Society to keep the costs down.

Since the launch of the *Magazine* there had been a policy of not printing the pedigrees or histories of individual families, which were considered to be of purely private interest. However, it was recognized that some members would be prepared to pay to have their researches published as a supplement. This was considered to be a good way of ensuring the pedigrees received 'a wide circulation and a reasonable prospect of perpetuity'. Several members took up the offer and privately printed supplements became a regular feature during the 1930s.

A new library card catalogue was compiled which though not perfect was a big improvement. Regular stock checks were taken against this new catalogue, cutting down significantly on the number of books that were 'lost'. Members requesting the staff to find books could be referred first to the catalogue, greatly reducing the call on staff time. The scale of charges was revised to make the collections easier to access, especially for 'members living in the country'. A whole day's search cost 10s. with shorter periods being charged *pro rata*, minimum half-a-crown. Non-members were charged double these rates.

While work continued on the Great Card Index it lacked the dynamism of the past. George Sherwood's index, which had begun in four boxes in 1911, had by 1932 reached three million slips. But the work was tedious and unrewarding and there was a constant call for volunteers. Being out of reach of London was no excuse since 'country members' were continually encouraged to make an index to their local parish registers or to the monumental inscriptions in the village churchyard. Few heeded the call. In 1931 only 6,667 slips were added; a far cry from the 100,000 or more that were being compiled in the early years. The index was also difficult to maintain. Careless searchers would return slips to the boxes in the wrong order and even put them in upside down.

Thomas Dale had pondered the problem in an address to the index sorters in 1934. He accepted that those behind the scheme had been 'idealists' and praised the indexers and sorters who 'laboured ungrudgingly for posterity'.[57] He attributed the falling off in interest partly to the energy of members being 'directed into other genealogical channels' and partly to the diversion of resources into typing existing slips rather than generating new ones.

Typing brought many advantages, making the slips easier to read for those sorting them into the index in the first place, as well as for searchers retrieving the information. Members were asked to subsidize this work, with two copies being made of any slips they requested, one of which the Society retained in place of the original handwritten version. The other great advantage was space. A cubic foot of shelf space could take 15,000 index slips (six drawer boxes), whereas the same space could accommodate up to 140,000 typed slips filed into bound volumes, as Boyd used for his Marriage Index.

As enthusiasm for the index dwindled fewer and fewer slips were added. The last addition recorded was a group of thirty slips from the India Office records filed in November 1938. After that various miscellaneous items were added, but only on a spasmodic basis and no record was kept. It was a valiant attempt to cross-reference genealogical information from a very wide range of sources, the likes of which would not be seen again until well into the computer age.

Percival Boyd, however, soldiered on and not content with his incessant labours on the Marriage Index began work on several other projects. One of these covered a selection of adult male burials in the London area from 1538 to 1853. He donated the resulting sixteen volumes, which became known as Boyd's London Burials, to the Society in 1935, being careful to point out they were far from complete. An announcement in the *Genealogists' Magazine* explained:[58]

Only males are included (children being omitted when so designated in the Registers), because for genealogical purposes the date of a man's death is more important than that of a woman who, unless she were sole or a widow, could not make a will except with the consent of her husband.

The sources used are not entirely clear but are believed to include eighty-seven volumes of parish registers held at the College of Arms, which had been copied and mostly indexed by Joseph Chester. Boyd is also likely to have consulted the extensive collection of transcripts of burials held in the Society's library.

Boyd's appetite for indexing knew no bounds and in 1935 he persuaded the Society to begin a collection of so-called 'family units'. His idea was to bring together on a single index sheet basic details of family groups from all kinds of records. Each sheet was to record an individual's dates of birth and death, their marriage or marriages, and the children with their marriages. References to residence, profession and wills were also to be recorded. Each child would then become a separate entry on their own which could be searched for their particulars, and so the index would go on through the ages.

Heralding the scheme as a 'new epoch in genealogy', the *Genealogists' Magazine* explained the thinking behind it:[59]

> There are three kinds of pedigree that are constructed by the genealogist; there is (1) the straight line of male descent; (2) the table of descendants; (3) the table of ancestors; with, of course, varying degrees of combination between them. The unit on which all these structures are based is the 'Family', which for this purpose may be defined as 'Marriage and its issue', and although reliable pedigrees can be constructed without the details of each 'Family', it is the bitter experience of most of us that we are unable to use these pedigrees because the information does not include the brothers and sisters. . . .In fact the Family is the one and only genealogical unit, and every genealogical structure is built up of a combination of these units.

The first volume completed consisted almost entirely of families of the Drapers' Company, of which Boyd was a member and had made a special study. Other volumes drew from sources such as Crisp's *Fragmenta Genealogica*, Sherwood's *Pedigree Register*, Harleian Society publications, and various pedigrees and family histories held by the Society. Boyd also embarked on a massive genealogical investigation, reconstructing families from entries in City of London church registers.

The project immediately ran into problems, however. Few volunteers came forward to complete sheets and provide details of their own families. The sheets show the work of relatively few hands and it is clear that for the majority Boyd was the principal author, with assistance from Sherwood and others.

Thirty-four volumes were compiled by 1951, covering families from all over the British Isles, but overall the family units scheme was a failure. The exception was London, which Boyd compiled himself bringing together another remarkable collection of material. He trawled through a wide range of printed and manuscript sources, extracting references to anyone who lived in the capital, entering the information on his unit sheets. In this, his last great work, Boyd used many of the sources that had helped with his other indexes, often making a note of the sources consulted at the foot of each family unit sheet.

The appearance of the first volume was announced in the *Genealogists' Magazine* in March 1939. On the outbreak of war, Boyd presented the collection to the Society, retaining it for his own use during his lifetime and he continued to make searches on behalf of enquirers. By the time of his death he had written nearly 60.000 sheets, which were bound in 238 volumes. This index became known as Boyd's *Citizens of London*, later changed to *Inhabitants of London* to reflect the fact that not all of the people listed were 'citizens' in the strict sense of being Freemen of the City.

John Beach Whitmore was the first to point out the value of this collection in an article published in March 1944.[60] First, although confined to London, the link between the City and county families all over the country made the collection of national importance, Whitmore noted. In the sixteenth and seventeenth centuries especially, younger sons of the gentry who were destined not to inherit land and titles often went to London to seek their fortunes in trade. Secondly, the collection covers the period when the North American and West Indian colonies were on the rise, with the corresponding growth in trade and emigration. Many London families were involved in one way and another, making it a useful source for Americans with pioneer British ancestry.

* * * *

For the Society's twenty-fifth anniversary, in 1936, Lord Farrer wrote an article, 'English Genealogy', in which he reviewed the growth of the Society and set out some proposals for its future development.[61] He reiterated the gigantic task before them in cataloguing and indexing all genealogical information and drew attention to the need for greater cooperation with other historical societies and bodies, such as the county record societies. The public library in particular, he argued, 'is destined to continue and to become an increasing factor in literary education'. The Society needed to cultivate better relationships with the major libraries across the country, and to become a 'recognized Clearing House for genealogical research', at least within England and Wales.

Such facilities would only be open to a certain class of person. 'It is of course grossly unfair that the Public Librarian should be expected to answer any Tom, Dick or Harry seeking his great-grandfather', Farrer noted. Many libraries 'get over this difficulty', he continued, by issuing students' tickets for their research branches, and 'I have heard that a small fee charged for such tickets covers expenses'. Thus, even in the 1930s the higher echelons of the Society still did not share Sherwood's conviction that everyone should have access to their past.

Farrer concluded his article with a list of the local repositories concerned. Fowler's model of county record offices had yet to take hold and for most counties one or more of the main libraries was still seen as the best point of contact.

The centrepiece of the Silver Anniversary celebrations was to have been an exhibition on genealogy and heraldry. In the event this had to be postponed due to the death of George V. It was eventually held a year later, in late June 1937 at Chaucer House. Over 1,200 people attended over six days, showing 'the extent to which the general Public are interested in the study of Genealogy and Heraldry'.[62]

Largely the work of Kathleen Blomfield, the exhibition was instructional rather than 'a mere display of curiosities', guiding newcomers through the steps to be taken in searching out their ancestry and introducing the various classes of records available. Portions of the Great Card Index were on display, as well as volumes from Boyd's Marriage Index and London Burials. Volumes of the indexes of marriage licences, the Apprenticeship Index, and parish registers were also shown, together with items such as family Bibles, probate records and company records. It was a format that was to be repeated many times over the years. The exhibition 'catalogue' in fact served as a textbook and included articles written by Society members. Many of these catalogues remained unsold and the members had to be encouraged to buy them at one shilling each.

With beginners' demands for information growing, the Society decided to produce its own comprehensive guide. *The Genealogist's Handbook* offered 'concise and accurate information about some of the more common sources of genealogical knowledge'.[63] Alongside guidance on how to use the different classes of record were descriptions of the Society's own collections, and the *Handbook* was aimed as much at the advanced genealogist as the beginner. Again Blomfield was a prime mover. The *Handbook* was first published in 1935 – at the price of 1s. – and reprinted in 1944 and again in 1948. The 1st edition coincided with the reissue of an earlier textbook, Phillimore's *Pedigree Work: A Handbook for the Genealogist*. This larger work was completely revised and updated by Bower Marsh, who died shortly before publication.[64]

Also published in this period was *Wills and their Whereabouts* by Bethell Godefroy Bouwens, a much-needed reference work on the complicated area of wills and probate records.[65] At its heart was an index of all the jurisdictions for the proving of wills, administrations and inventories, and an alphabetical calendar of existing probate registries. Though expensive at 8s. 9d. (plus 3d. postage), Bouwens donated a limited supply to the Society for sale at the discounted price of 6s.

In the days before electronic communication, private publication was the only means for genealogists to publicize their work. As interest in genealogy grew, the number of privately printed, small print-run family histories proliferated. Marshall's *Guide*, published in 1903, was hopelessly out of date and a new reference work on family histories was urgently needed. Theodore Radford Thomson attempted to fill the gap, publishing *A Catalogue of British Family Histories* in 1928. This purported to cover all books written as histories of English, Scottish, Welsh and Irish families. Lesser works, such as biographies, reprints from periodicals and 'mere pedigree collections' were not included. *Thomson's*, as it became known, was soon a standard work of reference and (under different editorship) remained in print well into the 1980s.

Farrer's notion of the Society as a genealogical 'clearing house' was already partly true. The copying of parish registers accelerated between the wars, and many volunteer copyists and typists, both members and non-members came forward to share this work. At Chaucer House the process was greatly speeded up by the purchase of an 'electric typewriting-machine' which enabled several copies to be made at one time. Transcripts were being received from all over the country for deposit in the Society's library and were building into a collection of national importance. Nowhere else was it possible to consult so many registers from so many different parts of the country in one place.

A listing of this collection was urgently needed and in 1937 the Society published *A Catalogue of Parish Register Copies*.[66] Edited by Blomfield, this was in fact a 2nd edition of the publication. The first had been compiled in 1924, covering the collection at that time, as a gift from Boyd together with a donation of £100 to buy copies of parish registers.

Next the Society turned its sights on copies of registers held elsewhere and in 1939 published the *National Index of Parish Register Copies*, the joint work of Blomfield and Col. H Kendal Percy-Smith. Some 3,000 transcripts of parish registers were listed, some partial, others complete. Conservative elements in the Society were against the project, however, arguing that it took up too much staff time and the Society should confine itself to its own collections. In the event, the Pilgrim Trustees charity provided a grant of £300 to cover the preparation and printing and once launched the sales of the *National Index* – at 3s. 6d. each – soon recouped these costs.

Blomfield extolled the virtues of transcription in a letter to *The Times*. Copying original registers, she explained, was the best way of safeguarding them against damp, fire or loss. Multiple transcripts should be made and then placed in different repositories to minimize the chance of loss through some catastrophe. One transcript should be handed to the church, as this prevented the handling of the original registers which may be in a dilapidated condition. The Society's proposal for a centralized register would 'ensure that no-one undertook to transcribe a parish register of which a transcript might already exist elsewhere unknown (this has not infrequently happened in the past)'. *The Times* devoted its leading article to backing the scheme.

The book was intended to be the forerunner of a more ambitious project – a National Index of Parish Registers (NIPR) – listing all known information on the registers of every ancient parish across the country. It would include the dates of surviving original registers, particulars of copies, notes of destruction or loss of originals, together with space to register additional information. A start was made but the Second World War intervened and it would fall to another generation of genealogists to launch the work.

Returned to full health, Boyd acceded again as chairman in 1938. Addressing the AGM, he said he regarded 'the Society and its collections as a sort of laboratory for the use of genealogists, the library providing the tools'.[67] He then referred to the work being undertaken in compiling the National Index which, he felt, would be the Society's most important project going forward. The aims should be to try and get the uncopied registers transcribed in the course of time. This would best be done locally and would require the Society to work closely with societies and individuals across the country. A small subcommittee had been formed to plan this work with Boyd as chairman.

Since the early days the Society had taken to heart the directions of the Founders that funds should 'not be wasted on dinners or excursions', but Boyd clearly felt that in some of its dealings the Society was too straightlaced. Coming from the City he was used to the conviviality of dinners and parties at which much business was done. He sought to inject something of this spirit into the membership, composed as it was of retired colonels, reverends and schoolmistresses.

He arranged a sherry party, held at Chaucer House on the evening of Tuesday, 18 April 1939. In an open invitation, in the *Genealogists' Magazine*, he explained:[68]

> Some centuries ago the Court of the Drapers' Company decided to have a dinner 'as it would be a good thing for the members to know one another better.' With a similar purpose I am hoping we shall have a large gathering of members and their friends on April 18th, when there will be opportunities which do not occur in the ordinary use of the Society's rooms for getting to know fellow members.

Some two hundred members and their friends attended – primarily from the Home Counties – and the event was heralded as a 'great success'.[69] Boyd, Sherwood, Blomfield and others gave a series of two-minute talks and there was the usual exhibition of books and manuscripts from the library.

Opportunities for members to meet occurred all too infrequently and many of those attending thought that 'the mutual help that they could exchange remains an untapped source'.

This source was to remain untapped, however. Although it was intended to mark a new departure, Percival Boyd's sherry party in fact signified the ending of an era – the Society's first and last hurrah of the inter-war years. The political situation in Europe was deteriorating and the Society, like the rest of the country, would be swept up in the storm that followed.

*　*　*　*

Chapter 6

'Beyond Mere Genealogy'

T he outbreak of war brought major changes to the Society. One of the first casualties was the lecture programme: travel restrictions, fuel shortages and the imposition of the blackout led to it being cancelled almost as soon as war was declared. In an effort to retain some semblance of normality, the rooms at Chaucer House were kept open during daylight hours from Monday to Friday. But with staff being called off to war service, Saturday opening had to be restricted from 10 am to 1 pm.

Facilities for borrowing books and manuscripts from the library were extended, as partial compensation. Members were allowed to borrow up to four books at one time, rather than the two they were allowed before, and to keep them for two weeks instead of one. Some of the printed books on the prohibited list (reference works and such like) could also be borrowed over weekends. Search services covering the library and collections were still available, by this time at the rate of 10s. per day or *pro rata*. A notable loss was the Honorary Librarian, H Kendal Percy-Smith, who was recalled to serve in the Indian Army. Godefroy Bouwens stepped in to fill his place.

Paper shortages were another inconvenience. The print-run of the magazine had to be cut back and those members who were late paying their subscriptions faced the risk of not being able to obtain the relevant back numbers to which they were entitled.

As the war progressed volunteers became difficult to come by and many of the Society's projects suffered as a result. Some members who were engaged on Air Raid Precautions (ARP) work, particularly those on switchboards, used the long intervals between calls to engage in a spot of indexing. Boyd was also robbed of his typists, severely impairing progress on the marriage index.

Some thought the Society could not survive. It would be better, they argued, for the records to be placed in safety and for the Society to close down for the duration of the war. Boyd, as chairman, and Blomfield, as secretary, resisted such moves. There could be no half measures. If the Society were to continue to function its records must stay in London and take the risk of destruction. However, after the nearby Guildhall Library was hit, the Society decided to send its collection of Poll Books and a few irreplaceable manuscripts to the country for safekeeping.

Boyd felt it his duty to spur the troops and in his chairman's column in the March 1940 edition of *Genealogists' Magazine* insisted that 'the activities of the Society continue as usual'.[1] With the lighter evenings, the lecture programme was restarted, including a keynote address by Fred Emmison – by now County Archivist of Essex – at the annual general meeting on 4 July.

As the bombs began to drop concern grew for the safety of the nation's historical records. In the First World War the main risk had been close to home – the pulping of records to meet demand for paper. But it was clear that this time round the risk from air warfare would be of a totally different order. During the 'phoney' war of 1939–40 custodians of records up and down the country began to take precautions to protect their treasures by means of evacuation, dispersal and duplication.

At the Public Record Office nearly 90,000 large packages were removed containing 2,000 tonnes of parchment and paper. These were dispersed to seven different refuges, including a prison at Shepton Mallet, a poor law institution at Market Harborough, Belvoir Castle, and several private houses. Some 30,000 feet of records were housed in London in an unfinished Tube line. A policy of dispersal was adopted as an additional measure of security, with certain classes of complementary records being divided so they were not all stored in the same place. Yet every record remained available for official use, and from November 1939 onwards the Search Room was open, although for genealogists the main offering was a monotonous diet of census returns.

Having cleared the public records, it was possible to use the safer parts of the building to shelter other archives such as those of the Archbishop of Canterbury from Lambeth, and of certain City companies. Many semi-public and private records were also evacuated.

Such precautions were not in vain. When air raids started Britain's repositories – generally housed in large buildings in the middle of major cities – found themselves in the frontline against enemy bombing. Night after night at the PRO trained staff dealt with incendiaries, twenty-three of which fell on the building in a single raid in 1941. In the East End and cities such as Birmingham, Coventry and Liverpool many churches were hit, in some cases leading to the loss or damage to parish registers. The Baedeker raids spread the bombing to the ancient cities where archives had been accumulating for many centuries. In April and May 1942 Exeter was attacked. The cathedral, city and county authorities had taken what precautions they could, including the evacuation of 25 tons of books and records but large collections remained. The Luftwaffe's bombs found the Probate Registry, the contents of which were entirely destroyed, while episcopal records stored in the Chapel of St James were scattered and damaged.

The Battle of Britain tested the precautions to the utmost, but there was no major case of evacuated records being destroyed. Nevertheless, some records suffered severely from the conditions in which they had been housed.

Underground cellars were often damp and the blocking of chimneys and windows caused mildew. One of the main causes of damage through bombing was from the breaking of mains and sewers. When the Chancery Lane Safe Deposit was flooded with sewage the solid concrete floors prevented the flood water from dispersing and many valuable records were damaged as a result.

Fire was another risk which caused particular problems for records often kept on metal shelves or in metal containers. In one City strongroom parchments lying on the red-hot metal curled into fantastic shapes and numerous seals melted, soaking the deeds to which they were attached and leaving the parchment transparent and brittle. The shortcomings in normal methods of storage were all noted and incorporated into guidance by the British Records Association (BRA).

In the days after Dunkirk the risk of invasion was real. As part of counter-preparations the country was subdivided into regions, each under the responsibility of a Regional Commissioner who was charged, among other things, with control of rescue and salvage. The BRA, together with the Historical Manuscripts Commission (HMC), provided the Commissioners with lists of important archives needing protection in an emergency. Fortunately these lists were never needed, but after the war they became the basis for the National Register of British Archives under the aegis of the HMC.

The Society pre-war work in copying parish registers had been widely applauded but it was recognized that such activities were of interest to a wider circle than just genealogists. As the project progressed the internal committee set up by Boyd in 1937 had been expanded to include other bodies, and become known as the Committee for Micro-filming Parish Registers. It was chaired by Charles Bigham, Viscount Mersey – who would later become the Society's President – and had the Archbishops of Canterbury and York as patrons.

It had been intended to formalize the Committee's work by forming an association to cover all aspects of the preservation, duplication and printing of parish registers. As well as the SoG, the association would have representation from the various parish register and record societies. The war intervened before the association could be formed and the general opinion was that this was not a propitious time to launch a new enterprise. Meanwhile, parish registers might be destroyed by enemy action without any copy having been made.

Although the more conservative element felt it was a diversion from the Society's original purpose, the executive saw that urgent action was needed and took the decision to press ahead with micro-filming on its own behalf. Office space and other facilities were found at Chaucer House, mostly on a voluntary basis.

Up to September 1940 the photography was done at a studio in London, and the registers brought there could be safely removed the same day. Where this was not possible arrangements were made for them to be housed safely overnight at the National Central Library. But by the height of the Blitz it was no longer expedient to continue micro-filming in London. Local centres were set up instead, within local, diocesan and county record offices, the registers being collected there and an operator sent to work on the spot. Some churches allowed the work to be done in their own vestries and even collected the registers of neighbouring parishes to be processed at the same time. Following a further grant from the Pilgrim Trust, the Committee was able to arrange for the attendance of an operator and their apparatus anywhere in England provided that at least 5,000 pages could be made available at each chosen centre.

The apparatus itself was based around the Graflex camera mounted on an adjustable stand. Each machine was fitted with a magazine able to take 100 feet of film, which was sufficient to photograph about 1,600 pages. The time of each exposure was automatically controlled by a foot pedal, which operated powerful lamps at each side of the stand for the period of the exposure. Two pages of a normal size register measured a little over an inch on the final film. The camera had a long depth of focus, so that even for very thick books no adjustment was required to keep the whole page in focus. Between two and three hundred pages could be photographed per hour provided the register was in a sound condition. Volumes in a poor state of repair were excluded from the scheme so that they were not damaged further by handling.

The Society lost a number of key personalities around this period. Lord Farrer, the third President, died in April 1940. He had maintained a keen interest in the Society's affairs, frequently attending committee meetings where he brought a sound knowledge of business, being a director of several railway companies. Also in 1940 came the death of William Bradbrooke, a surgeon and one of the Founder Fellows, at the age of 81. Most tragic of all was the loss of Lord Stamp, Farrer's replacement as President, who was killed in an air raid together with his wife and eldest son in April 1941.

Towards the end of the war conditions eased somewhat. With the worst of the bombing over people felt able to travel more and visits to the Society's rooms increased even beyond pre-war levels. In 1944 there were over 2,000 visits by members and a further 3,000 by non-members. Many of the enquiries came from American and Dominion servicemen stationed in Britain.

Nevertheless, the conditions at Chaucer House remained spartan. The building could only be heated for a few hours during the morning and on winter days temperatures were near freezing. Staff shortages were also a lingering problem. Ministry of Labour regulations prohibited anyone between the ages of 18 and 50 being employed in unscheduled occupations, forcing the Society to restrict opening hours.

Although the threat from enemy bombing receded, the country's records were not yet safe. With the Battle of the Atlantic restricting paper supplies, demand for waste paper grew and the Ministry of Supply stepped up its paper salvage efforts significantly. Large-scale 'paper drives' were organized around the country and, concerned that important records could get caught up in the paper sweep, the BRA secured the Ministry's permission to appoint referees to watch over what was collected. Ethel Stokes, Secretary of the BRA's Records Preservation Section, eventually organized some 700 local helpers, many of whom were already very familiar with their districts. She issued regular memoranda to keep them informed of developments as one class or another of the country's archives were marked down for destruction. Various Quarter Sessions records, parish registers, rate books and other records were saved as a result of these special rules being applied.

*   *   *   *

With the war over, the genealogical community attempted to return to where it had left off. But the energy of the pre-war years had dissipated. Percival Boyd continued to suffer ill-health and in 1948 stepped down from the executive committee for the final time. George Sherwood, though still in frequent attendance at the Society, was into his eighties. Neither could muster the drive they once had and the great indexing projects ground to a halt. Work on the Great Card Index had effectively stopped in 1938 and although Boyd continued to work on his marriage and other indexes progress was nothing like the previous rate. Paper shortages persisted for several years, curtailing the publication of books and other volumes including updated editions of the *Genealogists' Handbook*.

Meanwhile, the institutional landscape was undergoing significant change. Buoyed in part by post-war patriotism, a number of new organizations came onto the scene that would extend the study and scope of history in various directions. The Society could no longer regard itself as the sole guardian of genealogical interests.

One area of evolution was in heraldry. In 1947, whilst still a student at Oxford, John Brooke-Little founded the Society of Heraldic Antiquities. This aimed to do for heraldry what the SoG had done for genealogy; to extend interest among the general public, especially the young. Its focus was on heraldry, genealogy, precedence and related disciplines. The purpose, Brooke-Little explained, was 'to bring together in one Society all those who are interested whatever their age or experience'.[2] It would also 'try in some measure to make up for the deplorable lack of cheap, simple books on these subjects'. In 1950 the name was changed to the Heraldry Society, and in 1956 it incorporated and later became a registered charity. Brooke-Little entered the College of Arms and rose to become Clarenceux King of Arms, England's second highest heraldic office. He remained as chairman of the Heraldry Society until 1997 and then served as president until his death in 2006.

Local history was also experiencing a growth in popularity. There were many organizations involved in local history studies, ranging from scholarly projects, such as the *Victoria County History*, to national bodies, such as the Society of Antiquaries, through to local historical, archaeological and record societies. With Fred Emmison as their chief evangelist, George Fowler's ideas on county record offices were taking root with new services being formed across the country. The National Council of Social Service became interested in the issue. This was a government body charged with supporting personal and family life, and had instituted the creation of Citizens' Advice Bureaux during the early days of the war. It saw the study of local history as an activity to be encouraged but if it were to be made more accessible to the amateur cooperation between these various bodies needed to be improved.

In September 1947 the Council convened a conference, inviting representatives from historical societies and bodies, both national and local, from across England and Wales. As a result, a Central Local History Committee was elected comprising fifteen representatives, both expert and amateur. Its terms of reference were 'to assist in the development of the study of local history and to cooperate with other interested organisations in the achievement of its purpose'.[3] In December 1948 a second conference was called at which it was resolved to replace the provisional organization by a Standing Conference for Local History.

The Conference drew its membership from historians and historical societies all over the country, more than one hundred such bodies being represented at the 1949 annual meeting, including the Society of Genealogists. Rather than creating yet another organization for the study of local history, the object was to provide 'a parliament' at which existing bodies, societies and individuals could meet and discuss common problems. It aimed to assist and stimulate those already working in the field, while also encouraging others new to the subject. Many years later this model would prove useful in the genealogical world as well.

Several counties already had a local history committee or society which served as a liaison point between the various archaeological and record societies in the area, as well as a meeting ground for individual historians. This helped avoid overlap and duplication and encouraged cooperation on projects of mutual interest. The Conference set about replicating this approach across the country, aiming to stimulate the formation of such committees in every county. In 1948 seven committees had been set up, while a year later this had increased to thirteen.

Besides all local historical, archaeological and record societies, the Conference sought to ensure that education authorities, university extra-mural departments, and workers' education associations were represented, as well as Women's Institutes, museums and libraries. Arrangements varied from county to county, though sponsorship was generally provided by a county council or local education authority. Financial resources were never a major consideration, however, since most of the work was voluntary. The Conference issued a series of pamphlets offering advice on how to get started.

Within each area, a panel of experts would be established early on to help plan the practical work and research to be carried out by small groups in towns and villages. This was a democratic movement; it sought to reach out to ordinary men and women without any historical training, who were curious about the past history of their parish or neighbourhood but lacked the knowledge on how to find out more. People responded enthusiastically, through projects such as village exhibitions (often organized with the help of the Women's Institute), the recording of local dialects, and surveys of field and place names.

Genealogists were quick to recognize the importance of these developments. Writing in 1950, Leslie Dow encouraged members of the Society to work closely with their local committees.[4] Two areas, in particular, were worthy of attention, he advised: the transcription of parish registers and the collection of wills and deeds, which might often turn up at local level, for instance with landowners or solicitors. Dow's suggestions lacked any official endorsement, however, and the Society appears to have preferred to keep the Conference at arm's length. Such attitudes would come to characterize its dealings with many outside bodies in the years ahead.

In 1961 the Conference adopted the quarterly journal *The Amateur Historian* as its official organ, the journal having been started nine years previously by the documentary film-maker Terrick FitzHugh. The title was changed to *The Local Historian* in 1968. The Standing Conference itself was reconstituted in 1982 as the British Association for Local History, and today most local history societies are members.

Another new institutional arrival came from north of the border. Scottish genealogy, with its reliance on the clan system and separate legal structure, has always been a distinct area of study. The Society of Genealogists had addressed this to a certain extent, through lectures and within its publications, but in general tended to confine its interests to England and Wales. Sidney Cramer, a Dundee genealogist, became frustrated with the difficulties of making contact with others with Scottish interests. Cramer was hardly of sound Scottish stock himself: he came from a Jewish family of Russian and Lithuanian extraction, and his father was naturalized as a British citizen only in 1909. Nevertheless, he resolved to form a society, similar to the Society of Genealogists, possessing its own specialized library.

Cramer circulated some 500 newspapers within the English-speaking world seeking fellow genealogists with Scottish roots, from whom he obtained many interesting replies. Letters also appeared in the *Edinburgh Evening News*. At a meeting in Edinburgh on Saturday, 30 May 1953 the Scottish Genealogy Society was formed, with the objectives 'to promote research into Scottish family history and to advance and encourage the collection, exchange and publication of material relating to Scottish genealogy and family history'.[5]

The founding members began to collect printed books, manuscripts and pedigrees which built into an important library of Scottish genealogical material. They also started to collect microfilm and microfiche of old parish registers and census returns. A quarterly magazine, *The Scottish Genealogist*, was launched in 1954, first in typescript but soon afterwards in print. Other works have occasionally been published, such as the *Perthshire Hearth Tax* of the 1690s, *The Naming and Numbering of Scottish Regiments of Foot, Cavalry and Militia* and *A Dictionary of Emigrant Scots*. The Society was a pioneer in the recording and publishing of monumental inscriptions, work that continues through to the present day.

*   *   *   *

At Chaucer House, steady expansion of the library, even through the war years, had taken up all available space. The collections were regularly combed to weed out books that were obsolete or of little value, but this did little to ease the pressure. In any case, the lease was due to expire in 1953 and was unlikely to be renewed. If the Society were to continue to grow it would once again require a new home.

A hunt for new premises started according to an exacting specification. The building should be for the exclusive use of the Society, with room for expansion and capable of being reinforced to support the huge weight of filing cabinets and shelving. In addition, there should be facilities for flexible opening hours and proximity to good transport links.

With time on the lease ticking away, the Committee started to make enquiries in the late 1940s. But the property market in post-war London was hardly conducive to a move. The Society could not afford to buy and even the acquisition of a lease required the payment of a substantial premium for which it did not have the necessary capital.

Around 1951 Colonel and Mrs Hopkinson, both members of the executive committee, identified a suitable property in South Kensington, at 37 Harrington Gardens. It was an elegant Victorian house built in the early 1880s for the Vaughan-Morgan family, two of whom had lived there until recently. It was close to the museum quarter and several Tube lines, and most importantly, was structurally strong enough to meet the Society's requirements. There was a problem, however, in that under wartime regulations – then still in place – private dwellings could not be converted for other purposes without official permission. A period of protracted negotiations followed. The relevant regulation was repealed at a critical moment and the Society was able to secure a sixteen-year lease with a promise from the landlords of an extension later on.

The house consisted of a basement and two other floors sufficient to house a library, lecture room, members' room and offices. Three other floors would be let as self-contained flats. Society member G C Couldrick, a Fellow of the Royal Institution of British Architects, oversaw the necessary alterations and repairs, while the Chairman, Cregoe Nicholson planned the move of the library and collections. All was ready by early 1954 and the move took place over four days, 17–20 March, the very day the lease at Chaucer House expired. Members mucked in to pack and then unpack books and documents, in what one member dubbed 'Operation Backbend'. In all some 370 tea chests were transported across London, with the documentary and card index collections travelling separately.

Planning and execution of the move sapped the executive committee's time and energy during this period and there was little room for other projects. In 1953 a series of lectures was held to mark Elizabeth II's Coronation, some of which were published in the *Genealogists' Magazine*. A series of record office visits was also initiated, the first one being to London County Library. The year was marked by the death of Queen Mary, consort of George V, who had been the Society's Patron since 1919.

New technology began to creep in. Having led the way in the use of micro-photography to copy documents as a means of preservation, the Society eventually decided to purchase a microfilm reader so that the films made could be used on an everyday basis. 'Every large library in the country, from the British Museum downwards, has equipped itself to use this modern invention and our Society cannot lag behind.'[6] In 1956 £200 was raised, through an appeal, to purchase a suitable microfilm reader and the nucleus of a microfilm library. The tally of films soon ran into the hundreds, and eventually the thousands, and at the Society and elsewhere microfilm became (and in many cases remains) the main means of document retrieval.

Jeremy Gibson, one of the younger members, attempted to kick-start the National Index of Parish Registers project. Since the original publication in 1937 a card index of material for another volume had been kept at the Society. Most of this consisted of accessions to the library but it was recognized that there must be many more collections, and even single transcripts, in existence elsewhere, not least because of the transcription efforts undertaken during the war. Many of the new county record offices were also accumulating sizeable collections.

Gibson set about reorganizing the card index of pending material and adding new sources to it. He aimed to reissue the two volumes already published together with all new information received in one volume, arranged alphabetically by counties instead of in a completely alphabetical order by parish. Progress was slow, however, due mainly to a lack of volunteers. Gibson vented his frustration in a letter to *Genealogists' Magazine:*[7]

There are over 1500 members of this Society, and every one of them must have made use of copies of parish registers at some time. Genealogy should not be all 'take', and the Parish Registers subcommittee is appealing to members to 'give' something other than their subscription to the Society.

Although this was 1959, the notion of 'Country' and 'Town' members persisted. For the former, Gibson asked them to check whether the register of their local parish had been copied. 'It is far easier for individual members to negotiate with their own parish priest, who is probably a personal acquaintance, than for this Society to find a parson willing to part with his original register to an unknown transcriber.' The Society would provide specially ruled paper or typing paper for the task and advise on the correct layout. For 'Town' members, Gibson requested that they help out at Harrington Gardens, checking the index for accuracy before publication. The requests fell on deaf ears and it would be nearly ten years before the published index would see the light of day.

A correspondent, Horace Stone, urged more work to be undertaken on copying monumental inscriptions and headstones, which had received much less attention than the copying of parish registers. He recounted how in Essex boys from Brentwood School had been employed copying inscriptions in the surrounding parishes. His account of the project conjures up an evocative picture of short-trousered schoolboys in austere 1950s Britain:[8]

> After permission has been obtained to copy up a burial ground, the size of the party must be considered. Ten boys will copy about 400 inscriptions in a day. It is best to have two boys working together; each pair should be given a small, but fairly defined group of stones to copy so that as soon as they have finished the particular work they can be moved on to another area, if possible in a different part of the burial ground to give them variety. All work should be recorded in an exercise book with names in block capitals. Whoever is in charge should move about among the groups to sort out difficulties. The type of boy to whom this work appeals most is not necessarily one from the most academic form. It calls for plenty of drive, a sense of improvisation and above all a little humour.

With a conspicuous lack of regard for health and safety, he noted: 'A boy is just the person to enjoy a climb to a distant part of a church tower and a little excavation is well received.'

* * * *

The first major publication of the post-war period was John Beach Whitmore's *A Genealogical Guide*.[9] Genealogists had long been seeking a replacement for

George Marshall's landmark publication *The Genealogist's Guide*, the last edition of which appeared in 1903. Much genealogical material had been published in the intervening period and needed to be indexed. As well as individual family histories, these included pedigrees printed in county histories and in the transactions of archaeological and record societies.

Whitmore was another of the gentleman genealogists: a solicitor and former Army Major, who was active in the Harleian Society as well on the SoG's executive committee. He spent much of his time collecting genealogical material about the old boys of his public school, Westminster. In the late 1920s he began a set of notes based on Marshall's *Guide* for personal use, not intending them to be published. Over time, he and others began to see the value of publication but by this point the work had progressed to such a stage that a wholesale revision of the original *Guide* was no longer practicable. He decided instead to make it a distinct publication. Whitmore's *Guide* was not confined to pedigrees – which Marshall defined as 'any descent of three generations in the male line' – nor were the variants of names grouped in the same way. The first part, covering surnames from A to E, was published in 1947, followed soon after by two further volumes.

Guide to the Public Records, published in 1949, was the sixth official guide to the PRO's holdings and took the place of Giuseppi's two volumes from the 1920s, which by this time were out of print.[10] It was a substantial revision, covering the mass of material added to the public records over the previous twenty-five years. Again the *Guide* was published in parts as each was completed.

Both titles were useful in their way but as dry as dust. The new breed of amateur family history enthusiasts was looking for something altogether more educational and accessible. Thus, a new genre of popular genealogical textbooks began to emerge, aiming to take the subject to a public eager to learn how and where to get started.

First off the press, in 1953, was Leslie Pine's *Trace Your Ancestors*. Pine adopted a surprisingly chatty style for someone who was Editor of *Burke's Peerage and Burke's Landed Gentry*. A Member of the Council of the Heraldry Society, he already had several books under his belt, including *The Story of Heraldry*, a highly readable account of the subject from the earliest times. In *Trace Your Ancestors* he began:[11]

> Perhaps you have often wished that you knew more about your ancestors, where your family came from, and how you acquired the physical and mental characteristics which stamp you out as different from your fellows. It is a natural desire, and except in societies like that of modern, urban, rushing civilization, men everywhere have always wanted to keep some records of their forbears and the roots whence they sprung.

He went on to debunk all the reasons people might have for not tracing their family history – too expensive, only for 'high and mighty folk', fear of finding skeletons in the closet, etc. – before instructing his readers on how to get started ('It is a healthy and happy hobby, and you will enjoy yourself'), and taking them on a highly informative tour of the main classes of records.

In *Genealogy for Beginners*, published in 1955, Arthur Willis followed a similar approach, describing all the main classes of records and the repositories in which they were held. But he split the book into two, the second half (entitled 'A Genealogical Adventure') being written as a sort of detective story, describing his investigations into his own family tree. He recalled how, as a boy of 9, he had spent time with his grandfather in Ealing. Over the mantelpiece in the dining room hung a low-relief portrait of an elderly gentleman modelled in wax and enclosed in a red plush mount with heavy rococo frame. Beneath it hung several miniatures. Many years later, after his aunt's death, Willis inherited the pictures together with a collection of family documents. As is often the case, this inheritance proved to be the trigger that set him off in pursuit of his family, a hunt set out in an engaging way over the following sixty pages.

Writing in the preface to the 1st edition, he explained his motivations:[12]

> In making research into my own family pedigree I felt the need of an elementary guide on how to set about the undertaking, what to look for and where, the ordinary difficulties likely to be encountered and how they might be overcome. I was doing the research in spare time, so anything which would save me time investigating methods of approach would be valuable. I could find nothing in the way of textbooks, except two or three small handbooks, which by trying to embrace too much gave little information of value to me. I have found in another sphere how much a textbook is appreciated on the very elements of a subject, untrammelled by the complications of more advanced work, and I thought that an elementary book, answering queries and difficulties that I myself had met in my genealogical expedition, might be of value to others first taking up the subject, whether as a hobby or as profession.

The *Genealogists' Magazine*'s reviewer noted, 'the book bears the stamp throughout of having been written by a man who has learned and learned successfully from actual experience'.[13] The two-part approach was never entirely successful, however, and when it appeared in revised form, as *Introducing Genealogy* in 1961, Willis's account of his own research was greatly reduced, cut up and parts used as examples throughout the book.

English Genealogy by Anthony Wagner was a more scholarly work altogether. It attempted no less than 'a survey of English genealogy as a whole', endeavouring to 'give a picture of what is known and might be known of the ancestry of people of English stock'.[14] Wagner, a herald at the College of Arms, sought to place genealogy in a social and historical context, explaining its development and its implications. Written from a herald's point of view, the book is weighted towards the medieval or at least pre-Commonwealth period, when heralds were the leading authorities, as well as towards upper class families in general. Wagner lacked the common touch and the issues in documenting the labouring classes are little discussed. Nevertheless, *English Genealogy* was the first serious treatise on the contribution of genealogy to our understanding of history since the days of Horace Round, and in embracing social history broke new ground; it did much to enhance Wagner's reputation.

Another concern for newcomers was how to organize and present their information. In 1936, George Swinton, a former Lord Lyon King of Arms, had advocated a system of purpose-designed books for recording family information. Such books would be expandable in either direction – backwards as new information came to light and forwards as new generations were added – and would be preferable to notes on loose sheets of paper. In 1946 the publishers Feather Books Ltd actually produced such a volume, marketed as *The Family Book*. Running to sixty-four pages and priced at 7s. 6d., it was for keeping 'a record of the family, by the family, for the family' and was intended to replace the ponderous family Bible of Victorian times. Such systems were largely cosmetic and unlikely to satisfy the demands of serious genealogists.

Gerald Hamilton-Edwards again raised the issue in 1948, noting that there was no universally accepted way of recording genealogical data. He drew attention to a booklet entitled *How to Take, Keep and Use Notes*, by Dr J E Holmstrom, which dealt 'with the marshalling of information in a more general way'.[15] Hamilton-Edwards suggested using a series of record cards, some 5' × 3' and others 8' × 5'. The former would be used 'for small details, such as extracts from parish registers and other brief references, and the latter for longer material, such as extracts from wills and cumulative information about individuals from various sources'. He recommended using a large card for each individual, with the top-half given over to standard details of birth, marriage, death, etc., and the lower-half used to record additional information about the subject's life and career.

Hamilton-Edwards also discussed problems relating to classifying information, drawing up family trees (pedigrees), and copying documents where new photographic processes were coming into their own. Another system advocated at the time, named after the Danish genealogist Vilhelm Marstrand, relied on family unit sheets similar to those used by Boyd in his later indexes. In the event, it would be many years before suitable conventions and classification systems were agreed, and well into the computer age before the practical problems were fully solved.

One by one the Society's pioneers were fading away. Kathleen Blomfield retired at the end of 1950, after twenty years as Secretary. In all that time she only missed one executive committee meeting and her contribution to the Society had been enormous. In addition to the ordinary secretarial duties, she had overseen the removal from Bloomsbury Square to Chaucer House in 1933, been a key driver behind the Committee for Micro-filming Parish Registers, and had assisted with all the major pre-war publishing projects. She would be a hard act to follow. The executive committee presented her with a cheque in recognition of her long and valuable service and Blomfield settled down into what turned out to be a long retirement. She remained a frequent visitor to and volunteer for the Society, which later recognized her with an honorary fellowship. She died in November 1989, aged 95.

Percival Boyd passed away in April 1955 after years of poor health. His thirty-three years with the Society represented one of the most remarkable contributions to genealogy in Britain, before or since. His great Marriage Index was a work of outstanding importance, while his index of London burials and other materials were also substantial contributions. He continued working until the end and shortly before his death presented the Society with 300 volumes of pedigrees of his *Citizens of London*. As well as his industry, people remembered his genial nature and his ever ready willingness to help. As his friend William H Challen, noted: 'He was always intensely and lucidly interested in any problem', and had a great 'generosity in supplying information'.

Of the original founders, Charles Bernau and Richard Holsworthy had long since bowed out. George Sherwood, by this time the Society's Grand Old Man, soldiered on. As he approached his ninetieth year he was unable to visit Harrington Gardens as often as he once did, but remained a vice-president and through his second wife, Ethel, kept in close contact with the organization he had founded nearly fifty years before. His death in February 1958 severed the Society's last tie to its Edwardian founders. The torch passed to the next generation of genealogists who were to inject new energy not only into the Society but family history in general.

* * * *

Sherwood's last months at the Society coincided with the recruitment of an 18 year old who worked first as a research assistant and then for six months as librarian. Anthony Camp had been transfixed by genealogy since childhood and as a boy had 'collected the pedigrees of everybody and everything'.[16] He 'ransacked the local library' and 'extracted everything that might one day be put in a pedigree, covering the floor with enormous tables of the Royal Family written on the backs of National Savings posters'.

Such a mind was bound to make a major contribution to British genealogy, and so it was to turn out. Having graduated in history from London University, Camp returned to the Society becoming Director of Research, and eventually

Director. He would do for family history in the second half of the century what Sherwood had started during the first: help make it universally accessible and relevant.

Further impetus in this direction came from Cambridge. In 1950 a Heraldic Society was founded at the University but some of the members felt it should cover genealogy as well. At the beginning of the 1954 academic year a group of young genealogists – Malcolm Pinhorn (of Fitzwilliam College), Peter Spufford (Jesus) and Don Steel (Peterhouse) – formed a separate Cambridge University Society of Genealogists. Earl Mountbatten of Burma agreed to become its president and the Society of Genealogists' chairman, Cregoe Nicholson, one of its vice-presidents. It became affiliated to the SoG, the first organization to do so. Eventually, in 1957, the two university societies merged, the new organization adopting the name of Cambridge University Heraldic and Genealogical Society.

These three young turks – Pinhorn, Spufford and Steel – soon became active within the SoG and made a major impression on its affairs. Indeed, Don Steel had joined in 1948, at the tender age of 13. By the early 1960s, Pinhorn was chairman and Spufford was editor of the *Magazine*, while Steel took up Jeremy Gibson's work on the National Index. In 1963 Steel became the youngest Fellow, beating Gibson by a short margin.

One of Steel's first projects was to compile a list of members' interests as part of the Society's first list of members. Writing from his home in Morden, he circulated all of the 2,000 members with a form asking them to list the names and localities of families and districts in which they were interested, and any special interests such as 'European genealogy, the Army, newspapers, etc.' He also asked whether they were willing to help out with transcription and indexing. When published this was the first index of genealogical interests since Bernau's *International Genealogical Directory*, and the first ever to present an exclusively British listing.

The appointment of Lord Mountbatten as President of the SoG was another valuable development. Unusually for someone of such high birth, Mountbatten had a genuine interest in genealogy and, with illustrious connections to virtually all of the royal houses of Europe, had plenty to keep him busy. In his acceptance speech at the Society in 1957, he recounted how he turned to genealogy as a relaxation during his time in India and would work on it until the early hours. As often, his interest had been spurred originally by questions from his children, who pressed him to explain the various relations they visited in Germany and Sweden during the 1930s. His mother, the Marchioness of Milford Haven (who was born in 1863) was able to recall from memory some 1,500 names which Mountbatten then started to arrange into families. His eventual pedigree, dating back to the eleventh century, ran to thirty-one generations in the female line. Mountbatten contributed generously to Society appeals and also used his influence in various campaigns on fees and access to records. The Society benefited enormously from the relationship which lasted until shortly before his untimely death in 1979.

The Society thus approached its Jubilee Year of 1961 with new-found confidence. A number of special events were organized, including a sherry and cocktail party at Harrington Gardens on 8 May, the nearest convenient day to the actual Jubilee (based on the date of incorporation, 11 May 1911). A special issue of the *Magazine* was published in June including articles on the history of the Society and its current collections and projects, and in July a Jubilee Exhibition was held at Westminster Abbey. A new edition of *Wills and their Whereabouts* was also published, revised and updated by Anthony Camp.

The centrepiece of the celebrations was a Jubilee Lecture given by Sir Anthony Wagner, who by this time was Garter King of Arms. Wagner used 'Genealogy and the Common Man' to review the status of British genealogy at the middle of the twentieth century and set out what he saw as its path for future development.[17] A new edition of *The Complete Peerage* had recently been published. The fact that Wagner opened his lecture by welcoming this – an important work but hardly an everyday reference for most family historians – as 'the greatest genealogical event of our generation', suggested he was hardly in touch with 'the Common Man'. Nevertheless, he showed an astute awareness that genealogy was approaching a threshold.

Genealogists, he reminded his audience, had been called 'fools with long memories'. The reason for this scepticism, he believed, was 'a generalised reaction against the status-hunger, the passionate interest in social niceties, so easily turning to snobbery, long prevalent in England and much discussed at the present time'. It was not true, he insisted, that genealogy was only interested in the well-off or the upper classes:

> In England we have a wonderful abundance of records whereby the pedigrees of the poorest families can often be traced back for three or four centuries and sometimes much further still, while the technique of such research has been pursued and steadily improved for more than two centuries.

The information available is necessarily limited and 'the ancestor who emerges from the records as an individual is sadly rare in most times, places and stations'. Nevertheless, the information was there and both family and social historians had much to learn from it. 'The frontier region between genealogy and social history is a dangerous and difficult terrain, but I do not doubt that if the resources for its full exploration could be marshalled, results of the greatest importance to genealogists and historians alike would be forthcoming.'

What Wagner had in mind was for 'a comprehensive historical survey of English surnames'. Studying surnames, he argued, would tell us much about Britain's social development. What starts out as one name may diverge into different forms, not only in different families, but in different branches of one family. Conversely, names originally different may become assimilated into one form. Therefore, it is impossible to know the original form (and therefore the etymology) of a family name till it has been traced back to its earliest form by tracing the history of a family. Such a mapping of surname distribution and history would aid both family historians in the study of their own families, and social and local historians in their wider interests.

Wagner accepted this would be a major undertaking, but it was comparable, he argued, to existing programmes, such as the *Victoria County History* and the work of the English Place Names Society. As well as public and private benefactors, he thought important contributions might be made by kindred societies, similar to the Clan Societies of Scotland or the Family Associations of the United States, which brought together all those with interests in a particular name. Wagner also publicized the scheme shortly after in an article in the *Sunday Times*.

Prior to the lecture, Wagner had already discussed these ideas with the Marc Fitch Fund, of which he was a trustee. Marc Fitch was a successful businessman with a passion for all things historical. Soon after the war he had used some of his wealth to set up a charitable fund and from the 1950s onwards this became an important benefactor for family and local history projects. He was a keen supporter of the British Record Society, as well as editor of a series of BRS volumes on London probate records. His Fund made grants for research and towards the cost of publications on archaeology, history, historical geography, genealogy, heraldry and surnames, to the benefit of many hundreds of students and scholars.

Though the trustees had decided in 1960 to endow research into the history of English surnames, it took some time to find the right home for the work. Eventually, in 1965, a centre was established within the Department of English Local History at Leicester University under the leadership of Professor William G Hoskins. The Fund's support enabled the Department to appoint Richard McKinley as the Marc Fitch Reader in the History of English Surnames.

McKinley started with a study of East Anglia – chosen as a sufficiently large, self-contained and distinctive region – and began an intensive indexing and analysis of military survey and lay subsidy rolls for Norfolk from the early sixteenth century. The results, published some four years later, drew a number of interesting conclusions. For instance, McKinley was able to show there had been a great deal of movement over fairly short distances during the later Middle Ages, producing a distribution of individual surnames in geographically concentrated groups. Alongside this, there was considerable movement over greater distances and into the county from other regions.

This work was continued into the 1970s by McKinley and others, including Hoskins's successor at Leicester, Professor Alan Everitt. It built into an important body of work which, while of limited utility to family historians studying an individual surname, did much to aid understanding of migration and patterns of family movements.

* * * *

The release of the 1861 census returns, in 1962, put the Public Record Office under further strain. By 1963 the Office was receiving over 38,000 visits a year. Of those applying for readers' tickets, nearly half stated their primary interest was genealogy or family history, with the census returns of 1841, 1851 and 1861 being the main records consulted. Over 154,000 documents were produced to enquirers in the search rooms and the authorities could see this would rise further once the First World War records began to be opened up in 1965.

Conditions in the search rooms were virtually unchanged since the days of Sherwood and Fothergill, who had testified on the issue in their evidence to the Royal Commission in 1913. Chancery Lane was a century old and not adaptable to mechanical handling. Each document had to be fetched – and returned – by hand. The increase in the number and availability of records led to delays and at times considerable overcrowding. Stella Colwell, a professional genealogist, recalled her first encounter with the PRO 'in the sticky heat of July 1965':[18]

> it was a matter of securing a seat in the Long Room in Chancery Lane (and in those days you needed to be early or you had to queue), and of trying to find your way through the maze of references . . .

Since there were no indexes, locating a family or even a known address was no small undertaking. A researcher would have to order up a box of returns, which could often involve a wait of an hour or more. Once the box arrived from the store room it was a matter of scanning the original returns for the correct enumeration district, folio and page numbers. If this proved unsuccessful, the search territory had to be expanded into neighbouring districts. This made searching the census a time-consuming and laborious process and for Colwell 'the hot sticky heat evolved into the cold sweat of panic and disillusionment'.

Something had to be done. The Ministry of Public Buildings and Works agreed to fund a new building on the Chancery Lane site, including search room accommodation for 250 readers. 'We cannot but urge too strongly that this project should be given a high degree of priority', urged the Advisory Council on Public Records.

Technology was also seen as part of the answer and by the time the 1871 census was released, in 1972, the whole census series had been withdrawn from public use and replaced by microfilm copies. Some researchers welcomed this innovation but others sorely missed not being able to consult the records directly. Colwell first used the system on a visit to the new PRO centre in Portugal Street:[19]

The room was kitted out with high, unyielding tables, on which were set strange boxes with cards containing detailed instructions and diagrams on how to operate them. Working in close contact with other researchers, gazing into a box and winding a handle, I felt much as early textile factory workers must have done, as around me genealogists and others struggled to master the system, shiftily glancing at their neighbours to see how the reels should be mounted, and valiantly trying to decipher the cards. The Census overnight became remote, clinical, and curiously inaccessible. No longer could you flit from page to page, turn them backwards and forwards for more information, and thus the personal and intimate involvement with history was lost.

The camera lacked the subtlety of the human eye, so that it was difficult to make out the nuances of pen and pencil marks that cover many returns. Inconsistencies in exposure led to some pages being either too light or too dark, making them almost illegible. And if the reels were not mounted properly the films would become scratched and quickly degrade. Nevertheless, the new system was much easier to administer for both researcher and archivist. A microfilm could be collected in the search room within ten minutes of a request being made and eventually certain films were put on open shelves, 'arranged like a row of toys in boxes'.

The Registrar General was never sympathetic to the needs or interests of family historians and indeed the 1861 returns came close to being completely destroyed. Needing to make room for the new 1961 census and concerned about the confidential nature of the information, the Registrar had planned to have the whole census burnt once the 100-year closure period expired. Christopher Chataway, MP for Lewisham North, raised the issue in the House of Commons and succeeded in getting the issue reviewed. The Registrar and the government eventually back-tracked and agreed to transfer all the returns for England and Wales to the PRO; those for Scotland had already been available for some time, right through to the census of 1891.

In 1966 a review of the laws governing the registration of births, marriages and deaths was initiated and the Society again used this as an opportunity to press its demands for improvements and wider access. First, a greater range of information needed to be recorded, especially for deaths. The death certificates then in place were widely recognized as being inadequate. Since they recorded neither the date of birth or marriage, a death certificate was unable to prove a deceased person's identity. Thus many claims to property and inheritances could never be proven. Similarly, knowing that a person died in a certain year provided no link to their marriage or birth, and these could only be found with reasonable certainty within the BMD indexes if the name was fairly uncommon.

The Society championed the view that death certificates should record the deceased's place of birth and the names of the parents, the rank, profession or occupation of the father, and the date and place of marriage with the wife's maiden name. It should also show their marital status. Wagner had placed such a system at the top of his 'wish list' for improving genealogy in Britain:[20]

> If entries which link marriage entries with the parties' baptisms, or births, baptismal or birth entries with the parents' marriage, and death or burial entries with the deceased's birth and parentage, have been feasible in France and Germany for three centuries or more, and in Australia for one, they should by now be possible in England.

Secondly, the Society urged improvements in the indexes to the registers, for which the last major revision had been in 1912 when a mother's maiden name was included in the indexes to birth.

The main target, however, was again for public access to the registers themselves. Still no information could be supplied from the registers at Somerset House without obtaining a certificate, which then cost 5s. 3d each. Echoing George Sherwood's letter of some fifty years before, the Society pointed out that fees were being applied to records that were well past the 100-year disclosure point for public records. This was in contravention of the principle that public records should be freely available after a prescribed period. This situation was no different to that of wills, which were readily available at the Principal Probate Registry, the Society argued, and it again called for the earliest registration records to be deposited at the PRO.

Revisions to the civil registration system were eventually implemented in 1969, but without any changes in the conditions under which the public could access the historic registers.

While they found it hard to gain a hearing with politicians, genealogists were also struggling to be recognized in academic circles. In 1962 the International Congress of Genealogical and Heraldic Sciences, an international gathering of societies and researchers, held its meeting in Edinburgh. In his opening address the Scottish host, Lt-Col. Robert Gayre derided the fact that universities still tended to look down on genealogy. It was not considered a serious academic discipline and was seen as the preserve of those seeking personal and social aggrandizement. 'Even if this were so', Gayre went on, 'it would not destroy its validity as a scientific discipline, and the universities have been very remiss in not having given it its due place in their fields of study. I think that I am right in saying that we have still to wait to see the day when a chair or a department of genealogy is established in a British university.'[21]

Gayre drew attention to the significance of genealogy for the new science of genetics, which was then wrestling with Crick and Watson's discovery of DNA. Whether they were studying fruit-flies or man, all geneticists were dealing essentially with genealogical problems. The fact that some people could trace their thirty-two immediate ancestors was an invaluable source of information, Gayre argued, and it was time for British universities to interest themselves in the field.

*   *   *   *

Meanwhile work on the *National Index of Parish Registers* was gathering pace. Gibson's 1959 appeal had brought in new volunteers and by July 1960 drafts had been prepared for seven counties and slips had been made for all parishes in England and known copies entered. At this point Gibson decided he wanted to focus on his work on Oxfordshire registers and passed the project over to a colleague, Colin Field. Around this time Don Steel became chairman of the Society's Parish Register Sub-Committee and agreed to take on overall editorship. He decided to broaden the scope of the project to include information on bishops' transcripts – a decision that would delay publication further but much increase its eventual value.

In 1965 the work moved into its penultimate phase. All Anglican parishes for which reliable information was lacking were circulated, together with the secretaries of every Nonconformist church founded before 1837 for which registers could not be traced. Some 600 superintendents of Methodist Circuits and nearly all parish priests of Catholic churches founded before 1837 were also contacted. J R Cunningham of the LDS church made available extensive microfilm records and Edward Milligan, archivist of the Friends' House, Euston, provided access to Quaker registers. By January 1966, the preparation of the county lists was almost complete, and work commenced on a series of general articles to accompany the work.

Some thirty years after it was first conceived, the *National Index of Parish Registers* (NIPR) was eventually published in early 1967, aided by an interest-free loan of £4,000 from the Pilgrim Trust.[22] Reviewing the first volume in *Genealogists' Magazine*, Camp hailed it as 'a landmark in English genealogy'.[23] Around 200 people had worked on the project (including Steel's mother, Alice), making it the largest cooperative undertaking in the family history field up to that time.

With deposition of registers at a local record office still not a mandatory requirement, the *Index* proved a boon to family historians. Its volumes presented for each county an alphabetical listing of the parishes, showing the dates of the original registers (including any missing years) and where they were to be found, as well as similar information for bishops' transcripts, manuscript copies and any registers covered by a composite index such as Boyd's Marriage Index. Details of Nonconformist chapels within the parish and any special features, such as overlapping ecclesiastical jurisdictions, were also presented. By looking up a relevant parish a researcher was able to identify the existence not only of Anglican registers and their location, but also those of Catholic and other churches in the same locality. Despite its value, it proved difficult to maintain the momentum of the early work and by 1980 only six of the fifteen or so planned volumes had been published.

When Marc Fitch took over Phillimore & Co. in 1969, the SoG appointed the company as its official publishers. With a professional publishing office at its service for the first time, the output of publications under the Society's moniker greatly increased, providing much-needed extra income.

Commercial publishers also targeted this field during the 1960s. Following in the footsteps of Arthur Willis, Nancie Burns's book *Family Tree: An Adventure in Genealogy* presented research as a detective story, using her own family as an example. Frank Smith – a Society member – produced *A Genealogical Gazetteer* intended as a reference work on place names and ecclesiastical jurisdictions. Leslie Pine's contribution was *The Genealogist's Encyclopedia*, which claimed to be 'a complete guide for the student seeking to trace his family history'. In a review, Camp dismissed it gruffly as 'a rambling and rather gossipy general account of many things connected with genealogy and heraldry', since it lacked the conventional structure and comprehensiveness expected of an encyclopedia.[24]

Probably the most important book of this period was *In Search of Ancestry* by Gerald Hamilton-Edwards. A key figure in the Society during the post-war years, Hamilton-Edwards was the son of a lieutenant-general in the Royal Marines and had extensive Navy ancestry. From Keble College Oxford he went to University College London to take a Diploma in librarianship in 1929. One day he overheard a chance remark from a student, who was telling another that it was possible to trace one's ancestors through the wills at Somerset House. 'I was then struck by the thought', he wrote later, 'that I knew very little of my own paternal line and that it might be rather interesting to trace it. Little did I know of the formidable task in front of me!'[25]

After the war Hamilton-Edwards returned to his home in Plymouth and combined teaching and library work with freelance journalism and writing. He also undertook work for the National Register of Archives and was a fellow of the Library Association. In 1962 he moved to Oxford where he became closely involved with university life and compiled a series of entries for the *Dictionary of National Biography*. He joined the Society in 1942, became actively involved in committee work and lecturing, and was a frequent contributor to the *Genealogists' Magazine*. After moving closer to London, his portly figure was often to be seen at Harrington Gardens, immersed in lengthy conversations of genealogical detail, usually in the Members' Room where even in the 1960s tea and cake were provided.

His *In Search of Ancestry*, published in 1966, was well received, with one reviewer claiming 'no previous book has introduced the general reader so entertainingly and comprehensively to the search for his forbears'. Hamilton-

Edwards wrote in a light, engaging style and was on firmest ground in the areas he knew well from his own research – the services, East India and Scottish sources. The extensive bibliography was an important feature of the book and widely regarded as among the best of its type. *In Search of Scottish Ancestry* (1970) and *In Search of Army Ancestry* (1978) were also a success, although his final work, *In Search of Welsh Ancestry* (1986), was less well received.

*   *   *   *

Alongside Don Steel, Cecil Humphrey-Smith was another of the new generation of British genealogists. Having had an interest from an early age, in the mid-1950s he took up postgraduate research at the London School of Hygiene and Tropical Medicine, just yards from the Society's then offices at Chaucer House, Malet Street. London University's Department of Extra-Mural Studies invited him to give a series of six talks on heraldry and genealogy and within a few years these had grown to twelve- and twenty-four-week courses at centres across London and the Southeast.

In 1957, at a historical association in Sunbury-on-Thames, Humphrey-Smith gave a lecture on 'Introducing Family History'. He encouraged his audience, many of whom were new to the field, to look beyond the bare bones of their family trees and try to build up a more complete story. Subsequently, he frequently referred to this as a 'pioneering' address and claimed it to be the first use of 'family history' as a concept distinct from 'mere pedigree work and genealogy'.[26] Humphrey-Smith began writing and broadcasting on this theme and advocating a greater focus on family history education.

Humphrey-Smith's godfather was Julian Bickersteth, an Anglican archdeacon and a Canon of Canterbury Cathedral. Bickersteth was perturbed by the disruption that was beginning to affect family life in Britain and believed there was a need for the family to be studied more at academic level. Humphrey-Smith took up these ideas and in 1961 established a charitable educational trust for the study of the history and structure of the family. It was located at Canterbury, where a new university was already planned, and for which Bickersteth was also a prime mover.

The Institute of Heraldic and Genealogical Studies (IHGS) occupied medieval properties in Canterbury's Northgate. Its charter allowed it to provide 'for training, study and research in family history, for investigating means of harnessing the results of such research to other disciplines, as well as assisting amateur and professional bodies with related interests'. Having indicated initially that the Institute 'has no intention of forming yet another document and archive repository', this is exactly what it went on to do.[27] A library was set up which grew to become an important collection, especially relating to heraldry, and a quarterly journal *Family History* was launched.

Its first project was ambitious in the extreme: to compile an index to all the parish and non-parochial registers in England and Wales from the earliest through to the beginning of civil registration in 1837. This British Vital Records Index would mean 'that any person whose ancestral records are to be found in any parish can be located in minutes'.[28] A copy of each of the registers would be made in index form, checked against the originals and any bishops' transcripts, and then collated into appropriate areas. As if this were not enough, 'incumbents' (i.e. clergy) were to be 'encouraged and assisted in forming "family associations" of descendants of families anciently connected with their parishes and these will be persuaded to help in the preservation and maintenance of the places in which their roots were nurtured'. It would be a major task, Humphrey-Smith conceded, 'but there is enough American, Commonwealth and British money being spent fruitlessly and uneconomically on English ancestry research to do this job in less than 20 years'. If all those engaged in English genealogy agreed to 'pool their resources in the Institute's work' then the index could 'be produced well within our generation'.

These proposals did not go down well at Harrington Gardens, where they were seen as nothing less than an audacious land-grab for the Society's territory. It failed to support the scheme and, as a new organization with virtually no track-record, the Institute was unable to attract much interest from elsewhere. After a year or so the British Vital Records Index was quietly dropped and Humphrey-Smith turned his attentions to family history education where, he judged, it would be easier to make an impact.

For many people taking up family history during the 1960s it was their most scholarly activity since leaving school. While there was now no shortage of books and guides, there was also a real appetite for education, at least at a vocational level. Evening classes at schools and colleges and courses offered by workers' educational associations became the main outlet for this, as well as the extra-mural (but certainly not the history) departments of several universities. From his centre at Morley College, south London, Humphrey-Smith negotiated with London University for a Certificate in Family History Studies and subsequently for a Diploma. Other courses (some residential) were offered by the School of Education of the University of Kent at Canterbury, Oxford University's Department of External Studies, and Bristol University's Extra-Mural Department.

As family historians became more experienced, many saw an opportunity to turn their hobby into a career, or at least to make some pocket money out of it, by offering to undertake searches and research for others. These represented a threat to professional genealogists who were trying to run a business and had fixed overheads to meet. Many 'amateurs' were of limited ability, the professionals argued, or lacked the breadth of experience to cope with a full range of inquiries and so attempted to learn at their clients' expense.

Faced with increasing concerns about quality of work and scales of charges, Brian Brooks, of the genealogical practice Brooks & Simpson Ltd, called a meeting of professional genealogists to consider the issue. It was decided to set up the Association of Genealogists and Record Agents (AGRA)[29] as a professional body to establish and maintain standards of conduct and research in the profession. The Association set scales of minimum fees and charges 'in order to protect the public', and maintained lists of accredited genealogists, record agents and affiliates. It also provided a voice for the profession in wider discussions relating to the use, preservation and availability of records.

Membership was for those attaining 'a suitable standard of competence . . . practical ability and experience in the professional field'. Initially members were recruited by invitation only but later membership was opened up to anyone able to show suitable case work. Eventually, in the 1980s, formal standards were set based on attaining recognized qualifications. All members were required to adhere to a mandatory code of practice. In effect, the Association was little more than another club – a closed shop even – for those at the top of the profession and did little to stem the tide of amateurs and semi-professionals looking to make cash on the side. The 'amateur versus professional' issue rumbled on throughout the 1970s and 1980s and became the focus for much debate, some of it quite vitriolic.

*   *   *   *

By the mid-1960s, the Church of Jesus Christ of Latter Day Saints (also known as the LDS church or 'Mormons') was becoming an important force behind genealogy in Britain and around the world. Christianity has always placed a strong emphasis on the family and respect for family life. But uniquely among Christian denominations, the LDS church has elevated genealogy to a point of doctrine.

Mormons believe that families will be together after death and to ensure this they are exhorted to submit family genealogical data for what is known as 'temple work'. This involves the administration for the dead of three gospel ordinances – baptism, endowment and sealing. Baptism is similar to the rite practised in many churches and in this case involves immersion. Endowment is a course of instruction in the high standards of living expected by the church, requiring candidates to obey all the laws and ordinances of the gospel. The highest ordinance is 'sealing', whereby parents and children, and husbands and wives are linked together 'in an eternal family union'.

For LDS adherents eternity is spent with the family, resulting in intense interest in genealogy to find and identify family members. As the Mormon genealogist Archibald Bennett has written:[30]

Our mission in temple work, then, is to compile an accurate and complete record of our own family group, of the families of all who are descended from us, and of the families for every marriage of every progenitor (or direct ancestor) through whom our own life came; and to see that every requisite baptism, endowment and sealing is administered for them to enable them, if worthy, to inherit the highest exhortation of the celestial kingdom. In doing this we can inherit the highest joy.

Consequently, the compiling of family history and pedigrees grew to be an important part of the Mormon faith. In 1894 the Genealogical Society of Utah (GSU) was established in the Mormon capital at Salt Lake City, by church members. From a small room with a few books, the LDS Library grew quickly and by the early 1960s was the largest genealogical library in the world, housing over 60,000 books and other volumes, an elaborate card index running to some 22 million entries, over 250,000 pedigree charts, and many thousands of rolls of microfilm. While the Society of Genealogists was deciding whether to buy its first microfilm reader, the LDS Library had 200 modern readers for visitors to use. A staff of forty full-time researchers was employed to carry out research for church members from around the world. Many of these were natives of the countries concerned and so were both proficient in the local language and had a practical knowledge of the national genealogical system.

Britain was an important base for the LDS church from a genealogical point of view. It was one of the first places the missionaries visited in the 1830s, soon after the church's foundation. They found willing converts and by 1850 there were more than 30,000 church members in this country, more than in the whole of North America. In the early days membership was seen as a ticket to emigration by the poor and unemployed, who regarded crossing the Atlantic as a pilgrimage to a promised land. Later on the emphasis shifted to building the church within Britain but disillusionment with its teachings, as well as physical persecution, stemmed the growth. Anti-Mormon sentiment reached its height with a series of riots in 1911.

In the period between the wars, the church maintained an advanced research organization in Britain, at its peak engaging a staff of twenty-six full-time and about thirty part-time employees. This research was non-profit-making, a small charge just being made to cover the searcher's time. As was the practice elsewhere, classes were offered to church members to instruct them how to go about their family research and the very exact recordkeeping the church required for submission to the temple. Typically, these might comprise two three-quarter hour lessons per week, generally on a Sunday and Thursday. Trips were organized to Somerset House, the Public Record Office and other repositories. In addition, the church promoted the gathering of monumental inscriptions from churchyards. Usually these would be typed up and a copy given to the relevant library or county record office.

After the Second World War the church wound down its British-based research organization in favour of a series of libraries – also known as family history centres – associated with the many new missions being built up and down the country. Usually housed in a room in a church-owned meeting house, these centres offered help to members and non-members alike. An initial grant could be sought from the GSU to cover equipment costs and a starter kit of reference materials. Once up and running a library had to abide by certain criteria laid down by the church: it must be free of charge to all, be non-profit-making, be run by volunteers and not used to evangelize.

The activities of the LDS church proved a major impetus to the development of family history during the post-war period, both in Britain and the United States. In Britain, the church began microfilming in Co. Durham in 1948 under the auspices of J R Cummingham. Even before the war the church was experimenting with the use of microfilm and helped establish it as the accepted method of preserving and disseminating historical records. It was reliable, cheap and fast. With good readers and high standards of filming, microfilms became practical.

One of the pioneers of this work was Frank Smith, a British-born mining engineer from Doncaster. During the war Smith took an interest in the LDS's work on monumental inscriptions and became an active member of his local group. After emigrating to America in 1953 he joined the staff of the GSU as manager of the Research Department, where one of his first acts was to step up the microfilming programme. In 1956 Smith began a long association with David Gardner, another British émigré on the GSU staff, during the course of which they produced many guides and educational materials. The most significant was the three-volume *Genealogical Research in England and Wales*, for many years the most authoritative publication available. In 1958 they published *A Basic Course in Genealogy*, followed in the early 1960s by two useful genealogical atlases of Ireland and Scotland. Gardner was also a regular chaperone for travel study groups on family history to Britain from Utah's Brigham Young University.

By 1963 the church had produced more than 250,000 rolls of 100ft film, covering most European countries. Around 36,000 rolls had been produced for the British Isles, comprising some 40 million pages. As well as many parish registers, these included: the wills and probate records from twenty-six district probate registries and Somerset House, a vast collection that took eight years to film; the 1841 and 1851 census returns (and through to 1881 for Scotland); 1.5 million records from the National Library of Wales, including the bishops' transcripts and marriage bonds; and indexes to births, marriages and deaths for both Northern Ireland and the Irish Republic.

In the late 1950s a vault was opened in the Rocky Mountains that would protect these and the many other LDS records in the event that the Cold War then raging should ever turn 'hot'. This was (and still is) used to store the master copies of all the church's records and databases.

The church's effort to expand its collections brought it into conflict with the Society of Genealogists, many of whose members were suspicious of its motives. The GSU had supported many projects over the years, including some of Percival Boyd's work, and was becoming an important benefactor of genealogical research in Britain. It bought both Boyd's and George Sherwood's collections after their deaths, which were removed to Salt Lake City for microfilming.

In 1964 the church approached the Society with a view to an exchange of information, in particular access to its parish registers collection. The executive committee agreed to allow access to some of its records but when this became known several members urged an extraordinary general meeting be held to consider the issue. When the committee rejected their request, they summoned a meeting anyway at Harrington Gardens, which the chairman, Robert Garrett, declared invalid. Eventually it was decided, to avoid controversy, to permit access to secular records only.

In August 1969, to commemorate the seventy-fifth anniversary of the Genealogical Society of Utah, the LDS organized the World Conference on Records. For the first time on a world scale, the conference brought together genealogists, archivists, demographers and technical experts on microfilming and other methods of preserving records. The theme, 'Records Protection in an Uncertain World', emphasized the need for every nation or society to preserve its own records from wear, deterioration, neglect and natural or man-made disasters, and for collaboration between bodies and experts with relevant skills.

Around one-third of the 7,000 delegates attended lectures on British genealogy, with several eminent figures of the time invited as speakers. In addition to Don Steel, who gave a lecture on Nonconformist Registers, the British contingent included Fred Emmison, Peter Spufford, and Noel Currer-Briggs. For amateur family historians new to the field the Conference was a formative experience, and when they returned home it helped energize them in the new phenomenon sweeping British genealogy: local family history societies.

* * * *

In the early 1960s, genealogy in Britain was still highly London-centric. Apart from the Scottish Genealogy Society in Edinburgh, there were no groups or societies dedicated to genealogical issues within the regions. The Society of Genealogists might have dropped 'of London' from its title early on, but in practice it was very much a metropolitan affair. Its rooms and library were based in the heart of the capital and all of its meetings were held there. The local structure foreseen by the founders – based on a network of county secretaries and local groups – had never got off the ground. Only around half a dozen county secretaries were ever appointed and the system soon became defunct. In the malaise that set in after the war no one had the energy to revive it and the executive committee was too preoccupied with its own affairs to recognize the growing need for local initiatives and actions.

Attitudes in the SoG were highly insular. Just as the Society itself had resisted cooperation with bodies such as the Institute and the LDS church, so individual members (who tended to be relatively experienced) were reluctant to entertain the idea that they had anything to gain from fellow researchers. When Steel revised and enlarged the SoG's *Register and Directory* in 1966 take-up for the 2nd edition was disappointing: of 2,000 printed less than 100 were sold.[31] An anonymous correspondent, identifying themselves only as 'MEDVEP', pondered the reasons for this in a letter to the *Magazine*:[32]

> Although many do not like to recognise the fact, the average genealogist is basically a lone wolf. He does not want to share the information he has so carefully collected and is not interested in corresponding with others on the subject. He regards with horror the writer of enquiring letters, most of which (when legible) will not be of the slightest interest and more often than not will want something for nothing, but he will take any details offered in such letters and use them to his own advantage without acknowledgement. He does not in any case have any faith in the ability or knowledge of any genealogist other than himself. He does not submit a Birth Brief to the Society, and would not dream of copying his information, let alone an outline pedigree which would give his secrets away, for deposit there. . . . Those who are willing to correspond and exchange information are certainly a minority in the Society.

'MEDVEP's identity was never revealed but it was obviously someone very well versed with the Society and its workings. That they felt able to write in such barbed tones – and that the contribution was published – says much about attitudes in the Society at the time, particularly towards newcomers.

But the characterization was incorrect: not all genealogists were 'lone wolves'. While the enthusiasts in the Society preferred to go their own way, out in the country many of the new converts to family history were looking for help and support. They needed a means to exchange information and share their very specific local interests. Faced with a vacuum at the centre, family historians up and down the land started taking matters into their own hands.

In Birmingham, Dr Stuart Kingsley Norris, a surgeon at the Birmingham and Midland Eye Hospital, came up with the idea of a local society dedicated to genealogy and heraldry. He discussed the idea with John Sharp of Birmingham City Libraries and they subsequently set up the Birmingham and Midland Society for Genealogy and Heraldry (BMSGH), with Norris as chairman and Sharp as secretary. Norris had long associations with the Birmingham and Midland Institute, a foundation promoting science, literature and art in the city, and the BMSGH became affiliated to it. A consummate operator, for the inaugural meeting in February 1963, Norris managed to get himself onto both the Midlands radio and TV news, and be interviewed on the *Today* programme on the BBC Home Service.

Among the 118 members enrolling during the first year was Fred Markwell, a headmaster from Kings Heath. Markwell's interest in family history had been sparked a few years before through a chance meeting on holiday which set him off on a quest to trace his own ancestors and those of all that bore his surname. Like most newcomers, he had no instruction or preparation and initially worked in isolation. When he heard about the BMSGH he joined straightaway and soon became its honorary secretary, a post he held for ten years. 'I know of no other intellectual pursuit', he wrote later, 'which engenders such enthusiasm, which so easily gives a sense of pride in achievement, and which makes one so long to communicate with others and share one's triumphs.'[33]

Other local groups soon followed. In the Northwest, the Manchester Genealogical Society was formed out of a nucleus associated with the Avro Whitworth aircraft company; later Lancashire was added to its name. In nearby Cheshire, Philip Carr and Bertram Merrell founded the Cheshire Family History Society, the first to use the term 'family history' as opposed to 'genealogy'. Across the Pennines, the Yorkshire Archaeological Society set up a Family History and Population Studies Section, and on the south coast the Sussex Family History Group grew rapidly. Kent, Oxford (where Jeremy Gibson became a prime mover), and Norfolk and Norwich were also early arrivals. These locally based societies found a ready audience among amateur family historians. By the early 1970s the BMSGH's membership had reached 500 and the number attending the regular meetings grew from an average of 30 to 170.

What Fred Markwell called 'the Provincial Movement' brought new energy into the family history world. Many of the local societies' recruits were new to the field. Most were from middle or working class backgrounds – in many cases not having progressed beyond secondary education – with no expectations of finding an illustrious pedigree; they just wanted the thrill of the chase and perhaps to learn a little along the way. Evening classes in genealogy and family history proved extremely popular and local education authorities and workers' educational associations struggled to meet demand. Often the tutors were relatively new to family history themselves and kept barely one step ahead of their pupils.

Eva Beech, a member of the BMSGH, ran her first course at Hanley, Stoke-on-Trent, in autumn 1973. Following publicity on local radio and in newspapers, forty-eight people enrolled, mostly beginners. 'That first year as a tutor', she wrote later, 'began one of the most challenging periods of my life.[34] All my spare time was spent in gathering information and material, in preparing lectures, and in helping students with individual problems.' Running the first course in her area was 'pioneer work', with 'no one to tell me how or what to teach. I worked every lecture out myself, basing it on my own experience in tracing ancestors and on my reading.' Beech found it a rewarding experience and enjoyed watching her pupils grow, both in confidence and companionship. She gained much practical advice from them, too, especially about practical researches.

The camaraderie engendered by local societies and evening classes acted as a counterweight to the austere and unwelcoming environment found elsewhere. Archivists and librarians of the 1960s and 1970s did not quite know what to make of the new clientele – whom they rather cruelly referred to as 'genies' – that was descending on their hallowed repositories.[35] With microfilm and microfiche not yet widely available, research often involved handling original documents and archivists were taken unawares by the demands of a myriad of sweaty fingers. Documents had to be physically retrieved from strongrooms and vaults, and users frequently required help to read old handwriting or translate Latin entries. They also expected toilets, cloakrooms and refreshment areas, which had not been catered for previously.

The research process was costly and time-consuming. In the days before computers and email, relatives and archives had to be contacted by letter. All of the main repositories were in London with little duplication of records elsewhere. At a time when many firms still operated a fixed two-week holiday period in the summer, researchers had limited time during which to visit distant archives. When they arrived there were no indexes to census returns and few to any other types of record. Photocopying was new, expensive and not widely available.

A practice that appears especially quaint, to modern eyes, was the need to visit churches to view parish registers. Incumbents varied in their attitudes to genealogists' enquiries. A few clearly regarded them as cranks who had to be tolerated, but most were cooperative and sometimes took a personal interest in their search. Pauline Litton, an early recruit to the FHS movement, recalled widely differing receptions:[36]

> There were those who left the researcher in the vestry with the registers and an open cupboard containing the church silver; those who locked the researcher in a stone-cold room, with no toilet facilities, for an unspecified length of time; those who insisted that they look at the registers themselves and supply you with the results for a fee; those who stood there while you wrote out pages of entries, then counted them and charged 3d. per entry; and finally those who installed you in their own study, with heat and light, and who provided cups of tea.

Fred Markwell had similar experiences, ranging from one vicar who charged 4 guineas for extracting eleven entries, to another who waived his fee despite an extended search across several registers.

Family history societies' most important function was providing information and guidance. They produced regular newsletters to keep members in touch with the society's and each other's activities and these eventually expanded into full-blown journals. Many were of high quality and of interest not just to local members, reflecting the new corpus of knowledge from the growing membership. As well as lists of new members, which would be scanned eagerly for kindred souls, there were articles, revealing stories, and abstracts of local and national documents. Societies began to exchange journals and from this discussion of wider collaboration and cooperation began.

The Society of Genealogists viewed these developments initially with disdain and, once it was clear they could not be ignored, with suspicion. One response was for the Society to set up local groups of its own. Official backing for these was only ever lukewarm and the handful of groups that were formed were short-lived. In 1971, a 'Northern Group' was created for members with north of England interests – but held its monthly meetings in London. A further effort to form a Midland Group never got off the ground.

Jeremy Gibson was initially antagonistic to the idea of local groups, either within the Society or outside. He urged members to 'join their local historical societies, and work for the formation of genealogical sub-committees through those, instead of suggesting setting up quite independent local groups'.[37] Such societies tended to ignore genealogy because there were not enough genealogists as members and if they wished to change this they needed to get involved. Such an approach was far preferable to 'yet more specialist splinter groups', Gibson argued.

Another member, Michael Faraday, doubted 'the implication that people who live near one another have genealogical and archival interests in common and can effectively contribute to the genealogy of that district'.[38] Since people now moved around more, few lived in counties where their ancestors were located, Faraday argued. He urged, instead, the creation of local interest groups composed of any Society members with interests in a particular area and not necessarily based there. He added, rather pompously, 'it takes so many years to become even imperfectly familiar with the records and families of one county that I doubt most people's ability to contribute to the genealogy of another county. I doubt even more their wisdom in attempting to dissipate thus their energies.'

Faraday, of course, had completely missed the point. It was *because* people often lived far away that they needed a link to a locality they knew little about. And as for imperfect knowledge, many of those leading family history societies were already highly experienced researchers (albeit amateur) and only too ready to share their expertise with others.

Steel was supportive of local groups and critical of the SoG's failure to embrace them. Gibson and Faraday's arguments against this, he wrote to the

Magazine, cancelled each other out. Most genealogists were unlikely to join local history societies, as Gibson suggested, because they were not interested primarily in their 'home' areas; similarly, Faraday's suggestion for local interest groups would not work because members with relevant interests were too dispersed.

Moving to the heart of his argument, he went on:[39]

> With a membership of over three thousand, most of whom live out of easy reach of London, the Society is, in my view, in danger of degenerating into a subscription library. I feel that its character as a 'society' can be maintained only by the development of strong local groups, which will organize their own meetings, develop their own *esprit de corps*, give beginners the help they are so often crying out for, and sponsor local transcription and indexing work.

Steel felt 'the real future of the Society' lay in such a structure. It would offer existing members more while opening up the opportunity to campaign locally for new members. He ended with a warning:

> Such groups are likely to be formed in any case; we already have enterprising societies such as the Birmingham and Midland Society for Genealogy and Heraldry, and the Manchester Genealogical Society. I would much prefer them to be the supports of a strong central society.

It was already too late. The new societies were being built from the ground up and were developing their own character in the process; they had no intention of being mere branches of a 'strong central society'.

Fred Markwell was becoming well known in the family history world and a source of support for the new societies springing up around the country.[40] As the 'Provincial Movement' gathered momentum, Markwell saw there were exciting possibilities for cooperation. 'Just as the genealogist, working in isolation, misses so much, so too, regional societies can be greatly stimulated by close contact one with another', he wrote.[41]

One of his correspondents was Elizabeth Simpson, magazine editor for Cheshire Family History Society's northern branch. Markwell put her in touch with other societies and Simpson suggested they exchange magazines to save the cost of each society becoming a member of the other. She began to develop a nucleus of groups with mutual arrangements to exchange publications and other information.

While some societies were only too happy to cooperate in this way, others were reluctant to enter into reciprocal arrangements. She outlined her experiences in a letter to the *Genealogists' Magazine* in 1973:[42]

> Some are important genealogical societies which actually have written into their 'Aims' that they set out to further the interests of their

members and help other bodies with related interests. Others are strictly historical societies which seem to think that history and family history are two quite divorced subjects and should never be confused – or worse, connected. I have had some terrible rebuffs, with every reason under the sun quoted as to why 'they' will not swap 'their' publication for ours. In some cases I have persevered and striven until I have won – but in others, lack of time, and availability of unlimited postage, has forced me to give up.

To add insult to injury, many of these societies never returned the sample magazine Simpson had sent.

Simpson, too, became an advocate for family history nationally. In March 1972 she wrote to the *Observer* urging its readers to trace their ancestors, and received getting on for 400 replies. She also began teaching courses in the Northwest for the Workers' Educational Association and local education authority evening classes.

She and Markwell met with other recently formed groups, including the Society of Genealogists' Northern Group, and the idea of wider collaboration began to take hold. In September 1973 this collective sponsored a full-page advertisement in the *Genealogists' Magazine* calling for readers, particularly the Society's overseas members, to join local groups based near their British ancestral homes. Markwell had negotiated a 10 per cent discount on the £20 cost of the advertisement, so that it cost each of the nine societies just £2; nevertheless, such was the uncertainty at the time that some had to be convinced of the wisdom of the expense. While within the SoG, even the decision to run the advertisement drew the ire of some members.

As the winter of 1973 approached Simpson busied herself with arrangements for the combined group of nine societies to attend Heritage '74, a major history event being planned for the following year. As part of these preparations a meeting of the group was held in Birmingham in April 1974. While they tried to focus on the matter in hand, during the lunch and coffee breaks conversation kept drifting back to the opportunities for wider cooperation and the possibilities that lay ahead. Several of those present had engaged in similar discussions a few weeks before at a conference in Canterbury organized by the Institute.

Eventually, Steel decided the issue could be ducked no longer. He convened a meeting, again in Birmingham, to discuss a formal structure for collaboration between local groups. Markwell was keen that the BMSGH should not be seen as leading or sponsoring these activities and so was reluctant for the meeting to be held at the Birmingham and Midland Institute. Through Dr Marie Rowlands, of the Catholic Records Society, Steel arranged rooms at Birmingham's Newman College instead.

Around thirty persons representing some twenty groups and societies attended the meeting, held on 8 June 1974. These included, among others, Fred Markwell, Don Steel, Cecil Humphrey-Smith, and two enthusiastic newcomers: Royston Gambier of Kent FHS and John Rayment of Essex FHS. Lt-Col. Iain Swinnerton, chairman of the BMSGH, agreed to chair. However the SoG, sceptical and suspicious of where matters might lead, declined to send a representative. Simpson was also absent as she was on a family holiday in Ireland.

After considering draft proposals, a decision was taken to set up a new body with the provisional title: the National Federation of Family Historical, Genealogical and Heraldic Societies. Its aims were 'to co-ordinate and assist the work of societies or other bodies interested in family history, genealogy and heraldry; and to foster mutual co-operation and collaborative projects to help researchers'. It also aimed to represent the interests of its member societies, and family historians generally, especially in the preservation and availability of archival documents. Six of those present had been empowered to federate their societies immediately; others indicated their intention to do so once they had reported back to their committees.

A second meeting was held at the Albion Hotel, Brighton, in early August, on the fringes of Heritage '74. At this meeting, on the suggestion of Royston Gambier, the rather more concise title of Federation of Family History Societies (FFHS) was formally adopted.

Markwell confessed later that he had gone to the Newman College meeting with an open mind, not knowing what would result, if anything. But he left greatly inspired by what he felt was a historic occasion. His only regret was that the vital step of federation had not been made earlier.

With the formation of the FFHS the final piece of the jigsaw was in place. By 1974 the family history landscape looked very different to that that had existed just a decade before. For fifty years, since its foundation in 1911, the Society of Genealogists had been the pre-eminent force in genealogy in Britain. In a little over ten years, since the Society's Jubilee in 1961, all this had changed. The setting up of the Institute of Heraldic and Genealogical Studies had brought a new emphasis on education and professionalism; local family history societies and their eventual coming together in the Federation of Family History Societies created a powerful new force for family history at local level; and the arrival of the LDS church, with its virtually limitless resources, brought an important new sponsor for genealogical projects.

These four bodies – the Society, the Institute, the Federation, and the LDS church – were to shape family history in Britain for the next twenty-five years. For the Society, though, it meant accepting that its power and influence had been eclipsed, an idea with which many of its members would have difficulty coming to terms.

*   *   *   *

Chapter 7

Back to our Roots

Elizabeth Simpson arrived home from holiday to find a box of notepaper on her doorstep. Being highly appreciative of her organizational skills thus far, her 'friends' in the societies group had nominated her to become secretary of the new body. She used the notepaper to give notice of the Brighton meeting and after the successful outcome there set about building the Federation as a nationwide community.

Simpson promoted her exchange system for society journals and using the material she gleaned began writing the FFHS's own newsletter which was circulated to all members. This eventually acquired the title *Family History News and Digest*, a publication that continues to be produced to the present day. She worked tirelessly, writing articles for magazines, sending letters to newspapers and even being interviewed on the *Jimmy Young Show* on Radio 2. A flood of letters came back and when these became too much for her and her Cheshire helpers to deal with she packaged them up to correspondents in societies around the country. She hoped this would provide the basis for new societies in places where were none yet, or add to the numbers of small groups already formed.

The strategy worked. From the initial dozen or so societies at the time the Federation was set up, numbers grew steadily. The new people coming into the movement brought a wealth of experience. The groups so formed sought publicity and set themselves tasks to do, and thus projects were born. Simpson's energies did not stop at Britain's shores; she also kept a lookout for relevant English-speaking societies overseas and recruited them as well.

While Simpson did most of the work, she was aided by a dedicated team that included Iain Swinnerton, who had accepted the post of chairman and later president, and Royston Gambier, who served as treasurer. Simpson sent Swinnerton a carbon copy of every letter she wrote; a stickler for detail, he proved adept at keeping up with this flood of material.

One of the first things the Federation felt necessary to do was to mend fences with the SoG. A secret 'liaison committee' was set up, with Simpson and Colin Chapman representing the Federation and Sir Andrew Noble and Miss M Surry representing the Society. The group meet regularly during these early days, often at Sir Andrew's flat, to identify issues of mutual interest and discuss how to overcome the distrust.

At the Federation's first AGM, held in September 1975, a constitution was passed after much internal debate. This gave the Society a privileged status among the membership, specifically the right to nominate a member to the Federation's executive committee; a similar provision was extended to the Institute. The Society accepted and Noble was nominated to the role. Eventually such overtures were enough to convince the Society that the FFHS was not a threat but an ally and the liaison group was able to disband.

A series of twice-yearly conferences was initiated to enable everyone to keep in touch. Simpson would set up a registration desk at the door of the main conference hall and personally welcome and talk to every delegate as they arrived. Many of these became regular attendees and the volunteer backbones for their respective groups all around the country.

Societies embarked on a wide range of projects, from transcribing local censuses to recording monumental inscriptions, compiling marriage indexes and noting 'strays' (people from other areas encountered in local registers and records). More experienced members found themselves in demand as tutors for courses organized by local authorities and others. This, in turn, proved a good recruiting ground for new members, helping to swell local FHS memberships even further.

By the time of the tenth anniversary, in 1984, the Federation had a membership of 130, including sixty-five county and district societies, thirty-four overseas societies, as well as a number of one-name associations and specialist societies. Every county in England was covered and some, such as Cheshire, Kent, Middlesex and Surrey, had more than one. Seven local societies had memberships of over a thousand.[1] Even by conservative estimates, total membership of societies affiliated to the Federation was at least 50,000.

*   *   *   *

Don Steel recognized the arrival of the Federation as a watershed and attempted to steer the Society into reflecting on its own future. In June 1974 – the month that the Federation came into being – he wrote an open letter to the *Genealogists' Magazine* putting forward 'some personal (and highly subjective) points for discussion'.[2]

The Society had changed beyond all recognition over the last sixty years, Steel pointed out. In the early days it consisted of a small group of friends, mostly professional genealogists, retired professional men and gentlemen of private means. But by the 1970s there were well over 3,000 members, most of whom lived outside London and were in full-time employment.

'We are no longer a genuine *Society*', Steel explained, 'because most of the members do not have contact with each other.' There were no social functions, not even an annual dinner, he complained. Repeating his claim that the Society had 'become a subscription library', he noted that even this was not readily accessible by country members, and all they really received for their subscription was the magazine. This was not good value and consequently many members resigned after just a year or two.

Many genealogists were turning to local groups, he suggested, because 'the Society is too large to provide genuine fellowship'. Again he chastized the executive for what he saw as a missed opportunity:

> instead of welcoming, inspiring and co-ordinating these initiatives the Society has tended to ignore them. As a result most are now quite independent of what should (in my view) have been the parent body.

Broadening his criticism to other fronts, he noted the Society also had no education or training activities which members would find a great service. Consequently, individuals had been left to organize courses and conferences on their own initiative. The main gathering was the annual general meeting (AGM), 'Yet in our Society every effort is made to keep this a boring empty formality'. It would be much more effective, Steel argued, to have this as part of a study day, so people had more incentive to attend and could learn something while they were there.

The Society had done little to champion the cause of genealogy in the wider world, he added, in particular by providing courses at evening classes and university extra-mural departments. As a result such classes were developing outside the Society's influence.

Steel was active in all three of these areas – local branches, conferences and courses – in a private capacity because, he said, the executive committee was just not interested. The problem was 'an attitude which sees the Society as premises in London rather than a collection of people scattered geographically, but united through interest in genealogy'. From his experience in running courses and conferences up and down the country, he noted, 'it is simply not true that genealogists are interested solely in their own families and do not want to associate with others'.

Finally, Steel observed, the library itself was becoming less comprehensive, with indexing activities discontinued and shortage of funds and space affecting new acquisitions including members' own pedigrees. This detracted from the Society's cherished role as the national genealogical library. Bigger premises were urgently needed but the escalation in property values since the issue was first raised a decade before made this all the more challenging.

As Steel intended, his comments sparked intense debate. Robert Garrett, a former chairman of the Society, responded that frequent attention had been given to the search for alternative premises. Furthermore, he did not think that:

'letters of this nature which concern the policy of a Committee should be published without giving that Committee the opportunity to reply at the same time'.[3] Patricia Riach, another executive member, thought Steel knew the problems of lack of money, staff and space more than anyone and should 'refrain from destructive criticism'. Others were more supportive, such as a new member who wrote that he found 'those using the Society's rooms are very insular and private'. Local societies were not only more welcoming, but also in a better position to have information matching the searcher's interests.

Little by little, the Society's grandees took the criticisms of Steel and others to heart and began to accede to their demands. In June 1975, alongside the AGM a one-day conference was organized at Digby Stuart College in Roehampton, thus making the meeting a more educational and social occasion. This soon became a regular fixture. By 1977 over 350 Society members and friends were attending these events – many more than ever attended the traditional AGM.

* * * *

By this time Steel was actively involved in family history education, both formal and vocational. He had moved from speaking at lectures and conferences to organizing them. One of the first was for the Society's sixtieth anniversary in 1971, when he was course director for a residential weekend conference held at Bristol University. A further course followed in January 1972, also at Bristol. The success of these events convinced Steel of the need for regular and much-expanded provision of educational courses to meet the demands of family history enthusiasts.

His interest was also at a professional level. In the late 1960s and early 1970s while working in teacher training at Berkshire College of Education, Steel collaborated with a colleague, Lawrence Taylor, in producing a booklet for local teachers, suggesting for the first time how family history could be used as a means to excite children about the past. These techniques were applied successfully in a number of Berkshire and Hampshire schools, both primary and secondary.

Describing their approach in an article in 1970, Steel and Taylor explained that teachers increasingly sought to explain history through a child's direct experience, usually through local history studies.[4] The family as a focus for the child's environment had been neglected up to now and 'it is only very recently that educationalists have begun to appreciate the possibilities of using this theme in the classroom to illustrate the course of social and political change'. However, they went on, family history has a much wider application than this:

> In laying the emphasis, not so much on the family as a social institution,
> but on the child's personal researches, we see family history primarily as

a method of teaching historical techniques and as a natural integrator of many subjects. Over the past four years, we have worked with College of Education students in investigating the possibilities of this approach.

Children were encouraged to start by writing their own autobiographies and accumulating information on their own way of life so as to be able to make comparisons with previous generations. Then they were asked to consult family members to compile family trees and gather biographical information.

By tracing as many lines as possible instead of concentrating just on the male line, most children discovered that their ancestors came from a wide variety of social and occupational backgrounds. As their knowledge about the activities of these families grew, so did their understanding of national and local events. These became not a boring and meaningless set of facts to be learned by rote, but essential equipment in understanding the vicissitudes of their ancestors.

From the building up of family trees and the writing of biographies, most children proceeded to study a particular topic in depth, which led to a diverse range of projects. Some of the older children were even enthusiastic enough to want to investigate their families further back.

To take their approach to a national audience, Taylor and Steel organized a three-day conference, Family History in Schools, held at the University of Reading in September 1970. This was followed by a book with the same title, published in 1973, explaining how teachers could use family history as a gateway to the past. The book was aimed particularly at teaching for the 9–14 age group, but they knew from experience that their methods would also work for older teenagers and adults.

Once again, a new community was growing up and at a conference in Bournemouth in March 1976 the decision was made to set up an Association of Teachers of Family History. Its objective would be to promote family history education at all levels. Although anyone could become an associate, full membership was reserved for those with recognized teaching qualifications 'or substantial experience of teaching family history'. A committee was formed with the usual cast of names in a different permutation: Cecil Humphrey-Smith as chairman, Steel as vice-chairman, Elizabeth Simpson as secretary, plus others as treasurer and editor.

In the late 1970s Steel moved to become Education Officer at BBC Bristol, a public relations role for school broadcasting. The job involved substantial travel to schools around the west of England and provided the ideal platform to evangelize about his ideas to teachers and school bodies, something he continued to do for the remainder of his professional career.

Another of the early advocates was Stella Colwell, a professional genealogist and lecturer. Her involvement in family history education convinced her of the need for a national genealogical congress, as was already commonplace in other European countries. In 1973 she raised the issue at the Society's AGM. The accounts showed a surplus of £4,000, making it the Society's most successful year ever. Colwell suggested that the funds could usefully be put towards financing a conference which, she argued, ought to be one of the duties of a body such as the SoG. Although sympathetic to the idea, the chairman, Brian Fitzgerald-Moore, replied that repaying the mortgage and maintenance of the premises was far more important. Other committee members agreed. Not for the first time, conservatism won the day. Any thoughts that such a conference could be self-financing – or even profit-generating – never entered the equation; all the committee saw was work.

Undeterred, Colwell lobbied key people to support her and on 19 September convened a meeting to discuss the idea. Among those present were Fitzgerald-Moore, Don Steel and Malcolm Pinhorn, the veteran archivist Fred Emmison, John Brooke-Little founder of the Heraldry Society, and the SoG's Anthony Camp. Pinhorn was elected chairman of what became the working committee for the first English Genealogical Congress (EGC).[5]

The Congress was to be a four-day event, from Tuesday 26 August to Saturday 30 August 1975 at St Catherine's College, Cambridge. The Master of the Rolls, Lord Denning, agreed to be Patron, and George Squibb, Norfolk Herald, acted as President. Funding for the event was provided by the Wrythe Heraldic Trust and the SoG also provided a loan.

A fairly general theme was thought to be necessary for this first event to ensure it attracted a wide cross-section of people. The theme 'Family History and Demography' was eventually chosen, subtitled: 'the contribution which genealogists can make to historical studies'. The organizing committee wrote to genealogists and academics who they thought might be interested in providing lectures and seminars and most responded positively. Speakers were booked for a wide range of topics, such as 'Census Returns, the Family Historian and Social Milieu', 'The Records of the English Ecclesiastical Courts', 'The Relevance of Heraldry in Genealogical Research' and 'Family Reconstitution – Who Gets Missed Out?'.

The family history world had never seen anything like it. Unlike the international congresses held periodically in Europe and elsewhere, this event was aimed at the layman – the amateur – rather than the professional genealogist. As well as a full lecture programme, there were excursions to Norfolk, Essex and the city of Cambridge; a civic reception at the Cambridge Guildhall; a cocktail party hosted by the FFHS; and a banquet at which the main speaker was Michael Maclagan, Portcullis Pursuivant. Two exhibitions were mounted, one at the Fitzwilliam Museum and the other in Heffers' bookshop, illustrating different aspects of genealogy. There was also a special bookshop in the Congress office.

Over 180 people paid the £5 attendance fee (plus £32.50 for

accommodation), and the event was blessed by perfect summer weather. The Congress concluded with a lecture by Don Steel on the development of genealogical studies and the role of family history in the 1980s; and a debate which passed a series of resolutions on hot topics, such as the increase in fees for certificates.

The venture was a commercial success, too. After meeting all expenses and repaying loans from the Trust and the SoG, a modest profit was recorded. The organizers decided to use the money to make a grant towards the establishment of a National Pedigree Index, one of the ideas that had been discussed during the Congress debate. The balance was put aside towards future events.

Further Congresses followed, the second being again at Cambridge in 1978, this time on the theme 'The Theory and Practice of Genealogy – the contribution which genealogists can make to historical studies'.

The National Pedigree Index (NPI) was intended to be a central index of pedigrees researched or being researched within the British Isles. The qualification for a 'pedigree' was that used by Marshall nearly a century before: a descent of three or more generations in the male line. It was hoped the scheme would help to avoid duplication and put researchers in touch with others working on the same families.

Following positive reactions at the Congress, Colwell, Pinhorn and others took up the idea and in May 1976 an advisory committee was formed. While all those involved were prominent within the Society, including Anthony Camp, the executive committee was reluctant to back it and so the Index was not an official Society project. As an independent undertaking reliant on voluntary effort it struggled with the ambitious goals it had set itself. Although by then personal computers were becoming available, the organizers stuck to a system of paper slips filed in drawers – an arrangement with which George Sherwood would have been entirely at home.

The Index recorded the usual mix of information: details of surname being researched, period covered, places of residence and publications if any. For a small fee, to cover running costs, subscribers could request searches to be made in the Index for specified surname/county combinations. If a match were found the searcher was sent the name and address of the compiler, and if nothing was found their fee was returned.

By the early 1980s over 5,000 pedigrees were listed: a substantial number but still a drop in the ocean compared to the many tens of thousands of researchers participating in local family history societies. Various national and international directories also began to appear which were much more comprehensive, and of course computer-based resources. An attempt was made to differentiate from other indexes by emphasizing the NPI as a register of research actually carried out rather than just a list of people's 'interests'. In practice the distinction was pretty hollow.

Had it started a decade or more earlier, just as the local societies were becoming established, then arguably the NPI could have played a key brokerage role and become the national resource to which it aspired. Instead it attempted to go over the heads of the local groups (and their national Federation) and connect with individual genealogists directly without any organization or resources of its own. As such it was hopelessly ambitious and doomed to failure and in 1986 the organizers decided to call a halt to the project. The existing material was handed over to the Society for inclusion in its own index of members' interests.

*   *   *   *

One of the driving forces for the formation of the Federation was the International Congress of Genealogical and Heraldic Sciences (ICGH, the same meeting held in Edinburgh in 1962), which was due to return to Britain in 1976. Preparations for this were in serious trouble and the local societies had seen it as an opportunity to come together and make their mark.

Founded before the Second World War, the ICGH is the largest international gathering of genealogists and heraldic scholars. In 1972 the ICGH's Permanent Bureau approached Cecil Humphrey-Smith with a proposal that England should host the Congress in 1974 or 1976. He, in turn, approached Lord Mountbatten, as President of the SoG, and other organizations likely to be interested, such as the College of Arms and the Heraldry Society. The Congress was a highly formal occasion for which it was essential to have the backing at least of the College, as the national body for heraldry, and ideally royal patronage and government support.

Humphrey-Smith's Institute of Heraldic and Genealogical Studies took the lead and set up a working party that included Don Steel and Peter Spufford. The British Council and other bodies promised cooperation and Imperial College was chosen as the venue. The Society's first inclination, as usual, was to procrastinate. It failed to nominate a representative for the organizing committee, preferring to await a formal commitment from the College, which was an even more conservative body than the SoG. Sir Andrew Noble was appointed as a go-between for the two organizations, with a view to organizing a congress not in 1976, as the ICGH had requested, but in 1978.

As the months rolled on and no official support from these influential bodies was forthcoming, Steel and Humphrey-Smith realized they would have to take action. With Gerald Hamilton-Edwards, they put down a motion to the Society's 1974 AGM, held on 18 June, just ten days after the seismic events at Newman College. The motion called on the executive to appoint an official representative for the organizing committee and to set up its own subcommittee to handle the Society's involvement in the event.

The meeting convened with Lord Mountbatten in the chair. He made it clear he was taking a personal interest in the issue and had had discussions with the Earl Marshall and Garter King of Arms. However, he did not wish to be associated with any congress that did not have the 'active participation of the College'.[6]

Steel then spoke to the motion, explaining that both the Society and the College favoured a congress in 1978 but that no response on the matter had been made to the ICGH and was long overdue. Meanwhile, the local societies had federated and were intent on pressing ahead with an event in 1976. It was 'regrettable' that these different views were held and the ICGH could not be told that England did not want them in 1976 but would consider the matter just two or three years later. Seconding the motion, Hamilton-Edwards said so much enthusiasm had been shown at Birmingham and the counter-proposals had been so long deferred that he felt this unique opportunity could not be allowed to slip by.

Replying for the executive committee, the chairman Alexander Sandison stressed that the Society supported the idea of an internal congress but any such meeting without the College 'would be Hamlet without the Prince'. The points of disagreement were about timescale and to some extent scope. While others would do an excellent job, only the College had the resources to organize a 'first-class international congress'. Those intent on organizing an event in 1976 should think of it as a national convention instead. A pause of two years would, he argued, 'be a small price to pay for an event which . . . would be infinitely better and more broadly based'. He tabled a counter-motion which committed the Society to supporting an event in 1978.

Fred Markwell then addressed the meeting. Any Congress organized by the College would, he thought, be superb but he was sure very few local societies would want to support it. They wanted to do things together and had been awaiting this opportunity for years. Their congress might not be quite on the lines envisaged by the executive but it would be a voluntary effort done for their own sakes and for that alone would be worthwhile. The Federation was determined to go ahead with its plans in any event. Indeed, the Birmingham meeting had passed a resolution on the issue, noting: 'that the image of British genealogy which is presented to foreign visitors should reflect the broadly based appeal of the subject in this country and the increasing emphasis on "family history" rather than "mere genealogy"'. Markwell saw no reason why there should not be two conferences: 'Let the College have its own, but let these societies which have got together also have a go.'

For the genealogy establishment Markwell's comments were clear signs that these upstarts from the provinces meant business. Mountbatten replied, rather condescendingly, that while he 'greatly admired the achievements of Mr Markwell and his friends', their efforts would best be directed towards organizing an English Congress. Any attempts to rival the College were 'bound to be trouble'.

The meeting became increasingly log-jammed, with Steel and Humphrey-Smith insistent that the Society give the event its official backing, and Mountbatten and the executive adamant that official support from the College was required, with 1978 as the only practical timeframe. Rodney Dennys, who was Somerset Herald (although he was attending the meeting in a private capacity), confirmed that the College would prefer to wait. In the end Mountbatten realized that the Society risked being split down the middle and declined to put any of the tabled motions to the vote. Instead he made a proposal of his own: that further clarification should be sought from the Garter King of Arms, preferably involving leading figures from the Federation, such as Iain Swinnerton. This motion was carried and the AGM, one of the most acrimonious meetings in the Society's history, was adjourned.

Following the meeting Noble was dispatched to Amsterdam for discussions with ICGH officials. These served to clarify a number of misunderstandings on both sides and on return to Britain Noble was able to recommend to the executive that further steps should be taken. In September Dennys flew to Munich and, on behalf of the Society, the Federation and the Institute, formally invited the 13th International Congress of Genealogical and Heraldic Sciences to meet in England in 1976. The College indicated its 'goodwill' but was not party to the formal invitation. Neither was the Heraldry Society, which although unable to participate in the preparations promised its support. The ICGH, of course, accepted.

In announcing the move, the Society felt it necessary to stress that 'the Federation was not brought into being, as many people suppose, solely to run the 1976 Congress'.[7] The Federation had spun this line at the time of its formation and it had been picked up by the press. *The Times* reported that: 'The heraldic and genealogical societies of England . . . formed a federation to run the first international congress on their associated subjects in Britain.'[8]

The *ad hoc* working party became an official Organizing Committee chaired by Noble, with Steel as his deputy. Humphrey-Smith was to be the Congress's Secretary-General, Royston Gambier its Treasurer and Major R R Collins (another SoG Fellow) the Congress Organizer. Various subcommittees were also set up involving all of the organizations involved. Having overcome their mutual suspicion and distrust, the various bodies were at last working together and pulling in the same direction. The collaboration that ensued over the next twenty-four months helped bind the constituent bodies together and deepen relationships between them at both official and personal levels.

After two years' hard work, the 13th ICGH opened its doors at London's Imperial College on 31 August 1976, as the country basked in one of the hottest summers on record. This seven-day jamboree was packed with lectures and seminars covering all aspects of genealogy, family history and heraldry, from the esoteric and scholarly to beginners' guides. Almost everybody in the world of note in genealogy and related fields was in attendance, as well as leading historians, demographers and other specialists. Some 400 people from twenty-six countries attended full-time, while their numbers were swollen by hundreds more who attended part of the programme, especially at the weekend. Many of the lectures had an international flavour and around fifty were delivered in foreign languages.

The opening ceremony took place in Imperial's Great Hall where the Duke of Norfolk, Earl Marshal of England, gave the welcoming address flanked by mayors and lord mayors. The centrepiece of the ceremony was the inaugural address by Sir Anthony Wagner, Garter King of Arms, on the theme: 'Heraldry, Genealogy and History'. It was followed by the appearance of a trolley-load of Wagner's latest book for those who wanted a copy signed by the great man himself. In the adjacent Common Room there were bookstalls, including a Federation stand with many regional FHS journals – manned devotedly throughout by Elizabeth Simpson's husband, Philip.

Alongside this was the usual mix of exhibitions, including one of original records produced by Essex Record Office. Since heraldry was a central theme, the venue was adorned with heraldic displays masterminded by Cedric Holyoake, a key figure in the Heraldry Society. The reception area was bedecked with colourful armorial bearings and delegates received metal lapel badges bearing the Congress's heraldic badge. One of the highlights of the social programme was a visit to the Institute's premises in Canterbury followed by a medieval banquet and joust at Allington Castle.

The Congress turned out to be one of the high water marks for genealogy in Britain, an event that is still talked about more than thirty years later. More than any event up to that date it showed, in a very public way, that modern genealogy was more concerned with the pedigrees – and increasingly with the family histories – of the man in the street than with those of the nobility and gentry. The 'common man' had taken possession of genealogy from the intellectual elite. Reporting on the event at the time, Jeremy Gibson observed:[9]

> It was a really staggeringly successful exercise in co-operation between a multitude of societies and individuals. With such a spirit abroad, the future of family history in Britain looks bright.

* * * *

By the mid-1970s tracing one's ancestry was gaining an accepted place in popular culture and nothing reflected popular culture better than television. In the 1970s and 1980s – the period widely regarded as the 'golden age of television' – it would be 'the box' that would propel family history to the next level.

The '*Roots* phenomenon' hit Britain in 1977. Inspired by tales from his grandmother, Alex Haley, an African-American journalist and author, had spent twelve years researching the history of his family. As with most black Americans, the story led back to slavery on plantations in the deep South. But Haley claimed to have gone further: to be the first black American to have traced his family's roots back to their origins in Africa.

His extraordinary story was told in *Roots: The Saga of an American Family* published in America in 1972. The book was an overnight sensation. Coming just a few years after the civil rights campaign and the assassinations of Martin Luther King and Malcolm X, it tapped into a new consciousness among African-Americans. 'Every black American can trace his ancestry back through slavery to an African village', Haley noted in an interview.[10] 'When I tell my story, it's really the story of every black person . . .' He continued:

> Most of all, I hope my book gives black people a sense of where we came from, a sense of a proud heritage. We are a people who subtly have been made to hate ourselves, to hate our slave ancestry. Our lack of identity has made black people feel worthless. And I want to give back to black people their roots.

The book was turned into a TV series but with slavery still a sensitive issue the producers had problems selling it to a US network. When a deal was eventually struck, the ABC network decided to add to the drama by broadcasting all eight episodes on consecutive nights – the first time a series like this had ever been turned into a 'TV event'.[11] It was watched by more than 120 million people, the largest audience ever for an American TV programme up to that time.

When the British edition of *Roots* appeared, published by Hutchinson, it ran into controversy.[12] Shortly after publication the *Sunday Times* ran an article casting doubt on the story. The book contained numerous historical inaccuracies, the article asserted, and the author's genealogical research in Africa was open to question. Haley issued a rebuff, stressing that the book was a novel and not a biography and hence much of the story was imagined. But he was also forced to admit that certain details did not fit as well as he had made out. Haley later accepted that while his ancestor undoubtedly came from the Gambia, his origins could not be pinpointed to any particular village. Nevertheless, *Roots* remains a powerful and moving account of the appalling fate of thousands of Africans shipped into slavery – a period that neither the black nor white communities had wanted to visit in any detail.

The *Roots* TV series was shown in Britain in April 1977, three months after its American debut. The BBC, too, decided to broadcast it over consecutive nights. Haley stoked up interest with a strong performance on the BBC's Parkinson show, which one reviewer described 'as significant as last night's initial episode in the series'.[13]

In Britain, which had never had the civil rights struggle and was experiencing growing racial tensions, *Roots* was a siren call. Comedian Lenny Henry has written of how the programme transfixed the Caribbean community here, who had never seen 'their story' on television before. 'My mum talked to people on the phone for . . . two hours. She called every black person she knew and talked about it.'[14] For young black Britons, in particular, it was a source of tremendous pride. 'I remember going into school on the Monday', recalled Henry, 'and people somehow didn't mess with you that day because all the black kids had this look in their eyes that said you better back off.'

Many British West Indians had been brought up knowing nothing about slavery or Africa and as a result it forced them to change the way they thought about themselves. Doreen Lawrence, of the Stephen Lawrence Charitable Trust, has said: 'Until *Roots* came out I would never have seen myself as a descendant of a slave, that was never part of my background that I learnt growing up in the Caribbean.'[15]

For the white community, too, *Roots* stirred a longing to connect with the past. Their ancestors were not slaves, or slave owners, but the programme served to show that everyone, whatever their race or colour, had a history, a personal back-story. Playing this out on prime-time TV amplified the message. Record offices were besieged by visitors wanting to search out their own roots, and family history societies were inundated with letters and inquiries; memberships jumped markedly as a result. Within two years a further series of programmes was to consolidate family history's mainstream appeal.

Gordon Honeycombe, a former TV newsreader, had spent many years researching his ancestry.[16] His curiosity had been sparked as a teenager in Edinburgh when he came across an announcement for a marriage. He wrote to the man who sent him an account of his family written by an American, John S Honeycombe in 1907. John claimed to be a direct descendant of a Norman knight, Honi á Combat, who fought at the Battle of Hastings and was given lands in Cornwall. Later Honeycombe came across a house apparently linked to the family on an old map. In 1956, while studying at Oxford, he went to Cornwall with two friends to have a look at Honeycombe Hall near the village of Calstock. In the registers, then kept in the parish church, were several Honeycombes. Was there any connection, he wondered, between the house, the Cornish Honeycombes, the American correspondent and the man who got married in Edinburgh? Thus began what became a twenty-year search into his family tree.

Honeycombe found that everyone in the world of that name *was* in fact related: not only that, they were all descended from one man, Matthew Honeycombe, who lived in the Cornish village of St Cleer in the reign of Charles II. The story of the Norman knight was false, but Honeycombe Hall took its name from the valley in which it stood and, using medieval records, Gordon was able to show that the people who lived there around 1300 took their names from both. The Black Death forced them out but they remained in the Calstock area for over 400 years and from there spread to other parts of Cornwall and across the globe.

Bryn Brooks, a producer at the BBC, was looking to put together a TV series about family history and approached Honeycombe to front it. Gordon was a well-known face on British TV at the time, having spent twelve years reading the news on ITV, but had recently left to become a full-time writer and playwright. Brooks knew Honeycombe had an interest in genealogy, possibly through *Family Tree*, a half-hour programme made for Westward TV in 1973 which featured his researches.

Initially, Brooks had planned to look at various aspects of genealogy, with Honeycombe there just as a presenter. But when Gordon turned up with a suitcase full of information Brooks realized he would need to change tack. He decided to personalize the series, using Honeycombe's researches to demonstrate general principles of family history research which viewers could apply to their own families.

Don Steel was the series' main adviser and with all Honeycombe's records at his disposal set about weaving them into a story that was both entertaining and informative. He worked on every programme, though only appeared in one, and wrote a book to accompany the series. Various other experts were brought in to help complete the picture, digging up interesting information and filling in the historical and social background. Much of the series was shot on location, including numerous scenes in churches and record offices, and a very brief appearance at the SoG at Harrington Gardens.

Family History aired on Wednesday 21 March 1979, at 6.55 pm on BBC2, the first of a five-part series. In the opening shot, the tall and urbane Honeycombe was featured outside the church at Calstock, recounting the family legend about the Norman knight. 'It says that we were rich, we were brave, we were noble, but is it true?', he asked. 'We all have ancestors', he continued, 'and in this series I hope to encourage you to dig out yours.'[17]

The BBC publicity machine had been put into action beforehand, including a two-page feature in the *Radio Times*.[18] A week before the first broadcast a launch party was held at the PRO in Chancery Lane, to which the press, broadcasters and leading figures from the family history world were invited. The first programme was shown and Gordon and other Honeycombes posed for photographs and answered reporters' questions.

The exercise ensured a welter of press coverage, in the news as well as the TV pages of the newspapers. Critics generally gave it a warm reception. Many articles used it as an opportunity to explain the basics of family history, mentioning repositories such as the GRO, PRO and the SoG. 'Why news is a family affair', proclaimed *The Sun*, noting the fact that an ancestor had been a town crier in Jersey to observe 'Honeycombe was not the first newscaster in his family'.[19]

Family History was soon being called 'the English Roots', an appellation that irritated Honeycombe since he had not watched the US series and saw his own programme as having higher aims. He used his launch interviews to stress it was more than just the story of his own family, telling the *London Evening News*: 'What I have tried to do is to show the social history of England through the experiences of my family – how they moved during the industrial revolution in search of work; how they migrated like so many others to America and throughout Europe.'[20] He also saw it as a chance to inspire others, enthusing to one interviewer that genealogy 'gives you a sense of belonging: it makes history real'.

Again, the public responded in droves. The day after the first programme was shown record offices reported an unprecedented number of inquiries, and the BBC realized it had a hit on its hands. Don Steel's book, entitled *Discovering Your Family History*, was published the following year and became a bestseller. However, as a BBC employee he did not receive any royalties from it, an issue that rankled him greatly. The series was later repeated on BBC1 in March and April 1980, and again in 1982 and 1986.

*   *   *   *

In their attempts to be comprehensive, family historians often found themselves researching all occurrences of a given surname or its proven variants, whether or not it could be linked to their particular family line. George Sherwood had been one of these, his accounts of the Sherwood family being one of the first examples of what became known as 'one-name studies'. Many new recruits to family history were attracted by this approach, resulting in studies of more and more names. In certain cases a family association or society was formed (a model that had long been popular in the United States), but in others individuals retained the work as a private interest.

With the formation of the Federation attempts were made to accommodate these 'one-namers'. At its request, Frank Higenbottam started a card index of people with surname interests. This grew steadily until a notice was published in an American magazine, which brought a deluge of inquiries. Iain Swinnerton agreed to take over as 'registrar' and after thoroughly revising the index the Federation published it in 1977 as the *Register of One-Name Studies*. Some 300 one-name researchers were listed, a few of whom were becoming known to each other through Federation meetings. These 'one-namers' decided to organize a conference of their own.

Held in Leicester in 1978, the conference attracted a large number of one-name enthusiasts. At that time twenty-nine of the Federation's ninety-three member societies were one-name societies. But it was clear there were many more researchers who were not associated with, and did not wish to form, a one-name society as such. Instead, the idea was floated of forming an association of *people* undertaking the study of a single surname. The title Guild of One Name Studies was chosen and a steering committee set up. The term

Guild was adopted to emphasize that the members were all individuals practising a specific craft and using a wide range of methods, sources and knowledge.

Fred Filby, a Fellow of the SoG, took an active role, being both chairman and acting registrar, and printing newsletters on a Gestetner duplicator in his spare room. He wrote to all those on the original register inviting them to rejoin the new Guild and by the inaugural conference at Plymouth in September 1979, 162 members had registered. Over the next six years Filby personally answered over 10,000 letters, including many that resulted from his address being given out on a television programme without his permission. During the mid-1980s the Guild came to an agreement with the SoG to provide a postal address, from where it continues to operate.

There is no single definition of a one-name study and the Guild accepts a wide variety of approaches, provided the research is undertaken on a systematic basis. One-namers are interested in the genealogy and family history of all persons with a given surname (and accepted variants) over time, and 'true' one-namers do this on a worldwide basis. Typically, researchers collect information on the origin and meaning of the name; its relative frequency and distribution in geography and time; patterns of immigration and emigration; and name variants and 'deviants'. Clearly, this is only possible for relatively unusual surnames.

Interest grew rapidly; by 1989 there were some 1,100 surnames registered and in 1992 the Guild admitted its 2000th member. Today it has nearly 8,000 registered names. The Guild enables members to share ideas with others and to explore those aspects of family history peculiar to one-name studies, such as surname evolution and development, linguistic corruption and the geographical ramifications of a surname and its variants. In this respect surname research is quite similar to, and has made important contributions to, the academic study known as 'demography'.

As a historian, as well as a genealogist, Don Steel retained a lifelong interest in historical demography and did much to promote a better mutual understanding between these fields. In an article in the *Genealogists' Magazine* in 1970, he described how genealogy was key to understanding the family, which had by then come to be accepted as one of the most important contexts for historical studies.[21]

Steel observed how, starting in France, 'professional historians have now begun to make a serious study of the history of the family unit'. In Britain, these ideas were pioneered by the Cambridge Group for the History of Population and Social Structure, led by Peter Laslett and Anthony Wrigley.[22] 'As a result of this line of inquiry, genealogists are coming close to attaining the respectability achieved by local historians a generation ago', Steel observed. Drawing on his vast knowledge acquired as editor of the *NIPR*, he went on to describe, in scholarly detail, how the two communities needed to work together in future. He returned to the issue in a further *Magazine* article in 1997, reflecting on his own experiences with the one-name study of 'Kitchener', as well as developments in the academic field.[23] Another pioneer in this field was Francis Lesson, who published articles on surname distribution as early as 1964 and helped connect the genealogy community with the academic work on surnames being pursued by Hoskins, Everitt and McKinley at Leicester.[24]

*   *   *   *

By the mid-1970s the LDS church's influence on genealogy was clear for all to see, primarily as a result of its investment in computerization. The Church began using computers and volunteers to extract births, christenings and marriages from many countries during the 1960s. For temple work Mormons are primarily interested in knowing dates of birth/baptism and marriage. The date of death or burial is not a necessary part of the temple process, provided the person is known to be deceased, hence information on deaths was not collected in such a systematic manner. In 1969 a new system of submissions for temple work was introduced and all submissions, whether made by church members or extracted from original records, were recorded on computer.

Initially, the index to these computerized submissions, known as the Computer File Index (CFI), was only available within the Church, at its headquarters and library in Utah. The first issue was produced on microfiche in 1973. It contained all records submitted since October 1969, when the new system of computer submissions was introduced, together with some earlier records. There were some 20 million records in all, over half of which were for the British Isles.

On a visit to the US in 1976, Fred Filby was shown the CFI by the Genealogical Society of Utah. At that time it was only available to Mormon organizations within the US, although plans were in hand to provide it to the new libraries the Church was setting up in Britain. Filby asked whether it would be possible to make the index available for wider distribution. He was told this would be expensive because the computer would have to be reprogrammed to remove the information relating to the Mormon rituals. Filby said that did not matter; the Brits would be happy to have the index as it stood. In that case, he was told, the cost would only be a few cents per sheet.

Thus, as well as the core information on actual births, baptisms and marriages, the CFI fiches used around the world also included columns on the right-hand size listing a complex series of batch numbers. These could be baffling for the beginner, but for those who knew how to use them also provided a useful means of checking.

The SoG opened formal negotiations with the Genealogical Society of Utah and acquired its first copy of the CFI in 1977. Many family history societies and libraries soon followed; often the purchase required investment in reading machines as well since microfiche was a relatively new format. In the late 1970s the CFI was renamed the International Genealogical Index (IGI), a name that soon became known to family historians everywhere.

The fiches were small sheets of microfilm, about four inches by six inches, each containing 270 pages of entries, with about sixty names in each section. The microfiche was placed in a reading machine which magnified the individual pages on a screen where they could be read easily. However, to make copies of fiches a different type of machine was required, and hence the printouts were relatively difficult to obtain and expensive. Soon specialist services grew up at record offices and publishers providing these printouts.

The IGI was an immediate success and rapidly became a staple of the research process. While indexes, such as Boyd's Marriage Index, had been available before, none had been in such a usable format or so accessible. From a library, in Birmingham or Manchester for instance, it was possible to search the records of parishes on the other side of the country – Sussex, Norfolk, Cornwall, and so on. Thus, researchers were able to cover whole regions or subregions very quickly and by investing in printouts of their searches had useful reference material to which to refer later.

The system had two major limitations. First, no area was fully covered, so omission from the IGI was no guarantee that a record did not exist or could not be found. This was particularly the case for Catholic and Nonconformist churches, who refused the Mormons access to their records on religious grounds. Secondly, the IGI was an index to records rather than a record in itself. Researchers were warned to check original records, since not all information in the source was recorded and there was also the possibility of transcription errors. The Church did its best to maintain high standards, requiring each entry to be read twice. But reliance on volunteers, many of them not native speakers, meant errors were inevitable. Of course, many beginners and the less rigorous ignored the advice and took the IGI as a primary genealogical source.

With the Church investing $10 million per year in extraction, the IGI grew rapidly. Periodic updates were issued, with major editions in 1981, 1984, 1988 and 1992. By 1992 the worldwide edition of the IGI contained 187 million names, more than 72 million of which were for the British Isles. By that time even microfiche was becoming too bulky to store and the series moved to CD-ROM only, the 9,200 fiches being replaced by a set of fifty-six computer discs.

Even this rich treasure trove was not enough for some people, who enviously eyed the (literal) mountain of data the Church was accumulating in Utah and made special trips to the Mormon library in Salt Lake City.

*   *   *   *

Major changes were under way at the General Register Office during this period which would mobilize the family history movement in a way that had never been seen before. Growth of the welfare state and the need to know more about how people lived created a demand from policy-makers for more detailed statistical data. In 1970 the GRO was merged with the Government Social Survey to form the Office of Population Censuses and Surveys (OPCS), although it retained a separate identity, and in 1972 for the first time a professional statistician, George Payne, was appointed Registrar General. Under these new arrangements, the focus shifted away from the administration of registration and more towards the uses of the data derived from it and from the ten-yearly censuses and other social surveys.

To emphasize this new utilitarian approach, in 1973 the OPCS, including the GRO, moved from its long-standing home at Somerset House into St Catherine's House on London's Kingsway. The GRO had been there since 1837 and in the minds of many family historians 'Somerset House' was synonymous with the searching of indexes and the quest for certificates. Although they complained about the working conditions (a deputation from the SoG had visited in 1971 to discuss the overcrowded galleries and poor ventilation), many were sad to see it go.

New, more functional search rooms at St Catherine's House opened to the public on 2 January 1974. For a while these represented improvement, but before long there were complaints that they too were overcrowded, and in particular that the continual battering by an army of searchers was leading to rapid deterioration in the condition of the index books. 'At lunchtime on a weekday', noted the *Daily Telegraph*, 'the place is sometimes more like an ill-organized Boy Scout jamboree, as picnickers mingle with serious researchers thumbing through the index registers.' To add insult to injury, opening hours at the new building were cut with the loss of Saturday morning opening, which many researchers had found particularly convenient. Such concerns were soon put aside, however, as the family history community found something much more important to worry about than opening hours and the state of the indexes.

The Conservative administration of the time was keen to disperse government work away from London and asked Sir Henry Hardman to look into the issue. His report, released in 1972, identified the OPCS as a possible candidate. Specialist functions, such as medical statisticians should be kept in London, Hardman recommended, but clerical functions, many of which were inherited from the GRO, should be moved to Southport in Merseyside, where the GRO already had an office. This would include the public search rooms which dealt with over a thousand enquirers per day.

Genealogists were outraged. To lose the civil registration indexes from London would be like losing a right arm. A deputation from the Society, including Alexander Sandison, Don Steel and Anthony Camp met officials from the Registrar General's office on 23 October. They were told that it was impossible for the public search room to be separated from the other offices, and that consequently a move to Southport was inevitable. Adoption records and postal enquiries for early certificates were already handled from there and the move would streamline operation of the Office. The Society's representatives replied that if such a move were to take place it would be essential for a duplicate set of indexes (other than in microfilm form) to be made available at a London location.

They reasserted these views in a letter sent two days later, and also took the opportunity to again raise the issue of the early records being deposited at the PRO – something the Society had been campaigning for since its foundation. These older records should be transferred to 'public repositories which are open for longer hours and where long pieces of genealogical, demographic and historical research can be conducted without the necessity of paying fees'. The GRO had, apparently, already conceded such a transfer and was consulting the Society 'on the cut-off date to be adopted'.

In November, Lord Teviot, a member of the Society who had already written a letter to *The Times* on the subject, raised a question in the House of Lords. The Government's spokesman, Lord Wells-Pestell told him that the Registrar General was still 'working out which sections of his office are to be transferred' and that a 'decision will be announced early in 1975'. When Teviot questioned an earlier pronouncement that St Catherine's House was to be the GRO's permanent home, he was told that 'there had been a number of happenings since then, and the question of dispersal of Government staffs is a very important matter'.

The Government's assurances that discussions were ongoing and that no decision had been made seemed rather hollow; on the contrary, the decision to move the office to Southport appeared to be an 'open secret'. Following further questioning by Teviot in the Lords, the Society decided to open a wider front. At its invitation, representatives of fourteen organizations met at Harrington Gardens on 13 January 1975 with Sandison in the chair. It was decided to write a joint letter to *The Times*, to get Society members and others to write to their MPs and to stress the broad range of people who made use of the indexes in addition to genealogists.

Camp and Teviot drafted a letter, together with Dr A J Taylor, Director of the Society of Antiquaries, and Peter Gwynn-Jones, the Bluemantle Pursuivant of Arms. 'It is perhaps not often', they began, 'that the interests of historians are identical to those of the "man in the street", but they are clearly the same where the projected move of the public search room and records of the Registrar General from London to Southport in Merseyside are concerned.'[25] They went on to note the wide range of uses for index searches – for passports, pensions, insurance and legal matters as well as family history – for which the proposed postal search service 'would form no adequate substitute'. Moreover, the removal of the records would be 'a disaster for the historian', taking away a key part of the circle of London-based repositories used for 'all sorts of legal, literary, biographical, historical and genealogical research'. 'That one of these should be isolated two hundred miles from London is unthinkable', the letter concluded.

Nearly thirty organizations agreed to sign the letter but *The Times* was only prepared to print six signatures. It eventually appeared in the paper on 1 February, signed by Arthur Carr, Chief of Staff of the Salvation Army; G R Elton, President of the Royal Historical Society; Brian Fitzgerald-Moore, Chairman of the SoG; J N L Myers, President of the Society of Antiquaries; J B Taylor, Deputy General Secretary of the Workers' Educational Association; and Anthony Wagner, Garter King of Arms.

A further meeting with Lord Wells-Pestell at the Ministry of Health and Social Security was arranged to press home the point. The deputation used the meeting to reiterate the points made in their *Times* letter and raise some new ones. Anthony Johnson, for the Law Society, explained that solicitors across the country used London-based agents to do legal searches and that postal searches would be no substitute. Richard Wall of the Cambridge Group described the value of the indexes to academic researchers. Speaking in his capacity as chairman of the Association of Genealogists and Record Agents, Camp emphasized that a large proportion of professionals were London-based. Rodney Dennys said the College of Arms viewed the removal of the records 'with alarm', adding in high-brow tones the importance of 'the propinquity of the records in London'.

On being pressed by Teviot as to when a decision might be taken, the Minister said it would be in the interests of all if it were taken 'later rather than sooner'. This reply raised eyebrows around the table, as it was the first indication that all might not be lost. When they came out they briefed the press to this effect, leading to a short report on the meeting in *The Times* under the headline 'Decision to transfer registry is delayed'.[26]

Nothing was heard for several weeks, but eventually on 18 February Wells-Pestell announced in the House of Lords that the public search room was to remain at St Catherine's House. Reports were carried the following day in *The Times*, *Guardian* and *Daily Telegraph*, the latter observing that the proposed move had 'caused a storm of protest from numerous groups and organizations who claimed it would delay searches and cause grave inconvenience'. The Society had played a key part in the campaign, mobilizing other organizations and acting as a focal point for the discussions with government. Family historians were, at last, beginning to find a voice in the public arena. This voice would soon be heard again, this time in a battle over access to parish registers.

The legislation relating to parish registers in the early 1970s was archaic. The provisions of Rose's 1812 Act still applied: church incumbents could charge searchers for consulting registers in their possession and were under no obligation to deposit registers with record offices, which were in a better position to preserve them and make them available under controlled conditions.

Lord Teviot initiated a debate on the issue in April 1971, asking the government 'whether they would consider introducing legislation for the better preservation of parish records' and urging it to establish 'a central indexed copy of all parish registers at the General Registry Office'.[27] Replying for the government, Lord Aberdare showed little interest in further legislation. The Parochial Registers and Records Measure 1929 had empowered bishops to set up diocesan record offices to which incumbents could deposit registers if they so wished. Local authorities were also able to accept the deposit of records, but he felt no need to force the Church to act. As for a central index, it would 'provide no more than a partial duplication of information already available' and was ruled out on cost grounds. Existing legislation was 'adequate at the moment', Aberdare concluded, and it was down to church and state authorities to sort things out using the available powers.

The following year the General Synod of the Church of England passed the Parochial Fees Order 1972, substantially increasing the fees that could be charged for searching parish registers. A fee of 15 pence could be levied for every year of baptisms, burials or marriages consulted. Researchers might need to look at all types of entry over an extended period, which would amount to £45 for every century of registers investigated – a huge amount for the time. Genealogists saw the move as a deliberate act by the Church to extort money from them and complained about it at every opportunity.

Around this time the Synod also began discussing a revision of regulations set out in the Pastoral Measure of 1968. This established the principle that church property no longer required for ecclesiastical purposes and of historic importance should be preserved 'in the interests of the nation and of the Church of England'. The Measure related primarily to the fabric of church buildings and paid little or no attention to parish registers, nor even features such as family monuments, brasses and pews. The SoG urged that the opportunity should be taken to ensure the Measure was extended to include the contents of the parish chest and other muniments of historical value.

In the face of continual lobbying by Camp and others, the Synod began to consider an overhaul of the fee structure as part of the Measure's revision. In place of a flat fee, searches would be charged on an hourly rate, starting at £1 for the first hour and then 50 pence per hour after that. This was just one of a wide range of changes being proposed. The amended Measure would also relieve record offices from the obligation to charge fees for searches in deposited registers; require diocesan bishops to designate or establish diocesan record offices if that had not already been done; and provide for the periodic inspection of those registers remaining in parochial charge.

Teviot thought the Measure did not go far enough, and even members of the Synod accepted it had limitations. As a Synodical Measure – an internal church regulation – it failed to carry the weight of primary legislation; its provisions were essentially a code of practice with no means of enforcement. Also, due to the way the Church was structured, the Measure did not apply to Wales. In February 1976 Teviot introduced his own Parochial Records Bill in the House of Lords in an attempt to enact the changes through primary legislation.[28]

At the heart of the bill was a proposal to amend Rose's Act, which stipulated that parish registers were to be kept in iron chests, with a requirement that either they be placed in a modern thermostatically controlled safe or deposited in the diocesan record office. It received a sympathetic hearing; replying for the government Wells-Pestell said he welcomed the bill and would 'give it whatever help was necessary'. But without proper government sponsorship progress was slow and, although the issues were given a valuable airing, the bill never saw the light of day.

The General Synod passed the amending Measure in late 1977 and, after being rubber-stamped by Parliament, it received the Royal Assent the following year, as the Parochial Registers and Records Measure 1978. The Measure swept away both the 1812 Act and the 1929 Measure and replaced them with new provisions. With some minor amendments passed in 1992 and 2003, it remains the main statutory instrument governing the long-term care and preservation of and access to parish records in England and Wales.

Lord Teviot was, by this time, a recognized expert on records legislation and was effectively the genealogist's voice in Parliament. Charles, the 2nd Baron Teviot, had acceded to the House of Lords in 1968 on the death of his father. He was already a professional genealogist, working from home with his wife Mary, who was also his business partner. His success in initiating the 1971 debate, which stung the Church into action on parochial fees, ignited his interest in the policy aspects of records and he was drawn further and further in.

He returned to the fray in 1978 on the issue of access to the civil registration records. The holy grail for genealogists – sought since the days of Sherwood and Fothergill – was for the earliest civil registers (which was generally understood to be those more than one hundred years old) to be deposited at the Public Record Office, where they could be freely consulted alongside other public records. The stumbling block was the Public Records Act 1958 which specifically exempted the GRO registers from being classified as 'public records'.

Until the early 1970s there had been some flexibility in the system. The GRO agreed there was no reason why local superintendent registrars should not permit access to original registers held locally. General searches in the registers were allowed and were used mainly by historians requiring blocks of data, such as causes of death in relation to age and occupation, that could not be obtained from the indexes alone. In 1973, however, the Registrar General specified that such searches could only be permitted 'when the local registrar has the time to undertake the necessary supervision', and in August 1974 they were stopped altogether.[29] No statutory instrument was invoked to do this, the GRO simply claimed the volume of requests at local offices was 'beginning to reach quite unmanageable proportions'. There was a loophole, in that registrars could loan their registers to local county records offices where they would be under the supervision of local archivists. When historians promoted this idea in the journal *Local Population Studies*, the GRO closed off this avenue too.

Historians were furious. The decision had been taken 'without proper consultation or consideration of the implications', the journal noted in an editorial, and was contrary to 'increasing liberality and freedom on questions of access to records of all kinds'.[30] 'We do not know of any good reason why local students should be denied research access to the older civil registers. This is not a matter we shall be easily persuaded to drop.' When the protestors examined the legal situation in greater detail, they found that none of the Registration Acts actually prohibited local registrars or the GRO itself from granting the public access to any registration document. Nor did the 1958 Act prohibit public access to register copies – it simply said they were not 'public records'. Provided they remained under the Registrar General's charge, they could be deposited at the PRO or anywhere else. Indeed, the non-parochial registers had been transferred to the PRO on this basis as early as 1966.

Thus, both local and centralized deposit were feasible options. The local solution was, perhaps, to be preferred, since local authorities were already under an obligation to provide accommodation for the superintendent registrars and it was logical that their records should be deposited in local authority record offices. On the other hand, deposit of the Registrar General's registers at a central repository would represent a great national resource. In either case the obstacle was what looked to historians and family historians like bureaucratic intransigence on the part of the GRO.

In November 1978 in the House of Lords, Teviot introduced the Public Records (Amendment) Bill to implement the necessary changes.[31] It was a simple piece of legislation with just three clauses. Clause 1 amended the 1958 Act, bringing registers older than 100 years under the definition of public records. Clause 2 implemented associated provisions to the latest civil registration legislation, the Marriage Act 1949 and the Births and Deaths Registration Act 1953. Clause 3 was a standard legal clause, known as 'citation and commencement', stating when the bill's provisions would come into force.

This last clause was to be the measure's downfall. No date was given because neither the GRO nor the PRO was prepared to commit to a timetable. The GRO said it would only be able to transfer once all the registers had been microfilmed, which would take some time to complete; and the PRO could not agree to the plan because it did not have room to accommodate either the records or the public searchers. Although the Lords gave the bill a Second

Reading, the government concluded the plans were too costly and the measure was quietly dropped.

After a further abortive attempt in 1979, Teviot returned to the issue in 1983 with another measure, also called the Public Records (Amendment) Bill. It required the same transfer after 100 years but this time Teviot conceded the need for fees to offset the PRO's costs. Family historians would pay a daily fee to consult the civil registration records. This would still represent a significant saving, Teviot argued, over the costs of purchasing individual certificates, which by then cost £4.60 in person and £9.60 by post. Income from fees would be used to cover the PRO's investment in premises – a new building might be needed – equipment and staff.

But the principle of paying fees to access public records raised alarm bells. It would put these particular records beyond the reach of many of the scholars and other readers who needed to use them. More importantly, it could be the thin end of a very long wedge. If this point were conceded how long before the PRO started charging for access to the rest of its collections? The alternative was to rely on technology: simply microfilm the registers and sell copies to libraries and record offices throughout the country, as was already being done with the nineteenth-century censuses. A central reading room would still be required but it could be on a much smaller scale.

A correspondence on the issue developed in the letters pages of *The Times*.[32] One correspondent, Christopher Charlton, argued that access should not be limited to 100 years and claimed that fees of between £10 and £20 per day were being considered. An Elizabeth Stazicker replied that local records offices and libraries could not afford to purchase microfilm copies, as Charlton suggested, and it was important that the principle of charging in search rooms was resisted.

Anthony Camp waded in, arguing that the 'entire answer' was the deposit of the original registers in county record offices.[33] This would save the cost of microfilming and reduce the congestion in any central repository; its absence was 'an absurd omission'. Victor Gray, of the Association of County Archivists, replied that Camp's suggestion merely pushed the problem from the taxpayer to the ratepayer. Many record offices 'would find themselves quite unable to cope with the burdens of space and time which would be created by the transfer'.[34] The real problem was that the bill would release a projected 100,000 researchers on the PRO (or on local record offices if Camp had his way) 'without any financial provision for coping with them'.

An alternative model, pointed to by both sides, was the situation in Scotland. For many years, it had been the practice there for searchers to be allowed to search for a fee (then £7.50 per day) not only the indexes but also the original registers under supervision and without being under any obligation to purchase extracts. In addition, all the registers prior to 1875 had been microfilmed and were available through the branch libraries of the

Genealogical Society of Utah. The Scottish example proved the value of centralized access, but also that a fee system, based on reasonable charges, worked.

Eventually Teviot himself replied. In a letter published on 26 April 1983 he defended his proposals and said some of the figures being bandied about for search fees were 'excessive'. The 100-year period was a starting point which might be extended if 'public opinion will become sufficiently relaxed'. As for Camp's argument for local deposit, 'it would not be practicable to burden local registrars with making their registers available to the public. We are dealing with what essentially is a central government function.'

Teviot's bill had government backing and this time passed all its stages in the Lords. It was due to have its second reading in the House of Commons on 13 May 1983. Unfortunately, this was the day the general election was called. Parliament was dissolved and all pending legislation fell. In place of centralized public access to civil registration records the country got a second term of the Thatcher Government instead.

* * * *

Surprisingly, despite the ever-broadening interest in family history there was still no popular magazine. By the early 1980s the introduction of computer technology made the production of niche publications more feasible and titles began to appear catering for a wide range of interests. Michael Armstrong, a Cambridgeshire businessman and keen family historian, recognized an opportunity and decided to launch a title for this growing market.[35]

Armstrong had had an eclectic business career which included being an ambulance driver, selling pottery and running a fish and chip shop. Pottery was his greatest love, but the business experienced continual cashflow problems. To supplement his income he took to teaching family history at local evening classes and doing a little semi-professional family history research.

One night at an evening class in Huntingdon, an American woman whose husband was stationed at a US airbase nearby turned up with a copy of an American publication, the *Genealogical Helper*. 'Is there a similar publication here?', she asked. Armstrong told her that there was not, but the incident got him thinking. He arranged a meeting with East Midlands Allied Press (EMAP), a publishing firm in Peterborough that produced a number of popular magazines. Armstrong estimated the magazine would sell 25,000 copies every two months and would offer around three to six pages of advertising space. EMAP made it clear that the economics did not stack up. But the executive offered encouragement nevertheless: 'it might not work for us', he said, 'but why not have a go yourself?'

Armstrong mulled over the idea for several days. Other publishers were likely to have the same reaction, he thought. But his knowledge of family history also convinced him there was a market. Eventually, after discussing the issue with his wife Mary, he decided to take the plunge.

A neighbour, Ralph Braybrook, turned out to be a former Fleet Street journalist and now worked on a freelance basis for various newspapers and periodicals. He agreed to help launch the magazine, which was to be called *Family Tree*. The team frantically started gathering material and put the first issue together on Armstrong's dining room table.

The first issue of *Family Tree* hit the newsstands in November 1984, initially as a bi-monthly publication. Early issues had the feel more of a community newsletter than a national magazine. There were regular contributions from the Society, the Federation, the Institute and particular one-name groups. A series 'Meeting People' carried interviews with key personalities of the day, such as Charles and Mary Teviot, Don Steel and Elizabeth Simpson. And a series called 'Record Office Review' profiled a particular record office in each issue.

Armstrong's approach to market research seems quaint, if not naive, by today's standards. Being keen to reflect readers' views, he regularly included questionnaires enquiring what they thought about the magazine. The results were later printed in great detail – just the sort of information a competitor might need. Nevertheless, these analyses provide some interesting insights into the motivations of 1980s family historians. To the question 'What sparked your interest?' the top three answers in 1986 were: 'After the death of a relative', '*Roots*' and 'Gordon Honeycombe's TV series'. Half of readers were in the 26–50 age group and another 40 per cent were aged over 50.

From the questionnaires it was clear people were looking for practical, hands-on advice: 'how to' guides, questions and answers, and letters were all popular. As a result much of the 'community' angle (the Meeting People series and the one-name profiles) was dropped and the magazine gradually evolved a more educational approach.

'Diary of a Genealogist', a regular column written by Anthony Camp, proved especially controversial. The SoG's Director of Research used it to record the day-to-day goings-on in his life, from meetings with colleagues and other genealogical organizations, to tours abroad, and even his personal machinations with plumbing and who he met for dinner. The trouble was he covered a full calendar month on one page, so that readers were only ever given a taste of what was really happening. Important meetings would be flagged without mention of the outcome, whereas half the entries for any month recorded mundane tasks such as letter writing. Armstrong's surveys showed readers were divided on the issue, with the column having avid followers and detractors in equal measure. Eventually, in 1990, 'Diary of a Genealogist' was dropped, only for Camp to be brought back a few months later writing a bi-monthly contribution.

Never one to shy away from controversy, Don Steel used the columns of *Family Tree* to raise a series of issues regarding privacy and censorship in family history. In three articles published between January and March 1987, Steel looked at what he called 'the dilemma' faced by family historians, archivists and publishers, respectively. Always thoughtful and provocative, Steel used the articles to encourage family historians at large to think about the moral issues raised by their work. At the same time, he could not help taking a swipe at some of his fellow travellers in the upper echelons of British genealogy.

Of family historians, he asked whether they should disclose all the information uncovered during their researches.[36] Should they tell about more unsavoury aspects such as illegitimacy, prostitution, and adoption – things which can resonant over several generations? If so, should such information be made available to people other than direct descendants? And what should and should not be published? There was much concern at the time about the amount of information of all kinds being held on computers and organizations holding such data had recently been made subject to the Data Protection Act. Although this did not yet apply to family historians, Steel wondered whether it should and what rights this would give people to doctor the historical record. 'Would this be censorship, or merely the proper safeguarding of privacy?', Steel asked.

In the second article, entitled 'The Record Custodian's Dilemma', Steel had the SoG itself in his sights.[37] He was planning a book on the history of genealogy and family history and had written to the Society requesting access to its own archive. To Steel's surprise, the executive committee refused but offered to check particular points in committee minutes. He was also told that the committee 'is, of course, extremely anxious to see that the material is handled in a sympathetic manner', which Steel took as a request for favourable treatment. When he tried to engage the chairman on the matter, he was told that there were 'confidentiality' issues and the matter could not be discussed further.

Steel was rankled by this and described the case in detail in *Family Tree*. Why would a Society that 'claims to exist for the study of an historical subject', of which he had been a member for thirty-eight years and a Fellow for twenty-three, not let him see its own records for historical purposes? It was, he thought, uncomfortable for the Society, which was used to the role of record user, to be put in the role of custodian. Yet the case was typical of the principle, then under increasing public scrutiny, that everything is secret unless someone authorizes its official release. 'In any democratic society', Steel explained, 'the deliberations of elected representatives should be freely open to inspection by any member, with the exception [of] . . . certain cases where it is necessary to preserve confidentiality for a considerable length of time.'

The third article focused on issues in family history publishing which, he argued, touched on 'principles of free debate and discussion'.[38] He noted the importance of the national family history journals, such as *Genealogists' Magazine* and *Family Tree*, as forums for open debate. This was not a characteristic he found accommodated in *Family History*, the house journal of the Institute of Heraldic and Genealogical Studies. This had been edited since its inception in 1961 by the Institute's founder and principal, Cecil Humphrey-Smith. It was widely seen, said Steel, as 'little more than a propaganda sheet' for the Institute. He had also had a bad experience with *Family History News and Digest*, the Federation's journal, which had refused to publish a correction he sent in on an article it had run. Finally, he laid into the *Genealogists' Magazine* for having refused to publish a letter about the earlier incident with access to its records, contrasting it with the openness with which his former critique had been published in 1974. All of these examples, he concluded, showed 'the totally unacceptable face of censorship'.

The series, not surprisingly, got *Family Tree*'s letters pages buzzing. Lay readers described their experiences in unearthing skeletons and how they had approached matters. But the juiciest replies came from the genealogy establishment. Pauline Litton, editor of the Federation's magazine, wrote that Steel himself was guilty of censorship as a result of selective quotation on the *Digest* incident.[39] Humphrey-Smith replied loftily that the Institute was 'an educational body' rather than a genealogical or family history society, and its policy was not to publish 'correspondence or articles for general reading and entertainment which are devoid of original content, new ideas or the results of research work'. The fact that much of the journal was Humphrey-Smith's own personal memories, musings and self-promotion seems to have escaped him.

Humphrey-Smith had upset many people over the years, particularly through his forthright attitudes on 'professionalism' and his slights against amateurs entering the genealogy field. Enraged by his rebuff of Steel, Alan Kent wrote an article for *Family Tree* recounting his own unhappy experiences with publishing in *Family History*.[40] Humphrey-Smith had, Kent thought, made him look a fool because it was 'heresy against genealogy to disagree with the Institute over fundamentals'. *Family Tree* published a further response from Humphrey-Smith a few months later, accompanied by an editorial piece by Ralph Braybrook appealing for calm.[41] As a hardened journalist, Braybrook expressed dismay at the 'needle-sharp antipathy' and 'increasing spikiness' in the correspondence, which was worse 'from family history circles than from any I have encountered'.

The incident served to show the tensions underlying family history at the time. It was a small world full of big egos, strong personalities and littered with personal feuds. The Institute, in particular, had always been controversial. Its purpose had never been quite clear (was its focus 'the study of the family', as originally stated, or family history?); it evaded scrutiny by operating as a charity rather than as a membership society, yet it also ran a commercial research outfit; and, to the chagrin of other bodies, it had staked out a role as the guardian of professional standards.

*   *   *   *

For the Society the 1980s was a period of gradual, and often grudging, modernization. After many years as Director of Research, in 1979 Anthony Camp was made its first 'Director'. The change in title actually reflected a situation that had pertained for several years: that Camp's role was as much managerial and administrative as genealogical.

By this time the Society had over 5,000 members and was a substantial commercial operation. It received over 15,000 letters per year (an average of 300 per week), most of which Camp replied to personally. Circulation of the magazine was running at about 20,000 copies and income from publications was worth £13,000. About 3,300 non-members used the library (an average of twelve per day), bringing in further income of £5,500.

Shortly after his appointment, Camp used his address to the Society's day conference to offer a wide-ranging survey of its status and prospects.[42] After briefly reviewing past attitudes to genealogy, he stressed Anthony Wagner's 1961 lecture 'Genealogy and the Common Man' as a turning point that had opened the door to 'the complete transformation of the membership of the Society and of the interest in the subject in this country'. Indeed, during the 1960s overseas commentators had been struck by 'the curious "democratisation" of genealogy in England', something that was almost unknown in Europe.

Turning to the more recent scene, Camp acknowledged that the Society should have done more to capitalize on the immense interest in family history in the country at large. The growth of local family history societies was, he said, 'largely due, in the first instance at any rate, to a feeling of dissatisfaction with the services provided by the Society, particularly where newcomers were concerned'. The fragmentation and duplication of effort that had resulted from these local societies was, Camp said, 'a tragedy', though he accepted that local groups were much better placed than the SoG to help those at the grassroots.

He went on to review the Society's activities in various areas: indexes of members' interests; pedigrees in print and manuscript; parish registers; monumental inscriptions; emigration records; and apprenticeships and professions. In most cases his prescription was the same: more indexes. Monumental inscriptions, marriage licences, Poor Law records and poll books – all were candidates for indexing projects, to be undertaken either by the

Society or at local level. And by indexing, Camp meant traditional slip indexes filed in drawers, of the type used by Sherwood and Boyd.

Camp finished with a warning against the desire for easy answers which he saw amongst many newcomers:

> The Member in a hurry must be made to understand that there is nothing to be called 'instant genealogy', and that all those things done in a hurry will need to be done again. It is a slow and painstaking assemblage of detail which brings most satisfaction to the genealogist and family historian. He will not achieve anything if he is not willing to give patience and time to study, and to put something back which may help others. That perhaps is the whole crux of the matter.

Not all were convinced by Camp's ideas on indexing. 'Why', asked Iain Harrison in a letter to the *Magazine*, 'in 1979, are we still thinking in terms of poking ephemeral slips into index drawers?' The Society had recognized the potential of computers as early as 1967, and in 1973 had recommended methods and standards to facilitate electronic storage. Yet it continued to waste 'hundreds, if not thousands, of man-hours annually compiling indices that could be produced by machines in minutes'. 'Has the index itself become the absorbing interest of our members?', Harrison asked. This was just part of a wider broadside that also attacked the Society's facilities, attitudes to newcomers and publishing policy.

Space at Harrington Gardens had become tight almost as soon as the Society had moved in and as early as 1964 there was talk of needing to find new premises. When the freehold was bought in 1968 these plans were put on the back-burner, but by the late 1970s conditions were becoming intolerable. When, by 1978, no suitable alternative accommodation had been found, the executive set up a New Premises Committee to focus the search. As with the previous move from Chaucer House, the problem was partly affordability and partly the Society's exacting requirements. Few buildings had all the necessary features, from office space and a common room for members to floors that were strengthened (or capable of being strengthened) to carry the library's tremendous weight. This time there was a feeling that, for all its shortcomings, Harrington Gardens would be difficult to beat.

Eventually, in 1984, suitable premises were found at 14 Charterhouse Buildings near London's Barbican. This was a large and strong modern building built in the late 1960s for storing rolls of silk. There were three floors plus a basement and it had all of the features being sought, including good accessibility by public transport. The Society moved in over three weeks during July 1984 and opened its doors at the new location on Wednesday 1 August. Charterhouse Buildings remains the SoG's headquarters through to the present day.

For the Society's seventy-fifth anniversary in 1986 the usual celebrations were arranged. A one-day conference was held at Oxford alongside the Federation's half-yearly meeting. Such had been the suspicion towards the Federation, that in the twelve years since it had been formed this was the first time the two organizations had organized a joint event.

The centrepiece of the celebrations was a reception held at the Royal Overseas League on 26 June. At this meeting Sir Colin Cole, Garter King of Arms, presented Dr Chris Watts, chair of the executive committee, with the Society's grant of arms. As always with heraldry, the design was full of symbolism. The shield had an oak tree with its roots showing ('eradicated' in heraldic terminology), against a circular background reminiscent of ancient pedigrees with radiating lines. The supporters were two cranes, recalling the roots of the word 'pedigree' in *pied de gru*, and they were looking backwards to symbolize the genealogist's quest for the past. The motto was *Radices Quaeramus* – 'Let us seek our roots'.

Harrison, meanwhile, had become a strong advocate for computerization and campaigned for it at every opportunity. In a letter to the *Magazine* in March 1980, he offered a cogent analysis of the changes then affecting the family history world and the contribution computers could make in addressing them.[43]

'The irony of genealogy', noted Harrison, 'is that it is only made possible because we have such a vast accumulation of old records, and yet it is the volume of records that makes genealogy difficult.' As the attraction of family history increased, it was clear 'More documents will be handled, fingered, torn and withdrawn from use.' Furthermore, repositories were under financial pressure and it was likely less, not more, money would be available for archivists, accommodation, photography and printing. The situation was being compounded by family historians wanting to know more about their ancestors, resulting in bringing 'into our orbit new classes of records which, until a few years ago, were safe from our attention'.

The answer, Harrison argued, must surely lie in making best use of the technology of the day. 'In 1980 it is already quicker and cheaper to create a computer index than to write one manually', he noted. He called on the Society to 'give us an early and positive lead on the question of computers'.

In the face of these criticisms, a small *ad hoc* committee was set up under Alexander Sandison to look into the potential for the use of computers at the Society.[44] The committee identified four main areas. First, there were 'housekeeping activities' such as accounts, membership records, salaries and stock control. Secondly, there was word-processing, where standard packages could be used to ease the ever-growing demands of correspondence, especially as many of the enquiries were amenable to standardized replies. This would also improve the presentation of publications and allow them to be updated more quickly; 'sales even of single updated pages might prove profitable'. The next area was the library, where again standard packages could be used to catalogue the collections. Though this would bring many benefits, the scale of the task was immense.

Finally, there were 'genealogical applications' which offered 'fascinating possibilities'. The committee agreed reliance on index cards was 'absurd', but these old-fashioned methods could be used by volunteers working in their own homes. Computerized alternatives would require special equipment. However, the committee noted, 'hardware costs are falling and it may not be long before a minimal unit for entering data could be brought [sic] for a few hundred pounds and loaned to members for particular projects'.

Although home computers were becoming available, they were expensive and the situation where there was a computer in *every* home was still a long way off. Furthermore, these early computers required programs to be written from scratch for the most basic of tasks. Sandison explained how he wrote a program to extract and index names from a report. It took the computer six hours to process and sort 500 names. 'These programs to do the extraction and sorting took a month or so to write, but are available for my next project', he observed.

In practice, it would be several years before the Society acquired its first personal computer, and several more before it fully utilized the technology. In this it was no different to many other small organizations in Britain at the time.

When the membership records were eventually computerized in 1990 it revealed a fascinating picture of longevity. The member of longest standing was then Anthony Powell, the novelist, who had joined the Society in 1926 – some sixty-four years before. He was closely followed by Sir Anthony Wagner, who had joined the following year. A further eighteen serving members had joined before the Second World War, including the eminent archivist Fred Emmison, the Mormon genealogist David Gardner, the philanthropist Marc Fitch, and George Squibb, Norfolk Herald. In total, twenty-six people had been members for fifty years or more.

Meanwhile, the world was moving on. In one of his regular columns for *Family Tree* in February 1994, John Titford described a recent visit from Judith Reid, who ran the Genealogy and Local History search room at the Library of Congress in Washington, DC.[45] Reid had explained to him the workings of a new computer system taking off in the United States called 'Internet'. It allowed a searcher to find and retrieve electronic information of genealogical interest from all over the world. 'This surely, is what we'll all be using in a few years from now?', posed Titford rhetorically. In this – the first reference to the internet in a British genealogical publication – he was, of course, correct: the future of family history lay with technology.

*   *   *   *

Chapter 8

Swivel-Chair Genies

The arrival of personal computers in the late 1970s represents a key staging point in the development of family history. Genealogical information is ideally suited to automated processing and the 'micro computer', as it was known, gave family historians a powerful tool with which to store and process their data. It brought forward a new category of family historians, the computer genealogists – those (almost exclusively men) who were researching their family trees but also technically minded enough to get to grips with the new technology.

Leading the debate was Iain Harrison, a retired Flight Lieutenant from north Devon. In the face of what he saw as the SoG's sclerotic and bureaucratic approach, Harrison took it upon himself to wage a one-man campaign to promote the use of computers within genealogy in Britain. He contributed numerous letters on the subject to the *Genealogists' Magazine* and sponsored work on computerization techniques at the PRO, Kew.

Harrison set out the possibilities in an article in September 1980.[1] Such was the ignorance of computers at the time that he felt the need to spell these out at a very elementary level. Once information is entered and stored on a computer, he explained:

> The preserved information can be printed automatically in any chosen sequence. References can be presented in the original order, alphabetical, numerical or chronological. Alternative spellings of a single surname can be presented separately or together. Persons can be listed by age, geographic location or occupation. The machine can be instructed to repeatedly print all, or part, of the stored information, and each successive print-out will be updated to incorporate all additions and amendments entered since the previous printing. The print-out can be produced locally, or at another terminal positioned many miles away.

Whereas some saw computers as a means of speeding up the production of traditional indexes, Harrison recognized their potential in search, doing away with printed indexes altogether. 'Why not', he asked, 'leave all the references in the memory of the machine, and instruct it to list only those that may be relevant to our search?'

Genealogists, Harrison argued, needed to discard their old methods. This did not mean they should stop using original documents. 'Nothing equates to the sensation of handling old papers, but we must stop handling them for speculative searches. They have a life which is not only limited but is actually decreasing as genealogy increases in popularity.' What was needed was a massive programme of extraction of essential data 'from as many sources as possible'. This need not necessarily be indexed, simply stored in a systematic way – computers would do the rest.

Census records were an obvious candidate, Harrison thought, as well as the Registrar General's records, though they would have to be released to the public first. The Society's own records, such as the Great Card Index, Boyd's Indexes and the Document Collection could also be treated in this way. He even suggested his own coding system by which this might be done. It was called the Gendex Code and was based on the then standard 80 characters of a computer print-out, so that each entry occupied one line in a printed listing. It was essential, Harrison concluded, that individuals make a start on their own 'because modern technology will not await the ponderous deliberations of a committee'.

Harrison's article and an earlier contribution by Sandison stimulated much debate.[2] Major Riach urged the Society's *ad hoc* committee to provide clearer direction. Was it intended that the Society buy its own computer, he asked? If so, would it just be used for the Society's own records in the library or also for records held elsewhere, in which case the issue of standards arose. This need for standardized catalogues was also highlighted in a further contribution by Sandison himself. He also drew attention to issues in relation to computer languages (getting different machines to talk to each other), surnames (how to cope with variants), and limitations in searching large indexes. Colin Chapman, General Secretary of the FFHS, implored enthusiasts to explore all avenues and not get driven down 'one-way streets'.

Many family historians had taken tentative steps into computer genealogy but as soon as they encountered problems found they were on their own. There was no help available on programming problems, nor any centrally agreed standards for organizing and searching data. Individuals were working in isolation, continually reinventing the wheel.

Eventually, in 1982 the Society at last seized the initiative. At Camp's suggestion, it sponsored a seminar bringing together genealogists with computer interests for the first time. Called 'The Genealogist and the Computer', the seminar was organized by Peter Swann and held at Baden Powell House, south London, on 19 June. Academics and enthusiasts presented a series of papers describing their experiences with genealogical applications. One, 'Genealogy and Information', was presented by Conway Berners-Lee, a computing pioneer and senior researcher with International Computers Limited (ICL). His son Tim would go on to invent the World Wide Web – an innovation that transformed genealogy, alongside the rest of the modern world.

The seminar was a huge success and convinced Camp that the time was right to publish a new journal devoted to this fast-growing field. The *Computers in Genealogy* newsletter first appeared in September 1982. Edited by David Hawgood, a member of Sussex Family History Society, it aimed to cater for both amateur genealogists looking to purchase or use a personal computer in their research and computer professionals needing to process genealogical records. Such was the appetite for these new tools that within six months the newsletter had over 700 subscribers.

This interest transmuted into a separate Computer Interest Group, which held regular meetings at the Society including an annual one-day conference. The evening meetings for beginners proved especially popular, helping computer novices to find their way through what was a very confusing field.

As yet there was no established platform for personal computers and family historians were faced with an array of competing and incompatible hardware. Early consumer offerings such as the Sinclair Spectrum, Sinclair ZX and BBC Micro competed alongside hobbyist kits from the likes of Heath and Zenith, and even more exotic machines like the Tatung Einstein and the TDI Pinnacle. In a *Computers in Genealogy* survey in 1986, readers reported over fifty different computers in use from around thirty manufacturers.

With almost no genealogical software available for purchase, the Computer Interest Group and the *CiG* newsletter provided much-needed forums for people to learn from one another. Users reported on attempts to write their own programs to perform genealogical tasks, using the BASIC programming language, or on adapting other software, such as general-purpose databases and spreadsheets, for genealogical use. A whole cottage industry grew up as computer programmers wrote specialist genealogical programs or 'packages' tailored to the capabilities of particular hardware. Amongst these early offerings were: Easytree for BBC, written by Murray Kennedy; Belgen for BBC and Sinclair Spectrum, written by David Lane; and GG5 for BBC, written by David Barnard. Belgen was superseded by Heritage, a genealogy package for BBC Micros written to a specification produced by the Society.

One of the most popular of these early programs was Personal Ancestral File (PAF), a genealogical database developed by the LDS church. Files generated by PAF could be put on floppy disk and submitted to the Church's headquarters in Salt Lake City for merger into its central database, known as the Family Ancestral File.

The limitations of the early hardware were easily exposed. The filing system on a ZX81, for example, could only cope with sixty-five entries. Even a 1990-era BBC Micro could only hold 400 records in memory at one time, although this increased to almost 3,000 with a second processor. Programs and data had to be stored and loaded from cassette tapes and some systems needed to be plugged into a conventional television as a display unit.

The advent of Alan Sugar's Amstrad proved a gamechanger. Amstrad's PCW range offered much wider capabilities than its competitors. For the first time, consumers could buy an integrated unit comprising a central processor and keyboard, a monitor and floppy disks. Family historians were able to record not only their genealogical data, using programs such as David Loverseed's Genny, but could also use the PCW as a word processor, to write letters, articles and newsletters.

Ann Chiswell, of the Federation, spoke for many when she described the excitement of acquiring her first computer – an Amstrad PCW 8256.[3] 'I was spending every spare minute with the machine, and becoming so absorbed that sometimes I quite forgot mealtimes.' Her husband became so fixated on 'cracking' the database program that 'having to go to work during the day was a real nuisance to him'. It took the couple two months to learn how to enter a list of names into an index and get a print-out on continuous stationery. But having done this Chiswell soon found herself classed as an 'expert' and was offering advice to Iain Swinnerton, Elizabeth Simpson and others in the FFHS hierarchy.

In the mid-1980s, Amstrad, IBM and others began selling personal computers based on chips manufactured by the American company Intel. These used a new operating system – the basic programs that make a computer function – known as DOS, produced by a tiny start-up company called Microsoft. Within a few years personal computers based on Intel hardware and Microsoft software had become standard in the business world and were beginning to dominate home computing as well. The BBC Micro and all the other early runners gradually disappeared, together with their software, although some retained loyal followings for many years.

As well as doing everything its predecessors could do, the wider capabilities of the PC platform brought new possibilities. A new type of program, known as desktop publishing, allowed users to create text, headlines, borders and graphs, and then combine them as printed pages. Now, rather than just printing a plain narrative or a family tree, a family historian could annotate the output to make it more interesting and readable. They could even print their own booklets to share their researches with family and friends.

As the range of computers in everyday use shrank, the problem of interchanging data between machines became much easier. The predominance of the PC and the small range of operating systems in use meant that even machines from different manufacturers could read and write standard floppy disks that could be moved from one machine to another. This still left the problem of how to exchange information between different software programs. Since it received information from all over the world, from users using all types of different systems, the LDS church encountered this issue more often than most. In 1984 it released a specification, known as Genealogy Data Communications (GEDCOM for short), to allow the interchange of data between dissimilar systems.

GEDCOM uses a series of hierarchical 'tags' that identify various events and associated information commonly encountered in genealogical datasets. For instance, 'birth' could be a tag for an individual together with associated data on date, place, witnesses, etc. This approach proved extremely useful and by the late 1980s all major genealogical software packages supported the GEDCOM specification for importing and/or exporting data. Not all implementations were compatible with the specification, however, so that users were likely to lose fields when swapping between databases.

By the early 1990s, the amount of commercial software and shareware (software offered on a try-before-you-buy basis) had begun to increase. The market was dominated by US offerings. Alongside PAF, leading packages included Family Roots by Quinsept, Inc. and Roots III by Commsoft. Of the early British programs, only Pedigree – a PC-based variant of Easytree – survived the transition into the PC world.

As the market became more mature, the Computer Interest Group and its magazine adopted a less techie approach and developed wider appeal. Rather than being a forum for exchanging programming tips, the Group focused on problem-solving around commercial packages and offered more consumer-oriented guides to the growing mass of genealogical software. Similar computer groups – some with their own newsletters – began to spring up in local family history societies as well.

Technology was influencing family history in other ways too. Throughout the USA and UK enthusiastic micro owners were setting up electronic bulletin boards which were free for others to access and use. These boards were the electronic equivalent of the notice boards found in clubs where people could leave messages, advertisements, requests, etc. for all to read. Available around the clock, they offered other facilities only possible online, including private mail boxes for electronic mail. In addition to free boards, there were several commercial mail and bulletin board systems such as British Telecom's Telecom Gold. These commercial boards were run on large mainframe computers and offered access to vast databases, such as BLAISE (owned by the British Library), The Source, Dialog (both in the US), and World Reporter.

The more far-sighted in the family history community recognized the value of such services for genealogical enquiry. The amateur bulletin boards were free and designed to assist self-help groups like these. Such a network could link amateur researchers not just in the UK but throughout the world. Thus, a researcher living in Glasgow and needing to visit a churchyard in Massachusetts could post their enquiry to a central bulletin board. Here it might be read by a Massachusetts researcher in need of assistance with Scottish records, or by someone who already had the information and perhaps was even researching the same family. They could reply via the bulletin board or directly if the enquirer had left their contact details. The query would remain on the board so that others were free to add to it over time with their own comments and information, so that 'discussions' built up.

This was the theory, at least. In practice, these early services were clunky and only the most hardy computer enthusiasts made use of them. Transferring data internationally, for instance, required the user to dial into a specific UK node at the cost of a local telephone call. Only a small subset of family historians had computers and even fewer had modems, which at the time were still not standard equipment. Certain boards, known as newsgroups, did not require a dial-in connection; they could be accessed directly via a global network called the internet, then in a very embryonic state. At the time, virtually all internet access in the UK was via academic institutions.

The first dedicated genealogy newsgroup, net.roots, was launched in America in 1983.⁴ It was named after Alex Haley's *Roots* and represented the birth of genealogy on the internet. In 1987 a major renaming of all newsgroups was undertaken, as a result of which net.roots became soc.roots. 'Soc' stood for society, reflecting the fact that the group was of a social (as opposed to academic or technical) interest. It was followed in 1988 by the RootsWeb Surname List (RSL), a database of surnames being researched by people on ROOTS-L, the first genealogy mailing list. In 1995, ROOTS-L became the basis for RootsWeb, a community internet site that made genealogical data and research facilities freely available online to all genealogists.

Source material was the next to be hit by the computer revolution. Compact disc (CD) technology was slowly making its way from music to data storage. CDs could hold much more data than the floppy disks then in use, making them ideal for distributing large datasets.

Nigel Bayley, a Wiltshire businessman, was an early convert. His company, S&N Genealogy Supplies provided genealogy programs for the new Windows platform that was becoming popular on personal computers. Recognizing that the CD format was well suited for family history data, Bayley invested in one of the first CD writers – the equipment was the size of a suitcase. Before long he had published hundreds of parish records, directories and poll books on CD in a series called the British Data Archive. The series sold well and convinced him there was a real appetite for electronic data.

Next Bayley turned his attention to the census, which at the time was only available on film or fiche. This sort of information could never be published on CD, he was told – and certainly not as original images – because the datasets were simply too big. He experimented with various scanners and compression methods and eventually developed a system to publish the census on CD, using the Acrobat format developed by the computer company Adobe.

His friend and mentor Michael Armstrong ran a feature on the project in *Family Tree*. The article created massive interest and advance orders started to pour in. Bayley realized he had to bite the bullet. He remortgaged his house and risked everything to buy a full set of census fiches and the necessary equipment. Within a few years the company had published the full UK censuses from 1841 to 1901 on CD-ROM and had developed techniques to improve the image quality by the use of custom software and specialist equipment.

The LDS church was another early promoter of data products. Its 1992 edition of the IGI was offered on CD for the first time, although this was only made available to certain LDS family history centres and other institutions. Commercial publishers and family history societies also increasingly turned to CD as the medium of choice.

For researchers used to consulting records in paper indexes or on film and fiche, the potential to purchase a disk with millions of records was astounding. Writer John Titford recounted his first sight of the CD version of the IGI as a wondrous experience. 'Here was the IGI in all its glory', he wrote, 'You just type in the surname that interests you and you get a full listing of that name for the whole country concerned.'[5] He admitted to being 'gob-smacked' at being able to purchase the entire American telephone directory on CD – some 80 million names – for a mere $99. Genealogical disks remained expensive, however, and beyond the reach of many.

*   *   *   *

Following the arrival of the world wide web in the early 1990s, the amount of British genealogical content and services available online increased dramatically. In 1995 a dedicated newsgroup for the British Isles was launched, known in the rather obscure parlance of the day as 'soc.genealogy.uk+ireland'. As part of the preparations for this a group of enthusiasts got together to make British and Irish genealogy available on the web. The group – Malcolm Austen, Brian Randell, Alan Stanier, Phil Stringer and John Woodgate – were spread out across the country and had never actually met face to face, a foreteller of the remote collaboration that was set to be a hallmark of online genealogy.

At the time the web was only one of several services available via the global internet network. Services with obscure names such as 'Archie', 'Gopher' and 'FTP' allowed users to search newsgroups and other computer sites and to exchange information and files. But the procedures involved were extremely complicated. Each service needed a separate program, which had its own syntax and quirks. The system was cumbersome and bewildering for the newcomer.

The web, by comparison, was much more user-friendly. It enabled documents and databases held on computers all around the world to be linked together seamlessly into what appeared to the user to be a single large document. This 'document' could include not just text, but also pictures, sound and video. Users could browse the system, copying or printing off anything of interest to them, without needing to know where the information was stored or that multiple computers and sophisticated networks were involved in accessing it. Armed with these technologies, societies and individual researchers were able to create web pages that provided family historians with access to information more easily than ever before.

The enthusiasts' group set up a website that they called the UK&I Genealogy Information Service, which soon became abbreviated to 'GENUKI'. Their aim was to provide a gateway to the ever-growing body of genealogical information on Britain and Ireland. They structured the information into four levels based on localities. The first level corresponded to the British Isles as a whole. At the second level were the individual 'regions': England, Scotland, Wales, Ireland (Republic of Ireland and Northern Ireland), plus the Channel Isles and Isle of Man. The next level corresponded to individual counties, and the fourth to towns and parishes. Information was then subdivided within each of these levels according to the subject categories of the LDS Family History Library.

Rather than information resulting from genealogists' own researches, GENUKI concentrated on primary historical material. The earliest information sources included the complete texts of more than thirty PRO information leaflets (transferred from Malcolm Austen's website) and a complete address list for all the LDS Family History Centres in the British Isles. Original sources, such as volumes of Phillimore's Hampshire Marriage Registers, the Joiner Marriage Index for County Durham and the North Riding of Yorkshire, and a listing of officers and men who served at the Battle of Trafalgar, soon followed.

The site went live in March 1995, using the web address http://midas.ac.uk/genuki/. By October it was already hosting web pages for a number of family history societies, including Clwyd, Devon, Dyfed and Gwynedd. In November the Federation made its publication catalogue available on the site. Volunteers across the country began to contribute information on their societies and to populate the different county pages. Others created pages for individual parishes. By mid-1996 around forty regional family history societies – over one-third of the Federation's membership – had representation on the site, often through official channels. The site also provided links to material that could be found elsewhere on the internet, and in particular the World Wide Web, such as archives and major libraries.

GENUKI was hosted on servers across the country. As well as Manchester Computing Centre (where Phil Stringer worked) and the University of Newcastle (where Brian Randell was a lecturer), it involved computers at Oxford, Colchester, St Andrews and Dublin. By June 1996 the total amount of information generated or obtained by the service accounted for more than 30 Mbytes of computer storage. The Manchester server alone was serving up around 25 Mbytes of data per day to searchers in seventy different countries. Although paltry by today's standards – equivalent to just a handful of music downloads – at the time it represented a major step forward. Virtually none of this information had been available on the internet before and for the ordinary researcher it meant the horizons were being pushed back all the time. By the stage the GENUKI domain name was registered, in March 1998, the site held over 10,000 pages of genealogical information.[6]

The web was becoming contagious. Public bodies across the land rushed to set up websites for an all-too-grateful public. Of the national bodies, the Historical Manuscripts Commission is thought to have been the first to establish a presence online, in early 1995. Other pioneers included the National Library of Wales, the PRO, and the PRONI. Somerset Record Office was the first county record office to go online, in March 1996, followed soon after by Cumbria, Liverpool and Greater Manchester. National organizations such as the Society, the Guild and the Institute also launched sites around this time. Another gateway site or portal, called Familia, was launched in June 1997 providing details of genealogical holdings in public libraries in Britain and Ireland. In the US, Cyndi Howells set up a portal called Cyndi's List. Within two years it had links to over 30,000 genealogy sites worldwide, including many in the UK, arranged in over ninety categories.

The growth of commercial internet services brought these resources within the reach of a much wider constituency. Access providers such as CompuServe, Demon Internet and America-on-Line (AOL) allowed users to connect to genealogical resources (and much else besides) for a modest monthly fee and at the cost of a local call. They could use these services to communicate with others, acquire information, query databases and documents, download programs, and publish their own family histories. The family historian's world got bigger by the day.

Enterprising individuals recognized the increasing interest in using computers in genealogy as a commercial opportunity. Entrepreneurs sought to share their computer and family history expertise to offer services for this emerging market. S&N Genealogy Supplies – Nigel Bayley's company – led the field, selling genealogy programs and databases as well as publications. Ron City of PC Computer Services specialized in family history programs, while David and Jill Foster set up Pandect to support Family Tree Maker, a software program of American origin. Joe Houghton of Computing for Genealogists carved out a business selling his and others' books as well as a range of programs and databases. Other computer pioneers included Tony Reese of Bristol-based company TRACS specializing in Apple Macintosh computers, Trevor Rix of TWR Computing in Suffolk, and Genealogica, started by Mike Spathaky, a Leicester-based web designer.

David Hawgood, editor of *Computers in Genealogy*, and a leading light in the SoG's Computer Interest Group, was by now something of a computer guru. His *An Introduction to Using Computers for Genealogy* was much read by beginners, while his specialist publications, such as *GEDCOM Data Transfer – Moving Your Family Tree*, were sought out by those with more advanced needs. In 1996 he turned his attentions to the online world, publishing *Internet for Genealogy*, the first internet genealogy book written from a British perspective.

Not all were convinced of the net's virtues, however. Writing in 1995, Midlands genealogist Dr Peter Cooley noted:[7]

> It seems that every second family historian you speak to nowadays has heard of the Internet and the wonderful opportunities it may provide for them. Although I generally welcome new developments in genealogical computing with wholehearted enthusiasm, I feel bound to raise a strong note of caution on this occasion before there is a lemming-like stampede by genealogists with computers and modems determined to spend small fortunes browsing the Internet in the mistaken belief that somewhere is the one missing piece of data they have sought for years.

Referring to an article in *The Times* which described how Hawgood himself had discovered a distant cousin in Hong Kong via CompuServe, Cooley pointed out that only the initial contact had been via the internet. The real work of finding a common ancestor had required 'good, old-fashioned genealogy assisted by computer record-keeping'. The internet had a role in genealogy, Cooley concluded, but it was 'not a panacea'.

Another correspondent, H R Henly, replied that, far from a stampede, his approach, like that of others, had been very cautious. The internet was not a panacea but was certainly a useful tool. It was, he noted, 'unlikely that one will ever find detailed data such as births or baptisms on the internet on a comprehensive scale, but reference information in the form of indexes is likely to escalate, particularly if we, the active users of this information, encourage our individual societies to contribute any data that they have in machine-readable form'.[8]

* * * *

Paradoxically, the burgeoning interest in computer genealogy also benefited the conventional media. As well as books by Hawgood and others, computer topics became a staple of family history magazines, which by the mid-1990s were increasing in number. Until then Michael Armstrong and his team at ABM Publishing Ltd had had the field to themselves. *Family Tree* was well established, although it still looked and felt more like a community newsletter than a commercial publication. The intimate portraits of key figures from the family history world, featured in the early editions, were gone. But the magazine was still dominated by the 'official organs': the Society, the Federation, the Institute and the Guild each had columns in the monthly issue. Alongside these extensive coverage was given to readers' letters and contributions, as well as news from family history societies around the world.

The growing availability of computer programs and data products – microfilms, microfiche and CDs – did well for advertising revenues. In 1992 Armstrong attempted to capitalize on this by launching a quarterly sister publication entitled *Family Tree Computer Magazine*, edited by David Hawgood. It failed to take off, however: the computer enthusiasts wanted something more regular than a quarterly update, while those who had only a passing interest were reluctant to shell out for a second magazine. Within two years the venture was shelved and incorporated into the main publication, but Armstrong felt compelled to limit it to four pages 'until such time as there is a majority demand for more'.

A second attempt at diversification was equally unsuccessful. Armstrong saw that many articles submitted to *Family Tree* by readers were being turned down because they were too contemporary. He thought there could be an opportunity for a new magazine to cover the more recent past. The yardstick would be 'within living memory'. It would include stories from readers' own lifetimes and those handed down to them through their families. *Yesterday* launched as a bi-monthly publication in January 1996, edited by John Titford. In his introductory editorial, Titford enthused about it being 'an exciting opportunity for us to re-live some of those old memories, to realise that we're not alone in our recollections'. Readers were not so convinced and the magazine folded after a year or so. On another front, in 1989 *Family Tree* arranged a trip to the LDS Library in Salt Lake City, offering British researchers an opportunity to visit the world's largest genealogical library. It soon became an annual event, regularly attracting thirty to forty people, ending only in 2005.

Yesterday was partly a response to a newcomer on the block: *Family History Monthly*. Launched in October 1995, it was the brainchild of the London-based Diamond Publishing Group, led by Peter Doggett. Doggett and his team were catering for those new to family history and needing a firm grasp of the basics. The magazine had a much lighter, more accessible style. There were 'how to' articles designed to help the beginner get started and introduce them to the main classes of records. And for an increasingly celebrity-obsessed age, there was a strong focus on the rich and famous. Each issue included at least one article on a well-known personality, briefly describing their personal history (although little original research was undertaken) and the context and history of their surname. Delia Smith, Anthony Hopkins, Elizabeth Taylor, Sean Connery, Daniel Day Lewis and Joanna Lumley all featured in the early issues. Another innovation was the use of colour, something *Family Tree* had resisted, even though it had been commonplace in periodical publishing for some time.

Family History Monthly was just the first of several new publications to hit the newsstands. In 2001 the Public Record Office, together with a commercial partner, launched *Ancestors*. This was primarily a vehicle for the PRO and its projects, addressing family, military and local history. In 2003 Future Publishing Ltd, a publishing conglomerate active in many sectors, launched *Your Family Tree*. Future aims to dominate every market that it enters and follows a very different business ethos to the likes of Michael Armstrong. Its appearance on the scene signalled that family history had truly arrived: genealogy was now on the corporate radar.

As with all markets, the swelling up of entrepreneurial activity brought its fair share of failures, the most spectacular being a publishing venture called the Family History Club of Great Britain.

The Club was founded in 1990 by Welsh businessman Keith Park and his wife Tracey, 'for everyone interested in British or Irish ancestors'. The Parks launched a journal, *Family Twiglets*, and set about compiling a directory as a competitor to the *Genealogical Research Directory (GRD)*, an established and highly respected publication for which Elizabeth Simpson was the UK agent. The Club's version was to be aimed solely at British research. Park promised advertisers that he would be 'looking at an initial print run of 50–80,000 copies in paperback and 20–30,000 in hardback', adding that these figures 'may have to be drastically revised upwards'.[9] Such statements were incredible. At the time, the worldwide sales of the *GRD*, which was in its 15th edition and had built up a large following, were nowhere near that level.

With no established customer base or track record, Park had a problem: how to attract a sufficient number of contributors, who could then be relied on to buy the directory. He began harvesting names from family history society membership lists in ways that raised a fair amount of friction with society secretaries. Eventually officials of the Federation became involved.

By the time the *Family History Book of Knowledge* appeared, in 1991, the relationship between Keith Park and the family history establishment was fractious. In one article, Park lambasted officers of the Federation as an 'Eastern European communist style regime'. The Guild also came in for criticism and he dismissed those who did not agree with his method of working as 'dufflepuds, dim creatures that follow sheeplike'.

The Club continued to collect names for the next issue and, as with the first, all the entries were free. When the 1992 edition appeared it ran to more than 1,000 pages, containing entries from over 6,000 people. As a work of genealogical reference it was a useful source. But rather than concentrating solely on improving the directory, Park embarked on a series of increasingly ambitious and outlandish ventures. A National Portrait Directory was promised, 'giving people the chance to locate images of their ancestors in paintings'. The Lost Fortune scheme claimed to have information on unidentified monies in old bank accounts, while the Edwards Project aimed to collect information on claimants to a lost fortune.

The Family History Club's ambitions knew no bounds. Its Intelligence Database would 'record all known research interests in one single source'.[10] Its Book Reviews project would 'build a collection of reviews, covering all books (eventually) connected with family history, history of the UK, associated historic items i.e. military, transport, etc'.[11] The Time Travellers group aimed to compile 'a complete register of everyone undertaking one name studies, place studies or family reconstructions'. From a residential address in south Wales, the Club was seeking not just to duplicate but to better all that the Society of Genealogists, the Federation and others had achieved over more than eighty years. Most far-fetched of all was a database 'to record all known family tree data, fully linked up'. 'It will take years to build', reported *Family Twiglets* in March 1992, 'and has computer storage requirements beyond what is practical to use today. Keith has been looking at the design of this over the last year, and as yet the design is not complete.'[12]

Needless to say, the database never was completed. Like much of the Club's activities, it was wishful thinking on the part of the Parks. Club members soon became dissatisfied with the poor service they encountered and started to ask for their money back. People who had paid up-front for the next edition of the directory, promised for the autumn of 1993, also became concerned. Complaints began to flood in and the company came to the attention of Aberdare's Trading Standards department. When pressed Keith Park insisted that all was above board and that the book would eventually appear. BBC Radio's *Face the Facts* programme also investigated the Club's activities but the broadcast was aborted at the last minute.

Early in 1994 the Club wrote to members asking for donations, a clear sign that all was not well. A letter signed by Tracey Park claimed that government departments owed the company a substantial amount of money. In documents filed at Companies House around this time Keith Park noted that the 'directory has become so successful that it is now giving us problems due to its success'. The couple appear to have made genuine attempts to save the company, including an aborted deal with a local history publisher who planned to publish the 1993 directory at its own expense. In the end, these came to nothing. The Parks eventually sold the company to a businessman who subsequently disappeared, and they were left with a series of County Court judgments against them. The 3rd edition of the *Family History Book of Knowledge* never did appear and some 1,400 family historians each lost at least £20.

The Parks appear to have been dreamers, rather than fraudsters. There is no evidence that they deliberately set out to deceive anyone or that they acted with malice in any way. They just got carried away by their own ambitions and believed their own hype. But the episode served as a salutary lesson: the cosy world of the past was long gone. Family history was no longer a closed community but an open market, with all of the risks and pitfalls that that implied. *Caveat emptor.*

One positive outcome from the Family History Club debacle was that it convinced the Federation of the need to compile its own directory of research interests. The project was to be called the *British Isles Genealogical Register*, or *BIG R* for short. There would be separate sections for each English county, Scotland, Wales, Ireland, the Channel Islands, the Isle of Man and the Isle of Wight.

A trial run held in Cleveland in early 1993 proved very successful. Buoyed up by this, the Federation had 100,000 forms printed for distribution to member societies at the AGM in Norwich in April. Virtually all Federation members agreed to take part by distributing the forms in their next journal. The forms were little different to those used by Charles Bernau for his *International Genealogical Directory* ninety years before. Each had space for sixteen entries, listing the name being researched, location, county and period. There was no limit to the number of entries an individual could submit, provided they paid the entry fee of £1 per form.

BIG R set out to be as comprehensive as possible. For example, each variation of a name or location was to be counted as a separate entry, a practice that many societies did not follow in their own listings of members' interests. Concerted efforts were made to reach the many thousands of family historians who did not belong to organized societies, so as to spread the net as wide as possible. Once completed researchers would only have to consult one list to find people with the same or similar research interests. Separate county lists would also be available for those wishing to concentrate their interests in a particular locality.

Genealogists embraced the project with open arms. The Federation had estimated initially that it might cover 50,000 names. In the event, some 17,000 contributions were received covering 250,000 entries. Consequently, the entries took rather longer to process than was originally planned.

The project was a masterpiece of organization and a credit to the Federation's ability to mobilize the family history community. John Perkins, a member of the Federation's Computer Sub-Committee, acted as administrator. He assembled a small working group to oversee the project, backed up by a much larger team of volunteers spread across the country. At the peak of activity around 500 forms per day were being received. These were checked by validators with local geographical knowledge, who checked spellings and codings, before being passed to a group of eleven inputters.

The full *British Isles Genealogical Register* was eventually released in stages during summer 1994. Since it was much larger than intended, the county and other regional sections were produced on microfiche rather than in book form.

Further editions of *BIG R* were published in 1997 and 2000. But with the growth of internet facilities its role as a source of contacts diminished and the Federation later took the decision to discontinue it.

*   *   *   *

The burgeoning of commercial activity around family history needed an outlet. In North America, where entrepreneurialism was celebrated, commercial fairs had been a feature of the genealogical scene for many years. All Britain had was the English Genealogical Congress, which by this time had effectively developed into a summer school, with an intensive series of lectures spread out over five days. The format was already in decline. Numbers for the sixth EGC, held in Warwick in 1992, were half those at the previous Congress in Exeter three years before. Many family historians now looked instead to their local family history societies, which were becoming highly proficient in organizing first-class conferences and similar events.

Anthony Camp decided it was time to introduce the American concept to Britain and in 1993 persuaded the Society's executive committee to organize a Family History Fair. Its aim was 'to extend even further the appeal of family history research in response to the upsurge in public interest in recent years'. This was to be a purely commercial event, with no lecture programme. Exhibitors would include family history societies, dealers selling books, maps and postcards, professional researchers, suppliers of conservation materials, publishers, computer software developers, and help clinics.

Being new to the commercial arena, the committee was concerned that the Society did not overstretch itself. Booking a large hall would accommodate more visitors, but the price of the stalls might prove too expensive for the vendors and societies. Added to which, they had no idea how many people would turn up. If the fair proved a gigantic flop, the exhibitors could lose out, while the committee would have to answer to the Society's members as to why it had lost money on the event. It thus decided to err on the side of caution, booking the Royal Horticultural Old Hall, a modest-sized exhibition space in Vincent Square, Kensington.

By the time the doors opened, on Sunday 16 May 1993, it was clear the organizers had a problem: not too few people but too many. Around 2,000 were lining the square to gain admission and in parts the queue was three or four abreast. Some had arrived more than four hours before opening time. The venue was soon full to bursting and, for the sake of safety, people had to be admitted in small groups through the morning. A petrol station owner next to the Old Hall took pity on genealogists who were caught short and made his toilet available for those in the queue. Many did not bother waiting and went off to sample other London attractions instead.

It was an acute embarrassment and the Society was forced to apologize. In a statement, chairman Paul Blake described the event as 'a victim of its own success'.[13] The Society 'deeply regrets the inconvenience' caused to those in the queue, Blake went on, and hoped 'that they will support future fairs in larger premises'.

Many did come back. The following year, the event was held over two days in the much larger Royal Horticultural New Hall on Greycoat Street and ran without a hitch. The annual gathering soon became established as *the* event in the British family history calendar. In 1999, the Society decided to complement this with an additional and similar show in Birmingham, at the National Exhibition Centre. Called the 'Family History Experience', here the fair was only part of the concept. There was also to be a substantial lecture programme and half-day seminars for beginners covering family history research in general and the use of computers in particular. Advice clinics and access to the Society's resources were also expanded. The two-day event was held over a weekend in late September. By the time the doors closed on the Sunday evening some 4,000 people had passed through.

The success of the Society's efforts prompted other groups to try their hands with similar events. Within a few years successful fairs were being held regularly in places such as Preston, York, Leicester and Gateshead. Computer entrepreneur Mike Spathaky took the concept a stage further, launching GENFair, an online marketplace for societies and suppliers available all year round.

This online fair tapped into another emerging trend: e-commerce. The internet was no longer just a platform for family historians to communicate and access information but also for them to buy goods and services. GENFair offered not only transcriptions and indexes in microfiche, diskette, CD-ROM and booklet formats, but also membership subscriptions and other services. Banks were still reluctant to offer online payment facilities for societies and small merchants, so GENFair acted as a broker, handling all the credit card transactions and settling monthly with the suppliers.

Local societies soon recognized the potential, offering e-commerce facilities through GENFair on their own websites. After Nottinghamshire FHS launched its online purchasing facility in 1998 (also designed by Spathaky), internet sales of books and memberships brought in more than £450 within the first six weeks. Many of the overseas visitors took advantage of the ability to pay by credit card and joined for more than one year. The site aroused so much interest that the stock of back numbers of journals was exhausted for the first time.

*   *   *   *

Official systems, meanwhile, were being stretched to the seams by the demands placed on them by genealogists. By the late 1980s the General Register Office was handling more than 360,000 applications for certificates per year, equivalent to well over 1,000 every working day, the vast majority from family historians. This relentless increase in demand, together with outdated equipment and difficulties in recruiting and retaining staff in central London, meant that the civil registration system was gradually grinding to a halt.

Conditions were particularly acute in the public search room at St Catherine's House, which was receiving around 7,000 visitors per day. Some two-thirds of these were family historians, and a further 10 per cent were professional genealogists, academics or record agents. The remainder – around a quarter of users – were people making one-off visits, such as needing to obtain a copy of a certificate for a passport.

Everyday this motley ensemble of professionals, amateurs and the unsuspecting public joined an unsightly battle to search the public indexes. Summer was the busiest time, when British researchers making use of their summer holidays mixed with foreign visitors trying to establish their British roots. One researcher at the time offered this advice to anyone contemplating a visit:[14]

> You will need to be six feet tall to easily reach the top shelves that house the indexes, and have shoulders three feet broad to secure a place on the sloping desks where you can open and study them. Bulging arm muscles are needed, as each one is about 24 inches deep and 18 inches wide, and is quite heavy. A good swinging action is needed to swing the index from the shelf onto the sloping desk, and woe betide anyone who has nicked your space, as they are likely to receive an index on their head.

Space was tight and in the heat tempers often flared as everyone desperately tried to find what they wanted, usually on a one-day visit. Having found the correct reference, searchers needing to order a certificate had to join a long queue before being served by surly GRO staff.

At least day visitors were at an advantage in this respect. At the time St Catherine's House handled all search enquiries. Those who visited in person were able to apply for a certificate on the spot and to collect it three days later for just £5: this compared to the £12 charged to those who applied by post. If the full reference were not known, an applicant would be charged a further £12 for a five-year search in the indexes, only half of which was refunded if the search was unsuccessful. And on top of this, all postal applications took several weeks to process.

After intensive lobbying from the family history community, in December 1988 the government issued proposals for reforming and modernizing the civil registration system in England and Wales. Reminiscent of earlier proposals. these plans involved relocating much of the Office of Population Censuses and

Surveys (OPCS) from London to Southport, where certain divisions were already based. Both the Public Search Room and the OPCS Library, which were regularly used by the public, were to remain in London, as would the OPCS's work on population and medical statistics. This would free up facilities at St Catherine's House to improve the search rooms.

The move was completed by March 1991. As part of these changes, all certificate applications were now handled from Southport, so that the system was no longer weighted in favour of those able to apply in person at St Catherine's House. A new twenty-four-hour priority service was also introduced for anyone needing a certificate urgently and willing to pay a premium.

The respite was short-lived, however. Continual increase in demand meant the Search Room was soon as crowded as it had been before. As it turned out, external events forced the OPCS's hand. In 1994 the BBC Pension Fund, which owned the Kingsway building, sold it to property developers. The new owners made clear that they intended to redevelop the site and that the OPCS's lease would not be renewed when it ran out in 1999.

As luck would have it, another relocation was also in the offing. A new extension to the PRO at Kew had recently been built, allowing the older public records to be moved there from Chancery Lane. This left only the census returns on microfilm in the old building, which also needed to be relocated. The ideal solution, from the family historians' point of view, would be for the civil indexes and the census returns to be housed together.

The Society of Genealogists (through its Director, Anthony Camp), the Federation and others in the family history world began lobbying to this effect. For once the authorities proved receptive to the needs of genealogists and began concerted attempts to find suitable premises.

After months of searching and negotiation, in November 1996 the Office for National Statistics (ONS, the successor body to the OPCS) and the PRO signed an agreement for a new combined facility at Myddleton Place, off Rosebery Avenue, Islington. The new venture would be called the Family Records Centre (FRC). It was conveniently close to the London Metropolitan Archives and the SoG, making this area of north London a 'golden triangle' as far as family historians were concerned.

The Centre opened its doors to a welcoming public on Monday 10 March 1997. The old census rooms had closed the previous Friday, severing a 700-year link with recordkeeping on the Chancery Lane site. The birth, marriage and death indexes moved from St Catherine's House a few weeks later.

Family historians now had the use of a light and modern building spread across three floors. Down in the basement was a cloakroom and a large refreshment area with the latest vending machines. On the ground floor was a well-stocked bookshop, alongside the BMD indexes. The PRO occupied the first floor, with visitors being given a pass, a seat and a black box to access the microfilms as they were at Chancery Lane (the box was used to keep a film's place in the storage drawer). As well as the census records on microfiche and microfilm, there were PCC wills and Nonconformist records and a bank of computers equipped with FamilySearch, the computerized version of the IGI. Other innovations included a computer link to the Scottish General Record Office in Edinburgh, and a small library of family history reference books.

For researchers used to working elbow to elbow in the confines of Kingsway or Chancery Lane, it was genealogical heaven. They found the facilities much better organized and the atmosphere more relaxed. Visitors were now allowed to take bags in with them and to use pen, rather than pencil, as no original documents were kept at the Centre. 'Research in comfort at last!', 'Very impressive. Lots of room and freedom to move about', and 'Everything the old search rooms were not', were typical of the comments received at the time. Opening hours were soon extended, including Saturday opening (which had been usual at St Catherine's House but was new for the PRO).

As search rooms across the country became ever busier, more attention had to be given to security. Traditionally archivists had maintained a low-key approach, casting occasional causal glances around the room to make sure readers were treating the records with respect, or not slipping them into their bags. But with many documents small and easily removable, some users found the temptation to dishonesty difficult to resist. The old assumptions that those interested in archives were intrinsically honest no longer applied.

Almost all record offices required searchers to sign a register on each visit, but it was rare for this to be checked in any way. A number of offices considered introducing a reader's ticket, but since searchers often visited several offices on a regular basis it was recognized there would be value in a common system. Negotiations within the Association of County Archivists led to the introduction, in 1988, of a reader's ticket for the County Archive Research Network (CARN). Initially valid in twenty county record offices, CARN tickets required the applicant to register just once at any participating office, giving their name, address, telephone number and signature, together with some form of identification.

Repositories used the tickets to validate signatures in the daily register and in some cases they had to be surrendered for the production of documents. This was just part of a package of new security measures. Increasingly archivists took to counting out documents in small numbers rather than issuing them in big bundles; bags and briefcases were banned from search rooms; and security barriers were introduced. Users viewed these developments with frustration, especially those who had been visitors for many years, but they gradually came to be accepted as a necessary part of the record office experience. Other repositories soon joined the scheme and CARN tickets came to be accepted more or less nationwide.

The Family Records Centre only covered English and Welsh records. Scotland had long maintained a similar facility at New Register House, where researchers could mine a rich seam of genealogical sources. Whereas searchers south of the border had to be content with the indexes, in Scotland there was open access to the full registers on microfiche, from the beginning of statutory registration (1855) through to the present day. Pre-registration parish registers (in Scotland known as Old Parochial Registers or OPRs) and the 1841–91 census returns could also be consulted, as well as a range of secondary sources such as maps, directories and the complete FamilySearch on CD-ROM. Users paid a fee of £17 per day or, for professionals and other frequent visitors, £1,500 per year.

Despite having some of the best genealogical facilities in the English-speaking world, here too there was pressure to improve access even further. In this case it would mean making use of the new medium that was beginning to permeate the family history world: the internet.

* * * *

Ian Galbraith was a young information technologist with a strong interest in archives. In the late 1980s he had founded a company – the first in Europe – offering document scanning services and subsequently worked as a consultant for the PRO, the Courts Service, the Land Registry, the Irish General Register Office and other government departments. Galbraith realized that the new communication technologies were set to transform the world of archives and this shift offered an ideal opportunity to build a business.

In 1996 he approached the office of the Registrar General for Scotland (RGS) with a proposal: would the office give permission for its information to be put on the web and would it work with him to do it? The goal – to index 30 million records – was huge and Galbraith had relatively limited business experience. But such was the mystique surrounding the internet at the time, government departments like the RGS were prepared to give young entrepreneurs like him a serious hearing. It was the start of the 'dot-com' boom with new businesses springing up every day. Seeing an opportunity to be in the vanguard, the RGS eventually agreed – Galbraith could have the data.

With his brother, David, Ian Galbraith set up a company, Origins.net. The pair put in £200,000 themselves and set about raising another £2m to fund infrastructure and marketing. The service launched in the spring of 1998, offering access to the indexes of births, marriages, and deaths back to 1553, as well as the index to the 1891 census. The 1881 census was added soon after. It was the first pay-per-view genealogical website anywhere in the world, and the first to provide complete coverage of an entire country. Users paid £6 for a maximum of thirty specific searches in the indexes. They could then order the certificates or census entries at a cost of £10 each. All payments were made by credit card and processed on the site in real time.

The internet had been making its presence felt in the genealogical world for several years. Family historians were becoming used to exchanging information via email and newsgroups, to downloading software, to ordering books and CD-ROMs, and even to consulting free indexes compiled by volunteers and made available by family history societies or individuals' own websites. But Origins was different. Now, for the first time, genealogists were being offered original data (albeit in index form) from an official source on a commercial basis. A rubicon had been crossed. Once researchers experienced the ease of searching online they would not want to go back to purchasing data CDs or queuing at record offices. It would take several years for such services to become widespread, but the direction was already set.

Genealogy's old guard would take some convincing, however. Having recently retired from the SoG, Camp wrote a review of the Origins service that was extremely critical of the RGS's approach. Other formats for the index data had been withdrawn, Camp noted, in case they 'undermined the viability of the commercial operation now in position'.[15] Such a service was, he suggested, 'a very curious operation for a government department to be involved in'. It 'ruthlessly exploits' volunteers who had worked to index the OPRs.

His criticisms drew a response from Tony Reid, a professional genealogist based in Edinburgh, who expounded the benefits of the Scottish system. The Origins service, he insisted, was only possible because of the extensive work that had already been undertaken to computerize the indexes since the late 1980s. Scottish users experienced better quality of service (even without Origins) because they paid higher fees. Turning to Camp's central criticism, that only the indexes were available, Reid pointed out that at least it was a start and better than anything available in England and Wales. Compiling digital images of the certificates themselves would be an immense task: 'It will happen one day but not, I suspect, without adequate search fee income to part-fund the operation.'[16] Here was the rub; digitization was expensive and someone would have to pay.

In London, meanwhile, a group of computer genealogists had come up with another approach for accessing indexes online, making them a basis not for a business but for a community project. What, they reasoned, if this new medium were to be used as a platform for that staple of the genealogist over the last hundred years – transcription?

Ben Laurie and Graham Hart were professional programmers. Laurie, in particular, was a veteran of free (so-called 'open source') software projects on the internet including Apache, a program used to run web servers. In December 1997 they found themselves in conversation with Camilla von Massenbach, another experienced genealogist, about how many family historians were actually using the internet and where it might all lead. They realized that with its ease of use, worldwide reach and low cost of access the net was the ideal means to facilitate a transcription project. The question was, what could they transcribe?

Source records were out of bounds because they could not be distributed efficiently, but anything that had already been microfilmed or microfiched was a contender. The GRO indexes were the ideal candidate. They were the key records for locating a life event where the date was not known and an essential source for all family historians. If they could be put online and made searchable, research would be far easier. Apart from the obvious benefit of much quicker searches, researchers would be able to match up marriages, see the distribution of surnames across the years, track how people moved across the country and much else besides. Taking a hundred years as a cut-off point, the team estimated that there were around 100 million records (from 1837 to 1898) – a huge number, but with enough people it could be done and Laurie and his colleagues would still be young enough to tell the tale.

The prospects did not look good, however. The GRO closely guarded its indexes and had resisted every demand from family historians to make such information more widely available. Would they really give up their holy grail to a group of computer geeks without any guarantees of what would happen? Laurie and his colleagues decided it was worth a try. They contacted the Office of National Statistics, the GRO's parent body, which owned the indexes, and letters began to pass back and forth. Whether the ONS was influenced by the lead shown by its Scottish counterpart, or whether like the RGS it got caught up in internet frenzy is not clear, but for whatever reason it finally agreed.

In a letter to Laurie in July 1998, Elizabeth Wilson, head of certification services at the ONS, stated that the Office was prepared to grant permission to publish online for records over one hundred years old.[17] Access to the information would have to be free of charge and the relevant website would have to carry various caveats on Crown copyright and subsequent use. In a tacit admission of the criticisms made by genealogists over the years, Wilson added: 'It may also be wise to include a disclaimer about the accuracy and completeness of the indexes which are both very poor in the earlier indexes.'

Laurie and colleagues were taken aback by the response, but realized they had to get organized – in case the ONS changed its mind. The first issue was where to host such a large project. Substantial storage space would be required, not to mention bandwidth for users' searches. RootsWeb, the US-based genealogical data co-operative, stepped forward. It agreed not only to host the website, but also to provide all the equipment and day-to-day administration required. Not being marketeers, Laurie and colleagues settled on a simple descriptive name for the project. Thus, FreeBMD was born.

Using RootsWeb and other channels, the FreeBMD team appealed for volunteers to act as transcribers. Individual volunteers were grouped into syndicates, each being allotted a set of records to work on. Since most of the work was done remotely, syndicates did not need to be in the same geographical area, or even in the same country. Each was overseen by a coordinator who helped syndicate members and made sure the transcription was done to the right standards. Many transcribers agreed to buy the source material – the ONS fiches – themselves at the cost of £24 plus VAT per calendar year for each 'event' series (birth, marriage or death).

The task before them was formidable. Not only did the original registers have errors and omissions, many were handwritten and so very difficult to read. The films and fiches used had been created directly from these original books, but the transcribers soon found them to be incomplete. Some had pages missing or damaged, while others had been badly photographed.

After much effort, the FreeBMD database went live on 30 December 1998, containing some 20,000 entries. At first, it made little impact. The dataset was tiny and coverage patchy, so that the chances of a researcher finding a particular match online were extremely remote. But as time went on the network effect began to kick in. The new ways of working tapped into human resources on a scale that the genealogical community had never mobilized before. The basic transcription process – copying from original records and quality checking of the results – was essentially unchanged from the days of Sherwood and Boyd. But the way in which the new technologies allowed this to be replicated broke all barriers. Volunteers not just in Britain but around the world were able to work on the project, contributing as much or as little as they wished.

With such vast resources at its disposal, FreeBMD grew rapidly.[18] By March 1999, some eight weeks after the service had been launched, there were 100,000 entries online and by the end of the year well over 500,000 entries had been transcribed.

From then on FreeBMD was set on a course of near-exponential growth. Milestone after milestone was passed with accelerating speed: first one million entries (February 2000), then two million (May 2000), ten million (April 2001), and twenty million (October 2001). By the end of 2002, the database had over forty-five million entries and was being added to at the rate of two million records every month, contributed by a network of 5,000 transcribers. The milestone of 100 million unique records was reached on 16 May 2005, and 200 million just before the project's tenth anniversary in September 2008.

A project of this magnitude naturally attracted the interest of commercial rivals. The founders could easily have sold out and made a fortune. Sticking true to their ideals, however, they established FreeBMD as a registered charity, with Laurie, Hart, von Massenbach and a fourth colleague, David Mayall, as trustees. In 2003 the ONS relaxed the 100-year rule, allowing the project to work on more recent entries as well. Although the indexes are still far from complete, today the site regularly handles over 300,000 searches per day.

FreeBMD's success did not deter others from taking the commercial route. While many of these were start-ups, a 'bricks and mortar' company decided it would also chance its hand in the burgeoning genealogy market.

Title Research was set up in 1965 by Thomas Curran as a consultancy for probate professionals. It carried out research for solicitors trying to trace unknown or missing beneficiaries of wills and trusts. In the course of its work the company needed to consult the civil registration indexes on a daily basis and took the decision to scan and digitize these to increase the efficiency of its operations. Curran retired in 2000 and handed over the reins to his son, also called Tom.

The younger Tom Curran had recently joined the company from the media sector and knew all about the internet. There could be an opportunity, he thought, to use its rights to data from the civil registration and census indexes to create a profitable consumer website. Having obtained the necessary permissions from the GRO, he set up a new venture called 1837online.com.

Whereas FreeBMD had set out to transcribe and index each individual entry in the civil indexes, Title had contented itself with scanning and indexing complete pages of the index registers. It was these that were made available through the new business. The website launched in April 2003, offering access to the complete registration indexes for England and Wales from 1837 through to 2002. As with Origins, the website adopted a pay-per-view model.

The reliance on page scans rather than individual entries was not ideal for these purposes. Anyone looking for the birth of a 'Tom Curran', for example, might find it in a page where the entries ran from 'Crow' to 'Cutler'; only these first and last entries for each page were referenced. Since there were four sets of index registers per year (one for each quarter), a ten-year search might involve consulting up to forty separate page scans. The system was cumbersome, but the best available for those years not yet indexed individually by FreeBMD. Furthermore, 1837online was the only site offering digital scans of the original registers, which otherwise were only available at the FRC or on microfiche.

Family historians were prepared to overlook the system's shortcomings and, as with Origins and FreeBMD, flocked to the site in droves. In 2004 the company added consular records to its offering, allowing researchers to search for British nationals who were born, married or died overseas. Records from the two World Wars were also added, followed soon after by a full transcription, with digitized images, of the 1861 census. In December 2005, it acquired the records of the National Archivist (a private website), including passport applications and death duty records. In November 2006 Curran rebranded the site as Findmypast.co.uk, reflecting the much wider range of online records and services that were now available. However, Findmypast lacked the resources necessary to compete on the global stage and in 2007 Curran sold the site to Scotland Online. This, in turn, was acquired by the publishing conglomerate D C Thomson and rebranded as Brightsolid Online Publishing Ltd.

By this time Findmypast's main competitor was not Origins but MyFamily Inc., owners of the leading American website, Ancestry.com. The British obsession with family history had not gone unnoticed across the Atlantic and in 2001 MyFamily set up a UK office, determined to grab its share of this booming market.

The company's origins were in Provo, Utah, as a publisher of books for the LDS church, although it claims to have no formal association with the Mormons. With the arrival of the web, MyFamily moved into internet genealogy databases and by 2000 had established Ancestry.com as the largest online subscription-based genealogy site. It began looking for opportunities abroad and with its expanding customer base and rich history of records, Britain was the natural market to be in.

A UK-specific site, Ancestry.co.uk, launched on 18 September 2002. MyFamily had managed a coup by securing an agreement with the PRO for the rights to transcribe and digitize the 1891 census, one of the most recent then available. It also struck a deal with FreeBMD for access to its ever-growing fully indexed database in exchange for sponsorship of the voluntary transcription efforts. Other early Ancestry offerings included fifteen million names from parish and probate records in the UK and Ireland, and an electronic version of Pallot's marriage and baptism indexes covering some four million entries.

Within months of Ancestry's UK launch, there was yet another site vying for genealogists' attention and their money. Genes Reunited was a spin-off from Friends Reunited, a website that enabled people to reconnect with former schoolmates and work colleagues. The brainchild of a husband and wife team, Steve and Julie Pankhurst, Friends had a very different feel to other genealogy sites. It relied on communication rather than data, with people connecting with each other in what would become known as a 'social network'. This model could work equally well, they thought, in family history, allowing researchers to build extended family networks.

The Genes Reunited software enabled users to put their family trees online, either by building them from scratch or uploading existing data. They could also add individual photos and notes for each relation. The names from each tree were added to a central database and were accessible for anyone to search, but the full tree was only available to those authorized to view it by the member.

Genes was a genealogical directory for the internet age. Conventional directories only allowed researchers to search for relevant research interests in the most general way – whether someone was searching for a surname in a particular county or a particular period in time. In print, any more detail than this was totally impracticable. But with the net, the level of information that could be held and searched was unlimited. Added to this was the interactivity. Once a member (membership of the site was free initially) had identified another member with whom their trees overlapped, they could send them a message and request further contact. It was instantaneous and powerful. Often people found the site lifted 'roadblocks' they had been stuck on for years. Others discovered relatives they never knew existed, even living just a few miles away. The model was attractive but not enough to keep the punters coming back. Genes decided it too needed data to attract people back to the site and provide a source of revenue.

Thus, by the early 2000s Genes had joined Origins, Ancestry, Findmypast and the Genealogist (a genealogy website started by S&N's Nigel Bayley) in the clamour for historical data. Market economics now kicked in. Prices dropped while the range of information and services available to customers expanded. The ground rules were clear: this was now a battle for scale and only those with the most comprehensive customer offerings – which essentially meant the biggest datasets and best customer service – would survive.

Into this increasingly cut-throat world of internet commerce stumbled the hapless PRO.

* * *

The Family Records Centre, where the PRO was a partner, was proving hugely popular. In its first year of opening it received some 140,000 visitors, compared to the 28,000 who went to Chancery Lane, and the numbers kept on increasing. The new facility had higher capacity than those it replaced, but even here it was estimated that by 2003 the Centre would have reached saturation point. And this was without the impact of the 1901 census, which was due to be released in 2002. PRO officials foresaw this would bring an army of new researchers of all ages, which, together with increased visits from existing users, would cause an unprecedented upsurge in demand at the FRC.

Digitization was clearly the way to go. The 1901 census would be digitized and made available to researchers via the internet. This would be a huge undertaking. The census ran to more than thirty-two million names on something like 2.5 million pages. Nothing like it had ever been attempted before.

Financial restrictions on capital expenditure meant the PRO was unable to finance the project itself; it would have to seek commercial partners under the Labour Government's Private Finance Initiative (PFI). Advertisements were placed in December 1998, according to European procurement procedures, from which a short-list was prepared. The specification required that the contractor develop the system and undertake the indexing and digitization, as well as operate the project once it was made available on the internet. An online service was also to be made available at designated service centres, such as the FRC. The project was to be self-financing, with the contractor able to recover their full set-up and operating costs and the remaining revenues being shared equally with the PRO.

After due process, in October 1999 the PRO awarded the contract to the Defence Evaluation and Research Agency (DERA). The decision was surprising. As the name suggests, DERA's background was in defence: it was a government-funded agency undertaking research into defence systems, covering everything from biological warfare and new types of weapons to cybersecurity. As a research centre it was of the highest standing – employing the greatest concentration of PhDs in the country – but it had virtually no background whatsoever in consumer markets, which is what operating the service would effectively entail. At the time of the bid DERA was in the process of being privatized and within a few months was reborn as QinetiQ plc, a public company.

The PRO was keen to ensure that users were involved at every stage. Several open meetings on the project were held at the FRC during 1998 and 1999, and following the contract award a 1901 Census Project Advisory Panel was set up involving, in the management speak that now infected the PRO, relevant 'stakeholders'.

One of the Advisory Panel's main concerns was for the principle of free access to be retained. The contractor clearly had to make money, so there were no objections to charging for access via the internet, on a 'pay-per-view' or some other basis. But it was essential that access at the PRO itself remained free, especially as no microfiche version would be produced. The PRO eventually agreed to this, mandating that access to the electronic form of the 1901 census be made available free of charge at the FRC and a handful of other repositories.

So confident were those involved of a smooth launch that they allowed expectation of the project to reach fever pitch. In the months running up to the launch, the family history press was full of articles and adverts, and over the long Christmas holiday the story got taken up by the general press and broadcasters. *Ancestors* magazine, another of the PRO's commercial ventures, explained:[19]

> The 1901 teams at the PRO and QinetiQ have had a hectic few months doing the final checking and are looking forward to seeing the service go live on 2 January 2002. We know many hundreds of thousands (if not millions) are also eagerly awaiting this date. Many of you have asked whether the site will crash as everyone tries to access the site at 9am (GMT). We can assure you that QinetiQ have carried out numerous tests on the system. It has been designed so that if it should reach user capacity it will simply deny access to any new users. A message will be

displayed explaining that the site is busy and will advise users to try again later.

The worst fears of these *Ancestors* correspondents were realized. From the moment the site went live on Wednesday 2 January it struggled to meet demand as a combination of dedicated researchers and the mildly curious rushed to get a genealogical fix. Visitors were soon turned away but this did not stop the site from crashing repeatedly. By the weekend a restricted service was being offered. Attempts to increase access proved unsuccessful and by the beginning of the following week the site closed completely while the team considered what to do.

Under siege, the PRO blamed the media for raising awareness of the site to unsustainable levels. 'We didn't aim for publicity', announced a spokesman. 'We thought we would space it out, but the press found out and increased the numbers who knew about it. We understand the disappointment and frustration but it is a sign of the massive demand for family history.'[20]

The scheme had been controversial from the start: many in the family history community were hostile to the whole idea of commercial companies becoming involved with public records; another faction was sceptical of digitization and the increasing reliance on computers in genealogy. Each of these camps now felt their position had been vindicated and had no hesitation in saying so. *Family Tree* received its largest correspondence on any issue in the magazine's eighteen-year history.

As the facts were uncovered, one word was used over and over again: 'fiasco'. The genealogy establishment in particular felt let down. In the run up to the launch Richard Ratcliffe, the Federation's representative on the Advisory Committee, repeatedly called attention to experiences with other genealogy websites which had crashed during their early stages. In 1998, the Commonwealth War Graves Commission website had crashed within hours of putting its First World War Debt of Honour database online. A similar experience had befallen the release of the Ellis Island Immigration Centre records in the US, with the website receiving nearly fifty million hits in the first six hours. QinetiQ, however, maintained that it was confident it had set up a system that would cope with the demand.

Service was eventually restored some nine months later, a frustrating period during which access was only available through online terminals at the PRO and through old-fashioned fiche at Kew and certain local studies libraries.

Family historians were prepared to forgive the crashes; after all, demand is hard to predict and a new service is bound to attract attention during its early stages. What they could not forgive was the poor quality of the transcribing. As more people began to access the site it became clear that the quality of the data left much to be desired. Names and places had been copied incorrectly and whole households had been missed off. Whoever had done the transcription was clearly not familiar with nineteenth-century handwriting. Their ire was aggravated by the PRO's pay-per-view charging structure, whereby searchers were charged by the number of searches they made. The census could only be searched for individual people, rather than whole households, at a cost of 50 pence per person. Viewing the remainder of the household cost a further 50 pence and to see an image of the original census entry (essential given the poor transcription) cost a further 75 pence. Thus, researchers were faced with charges of up to £1.75 per household (or more if the entries cut across several census pages). Added to this was a cumbersome payment system involving either prepaid vouchers (which had to be bought elsewhere) or credit card payments (only valid over a forty-eight-hour period).

Two conservative MPs took up the issue and, together with *Family Tree*, started probing the whole 1901 story. It emerged that one of QinetiQ's subcontractors was Enterprise and Supply Service (ESS), the commercial arm of HM Prison Service. When it became clear that additional resources would need to be deployed for the transcription work to be completed on time, ESS had subcontracted a proportion of the work to commercial data input companies in India and Sri Lanka. Parliamentary questions revealed that almost 80 per cent of the transcribing had been carried out outside the UK, with both QinetiQ and the PRO involved in quality assurance checks. Another revelation was that of four organizations shortlisted for the contract only two provided full submissions. It left the impression that QinetiQ, a public sector body eager to find its feet in the commercial world, had been earmarked for the work from the outset.

The very public nature of the failure was a disaster for all concerned. For the PRO, embarking on its first major commercial venture, it raised doubts on the Office's ability to manage large projects and whether it was up to the demands of the online world. For the newly privatized QinetiQ, it damaged the company's reputation just when it was seeking to diversify outside of core defence markets. And for family historians, it served to show that the public records were now just a commodity, to be bought and sold like everything else. The episode left a bitter taste with many.

The National Audit Office's investigation into the project was particularly critical of the PFI arrangements, whereby revenues were to be shared between the two partners. It noted that changes in government policy meant that 'alternative licence arrangements . . . allow greater flexibility for commercial exploitation of public records than a more conventional PFI contract'. Proposals to digitize the 1881 and 1891 censuses, which were originally part of QinetiQ's ten-year contract, were put on hold.

Having been left to take the flak for the deficiencies of its business partner, the PRO's relationship with QinetiQ never recovered. The contract was terminated early and both parties attempted to move on and put the unhappy episode behind them. In 2002, the PRO became the National Archives

(TNA).[21] Ostensibly, the move was motivated by a merger with the Historical Manuscripts Commission, but one can imagine the marketing department's glee at the opportunity to ditch this damaged brand.

Marketing, contracts, private finance: it was all a far cry from 2 January 1992, when just 100 or so people formed an orderly line at Chancery Lane to view the 1891 census returns. Family history in Britain had travelled a long way in ten years.

* * * *

After the early success of *Roots*, *Family History* and similar TV programmes, genealogy had dropped off the broadcasters' radar during the late 1980s and 1990s. With the growth of the internet and in the wake of public interest in the 1901 census, the production company Wall to Wall decided it was time to return to the issue and approached the BBC about making a new series. One of the researchers on the show was Nick Barratt, a specialist in medieval archives, who had worked at TNA before leaving to work for the BBC and set up his own research company.

The producers looked at various formats for the programme. A game show was briefly considered, as was a magazine-style programme with members of the public. None of these seemed to fit the bill, however. In today's celebrity-obsessed age, the team reasoned, the programme needed big names if it were to make an impact. Eventually they hit on the idea of a social documentary using celebrities as presenters. The programme would not be *about* the celebrities but would be fronted by them, using the presenters' own family histories to illustrate wider social history. Barratt's company, Sticks Research Agency, was engaged to do the background research, interviewing the celebrities and their families, rummaging around in archives, and building a story for each episode that illustrated a particular element of Britain's social history.

Who Do You Think You Are? (*WDYTYA*) aired for the first time on BBC2 at 9.00 pm on 12 October 2004. The first episode featured the broadcaster and naturalist Bill Oddie. Wall to Wall had intended the programme to be about the industrial revolution, tracing the Oddie family's origins from Bill's family home in Birmingham back to Lancashire and Yorkshire, as Barratt's research had revealed. Oddie, however, only wanted to talk about his mother, whose death at an early age had had a dramatic effect on his life. Mrs Oddie, it turned out, suffered severe mental health problems and had been committed to a secure hospital. More than half the programme concentrated on this aspect before following the trail further north.

In the final scene, travelling back home on a train, Oddie vowed to the camera: 'I wish I knew then what I know now, I could have helped her.' It was great television and set the tone for all that was to come. At the heart of each episode would be a journey, both physical and emotional. This was no longer social history but personal heritage: a journey of self-discovery with family history as the vehicle.

WDYTYA was an immediate success. Within a few weeks the show was drawing in more than four million viewers, and the ratings kept on rising. In this first series, the last ten minutes of each episode featured Barratt with presenter Adrian Chiles giving tips on tracing a family tree. But this emphasis on the mechanics seemed almost incidental. Viewers were drawn to the stories, as familiar figures such as Sue Johnston, David Baddiel, Ian Hislop and Moira Stuart delved into their pasts. The ten-minute slots were dropped in subsequent series, although not before they had made a star of Barratt himself, who became the celebrity genealogist for the media age.

As with *Family History* a generation before, the programme spurred viewers into action. Record offices received thousands of enquiries after the first broadcast and in the months that followed visitors at many offices increased by up to a quarter. Applications for vocational and further education courses also rocketed, while numerous commercial and society websites reported record activity.

The programme has its fans and detractors in equal measure. The presentation can be formulaic, with the editing cut into bite-size chunks to keep the story moving along. Like much of history TV, there is a tendency to concentrate on the nineteenth and twentieth centuries, where there is a rich pool of photographs and moving images. No regard whatsoever is given for process: celebrities walk into archives – not just the search rooms but the vaults themselves – handle original records and manuscripts, and find what they are looking for within a few seconds. Internet sites are consulted and within a few clicks reveal up material that points the presenter on the next stage of their quest. Seasoned researchers, of course, know that this is all staged. But for those not so versed it can leave misleading impressions, in particular the expectation that if it is not online it is not worth searching for.[22]

To date, around fifty personalities have been featured on the show, which since Series 3 in 2006 has been broadcast on prime-time BBC1. Among the most memorable moments, TV hardman Jeremy Paxman was reduced to tears after discovering the conditions in which his ancestors worked in the Yorkshire cotton mills. African-Caribbean chef Ainsley Harriot was shocked to find he was descended from a white plantation owner who had kept slaves. And actress Amanda Redman found herself in an on-screen encounter with her mother, who revealed for the first time her experiences with domestic violence. As actor Robert Powell observed looking back on his adventure, 'There is no such thing as an ordinary family.'

Some of the most moving programmes have been those dealing with the Holocaust, a historical catastrophe that masks millions of personal stories. Chat-show host Jerry Springer's family was Jewish and escaped to Britain from

Germany just before war was declared. He discovered that both his father's mother and his mother's mother had met their deaths at the hands of the Nazis. Later the programme introduced him to a second cousin from Israel whom he never knew existed. 'The basic lesson of all this', Springer concluded, 'is "Hold on to your family"', adding: 'Who do I think I am? A link in the chain of a wonderful family. I'm blessed.'

The phenomenon has proved a huge money spinner for Wall to Wall, with *WDYTYA* becoming a brand in its own right. The programme has been shown around the world as well as spin-offs, featuring indigenous presenters, being commissioned in Australia, Canada, Ireland and the United States. In October 2007, BBC Magazines launched *Who Do You Think You Are? Magazine*, a monthly publication that includes material from the show. It followed hot on the heels of Who Do You Think You Are? Live, a family history fair held at London's Olympia in May of that year. The Society of Genealogists was a partner in the event, which subsumed the Society's highly successful Family History Show, by then in its fifteenth year.

With *WDYTYA* and its imitators, genealogy's journey from esoteric pastime of the upper classes to multi-million pound consumer market was complete. The brand has come to define family history in Britain today and has been one of the key factors behind genealogy's phenomenal growth in recent years. The show has awakened people's interest in the past as never before and given them the confidence to start their own personal journeys. Ancestry is now socially acceptable. If it is okay for actors, rock stars, TV presenters and sports personalities to delve into their family trees, then why shouldn't the rest of us? Whether your forebears were princes or paupers – the message runs – they are still *your* ancestors. They had a role in the scheme of things, not least in contributing their genes to you, and are just as worthy of research as monarchs and politicians. Newcomers and experienced researchers alike have been enthused to see how far the family history quest can take them. We are all the *Who Do You Think You Are?* generation.

* * * *

Chapter 9

The Family Helix

In the twenty-first century genealogy in Britain has truly come of age. Forces that had been building quietly over many years have come together in a way that has brought an interest in ancestry into the mainstream. Family history has thrown off its shackles and stepped into the limelight, proving itself to be an activity that is accessible, engaging and open to everyone. Technological advances make it easier for people to communicate and share their family information. Digitization has put a rich pool of historical data within the reach of anyone with an internet connection, while an emphasis on 'inclusion' and a bottom–up approach to heritage in cultural policy have led to new approaches to archives within the public sector. An activity that was once confined to a few is now practised and enjoyed by those of all backgrounds. Tracing one's roots has become part of the social milieu, and in particular part of the digital milieu – just another form of information that is there to be discovered, traded and shared online.

Family history today truly reflects Britain's multicultural society. Non-white faces were once a rare sight in repositories: in some respects they still are but this is because for most immigrant communities their ancestors are not to be found there. Online, however, interest is flourishing. Initiatives by the National Archives, immigrant genealogy projects such as Moving Here and Every Generation, and specialist resources being made available by commercial websites allow Asian, African-Caribbean and other immigrant communities to trace their heritage.[1] Such research can be more challenging than in the UK, not because the records do not exist but because the countries concerned are not able to invest in digital resources. Here, especially, progress is likely to depend on interest from commercial providers and/or the LDS church.

The 1901 census release and the success of *Who Do You Think You Are?* were clear milestones. Did they create the post-millennium family history boom or were they merely symptoms of it? Cause and effect are difficult to discern in any social situation but it is worth probing the point further.

As in crime novels, we have to think in terms of both motivation and opportunity. For those interested in tracing their roots, the opportunities certainly increased through more data and easier communication. But this in itself was not sufficient to initiate a boom. If family history had followed a 'business as normal' route then demand for the census would have followed the PRO's projections and researchers would not have been faced with blank screens in January 2002. Sometime around the late 1990s something else happened: a realization among the public at large not only that their personal heritage was there to be uncovered but that they *needed* to investigate it. The fusion of memory, media and record proved irresistible.

The millennium itself appears to have been a key factor. Although few went as far as depositing their own millennium time capsule (*Family Tree* offered readers the opportunity to have one buried for 200 years for £41), this landmark event – the flipping over of one century to another – made many think about the sweep of history and the fleeting nature of human lives. People saw the twentieth century – a period of two world wars, massive social change and great technological advances – slipping away and wondered what the next one hundred years would bring.

If they could not foresee the future, at least they could probe the past and new technology allowed them to do so in a way that was much more relevant and personalized. It gave them an interest they would never get from a textbook about dull historical figures with whom they had absolutely no association. It democratized history in a way that would have been impossible a generation before. The ordinary, everyday lives of our ancestors, people realized, held as much fascination as those they found in the history books. The social history movement of the 1960s came full circle as everyone developed their own personalized microhistory. History was now not just *about* the ordinary men and women who fell outside the traditional historical record, it was being *written* by them as well.

Alongside relevance, community was a motivating factor. Even in the 1990s family history was a fairly solitary undertaking. Family history societies offered fellowship for those who had the time (and inclination) for formal groups, but they had little to offer for those researching in a location a long way from where they lived. Early communication technologies, such as bulletin boards, were clunky and complicated and only appealed to the most tech-savvy enthusiasts. This made it difficult for researchers to share effectively. The internet with its instant communication and rich media environment changed all that. Communities built up around particular surnames, localities or other interests and took away the loneliness of the long-distance digger. Traditional societies, with limited budgets and information technology skills, tended to get left behind, however.

Long-standing arguments about 'breadth versus depth' continued: whether one should aim to find all possible ancestors or concentrate on the detailed stories of a few. New technology aided both approaches. Those who set out to be 'name collectors' found it possible to make a myriad of connections that allowed their family trees to grow in all directions. Trees with 5,000 or more names are not uncommon online. Similarly, those interested in just a limited number of lines found that the rich information available online (including indexes to offline records) allowed them to delve much deeper and develop a detailed picture of their ancestors' lives.

Commentators found it hard to ignore a phenomenon so firmly rooted in the public consciousness. Until this point genealogists had enjoyed a fairly benign press. To the extent it was covered at all, family history was seen as a harmless, if slightly esoteric, pastime and discussion was generally devoted to telling researchers' stories and helping people to get started. Now, in our more cynical age, the growing interest in tracing one's roots was exposed to probing media scrutiny.

The country being in the grip of 'a national obsession to find out who we are' was a frequent theme.[2] Reporters wrote of the 'hordes of researchers' descending on the National Archives and of 'document rage' as enthusiasts jostled against each other in crowded record offices. Genealogy websites, readers were told, were 'the most commonly visited on the internet after pornography'.[3] This assertion was not backed up by any quantitative information or quoted source but was repeated over again until it became a cliché. One commentator noted wryly the similarity between the two: 'What kept those family trees branching but endless sex, in ever changing permutations?'[4]

Viewing from afar, like spectators at a zoo, journalists peered into the family historians' world with a mixture of amusement and disdain. *Independent* columnist Terence Blacker saw family history as a means of glamorizing dull lives and a distraction from the demands of real families. 'At the moment when so many of us have become generally hopeless at maintaining family life, a connection with kith and kin safely dead offers a welcome refuge', asserted Blacker.[5] Mike Hume, writing in *The Times*, opined that the craze for 'DIY genealogy' was 'less about discovering how we lived then than distracting us from how we live now'.[6] It was, he added, 'a senseless waste of a life to interrogate the dead in search of an off-the-peg identity'.

Others saw an unhealthy combination of snobbery and inverted snobbery. Adherents were impatient to find that they were descended either from blue blood or from criminal rogues and poor immigrant stock. Through this 'strange duality . . . genealogy seeks to define us, not by our own achievements or character, but by our origins'.[7] *Times* columnist John Naish was more open-minded, observing that the reason investigators were drawn to the more lurid discoveries, such as illegitimacy, bigamy, adoption and criminals, was that they left stronger traces in the records.

Writing at the time of the 1901 census release, D J Taylor in the *Independent* was sanguine. The attraction, as he saw it, was the 'elemental sense of connection, purpose, the figure waving back from the crowd'.[8] 'One of the great discoveries of adulthood', he went on, 'is that families have secrets, great gaps, fissures and bits of bygone wool-pulling that no amount of senior-member reminiscence can ever explain away.' Taylor found it curious that one of the prime uses people found for new technology was to track down their forebears from a hundred years ago. But it was also comforting that in an age of mass culture, 'a part of the old-style mental outlook, the kind that in the Victorian age recorded generational descent on the flyleaf of the family bible, survives'.

Being steeped in the world of politics, media hacks could not help grinding political axes either. In the right-of-centre *Spectator*, Leo McKinstry accused institutions and libraries of using family history to 'exceed their Whitehall-imposed targets for visitor access'.[9] More importantly, genealogy, with its emphasis on illegitimate or foreign ancestors, was fashionable because it

> promotes two of the key politically correct themes of our times: first that Britain is essentially a land of immigrants so recent changes in our demography should be of no real concern; and second that families comes in all shapes and sizes, so breakdown in married life is an irrelevance. It is no coincidence that the BBC, the chief propagandist for the political values of our age, should be such an enthusiastic promoter of genealogy.

People were seeking 'an anchor in an increasingly fragmented world', McKinstry conceded. 'Mass immigration, the wilful destruction of our nationhood and the collapse of the traditional family' had created a need for belonging. But the family history boom had not led to a greater understanding of Britain's past. 'While we beaver away on the net or in archives, we have never been more ignorant about our island story. Genealogy is no substitute for a true sense of identity.'

From a similar perspective, Simon O'Hagan writing in the *Daily Telegraph* attributed the popularity of genealogy to the decline of traditional religious and family structures: 'People are now looking to their roots as something to cling on to. They see their ancestors as their identity.'[10]

From the opposite end of the political spectrum, *Guardian* journalist Jonathan Freedland found the 'democratising history' narrative perfectly in tune with his socialist beliefs.[11] Spurred on by the birth of his son Jacob, Freedland – a fourth generation of Jewish immigrants who came to Britain from Eastern Europe – felt compelled to find out more about his own roots. He chronicled his search in a moving book *Jacob's Gift*, which is part family memoir and part a reflection on the nature of roots and identity in the modern world.

The emotional impact on people who stumble across unpleasant discoveries in their research was another aspect to capture the media's attention. A pronouncement by the Society of Genealogists that amateur historians might need counselling to help them deal with the secrets they uncovered made a strong story. 'Why shaking the family tree can be bad for your health', proclaimed the *Daily Telegraph*.[12] The article quoted examples of researchers, one of whom had found her great-grandparents had never married and another who discovered the person she thought was her late uncle was in fact her father. Such coverage helped reinforce the notion of family history being a deeply personal and emotional activity, rather than just a pastime.

The influx of new practitioners seen over the last ten years has not always been welcomed by traditionalists. They complain of researchers with poor manners and selfish attitudes: people who take information and give nothing in return (sometimes without even saying 'thank you'), and then reproduce it online without permission or acknowledgement. This has made some reluctant to embrace the new technologies in case they 'get taken for a ride'. But this is not unique to the digital era. Even in the days of letter writing, genealogists and archivists were plagued by correspondents demanding 'all you have on Such And Such'. Those experienced in human nature as well as research learn to deal with these problems, probing enquirers' knowledge and motives and disclosing information piecemeal rather than in one fell swoop.

Are these casual researchers really 'family historians'? In the sense of their interest being converted into a lifelong hobby during the course of which they get drawn into a wider network of societies and enthusiasts, as happened in the past, then probably not. But everyone has a right to probe and to come to family history on their own terms. We can mourn the passing of the old order but that will not bring it back. Taking the most benevolent view, one could say that newcomers' behaviour is, perhaps, a result of ignorance rather than bad manners. If they understood how difficult things were 'in the olden days' then perhaps they would be more appreciative. On the other hand, how difficult is it to say thank you and observe basic social etiquette?

Rather more worrying is the issue of quality and accuracy in the new digital era. The problems here are threefold. First, massive commercial transcription projects are being initiated, many of which are undertaken 'offshore' in low-cost locations like India without proper oversight. Secondly, the internet is allowing self-taught and sometimes naive individuals to cobble together information from disparate sources without adhering to basic guidelines. Thirdly, the LDS church – which remains a powerful force in genealogy worldwide – is expanding its genealogical ambitions significantly, without the same checks and safeguards on the data that it has imposed in the past.[13] Thus, lax standards in research are being compounded by errors in the data sources being used.

All of this provides for a potent mix, making it near impossible for others to spot errors or to check a researcher's claims against original sources. As we have seen, self-delusion and even outright trickery are nothing new in genealogy. From the mythological pedigrees of the Middle Ages, through the unquestioning inquiries of the heralds, to the snobbery of the Victorian period, a grand lineage has always appealed to some. New technology merely perpetuates human frailties. But the scale of the problem is much greater now than anything faced in the past.

The internet is unregulated and difficult territory for any form of scholarship. In genealogy, people are becoming remote from the records and do not appreciate the importance of citing sources. At the same time, the provenance of the records themselves is being undermined. Whereas once a source such as the National Archives could be taken as a guarantee of authenticity, the fact that we are dealing not with original records but with digital facsimiles that have been copied and rekeyed *on a massive scale* means even these cannot always be trusted. We may have more data but without rigorous standards of referencing and quality control there is more scope for a false trail, whether intentioned or not. The 'serious researcher' has to tread carefully.

If genealogists only had the quality of their databases to worry about most would be happy enough. In fact, the cosy world of family history faces many challenges and seismic shifts in the research landscape are in the offing. These challenges come from three main directions. First, changing attitudes to personal data and the growing privacy culture. Second, the commercialization of family history and the resulting shift in ethos from that of a self-propelling community to a consumer market with buyers and sellers. Third, the rise in genetic genealogy which promises to revolutionize our understanding of ourselves, our families and our place in the wider human story. Let us deal with each of these in turn.

* * * *

As genealogical data has become part of the currency of modern life, concerns have risen about how such data can be used and who has access to it. Today, there are any number of reasons why unscrupulous individuals might seek to access sensitive personal information – financial or welfare fraud, trafficking of people and drugs, terrorism and organized crime. If a family historian can obtain a birth certificate for a baby who died, say in the

1960s, for research purposes then so can a criminal who might use that information to construct a false identity.

This has thrown attention on civil registration, the system of registering births, marriages and deaths through local registrars, which are then reported to the General Register Office in London. In Britain (or to be more precise in England and Wales), civil registration has remained largely unreformed since the early nineteenth century. Paper proliferates, with little use of modern technology and few safeguards against the records being used in support of fraud or identity theft. Even without taking the needs of genealogists into account, the system is not up to the needs of a modern society. Governments of all complexions have dragged their heals on the issue of reform and recent experience in this area has been a catalogue of inaction, missed opportunities and unedifying climbdowns.

Civil registration was not set up for genealogists but as one of the main users of the service they have always maintained a close interest in its operation and policies. Their main concern is that, unlike other public records, the historic registration records – those over 100 or so years old – remain closed. Instead they are saddled with paying £9.25 for certified copies of certificates containing a minimal amount of information and which, once the relevant data has been extracted, are of no further use. As we have seen, time and again genealogists have called for these historic records to be opened to public view, preferably through being deposited at the National Archives. The strictures on certified copies should be relaxed, so that researchers can obtain the information more cheaply through non-certified copies or simple photocopies. Certified copies could then be reserved for certificates issued for official purposes, such as passport applications.

The demands seem clear enough and there has even been a broad measure of agreement in official circles about what needs to be done; but the mandarins and politicians have moved at a sclerotic pace.

By 2000, after another shuffling of the chairs in Whitehall, the General Register Office was part of the Office for National Statistics (ONS). Nearly ninety years after George Sherwood had complained to the Royal Commission that the GRO indexes were 'inadequate and insufficient', virtually nothing had changed. The 1988 reforms had led to improvements in the search facilities and the opening of the Family Records Centre, but the registration system itself had not been touched.

A series of policy documents and consultation papers followed one after another, each appearing to go over the same old ground. After having set up a series of working groups to look into the issues, the Conservative government published a Green Paper in 1988, followed in 1990 by a White Paper with specific legislative proposals. These got nowhere and private legislation intended to force the issue of access to the older records was unsuccessful. The Labour government returned to the matter in a consultation paper in 1999, followed in 2002 by yet another White Paper.

The political climate in relation to personal data had changed considerably over this period, in the face of a growing privacy lobby and human rights culture. Family historians thus found themselves confronted in 2002 with proposals much more draconian than those of a decade before. A central concern was the problem of people buying birth certificates to create false identities. The 1990 White Paper had advocated a simple solution: that all copies issued be non-certified. Those who needed a certified copy would be required to complete a more comprehensive application form resembling that for a passport. By 2002 these provisions had been reined in, so that even non-certified copies were to be of an abbreviated form, omitting key information such as addresses, occupations and causes of death. Only 'individuals and members of their families' having 'legally prescribed access' would be entitled to full certificates, though the means by which they were to establish their entitlement was not clear.

The White Paper also muddied the waters on historic records. The 1990 proposals had recommended that records be made publicly available when they were seventy-five years old. Even this seemed unduly restrictive to some and there were provisions for death and marriage records to be released earlier if Parliament agreed. But the 2002 paper increased, rather than decreased, the timeframe and used the phrase 'records relating to persons born over 100 years ago'. This reference to *persons* rather than *records* was not helpful, since it linked all an individual's records to a single release date. Potentially, it could mean that if a person died aged 90 their records would be released in ten years' time, whereas if a baby died researchers would have to wait a hundred years to see the record.

Genealogists viewed the proposals with alarm. The prospect of restrictions in accessing the civil records was bad enough but the removal of key address, occupation and cause of death information would severely undermine their value. The places of birth, death and marriage would remain public, but would be of limited utility as most births now take place in hospital. Genealogists often used information from the death certificate to link to coroners' reports and to service and professional records; a jump that would be much harder to make in future. Other countries, notably Australia in the English-speaking world, draw distinctions between modern and historic records but most do not impose a blanket release date. Indeed, rarely are death records restricted for more than twenty-five or thirty years. Marriages tend to be restricted for forty, fifty or seventy-five years and births for seventy-five or a hundred years. Having long enjoyed unfettered access (albeit at a price), family historians in England and Wales now faced the prospect of one of the most restrictive regimes in the world for accessing civil records.

Eyebrows were raised even further when researchers read how all this was to be achieved. In order to produce the shortened certificates, from which salient details had been removed, the ONS was proposing to transcribe all the certificates issued over at least the last seventy years into a vast new database. This amounted to around 300 million entries, accruing at a rate of 1.6 million a year. What was more, consideration was to be given to linking an individual's entries together to create a 'through-life record'. In the wake of the 1901 census fiasco and a similar failing with the passport system, the public sector's ability to successfully implement major IT projects had already taken a knock. The prospect of civil servants transcribing almost a hundred years' worth of entries and then linking them all together in a massive family reconstruction programme beggared belief. Anthony Camp expressed the reservations of many when he wrote:[14]

> From an organization which has shown so little interest in the needs of genealogists, the suggestion is frightening. In the past thousands were given wrong certificates or told that none existed. Now we have the prospect of erroneous matches and false errors which once perpetuated will remain on record and be impossible to correct.

The White Paper was followed in 2003 by a consultation document setting out the proposals in more detail, and in 2004 by legislation giving effect to the changes in the form of a Regulatory Reform Order – an administrative provision that avoided the need for primary legislation. Genealogists mounted a vociferous campaign, accounting for some 2,300 of the 3,400 responses to the consultation document. In response to this lobbying, the government agreed to reduce the restrictions on birth records to seventy-five years and on deaths to twenty-five years, as in the Scottish system. Occupations were also to be retained on certificates. These were minor victories but the thrust of the proposals remained unaltered, including the creation of the new database based on the GRO's centralized records rather than the local originals.

In the end it was MPs who saved the day. Parliamentary Select Committees expressed grave doubts about the proposals and refused to back them. The government was left with no choice but to withdraw the Regulatory Reform Order on the Modernisation of Civil Registration. It was back to square one.

In the absence of all-encompassing legislation, matters now proceeded along different tracks. After yet another consultation paper in 2005, new governance arrangements were introduced passing responsibility for register offices to local authorities and under a 2007 Act registration officers became local authority employees. At the same time new systems were introduced enabling officers for the first time to record entries online.

The need to reconcile the very real concerns about privacy and personal information with those of legitimate historical enquiry is a difficult balancing act. To date, British family historians have escaped the worst excesses of the state in restricting access to their core dataset but the reprieve is likely to be temporary. Governments around the world are tightening up on records of vital events. Although at present the UK government has not tabled any specific policy proposals, it seems only a matter of time before access is more heavily restricted. Since the indexes are widely available in the public domain and are being transcribed, prohibitions could only be made in relation to obtaining certificates or the information they contain.

* * * *

A second set of challenges facing family history are the related issues of digitization, commercialization and community. The release of original archival material in digital form is both a driver of the current boom and also an inevitable consequence of it. As demand for historical material has grown, archivists and administrators have looked to digitization as a means of making records more widely available, while at the same time constraining demand on physical facilities. Digitization is a costly and complex process, however, that has proven to be beyond the capabilities of either the public sector or the traditional genealogy community. As a result, it has been left to commercial companies to fill the gap, acquiring an ever-wider array of digital records and resources to meet expanding market demand. As with the discussion of privacy, the recent story starts with the ineptitude of the GRO.

Following the collapse of its modernization proposals in 2004, ONS announced that all birth, marriage and death records for England and Wales back to 1837 would be digitized and the indexes made available over the internet. This project, known as DoVE (Digitization of Vital Events) was just one element of a wider scheme. The EAGLE (Electronic Access to GRO Legacy Events) project would introduce a more efficient system of recording and tracking customer orders within the GRO at Southport, including access to the digitized information. A third project – MAGPIE (Multi Access to GRO Published Index of Events) – would provide online indexes to the newly digitized records via the internet. In 2005 the contract for DoVE was awarded to Siemens IT Solutions and Services Ltd, with rollout set for April 2008. As usual with such projects, the work would be 'offshored', with the data capture and verification undertaken in Chennai, India.

The Federation urged the GRO to use this unique window of opportunity to upgrade the indexes. In February 2006 the GRO confirmed that the digitized indexes produced under DoVE would include a number of enhancements across the whole series from 1837. Birth indexes would show the mother's maiden surname (previously only included from 1911); death indexes would show the age at death (previously only included from 1866); and marriage indexes would show the surname of the spouse (previously only included from 1912). The first two forenames were also to be shown in full, not just initials.

A veil descended over the scheme as the contractors got down to work. But despite assurances in ONS press releases, it soon became clear that all was not right with DoVE and its associated projects. Reports began to appear in the family history and IT press about delays. The deadline for scanning the birth indexes and loading the data onto EAGLE came and went. Then, in July 2008 the inevitable announcement came: the contract with Siemens was being terminated 'by mutual agreement'. Only around half of the work had been completed and without a full set of digitized records the long-sought-after online index could not go ahead.

The situation was not helped by yet another change of home for the GRO, this time from the ONS to the Identity and Passport Service (IPS). The IPS is an executive agency of the Home Office responsible for issuing passports and overseeing the then-Labour government's identity card scheme. Its instincts are towards privacy and the withholding of data rather than free and open disclosure. The decision to bring the GRO under the IPS umbrella was taken from the standpoint of safeguarding people's identities and providing more secure documentation. Family historians, with their endless requests for free and open access to everything, were seen as an irritation and were hardly likely to be a priority for an agency headed not by a public servant but a chief executive. And so it was to prove; one of IPS's first acts after acquiring the GRO was to stop the release of the current-day BMD indexes to commercial providers. To compound matters, the collapse of DoVE came just as the financial crisis broke and the money ran out. The whole digitization initiative was left in limbo while the GRO's new masters at the IPS pondered what to do.

The ire of family historians was all the louder for the fact that they had no paper backup. In anticipation of the new online system and to free up room at the Family Records Centre, in October 2007 the paper ledgers containing the BMD indexes were withdrawn. The Federation, the SoG and others complained that this was precipitate. Under its founding legislation, the GRO had a statutory duty to provide public access to a complete set of the indexes. But there was nothing in the 1836 Registration Act to say what form such indexes should take (how could the drafters then have anticipated modern technology?). The GRO maintained that provision of microfiche copies at certain locations around the country was sufficient to fulfil this obligation. For many this seemed to be bending the rules beyond what was acceptable; and in any case, microfiche indexes had always been more difficult to use than paper. Only six centres now held the full indexes and under the new policy other repositories and commercial websites were prevented from obtaining the most recent updates either on microfiche or electronically. This was a complete volte face on the part of the GRO, which just four years before had relaxed the licensing conditions on the indexes so that they could be made available online.

The Family Records Centre was not one of the six designated sites because in March 2008 it had been closed down. The availability of online indexes would, the ONS reasoned, 'permit other approaches to providing public access'. Since opening its doors in 1997 the FRC had proved a huge hit with family historians. As a partnership between the ONS and TNA it provided a 'one-stop shop', with all of the most significant records available under one roof and at an easily accessible London location. As well as anticipating the arrival of DoVE, its closure appears to have been influenced by matters closer to home. The ONS was having to leave its offices in Pimlico and needed a new building, while TNA was looking to save £1 million a year in rent to help meet swingeing budget cuts. Closure of this popular facility thus helped both bodies.

The ONS was the first to depart, in November 2007. Its much-thumbed set of BMD indexes, consulted by literally millions of searchers over the years, were boxed up and sent to storage in deepest Dorset. The FRC finally closed its doors on 15 March 2008 – almost eleven years to the day since its first opening – with TNA staff and services being transferred to refurbished and extended facilities at Kew. Researchers flocked to the Centre during its final weeks and on the last day staff effectively found themselves facing a sit-in. As time ticked down, they announced 'fifteen minutes', then 'ten minutes', then closure. No one moved and a chorus of boos and groans rose from the assembled company.

The dismal failure of the DoVE initiative was in marked contrast to the situation in Scotland, where digitization was proceeding apace. The tie-up with the commercial start-up Origins.net was working well and in 2001 the General Register Office for Scotland announced funding for the next phase involving the digitization of all Scotland's civil registration records. The DIGROS (Digital Imaging of the Genealogical Records of Scotland) programme aimed to image all historical records and to have them available online by the end of 2002. The more modern records would not be viewable online, although they could still be seen at Edinburgh's New Register House. At the same time, work began on digitizing the 1891 and 1901 Scottish censuses.

Projects proceeded smoothly, with only minor delays. The datasets were much smaller than those for England and Wales, although still a substantial undertaking. Nevertheless, the authorities in Scotland had succeeded where their counterparts south of the border had failed. Speedy implementation was aided by the fact that in Scotland many of the measures did not require primary, or even secondary, legislation. But the choice of approach was also a factor. Unlike Siemens, Origins (now rebranded as ScotlandOnline) was a company rooted in the genealogical community; it understood the data and what users expected and required.

Faced with indeterminate delays, the market stepped in to fill the void left by DoVE. Only the GRO had access to the full registers but at least commercial providers could improve on the indexes. FreeBMD, the volunteer indexing project, continued to make good progress but was still nowhere near completing the full run. Indeed, the task became the more formidable as the transcribers moved towards the present as the number of entries in any given year increased. Findmypast and *The Genealogist* each embarked on separate initiatives to produce searchable indexes from the beginning of civil registration. In effect, this was a vindication of the approach advocated by Camp – that the genealogical community was better off handling such projects by itself (although he had favoured the Genealogical Society of Utah to do the work).

By now digitization had become part of these genealogy companies' *raison d'être*. To meet the demands and expectations of the 'Who Do You Think You Are? Generation', businesses needed to deliver data, and lots of it. First off were the censuses. After the 1901 debacle, TNA realized it was best to stick with contractors who had a strong grounding in the sector. Ancestry was given the contracts to digitize the 1851, 1871 and 1891 censuses, while Findmypast won the contract for 1861 and gained the rights to the 1901 dataset through its acquisition of GenesReunited (which in turn had acquired them from QinetiQ). By mid-2006 all of the censuses then released were available online, albeit at different websites. (The 1881 census had been released on the LDS FamilySearch website in 2003.) In December 2006, in response to a Freedom of Information ruling, TNA announced that the release of the 1911 census was to be brought forward by three years, from 2012 to 2009.

With the censuses covered, companies turned their attentions elsewhere, signing up the rights to public records wherever they could find them. First World War service and pension records; British Army service records back to the Napoleonic Wars; passenger lists both inbound and outbound; Nonconformist registers; London parish registers and other parochial and local authority records; the probate calendar of wills and administrations: in recent years all of this information has become available online through commercial websites. However, the holy grail of genealogists over the years – a fully searchable database of pre-1837 BMDs – is still some way off. The dreams of the SoG's pioneers, of the British Vital Records Index of the 1960s, and even of the maverick Keith Park have yet to be realized; but significant collections are already available online and it is only a matter of time before a complete collection emerges.

In one of the most ambitious programmes of its kind, the British Library has launched a partnership with Brightsolid (owner of Findmypast) to digitize up to forty million pages of historic newspapers. This deal is significant for two reasons. First, it demonstrates how progressively greater efficiencies are allowing the digitization process to be scaled up to ever larger archives. Secondly, it shows mass digitization moving beyond the realm of official records as rights holders become more aware of the opportunities opened up by digital access.

Online archives may help to democratize history but they also serve to privatize it. In allowing companies to compete for access to historical records we have ended up with a series of walled gardens, each of which can only be entered by paying a subscription. A researcher has to be well heeled to afford them all. Moreover, in some cases digital records are being offered in place of physical ones rather than as an adjunct. This puts the very principle of free access to public records – which has been enshrined in archive legislation for over 150 years – at risk.

As recently as a decade ago the idea of selling access to genealogical information was greeted with great hostility by the family history community. Subscription websites are now universally accepted, even by the 'old school' researchers, because they feed the genealogists' constant appetite for more data. Under this new model, historical data is treated as a commodity and family historians are reduced to being mere consumers. As in a restaurant, they are presented with a menu of the services on offer and the price to be charged, and – like punters in every market – will shop around for the vendors offering the best deal.

There is little public scrutiny over the terms under which these companies undertake digitization, the standards they need to maintain, or the profit they are allowed to make. As a result, our national heritage is being used as a cashcow by businesses, some of whom are not even based in Britain. Of course, digitization is an expensive business and someone has to pay. However, the market situation we have been left with was not inevitable but the result of archival policy and the inability of the public sector to manage large projects effectively. With foresight, England's public records could have been offered through a public portal, as they are in Scotland or some Australian states, where it is clear that the fees paid are being used to support archive management rather than commercial businesses. Much more needs to be done to regulate how these companies operate and ensure they give more back to the genealogical community as a whole rather than just to their shareholders.

Genealogy companies' ambitions do not stop with the raw data, however; they are after our finished research as well. All of the sites offer facilities for subscribers to upload their family trees but anyone tempted to do so would be advised to read the small print. Companies often claim the copyright in data submitted in this way and once uploaded to a commercial server the owner can be left with little say over how their information is used.

Thus, the prevailing ethos is that of a market rather than a community; of competition rather than cooperation. To the extent researchers are willing to collaborate at all these days, it is online in relation to their own family tree, family name or location. Wider community projects have gone by the wayside because commercial companies are able to resource and manage such activities much more effectively. Pauline Litton, a life vice-president of the Federation, has observed that:[15]

A generation of co-operation, of individuals meeting, talking, arguing, working together for the benefit of family history, is in danger of being replaced by one many of whose members sit in front of a computer, talking but putting nothing back into our hobby.

The result has been a marked shift in power. Whereas once a researcher's allegiance was to a family history society or the Society of Genealogists, now their affinities are to commercial websites. With limited resources and largely volunteer structures, the traditional genealogy institutions were slow to adapt to this new world order and to reap its benefits. Membership of family history societies has not grown at anything like the rate of online sites. The major projects initiated and managed by the community in earlier times – such as transcribing parish registers, copying monumental inscriptions and cataloguing local records – now look small beer compared to what is available within an ever-widening market. Many societies still rely on book, CD and microfiche sales for a substantial part of their income, products that have much less appeal than hard data delivered at the click of a mouse.

When the Federation gathered in Loughborough for its thirtieth anniversary conference in August 2004, the tensions between the 'old' and the 'new' order were simmering beneath the surface. The conference was a five-day affair with top billing given to the great and the good of the family history world. Alongside Sarah Tyacke, Keeper of Public Records for England and Wales, and Dr Ruth Paley of the House of Lords Library, there were leading academics in local and family history, as well as speakers from Australia and the United States including a contingent from the LDS Library in Salt Lake City. Only the most ardent genealogists would spend five days at a conference, or could afford the £320 fee. Delegates listened attentively to the lectures, and watched awards being given to young people, the best family history journals (appropriately entitled the Elizabeth Simpson Award), and the best websites. Then – in line with the

1970s theme – they danced the night away to the 'Marcus Daniels discotheque'. Save for the website awards, they might just as well have been back at Newman College, where their community was born. Except that the conference had only been made possible by a US$10,000 donation from Ancestry.co.uk, a new arrival keen to build up its market profile. Little did the stalwarts of the Federation know that within a few years it would be to Ancestry, rather than to the FFHS, that many family historians would owe their allegiance.

The Loughborough event was the last major gathering of its kind organized by the Federation and in effect can be seen as the end of the community era. The voluntary model that had sustained family history since the 1960s was now pitched against major corporations. Committed as they were, the enthusiasts of the Federation and its local societies could not compete against the might of corporate organization, planning and marketing. That it was losing the race became obvious to all in 2008 with the closure of its online offering FamilyHistory Online. This website had been set up as a gateway to the data resources (mainly BMD transcripts and monumental inscriptions) held by local societies. Users accessed the data on a pay-per-view basis with the fees being fed back to the relevant society. The site was clunky and prone to crashes and the Federation decided it could not raise the investment necessary to keep it going. Poor business decisions also curtailed the publishing activities which were previously a major source of income.

Problems with the National Burial Index epitomize the difficulties. This is a major project, coordinated by the Federation, to provide family historians with a resource for finding burials, complementing the *International Genealogical Index* which covers mainly baptisms and marriages. Work began in 1994 with burial records being transcribed and computerized, mainly by family history societies. Cracks in the traditional community model were already beginning to show. Volunteers – who had always been difficult to find – were thinner on the ground than ever, especially for the crucial checking tasks. It took seven years, until 2001, for the 1st edition to appear, and there were many complaints about accuracy. A 2nd edition followed in 2004, raising the number of entries from 5.4 million to 13.2 million, followed by a further release in 2010 with over 18.4 million entries. Its continuation as a CD-ROM product at a time when so much data is available on a subscription basis looks outdated, but in the absence of an online platform is the only option.[16]

With its own membership base and professional staff, the SoG should have been better placed to capitalize on the new commercial world, but here too problems have ensued.

The Society was an early convert to digitization and in 2000 signed a contract with Origins to provide exclusive online access to its collections and indexes. This has seen some of the Society's treasures placed online, including Gerald Fothergill's *Apprentices of Great Britain*, Percival Boyd's great indexes (Marriage Index, Inhabitants of London, and London Burials), and important collections of eighteenth- and nineteenth-century marriage records. These landmarks of British genealogy have been given new life in the online world. There is also a facility by which members may share their own data collections.

However, the income from Origins has not been sufficient to offset the difficulties experienced elsewhere. A decline in the sale of books, stagnant membership levels and a spiralling cost base have hit the Society hard over recent years. Overseas membership, in particular, has fallen off sharply in the face of alternative offerings from commercial websites. For its centenary in 2011, the Society celebrated its undoubted achievements over the last hundred years and sought to look forward to the challenges to come. But as with the Federation, it is difficult to avoid the conclusion that this behemoth of British genealogy is struggling to find a role in the new commercial landscape.

*   *   *   *

Alongside the changes coming from the digital world, family history has to face up to developments in the fast-emerging field of genetic genealogy. Here, too, we are seeing the rise of entrepreneurial businesses and the creation of new communities of interest that challenge the established order.

Genealogists have long been interested in the overlap between their field and the science of genetics. As early as 1875 George Darwin, a son of Charles Darwin, used surnames to estimate the frequency of first-cousin marriages and calculated the expected incidence of marriage between people of the same surname (known as 'isonymy'). For Britain, he estimated the proportion of cousin-marriages to be between 2.25 and 4.5 per cent, with the practice being rather more common in the upper classes than in the general rural population. (Famously, his parents, Charles Darwin and Emma Wedgwood were first cousins, as were Queen Victoria and Prince Albert.)

Following the brush with the pseudo-science of eugenics, it was not until the second half of the twentieth century that genealogists such as C Harold Ridge and H L White returned to the issue, attempting to set out a 'scientific genealogy' that reconciled genealogists' experiences with accepted scientific knowledge.[17] Ridge discussed, among other things, inherited malformation related to the male Y-chromosome, quoting as an example the finger deformation (syndactylism) which appears on the tomb effigy of John, 1st Earl of Shrewsbury (1390–1453). A scientific paper published in 1963 described variations of the syndrome known as *brachydactyly* (short digits) and associated anomalies based on a study of 600 descendants of an American family of Staffordshire origin.[18]

Although speaking different languages, the two communities eyed each other with interest. Geneticists used family pedigrees – sometimes in association with genealogists – to study the inheritance of physical traits and diseases, while genealogists sought to understand how such science might one day be used to unlock lineages that lie beyond the written record. Only in the late 1990s was the connection finally made.

The invention of genetic fingerprinting by Professor Alec Jeffreys at Leicester University in 1984 brought modern genetics out of the laboratory and into everyday life. DNA – deoxyribonucleic acid – is the material from which genes are made. Human beings carry some 30,000 genes arranged across forty-six chromosomes that together hold all the genetic information which makes each individual. The DNA molecule is extremely complex, consisting of four types of chemical code – known as bases – wound together in the now-famous double helix structure. Since its discovery by Crick and Watson in 1954, scientists had observed that certain sequences of bases occur again and again through the length of the molecule. Jeffreys's technique created a unique genetic blueprint that allowed a person to be identified based on these recurrent sequences in their DNA. The first applications were in forensic science – using DNA evidence to link a suspect to a crime scene.

Importantly for genealogists, the genetic blueprint is inherited directly from each of the individuals' parents and relates to the parents' own DNA fingerprint. This meant it could be used to link samples from different people in situations where paternity needed to be established, such as wardship or divorce proceedings, intestacy disputes, or immigration applications.

There are two types of DNA: nuclear DNA, which is found in the nucleus of a cell, and mitochondrial DNA (mtDNA), which is found outside the nucleus. Nuclear DNA (also known as Y-DNA because it is carried through the male Y chromosome) is passed from father to son while mitochondrial DNA is inherited by both sexes from the mother alone. In a stable population this means that one mother will eventually pass her mtDNA to all females within her line; thus mtDNA can be detected many, many generations later. Scientists realized that these two instances could each be used as genetic markers. Y-DNA should be a marker for the paternal line, while mtDNA should be a marker in the maternal line.

Scientists set about investigating these theories and in a series of breakthroughs in the late 1990s produced stunning results. The Y-DNA theory was first proved by Professor Michael Hammer, a molecular geneticist at the University of Arizona. In a paper published in *Nature* in

1997, he and his co-investigators showed how a particular marker was more likely to be present within certain groups of Jewish men who were traditionally thought to share the same ancient lineage. With Bennett Greenspan, Hammer later co-founded Family Tree DNA Inc., the first of a new type of genealogy business aiming to commercialize genealogical DNA testing.

The innovation in mtDNA came in Britain where Professor Bryan Skyes, a molecular biologist at Oxford University, was assessing DNA samples from archaeological digs. After examining 6,000 random samples of mtDNA collected from women and men across Europe, he concluded that virtually all of them could be put into one of seven genetically related groups. These findings were profound: they implied that all modern Europeans were descended from one of just seven women who each lived within the last 50,000 years. Sykes later wrote a popular account of his research in a bestselling book, *The Seven Daughters of Eve*[19] Here he gave these seven 'clan mothers' names, such as *Ursula* and *Helena*, and developed a series of fictional narratives describing roughly where and how they would have lived.[20]

When the book was published in 2001 Sykes's lab at Oxford was inundated with requests from genealogists wanting to use DNA-based genetics to trace their ancestry. His company Oxford Ancestors, the first British-based genetic genealogy enterprise, met this need and was soon joined by several others. Next, Sykes turned his attention to Y-DNA. Taking sixty men bearing his surname at random from the phone book, he found that around 70 per cent of them were all descended from a common ancestor, an original Mr Sykes who lived in the 1300s. The remainder, who did not share the same DNA markers, Sykes put down to being the result of adoption or illegitimacy.[21]

The implications of these advances were not lost on genealogists. Y-DNA is passed intact from father to son down through the generations in the same way (in Western cultures at least) that surnames are. Barring a non-paternity event, the surname and Y-DNA travel through time in tandem. DNA investigation had now reached a stage that would allow family historians to confirm the links between branches of families having the same or similar surnames where the documentary evidence was otherwise lacking, and even to assume their origin from a single putative ancestor.

The possibilities were especially attractive for those undertaking one-name studies, who already had a captive population and a good base of corroborative written evidence. Pioneers such as Arthur Carden and Chris Pomery expanded their one-name studies to embrace DNA information, generally Y-chromosome signatures.

Y-chromosome testing relies on matching certain genetic markers that are known to change from time to time due to random mutations. Markers are chosen such that men whose common ancestors lived millions of years ago show many differences, whereas men with a common ancestor within the past 1,000 years show identical numbers of repeats. A Y-chromosome analysis typically looks at around ten to fifteen of these markers. Different laboratories may use slightly different sets of elements, however, meaning the results are not always directly comparable.

The technique is particularly useful in tracing the roots of émigrés to America or elsewhere who left no other clue as to their British origins. The Lockwood family of New Hampshire, for example, had worked out that their ancestor John Lockwood went to New England in the early seventeenth century because his name was on a ship's passenger list. But they did not know whether he was from Suffolk or Yorkshire. Using Y-DNA matching, Sykes's team was able to direct them towards the Suffolk Lockwoods as the most likely origin. Others are less fortunate. One twenty-strong family clan gathered for a reunion only to discover that the president of the clan had the wrong DNA – one of his ancestors must have been illegitimate or adopted.

These innovations provided something of a boost for surname research, although not all of the groups so formed considered themselves 'one-namers' or joined the Guild of One Name Studies. On the contrary, companies such as FamilyTree DNA and Ancestry set out to colonize this new territory for themselves, encouraging genealogists to see them not as laboratories providing a testing service but as 'communities' within which to base their projects. This is yet another example of how traditional communities, such as the Guild, have lost influence in recent years, as their power has leaked away to commercial interests.

Just as in the use of DNA evidence in a court of law, genetic genealogy is not foolproof. Genetic testing is a probabilistic technology. It shows that two individuals are related but is not in itself proof of paternity (or even of maternity). The same results could be achieved by any number of genealogical relationships. With Y-DNA, for instance, an individual's father could be anyone sharing the same male line, such as an uncle or a male cousin, and the results would still be preserved, a situation known as 'false paternity'. What is more, the 'basic' Y-DNA and mtDNA tests only capture the extremes of the genealogical tree – the pure paternal line (father's father's father, etc.) and the pure maternal line (mother's mother's mother, etc.). New techniques are expanding the scope and applicability of DNA analysis even further, opening up the vast areas in the middle where descent is through male and female lines in any combination. These techniques track more recent mutations that are detectable across both sexes, producing a fine-grained genetic signature.

Such techniques would be tremendously powerful. They could, for example, be used to verify ancestral lines through any given path of descent. They could be used to determine ancestry where the lineage is not known, for instance because of illegitimacy, naturalization or a legal change of surname. And they could be used to find the paternal lines of adopted children; in previous centuries 'adoption' used to be relatively informal within families and communities and was not documented. But for all of this to work the companies concerned need to build up large databases within which to mine the information. Hence, the emphasis on developing their own communities through which they seek to capture each project's genetic information.

Long-standing one-namers now see traditional and new techniques as complementary. Genetic genealogy is a way of supporting and accelerating traditional documentary studies and requires parallel documentary investigation. DNA analyses do not produce a family tree but they are a tool to help document a family tree, either as part of a surname project or standalone research. Around 200 Guild members are now following these so-called 'dual approach' projects, although this is only a small fraction of the almost 8,000 names registered.

Reflecting on the experience of the Pomery One Name Study – one of the longest running – author Chris Pomery has noted:[22]

> DNA results can be sorted into 'genetic families' based upon the raw DNA results alone, but thereafter the analysis of trees and how they link together is driven by contextual data and documentary evidence. The overall aim of a dual-approach project is to produce a set of combined data that is internally and externally consistent.

In the Pomery case fifty-five trees of UK origin have been identified, thirty-nine with emigrants and eight with no living descendants in the UK. These are characterized by twenty-four distinct DNA signatures, of which nineteen are unique, with convergence and clustering around a village in south Devon, the likely 'ancestral home'.

These results, and similar findings in projects such as the Carden and Meates DNA projects,[23] suggest that many, if not most, uncommon British surnames could eventually be shown to share a single male ancestor within genealogically relevant timeframes. They may also show that certain surnames are derivations or corruptions of others, leading to so-called surname 'super-groups'. Recent scientific research has even suggested that it may be possible to create a genetic map of the whole country, based on how certain genetic differences are shared by families originating in the same locality as well as by those sharing the same name.[24] One potential application could, quite literally, be 'arresting': harking back to Jeffreys's original breakthrough, researchers have suggested that such databases might one day be used to predict the surname of a suspect using DNA from a crime scene!

A further group of genetic tests, known as autosomal tests, is also available. These attempt to measure an individual's biogeographic origins by identifying particular markers, called ancestry informative markers (AIM), that are associated with populations from specific geographic areas. Autosomal DNA tests purport to express a person's genetic ancestry in proportional terms based on certain regional or ethnic groups. Companies providing these tests define the groups and subgroups in different ways, but generally four main groups are identified: European and Near Eastern (or Caucasian), South and East Asian (Asian), Sub-Saharan African (African), and Native American (Amerindian). Thus, a white Briton's ancestry might be expressed as 80 per cent Northwest European, 15 per cent Mediterranean, 3 per cent North African (all subgroups of European), and 2 per cent Sub-Saharan African. This suggests, perhaps, that their ancestors originate mainly in northern Europe (Anglo-Saxon, Norman, Viking, etc.), but at some stage over the last several thousand years have also received DNA from southern Europe (via the Romans perhaps?) and further afield. A surprising aspect of such tests is the extent to which people all over the world carry DNA associated with categories outside their purported 'racial group' (in this case North African and Sub-Saharan African). It suggests migration and interbreeding were much more common in the ancient past than previously supposed. Although revealing in scientific terms, autosomal tests are less interesting to genealogists, other than for curiosity value, since they relate to times well beyond the historical record.[25]

As with any emerging technology, genealogical DNA testing is changing rapidly. Scientists continue to push the boundaries in how the tests can be used, while new companies are springing up to exploit and commercialize the technology. Indeed, the whole market has something of the Wild West about it. Costs of testing and quality of service vary dramatically, while consumers often have little idea of what they are buying or what it will show. An investigation by consumer organization Which? found discrepancies in how different companies reported results.[26] One hedged its bets by saying a given sample indicated somebody of 'Polish, Arab or Irish descent'. There are privacy concerns, too. Hidden in the small print can be clauses that allow companies to store samples for up to twenty years, share the data with other organizations that conduct similar research and share the results online. Until recently the whole field of direct-to-consumer DNA testing was completely unregulated. New standards unveiled by the Human Genetics Commission in 2010 aim to ensure that the companies selling such tests follow basic principles of consent, data protection, truth in marketing, scientific rigour and balanced interpretation.[27] This is only a code of practice, however, and does not have force of law.

*   *   *   *

What will family history look like in the future? What is our generation leaving for our descendants to uncover? Sadly, the answer appears to be 'not as much as we should'.

In our own age, social patterns and behaviours are changing in ways that could make life for future family historians very difficult indeed. Virtually every form of documentation and written record that current-day genealogists rely on in looking at the past is under threat. Letter writing and diaries are a dying medium as people turn to email and other forms of digital communication. Family Bibles are no longer kept. Local newspapers, so often a rich source for the family historian, appear to be in terminal decline. Fewer and fewer people are joining collective organizations with membership records, such as trade unions, churches, clubs and societies, and voluntary organizations. Meanwhile, greater mobility means fewer of us live in or have connections with the areas in which we were born.

As a society we have never had such ready access to data and information. But in our 24/7 world, so much of it is fleeting and trivial. Emails, blogs and texts may say a lot but they mean very little. It is difficult to convey anything thought-provoking, sensitive or loving in an email; and even if we could would we print it off and tie it up with red ribbon for our descendants to uncover in a hundred years time? Many public authorities and businesses are going the same way, holding records only in digital form with no paper back-up. In our throw-away society even the notion of heirlooms – much-loved possessions that get handed down through a family – is under threat. Are we to hand down the IKEA furniture? There is a real risk of us being the 'lost generation' in terms of what we leave for the future.

Surely in this audiovisual age we will leave a visual record? Digital cameras and mobile phones have made it easier than ever to capture our everyday lives, allowing us to snap everything from a family wedding to a Friday evening in the pub. But once taken our photos tend to get forgotten. They accumulate as reference numbers on hard disks and memory sticks and rarely get printed to paste into albums. How many of us stop and take time to filter the profound from the frivolous; to earmark what we want not just to keep but to *preserve*? Family photographs of the late nineteenth and early twentieth century survived because they were viewed as special. At the time, photographic (and later film) imagery was sufficiently novel and expensive to be valued and kept. Can we say the same about images and other communications uploaded to Facebook or YouTube? And in any case, what guarantees do we have about the longevity of the web as a long-term storage medium?

This raises another issue: technical obsolescence. In 1984 the BBC launched a partnership with a number of computing firms to mark the

900th anniversary of Domesday Book. Over one million people participated in the project, many of them schoolchildren. They wrote about the geography, history or social issues in their local area and linked this to maps, photos, videos and statistical data. The information was stored on an innovative form of laser disc technology manufactured by Phillips. Around the millennium – just some fifteen years later – there were concerns that the discs would become unreadable as computers and drives capable of accessing the discs were becoming rare. In 2002 the BBC had to launch another project to recover the information and store it in a more durable format.

The Domesday Project is a prime example of digital obsolescence. Modern technology is advancing at such a pace that there is no guarantee any data committed to digital form today will be accessible in five, ten or twenty years time. Within the last twenty years cassette tapes, five-inch floppy disks, three-inch floppy disks and a host of little-known proprietary formats have all become outdated media. Compact discs (CDs) and digital video discs (DVDs) are set to go the same way. All magnetic storage media degrade over time, requiring constant attention to keep them in a readable state. There is a risk that any information stored in this way gets lost from the historical record without major restoration efforts, as is the case now for early twentieth-century films. As technology has evolved and costs of storage have plummeted, it is now more effective to store personal media online, using the internet like a massive filing cabinet. But here, too, there is no guarantee of permanence since software is continually changing. Even if the data can be located in thirty years' time, the programs then available might not be able to read it. And this assumes that the company running the server is still in business.

The preservation and conservation of data within the digital space is becoming a major issue for professional archivists and amateur historians alike. It would be ironic, to say the least, if the digital technologies that have done so much to open up the past to current-day family historians also led to our own times being obscured from future generations of researchers. The prospect of contemporary society being lost in some digital black hole which it is impossible to peer into is a very real one. Professionals and amateurs both need to do more to ensure this does not happen.

In terms of future records, the prospects for 'official sources' are of most concern. The three sources that have been the staple of genealogists over generations – parish records, civil registration records and census returns – are all, for various reasons, under threat.

Parish records are becoming less useful to family historians for a simple reason: organized religion is playing a less important part in people's lives. As is well known, church attendance has been on the decline for many years. But for much of the post-war period, even if people did not go to church regularly they at least did so for notable 'life events': to get married, to have their children baptized and for their funeral service. Although precise figures are lacking, nowadays church records capture a much smaller proportion of the population in this way.

This puts a much greater emphasis on the civil registration records in tracing people's vital events. Here, as discussed earlier, the family historian comes up against the growing privacy culture. The prevailing mood among policy-makers and citizens at large is in favour of less rather than more disclosure of personal data. In the future, those probing their ancestry will almost certainly be doing so within the context of a much more restrictive regime in terms of access to vital records.

So, parish and civil registrations records may not be available, but surely the census is safe? Alas, this is not so. Governments have always had a rather schizophrenic attitude to the census, eagerly devouring the information it produces but baulking at the ever-increasing costs. The latter view has finally prevailed and in 2010 the Coalition government announced that the 2011 national census would be the last. At an estimated cost of around £480 million, it was, according to Cabinet Office minister Francis Maude, 'an expensive and inaccurate way of measuring the number of people in Britain'.[28] The government will examine alternative and cheaper ways to count the population more regularly, using existing public and private databases, including credit reference agencies.

The needs of family historians have never been a factor in the design of the census; one of the pieces of information they find most useful – a person's place of birth – has not even been recorded since 1951. If the census as we know it is abolished, its genealogical function will need to be met in some other way. Most likely, this means ensuring more information is recorded on birth, marriage and death certificates so as to make it easier for the historians of the future to untangle the complicated relationships that exist in many modern families.

From the genealogists' point of view, changing attitudes towards marriage are of particular significance here. The number of marriages peaked in 1972, at around 426,000.[29] Since then there has been a steady fall in the number of people marrying and an increase in cohabitation. In 2008 there were around 270,000 marriages in the UK, the lowest figure since 1895. By contrast, around one-quarter of unmarried people between the ages of 16 and 59 were cohabiting. Around 46 per cent of children are now born – to use the old-fashioned phrase – 'out of wedlock'. This proportion has risen by more than 50 per cent since 1991, when 30.2 per cent of children were born to unmarried mothers (which is not to be confused with the much-maligned 'single mothers'). Within a few years we are likely to see a situation where more than half of children are born outside marriage, even though the majority will be the result of stable relationships. The trend is particularly marked for those born after 1970. For many in this generation cohabitation is not a precursor to marriage but a life choice. Their path will never be captured in the historical record, either by religious or civil institutions. Of course, their families will know who they are – and hopefully they will pass on their ancestral stories – but the point is that they will leave no mark in any official system.

The decline of marriage and new definitions of the family – which now includes civil partnerships where children may also be involved – has other implications. The fact that fewer people are inheriting their surname from their parents or grandparents is of more than just a methodological inconvenience for family historians. It changes the whole genealogical narrative; how we as a society think about ourselves and our heritage, and the version of history that we hand on to future generations.

Cohabiting couples and those in civil partnerships sometimes choose to hyphenate their names and the children take this merged identity. In other cases they are given the surnames of the father (because it is conventional) or the mother (because they bore them). Added to this is the case of second marriages, where the mother might take the name of her new husband but the children retain the original family name. A national newspaper recently reported an increasing incidence of couples 'meshing' their surnames when they marry. Thus, a Mr Jones and Ms Smith might become Mr and Mrs Jonesmith. According to some estimates, even among couples marrying only around half of women now take their husband's name.

It would take a work of sociology or psychology to explain how such changes impact on a family's sense of identity and that is not our purpose here. Whatever the effect, it certainly makes for complicated genealogy. A society where names are passed on not by the patrimonial system that has existed for at least 800 years, but by some other convention is a society with a very different view of itself and very different social mores. Families matter and how we choose to call ourselves matters to our understanding of our own history.

Even the new genetic technologies may not be able to help us here. If the link between male-line Y-DNA and hereditary (male line) surnames continues to be eroded, then in a few generations surname-based DNA projects will be much more difficult to undertake. At the same time, isolated populations, with their distinctive genetic codes, are being diluted, meaning that future analyses will be far less informative. Modern DNA is an increasingly homogenized soup and there is a danger that just as we are learning to decode the data, the signal is being lost.

Will the popularity of genealogy continue? Clearly, this is a maturing field. Factors that have contributed to the current boom – advances in technology, the ready availability of data, people's desire (for whatever reason) to connect with the past – are not going to go away. Less certain is whether it will remain a lifelong hobby or just something that people dip into and then move on. As data become ubiquitous, we can envisage a point where most (even all) genealogies of British families will have been documented and are publicly available. At that stage, once people find that their ancestry is just something to be downloaded rather than researched, family history may well lose its appeal. So we should be thankful that we live in a time when all the pieces of the ancestral picture are available to us, but there is still much to discover. We may, in fact, look back on this as Genealogy's Golden Age.

*   *   *   *

Bibliography

The text draws on a wide range of sources. The minutiae of the genealogy world over the last 100 years are chronicled in two periodicals:

Genealogists' Magazine, Society of Genealogists, London. Published quarterly since 1925. The publication was originally entitled *The Genealogists' Magazine*, 'The' later being dropped from the title.
Family Tree, ABM Publishing, Huntingdon. Published monthly since 1984. Variously known over the years as *Family Tree* and *Family Tree Magazine*.

Other periodicals serving as journals of record for late nineteenth- and early twentieth century genealogy are: *The Pedigree Register*, *The Ancestor* and *Notes and Queries*. References are provided throughout the text but the following can be considered as key sources for further reading on relevant themes.

General, Historical and Sociological Perspectives on Genealogy

Donald Harman Akenson, *Some Family: The Mormons and How Humanity Keeps Track of Itself* (Montreal and Kingston: McGill-Queen's University Press, 2007).
Terrick V H FitzHugh, *The Dictionary of Genealogy*, ed. Susan Lumas (London: A&C Black, 1985, repr. 1998).
David Hey (ed.), *Oxford Companion to Family and Local History*, 2nd edn (Oxford: OUP, 2008)
Elizabeth Shown Mills, 'Genealogy in the "Information Age": History's New Frontier', *National Genealogical Society Quarterly* 91 (2003), 260–77.
Robert M Taylor and Ralph J. Crandall (eds), *Generations and Change: Genealogical Perspectives in Social History* (Macon, GA: Mercer University Press, 1986).
Anthony Wagner, *English Genealogy*, 3rd edn (Chichester: Phillimore & Co., 1960, repr. 1983).
Anthony Wagner, *Pedigree and Progress: Essays in the Genealogical Interpretation of History* (Chichester: Phillimore & Co., 1975).

Genealogy and Specific Periods and Themes

Raluca L Radulescu and Edward Donald Kennedy (eds), *Broken Lines: Genealogical Literature in Late-Medieval Britain and France* (Turnhout: Brepols Publishers, 2008).
D E C Eversley, P Laslett and E A Wrigley, *An Introduction to English Historical Demography: From the Sixteenth to the Nineteenth Century* (London: Weidenfeld & Nicolson, 1966).
W Raymond Powell, *John Horace Round: Historian and Gentleman of Essex* (Chelmsford: Essex Record Office, 2001).
Don J Steel, 'Genealogy and Demography', *Genealogists' Magazine* 16 (1970), 203–11.

Scientific Perspectives, Especially in Relation to Genetics:

Robert A Peel (ed.), *Human Pedigree Studies: Proceedings of a Conference organised by the Galton Institute* (London: Galton Institute, 1998).
Chris Pomery, *DNA and Family History: How Genetic Testing Can Advance Your Genealogical Research* (London: The National Archives, 2004).

Brian Sykes, *The Seven Daughters of Eve: The Science that Reveals our Genetic Ancestry* (London: W W Norton, 2001).
Brian Sykes, *Blood of the Isles* (London: Bantam Press, 2006).

Use of Computers in Genealogy:
Peter Christian, *The Genealogist's Internet*, 4th edn (London: The National Archives, 2009); see also Peter Christian's 'British Genealogy on the Internet' timeline: http://homepages.gold.ac.uk/genuki/timeline/.
David Hawgood, *Computers for Family History: An Introduction* 4th edn (Hawgood, 1992).

History of Records and Archives
Patricia Bell, 'George Herbert Fowler and County Records', *Journal of the Society of Archivists* 23/2 (2002), 249–63.
Anthony J Camp, *Wills and their Whereabouts* (London: Anthony Camp, 1974).
Fred G. Emmison, *Archives and Local History* (London: Methuen & Co., 1966).
Edward Higgs, *Making Sense of the Census: The Manuscript Returns for England and Wales 1801–1901* (London: Public Record Office, 1988).
David Iredale, *Enjoying Archives* (Chichester: Phillimore & Co., 1973, repr. 1985).
G H Martin and P Spufford (eds), *The Records of the Nation: The Public Record Office, 1838–1988. The British Record Society, 1888–1988* (Woodbridge: The Boydell Press, 1990).
M Nissel, *People Count: A History of the General Register Office* (London: HMSO, 1987).
Stuart A Raymond, *Parish Registers: A History and Guide* (Bury: Family History Partnership, 2009).
Registrar General, *The Story of the General Register Office and its Origins from 1536 to 1937* (London: HMSO, 1937).

Notes and References

Chapter 1

1. Donald Harman Akenson, *Some Family: The Mormons and How Humanity Keeps Track of Itself* (Montreal and Kingston: McGill-Queen's University Press, 2007), p. 129.
2. 1 Timothy 1: 4.
3. Adherents of the LDS church take the Bible as literal truth. The website of one genealogy company associated with the Mormons includes the following statement: 'Various genealogies have been compiled for royal and noble lines. Some of these connect with the Bible genealogies which continue back to Adam and Eve. Although it may be reassuring to some to think they have connected their lines back to the earliest times, such compiled genealogies contain many errors. None of these genealogies have been proven. Some pedigrees include the names of various gods from which the earliest ancestors of their peoples supposedly descend and which come from early folk tales or mythology. It is practically impossible to separate the fact from the fiction. At this point it is not possible to document a lineage back to Adam.' www.progenealogists.com/greatbritain/medieval genealogy.htm.
4. The origins and shortcomings of the genealogical activities of the LDS church are discussed at length in Akenson, *Some Family*.
5. Jane Qiu, 'Inheriting Confucius', *Seed Magazine* (13 Aug. 2008). http://seedmagazine. com/content/article/inheriting_confucius/.
6. Anthony Wagner, *Pedigree and Progress: Essays in the Genealogical Interpretation of History* (Chichester: Phillimore & Co., 1975), p. 2.
7. Akenson, *Some Family*, p. 108.
8. Alex Haley, *Roots: The Saga of an American Family* (London: Hutchinson, 1977).
9. Don J Steel, *Discovering Your Family History* (London: BBC Books, 1980), p. 11.
10. Quoted in: John Rayment, 'The Functions of a Family History Society', *Family Tree* (Jan. 1989), 10.
11. Henry Byron Phillips, 'International Congress of Genealogy Day', *Utah Genealogical and Historical Magazine* 6 (1915), 166.
12. Lester J. Cappon, 'Genealogy: Handmaid of History', *Special Publications of the National Genealogical Society* 17 (1957), 1.
13. George F T Sherwood, *The Pedigree Register* 1 (1910), preface.
14. Ibid.
15. For further discussion on this point see: Akensen, *Some Family*, pp. 217–26.
16. Ibid., pp. 84–123.
17. It should be noted that the terms patrilineal and matrilineal refer to the tracing and recording of ancestry only and should not be confused with patriarchal and matriarchal, referring to the holding of power. Anthropologists have noted matriarchal societies where genealogical descriptions are both patrilineal and matrilineal, and similarly for patriarchal societies.
18. 'Brits' Family History Knowledge Worst in Europe', The Generations Network, Inc. (Ancestry. co.uk press release, 13 Dec. 2007). See also a similar survey: 'Brits' Startling Lack of Basic Family Knowledge Revealed' (14 Dec. 2006). Both accessible at: www.ancestry.co.uk. Such surveys are, of course, designed to promote commercial services and so have to be viewed with caution. In this case the research was undertaken

by independent market research organizations and appears to provide legitimate comparisons.

19. Gerald Fothergill, 'Genealogical Letters: Fothergill', *The Pedigree Register* 3 (1914), 110–12.
20. 'Online Family History Boom Reveals Five Million Secrets . . . and Counting', The Generations Network, Inc. (Ancestry.co.uk press release, 13 Sept. 2007). Accessible at: www.ancestry.co.uk.
21. Anthony J Camp, *Everyone has Roots: An Introduction to Genealogy* (London: Star Books, 1978), p. 146.
22. Frederick S Snell, 'The Study of Ancestry: Some Reflections', *The Pedigree Register* 2 (1910), 3.
23. Steel, *Discovering Your Family History*, p. 6.
24. Camp, *Everyone has Roots*, pp. 165–6.
25. Ibid., p. 154.
26. Ibid., p. 155.
27. Joseph G B Bulloch, 'The Problems that Now Confront Us', *National Genealogical Society Quarterly* 1 (Oct. 1912), 39–41.
28. Arthur Adams, 'The Historical Society and Genealogical Records', *Wisconsin Magazine of History* 7 (Sept. 1923), 59.
29. Robert Resta, 'A Brief History of the Pedigree in Human Genetics', in Robert A Peel (ed.), *Human Pedigree Studies: Proceedings of a Conference Organised by the Galton Institute* (London: Galton Institute, 1998), p. 77.
30. Elizabeth Thomson, 'Human Pedigrees and Human Genetics', in Peel (ed.), *Human Pedigree Studies*, p. 46.
31. Peter Spufford, 'Genealogy and the Historian', *Genealogists' Magazine* 15 (1967), 447.
32. W G Leveson Gower (ed.), *The Register of the Christenings, Burials and Weddings within the Parish of St. Peter's Upon Cornhill, London*, Harleian Society Register Series (London: Harleian Society, 1878), preface.
33. Robert M Taylor and Ralph J Crandall, 'Historians and Genealogists: An Emerging Community of Interest', in Robert M Taylor and Ralph J Crandall (eds), *Generations and Change: Genealogical Perspectives in Social History* (Macon, GA: Mercer University Press, 1986), p. 16.
34. Charles Bolton, 'The New Genealogy', *Utah Genealogical and Historical Magazine* 4 (1913), 127.
35. Arthur Adams, 'The Development of Genealogical Study through a Century', in William C Hill (ed.), *A Century of Genealogical Progress: Being a History of the New England Historic Genealogical Society, 1845–1945* (Boston, MA: New England Historic Genealogical Society, 1945), p. 65.
36. See for instance: D E C Eversley, P Laslett and E A Wrigley, *An Introduction to English Historical Demography: From the Sixteenth to the Nineteenth Century* (London: Weidenfeld & Nicolson, 1966).
37. Wagner, *Pedigree and Progress*, p. 8.
38. Ibid., preface.
39. Ibid., p. 10.
40. Ibid., p. 7.
41. Anthony Wagner, 'Genealogy and History', transcript of a radio talk broadcast on the Third Programme, 26 Aug. 1960. BBC Archives, Caversham.
42. Each of these schools can trace its origins to the 'people's history' movement of the 1960s and 1970s inspired by the historian E P Thomson and others. In his ground-breaking

book *The Making of the English Working Class*, Thomson told the forgotten history of Britain's industrial workers in the late eighteenth and early nineteenth centuries. His 'history from below' focused on telling stories of people who had traditionally been excluded from an elite history dominated by politics, foreign policy and male worthies.

43. William Weinstein, 'I Married a Genealogist', *Family Tree* (July 2003), 25.

Chapter 2

1. For an introduction to the history of parish registers see: Stuart A Raymond, *Parish Registers: A History and Guide* (Bury: The Family History Partnership, 2009).
2. For detailed discussion of the history of census taking see: Edward Higgs, *Making Sense of the Census: The Manuscript Returns for England and Wales 1801–1901* (London: Public Record Office, 1988); Muriel Nissel, *People Count: A History of the General Register Office* (London: HMSO, 1987); and the 'History of the Census' section at the Vision of Britain website: www.visionofbritain.org.uk.
3. Registrar General, *The Story of the General Register Office and its Origins from 1536 to 1937* (London: HMSO, 1937), quoted on the Vision of Britain website: www.visionofbritain.org.uk.
4. Nissel, *People Count*, p. 48.
5. Ibid., p. 53.
6. Ibid., p. 63.
7. The 1931 census schedules, enumeration books and other documents were held in an Office of Works furniture store in Hayes, Middlesex. On the evening of 19 Dec. 1942 the store was gutted by fire; there was no enemy bombing in the area and the cause was never identified. The resulting investigation is described in a letter in the National Archives: RG20/109, http://yourarchives.nationalarchives.gov.uk/index.php?title=1931_Census.
8. For detail on the origins and history of wills see: Anthony J Camp, *Wills and their Whereabouts*, 4th edn (London: Anthony Camp, 1974).
9. Stacey Grimaldi, *Origines Genealogicae; or, The Sources Whence English Genealogies May Be Traced* (London, 1828).
10. George F T Sherwood, *A List of Persons Named in the PCC Wills Proved in the Year 1750: Register Greenly* (London, 1918). Quoted in: Anthony J Camp, 'The Genealogist's Use of Probate Accounts', in G H Martin and P Spufford (eds), *The Records of the Nation: The Public Record Office, 1838–1988. The British Record Society, 1888–1988* (Woodbridge: The Boydell Press, 1990).
11. For an authoritative account of the history of public recordkeeping see the collection of essays in G H Martin and P Spufford (eds), *The Records of the Nation: The Public Record Office, 1838–1988. The British Record Society, 1888–1988* (Woodbridge: The Boydell Press, 1990).
12. Elizabeth M Hallam, 'Nine Centuries of Keeping the Public Records', in Martin and Spufford (eds), Records of the Nation, p. 35.
13. Ibid., p. 23.
14. David Iredale, *Enjoying Archives* (Chichester: Phillimore & Co., 1973, repr. 1985), p. 11.
15. Ibid., p. 12.
16. Ibid., p. 13.
17. Hallam, 'Nine Centuries of Keeping the Public Records', p. 38.
18. Ibid., p. 39.
19. Iredale, *Enjoying Archives*, p. 15.
20. Hallam, 'Nine Centuries of Keeping the Public Records', p. 40.
21. Simon Fowler, 'Our Genealogical Forebears', *History Today* (March 2001), 42–3.

22. Jane Cox, 'The Evidence of Every Man's Particulars: Thoughts of the Public Record Office on its 150th Anniversary', *Genealogists' Magazine* 22 (1988), 412.

23. The principal guides are S R Scargill-Bird, *A Guide to the Principal Classes of Documents Preserved in the Public Record Office* (London: HMSO, 1891); and M. S. Giuseppi, *A Guide to the Manuscripts Preserved in the Public Record Office*, 2 vols (London: HMSO, 1923–4).

24. An independent review, published in 2009, recommended a reduction of the thirty-year rule; the government subsequently decided that, except for certain classes of records, the disclosure period should progressively be reduced to twenty years. The change will occur over a ten-year period from 2013 onwards, with two years' records being released to the National Archives each year, rather than one. At the same time more bodies will be subject to the Freedom of Information Act.

25. Jane Cox, 'The Strongbox of Empire – Shut', *Family Tree* (Feb. 1997), 26.

Chapter 3

1. More specifically, 'pied' comes from the Latin *pes* (foot) and 'grue' from Latin *grus* (crane). The Middle French form is sometimes written as 'pié de grue'. An alternative suggestion is that the term 'pedigree' derives from the Norman French *par degrés* 'by degrees' – which is how the names in a genealogical tree are listed – but supporting evidence is lacking.

2. For further discussion see: Richard McKinley, *A History of British Surnames* (London: Longman, 1990) and David Hey, *Family Names and Family History* (London, Hambledon, 2000).

3. Raluca L Radulescu, 'Genealogy in Insular Romance', in Raluca L Radulescu and Edward Donald Kennedy (eds), *Broken Lines: Genealogical Literature in Late-Medieval Britain and France* (Turnhout: Brepols Publishers, 2008), pp. 7–25.

4. Julia Marvin, 'Narrative, Lineage, and Succession in the Anglo-Norman Prose *Brut* Chronicle', in Radulescu and Kennedy (eds), Broken Lines, pp. 205–20.

5. Lesley Coote, 'Prophecy, Genealogy, and History in Medieval English Political Discourse', in Radulescu and Kennedy (eds), *Broken Lines*, pp. 27–44.

6. Olivier de Laborderie, 'A New Pattern for English History: The First Genealogical Rolls of the Kings of England', in Radulescu and Kennedy (eds), *Broken Lines*, pp. 45–62.

7. Edward Donald Kennedy, 'The Antiquity of Scottish Civilization: King-Lists and Genealogical Chronicles', in Radulescu and Kennedy (eds), *Broken Lines*, pp. 159–74.

8. Coote, 'Prophecy, Genealogy, and History', in Radulescu and Kennedy (eds), *Broken Lines*, pp. 42–3.

9. For images of the Edward IV Coronation Roll see: http://libwww.freelibrary.org/medievalman/.

10. Emilia Jamroziak, 'Genealogy in Monastic Chronicles in England', in Radulescu and Kennedy (eds), *Broken Lines*, p. 122.

11. Wagner, *English Genealogy*, p. 353, quotes the case as being in 1378, which would date it before Richard II's invasion of Scotland in 1385 during which the similarity between the Scrope and Grosvenor arms came to light. This appears to be an uncharacteristic typographical error.

12. Ibid., p. 356.

13. John Spence, 'Genealogies of Noble Families in Anglo-Norman', in Radulescu and Kennedy (eds), *Broken Lines*, pp. 63–78.

14. Jon Denton, 'Genealogy and Gentility: Social Status in Provincial England', in Radulescu and Kennedy (eds), *Broken Lines*, pp. 143–58.

15. Alison Allan, 'Yorkist Propaganda: Pedigree, Prophecy and the "British History" in the Reign of Edward IV', in Charles Ross (ed.), *Patronage, Pedigree and Power in Later Medieval England* (Gloucester: Sutton, 1979), pp. 171–92.

16. Denton, 'Genealogy and Gentility', in Radulescu and Kennedy (eds), *Broken Lines*, pp. 157–8.

17. John Horace Round, *Studies in Peerage and Family History* (London: Constable & Co., 1901), pp. 307–8.

18. Patric L Dickinson, 'The Heralds and Genealogy', *Genealogists' Magazine* 21 (1984), 145.

19. For general discussion and bibliography of the antiquarian movement see: 'The Antiquarian Tradition', in David Hey (ed.), *The Oxford Companion to Family and Local History*, 2nd edn (Oxford: Oxford University Press, 2008).

20. Wagner attributes this as *Succint Genealogies of the Noble and Ancient Houses of Alno, or de Alneto, Broc of Shepdale . . . and Mordaunt of Turvey . . .*, by Robert Halstead, the pseudonym of Henry Mordaunt, Earl of Peterborough. Wagner, *English Genealogy*, p. 399.

21. Nia M. W. Powell, 'Genealogical Narratives and Kingship in Medieval Wales', in Radulescu and Kennedy (eds), *Broken Lines*, p. 175.

22. *Wagner, Pedigree and Progress*, p. 2.

23. George D. Squibb, 'Visitation Pedigrees and the Genealogist', *Genealogists' Magazine* 13 (1960), 225.

24. Wagner, *English Genealogy*, p. 368.

25. Philip Styles, 'The Heralds' Visitation of Warwickshire, 1682–3', *Transactions of the Birmingham Archaeological Society* 71 (1953), 47.

26. Rosemary Sweet, '"Mere Dull Description": Antiquarianism and Local History in the Eighteenth Century', *The Local Historian* 38 (2008), 245.

27. Peter Christie, 'The Gentleman's Magazine as a Source for the Family Historian', *Genealogists' Magazine* 20 (1981), 238–9.

28.. The term 'magazine' originally meant a military storehouse.

29. Julian Pooley and Robin Myers, 'Nichols Family (per. c.1760–1939)', *Dictionary of National Biography* (Oxford: OUP, 2004), online edn: www.oxforddnb.com/view/article /63494 doi:10.1093/ref:odnb/20118.

Chapter 4

1. Hannah Barker, 'Debrett, John (*d.* 1822)', *Oxford Dictionary of National Biography* (Oxford: OUP, 2004); online edn, Jan. 2008. www.oxforddnb.com/view/article/7403.

2. George Burnett, *Popular Genealogists or The Art of Pedigree-Making* (Edinburgh, 1865).

3. Ibid., p. 4.

4. Ibid., p. 5.

5. Ibid., p. 20.

6. Edward A. Freeman, 'Pedigrees and Pedigree Makers', *Contemporary Review* 30 (1877), 11–41.

7. Fowler, 'Our Genealogical Forebears', *History Today* (March 2001), 42–3.

8. Richard Sims, *A Manual for the Genealogist, Topographer, Antiquary and Legal Professor* (London: Avery, 1856, repr. 1888).

9. *Notes and Queries* 2nd series 5 (1852), 297 and 353–4.

10. The society is referenced at: *Notes and Queries* 7th series 4 (1887), 68 and 234; and 11th series 3 (1911), 266.

11. *Notes and Queries* 10th series 4 (1905), 230.

12. *Notes and Queries* 2nd series 6 (1858), 307–8. And replies pp. 307, 378, 438.

13. *Notes and Queries* 2nd series 6 (1858), 481.

14. *cacoethes scribendi* translates as 'the irresistible urge to write' and *amor nummi* as 'the love of money'.

15. Peter L Gwynn-Jones, 'The Harleian Society 1869–1994', *Genealogists' Magazine* 24 (1994), 508–9.

16. See Chapter 2.

17. Peter Spufford, 'The British Record Society: A Centenary History', *Genealogists' Magazine* 22 (1988), 323. A longer version of the same paper appears as: Peter Spufford, 'The Index Library: A Centenary History', in G H Martin and P Spufford (eds), *The Records of the Nation: The Public Record Office, 1838–1988. The British Record Society, 1888–1988* (Woodbridge: The Boydell Press, 1990).

18. Ibid. (in *Records of the Nation*), p. 123.

19. For discussion on the history of transcribing and printing parish registers see a series of articles by John Titford on 'Printed Parish Registers' in *Family Tree* (April 1999), 25–7; (June 1999), 61–2; (Aug. 1999), 25–7; (Oct. 1999), 58–9. Two important reference works here are: John Southerden Burn, *The History of the Parish Registers in England*, 2nd edn (London: Smith, 1862); and J Charles Cox, *The Parish Registers of England* (London: Methuen & Co., 1910).

20. Quoted in Richard Sims, *A Manual for the Genealogist, Topographer, Antiquary and Legal Professor*, 2nd edn (London, 1861), p. 357.

21. Titford, 'Printed Parish Registers', *Family Tree* (April 1999), 25.

22. Ibid., p. 26.

23. Ibid.

24. Titford, 'Printed Parish Registers', *Family Tree* (Oct. 1999), 59.

25. W G Leveson Gower (ed.), *The Register of the Christenings, Burials and Weddings within the Parish of St. Peter's Upon Cornhill, London*, Harleian Society Register Series (London: Harleian Society, 1878), preface.

26. John Amphlett, 'Genealogy', *Popular Science Monthly* 13 (Sept. 1878), 583–6.

27. *East Anglian Daily Times* (4 May 1922).

28. The real name of 'Plantagenet Harrison' was George Henry Harrison. He was born in 1817 at Whaston in the North Riding of Yorkshire and embarked on a military career – effectively as a mercenary – that took him to conflicts in Europe and South America. He obtained the rank of brigadier-general in the Peruvian army before returning to England in the 1850s. In 1858 he petitioned the Lords as 'George Henry de Strabolgie Plantagenet Harrison', and claimed the title of Duke of Lancaster as heir to the whole bloodline of Henry VI. He spent much of his time in the PRO trying to substantiate this claim. 'Plantagenet Harrison Knowles', *Notes and Queries* 170 (1936), 141–2.

29. Peter Weinrich, 'J. H. Round: Facts and Evidence in Family Trees', *Family Tree* (Aug. 1999), 49.

30. Frank I. Stenton, 'Round, John Horace (1854–1928)', in *Dictionary of National Biography* (1937).

31. W Raymond Powell, *John Horace Round: Historian and Gentleman of Essex* (Chelmsford: Essex Record Office, 2001), p. 52.

32. Stenton, *DNB* (1937).

33. William Page (ed.), *Family Origins and Other Studies by the Late J. Horace Round* (Glasgow: The University Press: 1930), pp. 170–1. The distinguished genealogist Sir Anthony Wagner suggests adding to this list pedigrees whose errors rest on a strained or

erroneous but not dishonest interpretation of genuine evidence. Wagner, *English Genealogy*, p. 358.

34. John Horace Round, 'Historical Genealogy', in Page (ed.), *Family Origins and Other Studies*, pp. 1–12.

35. Ibid., p. 11.

36. John Horace Round, 'An Approved Pre-Conquest Pedigree', in Page (ed.), *Family Origins and Other Studies*, p. 13.

37. For an account of a dispute between Cokayne and Joseph Foster regarding some of these manuscripts see John Titford, 'The Chester Manuscripts and the Harleian Society: Quaritch and Foster vs Cokayne and Armytage', *Genealogists' Magazine* 25 (1997), 401–6.

38. For a history of *The Complete Peerage* see Geoffrey White, 'The Complete Peerage', *Genealogists' Magazine*, 7 (1942), 253–7; for Round's involvement see Powell, *John Horace Round*, pp. 171–7.

39. John Horace Round, *Studies in Peerage and Family History* (London: Constables, 1901), p. 16.

40. *The Ancestor* 9 (1904), 104.

41. Powell, *John Horace Round*, p. 50.

42. Ibid., pp. 145–64.

43. Wagner, *English Genealogy*, p. 395.

44. Powell, *John Horace Round*, p. 165.

45. *The Ancestor* 12 (1905), 1.

46. Wagner, *English Genealogy*, p. 395.

Chapter 5

1. The Sherwood Collection, Society of Genealogists, London. Unpublished letters.

2. Dorothy Maltby Verrill, *Maltby-Maltbie Family History* (Newark, NJ: Birdsey Maltbie, 1915), p. 397.

3. *Notes and Queries* 10th series 6 (1907), 347.

4. *Notes and Queries* 10th series 8 (1907), 52.

5. *Notes and Queries* 9th series 7 (1901), 426–7.

6. Charles A. Bernau, *The International Genealogical Directory* (Walton-on-Thames: Bernau, 1907), p. 4

7. Ibid., p. 8.

8. *The Pedigree Register* 1 (1907), 48.

9. Charles A. Bernau, 'The Genealogy of the Submerged', in Charles A. Bernau (ed.), *Genealogical Pocket Library*, vol. 3, *Some Special Studies in Genealogy* (Walton-on-Thames: Bernau, 1908).

10. *Notes and Queries* 10th series 6 (1906), 48.

11. *The Pedigree Register* 2 (1910–13), preface.

12. *Notes and Queries* 10th series 11 (1909), 5.

13. Ibid., p. 78.

14. Malcolm Pinhorn, 'Foundation of the Society of Genealogists: A Footnote', *Genealogists' Magazine* 22 (1987), 179–81.

15. Ibid.

16. Ibid.

17. *Notes and Queries* 11th series 1 (1910), 285.

18. Ibid., p. 337.

19. *Notes and Queries* 11th series 1 (1910), 401–2.

20. Ibid., pp. 510–11.
21. R M Carne, 'C. A. Bernau', *The Midland Ancestor* 26 (1972), 6.
22. Pinhorn, 'Foundation', *Genealogists' Magazine* 22 (1987), 180.
23. *The Pedigree Register* 2 (1910), 33.
24. Lady Elizabeth Cust (d. 1914), daughter of the 5th Earl of Darnley, was married to Sir Reginald Cust, Kt.
25. Pinhorn, 'Foundation', p. 180.
26. Ibid.
27. Ibid.
28. One reason for the delay was objections to the new body by the College of Arms. See Patrick Dickinson, '1911 and All That: The Heralds and the Society of Genealogists', in *Society of Genealogists: A Century of Family History* ((London: Society of Genealogists, 2011).
29. More precisely, 'of London' was dropped from everyday usage in 1914 and from the legal articles in 1924.
30. Ibid.
31. By the time of the First Annual Report in 1912, fourteen fellows and members were listed as professionals.
32. *The Pedigree Register* 3 (1915), 352.
33. Society of Genealogists, *Annual Report* (London: Society of Genealogists, 1916), p. 6.
34. Anthony J Camp, 'Mad Annie Druce and the Saving of the Census', *Family Tree* (Jan. 2002), 4–6.
35. Ibid., p. 5.
36. *The Pedigree Register* 2 (1911), 221.
37. Royal Commission on Public Records, *Second Report* (London: HMSO, 1914), 44–6 and 290–1.
38. Royal Commission on Public Records, *Third Report* (London: HMSO, 1915), 40–3.
39. Royal Commission on Public Records, *Second Report*, 294–5.
40. George F T Sherwood, 'Public Records', *The Pedigree Register* 3 (1913), 193–6.
41. For Fowler's life and work see Patricia Bell, 'George Herbert Fowler and County Records', *Journal of the Society of Archivists* 23/2 (2002), 249–63; and Margaret Deacon, 'Fowler, George Herbert (1861–1940)', *Oxford Dictionary of National Biography* (2004.)
42. Bell, 'George Herbert Fowler', p. 251.
43. Ibid., p. 253.
44. Ibid., p. 254.
45. *The Genealogist* 38 (1922), 3.
46. *Genealogists' Magazine* 1 (1925), 1.
47. *Genealogists' Magazine* 2 (1926), 65.
48. *Genealogists' Magazine* 4 (1928), 73.
49. *Genealogists' Magazine* 5 (1929), 1.
50. *Genealogists' Magazine* 4 (1928), 97.
51. *Genealogists' Magazine* 2 (1926), 1.
52. 'An Index to Marriages', *Genealogists' Magazine* 1 (1925), 72.
53. Percival Boyd (ed.), *A Marriage Index on a New Plan* (London: Society of Genealogists, 1928).
54. Anthony J Camp, 'Boyd's Marriage Index', *Family Tree* (July 1985), 10.
55. For the BRA's origins and work see Oliver Harris, 'The British Records Association', *Family Tree* (Dec. 1988), 5–6.
56. 'The Society's Reception', *Genealogists' Magazine* 6 (1934), 349.

57. T C Dale, 'The Society's Card Index', *Genealogists' Magazine* 6 (1934), 453–6.
58. *Genealogists' Magazine* 7 (1935), 23. 'Sole' here means a spinster.
59. 'A New Epoch in Genealogy', ibid., p. 26.
60. John Beach Whitmore, 'Boyd's Citizens of London', *Genealogists' Magazine* 9 (1944), 385.
61. Lord Farrer, 'English Genealogy', *Genealogists' Magazine* 7 (1936), 179–81.
62. 'The Genealogical and Heraldic Exhibition', *Genealogists' Magazine* 7 (1937), 575.
63. 'The Genealogist's Handbook: Being an Introduction to the Pursuit of Genealogy', *Genealogists' Magazine* 7 (1935), 195.
64. W P W Phillimore, *Pedigree Work: A Handbook for the Genealogist*, 3rd edn rev. by Bower Marsh (London: Phillimore & Co., 1936).
65. Bethell Godefroy Bouwens, *Wills and their Whereabouts* (London: Bouwens, 1939).
66. Society of Genealogists, *Catalogue of the Parish Registers in the Possession of the Society of Genealogists* (London: Society of Genealogists, 1937).
67. 'Annual General Meeting', *Genealogists' Magazine* 8 (1938), 141.
68. 'Chairman's Page', *Genealogists' Magazine* 8 (1939), 280.
69. 'Mr Boyd's Sherry Party', *Genealogists' Magazine* 8 (1939), 335.

Chapter 6

1. *Genealogists' Magazine* 9 (1940), 14.
2. *Genealogists' Magazine* 10 (1948), 270.
3. Leslie Dow, 'The Standing Conference for Local History', *Genealogists' Magazine* 10 (1950), 571.
4. Ibid.
5. 'The Scottish Genealogy Society', *The Scottish Genealogist* 1 (1953), 4.
6. 'Microfilms', *Genealogists' Magazine* 120 (1956), 203.
7. *Genealogists' Magazine* 13 (1959), 84.
8. H J W Stone, 'A Comprehensive Plan for Copying Churchyard Inscriptions', *Genealogists' Magazine* 12 (1955), 54.
9. John Beach Whitmore, *A Genealogical Guide* (London: The Harleian Society, 1947).
10. See Chapter 2.
11. Leslie G Pine, *Trace Your Ancestors* (London: Evans Brothers, 1953), p. 9.
12. Arthur J Willis, *Genealogy for Beginners*, 3rd edn (Chichester: Phillimore & Co., 1955, repr. 1976), p. 6.
13. 'Genealogy for Beginners', *Genealogists' Magazine* 12 (1955), 67.
14. Wagner, *English Genealogy*, p. 5.
15. Gerald Hamilton-Edwards, 'The Physical Side of Genealogy', *Genealogists' Magazine* 10 (1948), 225–8.
16. Camp, *Everyone has Roots*, p. 9.
17. Anthony Wagner, *Genealogy and the Common Man: Society of Genealogists Jubilee Lecture* (London: Society of Genealogists, 1961). Later reprinted (with a postscript on subsequent developments) in Wagner, *Pedigree and Progress*, pp. 144–55.
18. Stella Colwell, 'A Genealogist's View of the Public Records: Ideals and Reality', in Martin and Spufford (eds), *Records of the Nation*, p. 151.
19. Ibid.
20. Wagner, *English Genealogy*, p. 420.
21. 'Demand for a Chair of Genealogy', *The Times* (12 Sept. 1962).
22. Society of Genealogists, *National Index of Parish Registers*, vol. 1, *General Sources of*

Births, Marriages and Deaths Before 1837, ed. D J Steel (London: Society of Genealogists, 1968).

23. Anthony J Camp, 'The National Index of Parish Registers', *Genealogists' Magazine* 15 (1967), 331. See also later review by Peter Spufford: *Genealogists' Magazine* 16 (1969), 55.

24. *Genealogists' Magazine* 16 (1969), 101–2.

25. Gerald Hamilton-Edwards, 'Six Generations', *Genealogists' Magazine* 10 (1948), 141.

26. Cecil Humphrey-Smith, 'Editorial', *Family History* 25/202 (2010), 49. In a similar article, Humphrey-Smith claimed the 1957 lecture 'created family history as a distinct subject which brought the individuals in the family tree "to life" in their historical context': 'Editorial', *Family History* 23/190 (2007), 42. And in a further article he asserted that he 'first launched family history as a distinct subject more than 60 years ago': *Family History* 24/197 (2008), 338. While the compiling of a family tree would have characterized most researchers' approach at the time (simply because of the limitations of data), Humphrey-Smith was far from being the first to use the term family history, nor even the first to draw the distinction. As noted in previous chapters, the term was in widespread use throughout the nineteenth century and Horace Round himself used it in the title of one of his publications (Round, *Studies in Peerage and Family History*).

27. 'The Institute of Heraldic and Genealogical Studies', *Genealogists' Magazine* 14 (1962), 95.

28. 'The British Vital Records Index', *Family History* 1/1 (1962), inside cover.

29. Later changed to the Association of Genealogists and Researchers in Archives. See 'Association of Genealogists and Record Agents', *Genealogists' Magazine* 16 (1969), 116.

30. Archibald F Bennett, *A Guide for Genealogical Research* (Salt Lake City: Genealogical Society of the Church of Jesus Christ of Latter-Day Saints, 1956), p. 16.

31. Don J Steel and A E F Steel (eds), *Register and Directory 1966* (London: Society of Genealogists, 1966).

32. *Genealogists' Magazine* 17 (1973), 270.

33. Fred C Markwell, 'Co-operation in Family History', *Genealogists' Magazine* 17 (1974), 618.

34. Eva Beech, 'A Genealogy Class in North Staffordshire', *Genealogists' Magazine* 18 (1975), 203.

35. Elizabeth Shown Mills, 'Genealogy in the "Information Age": History's New Frontier', *National Genealogical Society Quarterly* 91 (2003), 260–77.

36. Pauline Litton, 'The Changing Face of Family History', *Family Tree* (June 2002), 29–30.

37. *Genealogists' Magazine* 16 (1970), 289.

38. Ibid., p. 291.

39. Ibid., p. 361.

40. For first-hand accounts of the period leading up to the formation of the Federation of Family History Societies see Elizabeth Simpson, 'The Federation of Family History Societies', *Family Tree* (July 1991), 18; Pauline Saul, 'The Federation of Family History Societies: Part II', *Family Tree* (Aug. 1991), 18–19; Colin Chapman, 'Founding the Federation', *Family Tree* (Jan. 2005), 62–4.

41. Markwell, 'Co-operation in Family History', p. 618.

42. *Genealogists' Magazine* 17 (1973), 448–9.

Chapter 7

1. These societies were the Birmingham and Midland Society for Genealogy and Heraldry (3,400), the Cornwall Family History Society (1,291), the Devon FHS (1,620), Essex

FHS (1,020), the Society for Lincolnshire History and Archaeology (Family History Section) (1,020), Northumberland and Durham FHS (1,172) and Sussex FHS (1,020). Gerald Hamilton-Edwards, *In Search of Ancestry*, 4th edn (Chichester: Phillimore & Co., 1966, repr. 1983), p. 155.

2. *Genealogists' Magazine* 17 (1974), 559–60.
3. Ibid., p. 621.
4. Don J Steel and Lawrence Taylor, 'Family History in the Classroom', *Genealogists' Magazine* 16 (1970), 329–33.
5. The term 'English Genealogical Congress' was also used for the Institute's conference held on 5–7 April 1974 at Elliot College of the University of Canterbury. This was a one-off event and Colwell's Congress (in 1975) is widely credited as the first EGC as it was the forerunner of a series.
6. 'Annual General Meeting', *Genealogists' Magazine* 17 (1974), 590–3.
7. 'Editorial', *Genealogists' Magazine* 17 (1974), 645.
8. *The Times* (10 June 1974).
9. J S W Gibson. 'The Congress: A Personal Impression', *Genealogists' Magazine* 19 (1977), 16.
10. Peter Strafford, 'A Black American Finds his Roots', *The Times* (1 Dec. 1976).
11. Another reading of ABC's decision is that it was nervous about public reaction and used the consecutive airings to get the transmission out of the way as quickly as possible.
12. Mark Ottaway, 'Tangled Roots', *Sunday Times* (10 April 1977), 17. For a fully referenced account of the controversies surrounding *Roots* in the USA and Britain see the entry: 'Roots: The Saga of an American Family' in Wikipedia, http://en.wikipedia.org
13. Michael Church, 'The Genealogy Experience', *The Times* (9 April 1977). Accessible at: www.timesonline.co.uk.
14. 'Going Back to my Roots', BBC News Online, 23 March 2007, http://news.bbc.co.uk.
15. Ibid.
16. As well as published sources, this section draws on personal correspondence with Gordon Honeycombe in Perth, Australia.
17. *Family History*, original programme script 1979, BBC Archives, Caversham.
18. 'Root and Branch', *Radio Times* (17 March 1979).
19. *The Sun* (21 March 1979).
20. 'TV Man Tracks Down his Family Tree', *London Evening News* (6 March 1979).
21. Don J Steel, 'Genealogy and Demography', *Genealogists' Magazine* 16 (1970), 203–11.
22. See D E C Eversley *et al.*, *An Introduction to English Historical Demography* (London: Weidenfeld & Nicolson, 1966)..
23. Don J Steel, 'Walls and Bridges: The Case for Co-operation between Demographers and Family Historians', *Genealogists' Magazine* 25 (1997), 504–8.
24. Francis Leeson, 'The Study of Single Surnames and their Distribution', *Genealogists' Magazine* 14 (1964), 405–12; and responses: 'Surname Distribution', *Genealogists' Magazine* 15 (1965), 78–9.
25. *The Times* (1 Feb. 1975). For a general account of this period see Anthony J Camp, 'Somerset House does Not Go to Southport', *Genealogists' Magazine* 18 (1975), 67–75.
26. *The Times* (23 Jan. 1975).
27. 'Parish Registers: House of Lords Debate', *Genealogists' Magazine* 16 (1971), 589–603.
28. 'Parochial Records Bill: House of Lords Debate', *Genealogists' Magazine* 18 (1976), 278–87.
29. Anthony J Camp, 'Facing the Future: The Challenge of the Citizen's Charter for the Registration Service', *Genealogists' Magazine* 24 (1993), 331.

30. Ibid., pp. 331–2.
31. 'Public Records (Amendment) Bill: House of Lords Debate', *Genealogists' Magazine* 19 (1978), 304–6.
32. See letters pages of *The Times* (31 March, 11 April, 27 April 1983).
33. *The Times* (15 April 1983).
34. *The Times* (22 April 1983).
35. Michael Armstrong, 'Family Tree: The First Ten Years', in *Ten Years of Looking into the Family Tree* (Ramsey: ABM Publishing, 1994).
36. Don J Steel. 'The Family Historian's Dilemma', *Family Tree* (Jan. 1987), 16.
37. Don J Steel. 'The Record Custodian's Dilemma', *Family Tree* (Feb. 1987), 28–9.
38. Don J Steel. 'The Dilemma of the Publisher', *Family Tree* (March 1987), 19–20.
39. 'Censorship and the Family Historian', *Family Tree* (May 1987), 32–3.
40. 'A Kind of Censorship?', *Family Tree* (June 1987), 23.
41. *Family Tree* (Aug. 1987), 4.
42. Anthony J Camp, 'The Society in a Changing World', *Genealogists' Magazine* 19 (1979), 382–92.
43. *Genealogists' Magazine* 20 (1980), 12.
44. *Genealogists' Magazine* 20 (1980), 37–9.
45. John Titford, 'At a Touch', *Family Tree* (Feb. 1994), 11.

Chapter 8

1. Iain R Harrison, 'An Eye to the Future: Uses of the Computer in Genealogy', *Genealogists' Magazine* 20 (1980), 81–4.
2. Selections of letters were printed as: 'Computers in Genealogy: A Symposium', *Genealogists' Magazine* 20 (1980), 126–30, and 160–1.
3. Ann V Chiswell, 'Family History with the Amstrad PCW 8256', *Family Tree* (May 1986), 5.
4. For a history of these newsgroups see Margaret J Olson, 'Historical Reflections of the Genealogy Newsgroups', http://homepages.rootsweb.ancestry.com/~socgen/Newshist.htm. For the history of ROOTS-L and RootsWeb see www.rootsweb.com/roots-l.
5. John Titford, 'At a Touch', *Family Tree* (Feb. 1994), 11.
6. GENUKI can now be accessed at www.genuki.org.uk.
7. Peter Cooley, 'Perils of the Internet', *Genealogists' Magazine* 25 (1996), 192; repr. from *Computers in Genealogy* (Sept. 1995).
8. H R Henly, 'Perils of the Internet Overstated?', *Genealogists' Magazine* 25 (1996), 230–1.
9. Michael Armstrong, 'This May Interest You . . .', *Family Tree* (Oct. 1995), 48–9.
10. *Family Twiglets* (March 1992), 11.
11. *Family Twiglets* (May 1992), 8.
12. *Family Twiglets* (March 1992), 12.
13. Michael Armstrong, 'Society of Genealogists' Family History Fair', *Family Tree* (July 1993), 44.
14. S K Elliot, 'A Rough Guide to St Catherine's House', *Family Tree* (Aug. 1990), 20.
15. Anthony J Camp, 'Have your Credit Cards Ready: Scottish Indexes on the Internet', *Family Tree* (July 1998), 17.
16. Tony Reid, 'Origins on Internet: Is it Good Value for Money?', *Family Tree* (Aug. 1998), 56.
17. The letter is still accessible at the FreeBMD website: http://freebmd.rootsweb.com/ons.gif. The announcement on the RootsWeb website is at: http://freebmd.

rootsweb.com/980926.html.
18. The site's evolution is chronicled at http://freebmd.rootsweb.com/news.html.
19. '1901 Census Online: Countdown Commences', *Ancestors* (Jan. 2002).
20. 'Census Website is Closed After 30m Hits a Day', *Daily Telegraph* (8 Jan. 2002). Accessible at: www.telegraph.co.uk.
21. A marketing invention, not observed here, is that the definite article in the organization's name should always be written with a capital T (i.e. The National Archives), possibly to distinguish it from the US body of the same name. Hence, TNA.
22. Even today, it is estimated that worldwide less than 5% of genealogical records are online and still less thaan 10% of the LDS collection is digitized. Sharon Hintze, 'The Past, Present and Future of Records Preservation and Public Access', Society of Genealogists Centenary Conference, 7 May 2011.

Chapter 9
1. See for instance: Moving Here, www.movinghere.org.uk; Every Generation, www.every generation.co.uk; and the Caribbean GenWeb Project, www.rootsweb.com/~caribgw.
2. Elizabeth Grice, 'Who are we? Researching Family History', *Daily Telegraph* (4 Nov. 2006). Accessible at: www.telegraph.co.uk. John Naish, 'Lost Generations Game', *The Times* (4 Nov. 2006). Accessible at: www.timesonline.co.uk.
3. Leo McKinstry, 'Sorry But Family History Really is Bunk', *The Spectator* (29 April 2008). Accessible at: www.spectator.co.uk.
4. Susannah Herbert, 'A Census for the Sad', *Daily Telegraph* (6 Jan. 2002). Accessible at: www.telegraph.co.uk.
5. Terence Blacker, 'A Family Tree is So Much Less Trouble than a Family', *Independent* (1 Oct. 2004). Accessible at: www.independent.co.uk.
6. Mick Hume, 'Root Around for your Family Tree If you Must, But then Get your Own Life', *The Times* (17 Dec. 2004). Accessible at: www.timesonline.co.uk.
7. McKinstry, *The Spectator* (29 April 2008).
8. D J Taylor, 'Unearth your Family's Murky Past on the Internet', *Independent* (3 Jan. 2002). Accessible at: www.independent.co.uk.
9. McKinstry, *The Spectator* (29 April 2008).
10. Simon O'Hagan, 'A Quest to Unlock the Secrets of our Ancestors', *Daily Telegraph* (6 Jan. 2002). Accessible at: www.telegraph.co.uk.
11. Jonathan Freedland, 'We All Need a Story', *Guardian* (14 April 2007). Accessible at: www.guardian.co.uk. Another article sympathetic to the democratizing history view is: Ben Macintyre, 'Myfamilyandotherweirdos.com', *The Times* (11 June 2005). Accessible at: www.timesonline.co.uk.
12. Elizabeth Day, 'Why Shaking the Family Tree Can Be Bad for your Health', *Daily Telegraph* (16 April 2005). Accessible at: www.telegraph.co.uk.
13. For discussion of the LDS programme see Akenson, *Some Family*, pp. 185–215.
14. Anthony J Camp, 'Proposed Reform of the Registration System: Vital Change or Dog's Dinner', *Family Tree* (July 2002), 29.
15. Litton, 'The Changing Face of Family History', *Family Tree* (2002), 30.
16. Earlier edns of the NBI are available on the Findmypast website on a subscription basis.
17. C Harold Ridge, 'Scientific Genealogy', *Genealogists' Magazine* 11 (1951), 137–40; and H L White, 'More Scientific Genealogy', ibid., pp. 173–6.
18. Referenced in Francis Leeson, 'Genealogy and Medicine', *Genealogists' Magazine* 15 (1968), 600–1.

19. Brian Sykes, *The Seven Daughters of Eve: The Science that Reveals our Genetic Ancestry* (London: W W Norton, 2001).

20. Researchers have now identified a total of around 36–7 'clan mothers' on a global basis.

21. Akenson, *Some Family*, offers a critique of Sykes's work. He points out that the false-paternity rate could be significantly higher than the 1.3 per cent claimed, while still preserving the Y-chromosome inheritance observed by Sykes. This is because there are various illicit (including incestuous) paths that preserve the integrity of the Y-chromosomal signature. His conclusion is that 'an assemblage of samples of Y-chromosome material from present day males of a specific lineage can never result in the confirmation that the genetic pedigree is the same as the social lineage that forms the documented genealogical narrative of the family involved (and this no matter how high the documentary standard of the paper genealogy'. Ibid., p. 280.

22. Chris Pomery, 'The Advantages of a Dual DNA/Documentary Approach to Reconstruct the Family Tree of a Surname', *Journal of Genetic Genealogy* 5/2 (2009), 93.

23. For the Carden and Meates DNA projects see respectively: www.one-name.org/profiles/carden.html and http://meates.accessgenealogy.com/index.html.

24. 'Population Structure and Genome-Wide Patterns of Variation in Ireland and Britain', *European Journal of Human Genetics* 18 (Nov. 2010), 1248–54 doi:10.1038/ejhg.2010.87. The researchers attribute these patterns to the fact that long ago people tended to marry within their own community. After many generations, the different villages developed their own genetic fingerprints, so that scientists can now detect that distant kinship.

25. The most high-profile scientific activity in this area is National Geographic's Genographic Project, a major international research initiative to track human migrations and to better understand the connections and differences in the human species. http://genographic.nationalgeographic.com.

26. 'We Reveal Online DNA Tests are Waste of Money', *Which?* (4 July 2008). Accessible at: www.which.co.uk.

27. Human Genetics Commission, *Common Framework of Principles for Direct-to-Consumer Genetic Testing Services* (London: Human Genetics Commission, 2010). Available at: www.hgc.gov.uk. Due to National Health Service reorganization, the future of the HGC is now in doubt.

28. Christopher Hope, 'National Census to be Axed After 200 Years', *Daily Telegraph* (9 July 2010). Accessible at: www.telegraph.co.uk.

29. Figures here are extracted from: *Social Trends*, 39th edn (London: TSO, 2009), 18–22.

Index